LONDON
1753

Douze des cris de Londres, dessigner de après Nature et Graver à l'eau forte par Paul Sandby

London 1753

SHEILA O'CONNELL

with contributions by

Roy Porter, Celina Fox & Ralph Hyde

11/06

DAVID R. GODINE · *Publisher*

BOSTON

The Trustees of The British Museum gratefully
acknowledge the generous support of Jacqueline and
Jonathan Gestetner towards the production costs of
this book.

Frontispiece: Etching from the series
Twelve London Cries Done from the Life, Part 1st
by Paul Sandby, 1760 (cat. no. 1.47)

First published in 2003 by The British Museum Press
A division of The British Museum Company Ltd
46 Bloomsbury Street, London WC1B 3QQ

First U. S. edition published in 2003 by
David R. Godine · *Publisher*
Post Office Box 450
Jaffrey, New Hampshire 03452
www.godine.com

ISBN 1–56792–247–3

Designed and typeset in Ehrhardt and Caslon
by James Shurmer

FIRST U.S. EDITION
Printed in Great Britain by The Bath Press, Avon

CONTENTS

PREFACE AND ACKNOWLEDGEMENTS

In 1752 Britain at last joined the rest of Europe in accepting the reformed calendar that Pope Gregory XIII had introduced on the Continent in 1582. From then on the new year began on 1 January rather than on the Feast of the Annunciation, 25 March. In 1752 eleven days were famously lost to the British between 3 and 13 September in order to counteract the accumulated arithmetical and astronomical errors of the old Julian calendar. Only the Exchequer refused the change, and so our tax year – to the bewilderment of the world – still ends eleven days after 25th March on 5th April. Britain had moved from the 'Old Style' to the 'New Style'. And one year later, in 1753, the British Museum was founded.

The London that witnessed these innovations was in the process of transformation from the capital of a developing economy to the centre of a new empire. Great Britain was itself a new country, the Parliaments of Scotland and England having been united only in 1707. In 1746 the claims of the Stuart monarchy were finally expunged at Culloden; in 1760 the German-speaking George II died and his young London-born grandson became George III; in 1763, at the end of the Seven Years War, Canada, India and much of the Caribbean came under British control. This exhibition looks at London, already the largest city in Europe and probably the most cosmopolitan in the world, during these crucial years, for it was in the city of Johnson and Garrick, Hogarth and Reynolds, that Parliament set up the first national museum in the world.

The exhibition is primarily one of prints and drawings, and we have taken the opportunity of the British Museum's 250th anniversary to show different areas of London at the time of its foundation as well as some less well known parts of its holdings. As always, these are largely made up of private collections, generously given to the Museum over the centuries. The Crace collection of more than six thousand prints and drawings (together with maps, now in the British Library) was put together by Frederick Crace and sold to the Museum by his son in 1880. One of the extra-illustrated volumes of Thomas Pennant's *Some Account of London* bequeathed by John Charles Crowle in 1811 is included in the exhibition, together with three large watercolours by Thomas and Paul Sandby that were long ago extracted and unfolded for safer keeping. The Museum's collections of trade cards - fine examples of Rococo design as well as documents of everyday life - are frequently consulted by researchers but rarely displayed. More than four thousand trade cards came to the Museum in 1818 as part of the collection of ephemera created by Sarah Sophia Banks, sister of Sir Joseph Banks, one of the Museum's early Trustees. A further nine thousand trade cards were bequeathed in 1959 by the historian of London trades, Sir Ambrose Heal. The important collection of playing cards is represented by two packs, one from the collection of 1,660 packs bequeathed by Lady Charlotte Schreiber in 1895. In 1891 Lady Charlotte gave a collection of nearly seven hundred printed fans, one of which is included in the exhibition. Also shown are examples from the Museum's enormous collection of portrait prints. They include a print from the thirteen volumes of theatrical subjects purchased in 1818 as part of the library of the classical scholar Dr Charles Burney, and others from the collection of eight thousand mezzotints bequeathed in 1902 by William Eaton, 2nd Baron Cheylesmore.

The Museum's outstanding collection of political and social satires is better known. Ten thousand prints were purchased in 1868 from the estate of Edward Hawkins, formerly Keeper of the Department of Antiquities; about 1,400 satirical prints had already entered the Museum with the collection of Sarah Banks and others have continued to be added by gift, bequest and purchase. The value of the collection of satires is greatly enhanced by the catalogues by F. G. Stephens and M. Dorothy George, a distinguished scholar whose *London Life in the Eighteenth Century*, first published in 1925 and still in print, remains essential reading for the social history of London in this period.

The exhibition also includes objects from other parts of the Museum: a full set of all the coins in circulation in mid-eighteenth-century London, a document from the early days of banking, medals commemorating victories in battle, and tokens and metal season tickets to places of entertainment (among them examples from the gift in 1906 of Sir Montague Guest, son of Lady Charlotte Schreiber). A magnificent Hellenistic bronze head represents acquisitions of the Museum's first decade, and a Roman marble bust demonstrates the taste of Grand Tourists. Examples of the luxury goods enjoyed by wealthy Londoners include Bow and Chelsea porcelain, glass, jewellery and watches, and a display of Chinese export ware.

We are grateful for the loan of John Rocque's magnificent map of London from the British Library, where Peter Barber, Debbie Hall, Kumiko Matsuoka and Barbara O'Connor could not have been more co-operative. Natasha McEnroe and the trustees of Dr Johnson's House agreed with great enthusiasm to lend a copy of his *Dictionary of the English Language*. Rhian Harris and Jane King facilitated the loan from the Foundling Museum of a group of poignant tokens left by mothers with their babies. Colleagues at the Museum of London allowed access to collections in areas not held in the British Museum, and we are very grateful for the loan of a ravishing piece of Spitalfields silk, a pair of shoes made in the City, a medicine bottle distributed by the leading cheap print publisher of the day, a set of cockspurs and two shop-signs; Antonia Charlton, Karen Fielder, Daniella Rizzi, Alex Werner and, especially, Edwina Ehrman were extremely helpful at all stages from selection onwards. Private collectors have also been kind enough to lend four fine watercolour designs for shop-signs, a silver season ticket and a set of rules for cock-fighting.

We would not have been able to put on this exhibition or to publish a catalogue of this quality without the help of a number of donors. The Corporation of London is an especially appropriate sponsor, as is the Golden Bottle Trust with its long history in Fleet Street. One of the City Livery Companies, the Salters', has also lent its support. Private individuals have been particularly generous; we are grateful to Francis Finlay, Jonathan and Jacqueline Gestetner and others who wish to remain anonymous.

The author wishes me to thank Celina Fox and Ralph Hyde, not only for contributing essays to the catalogue, but for sharing their expertise in many ways. Antony Griffiths helped to devise the structure of the exhibition and read and commented on the entire text of the catalogue. Catalogue entries have been provided by Barrie Cook (1.41, 1.42 and 1.43), Mark McDonald (3.42, 3.43, 3.87, 5.85), David Rhodes (1.31) and David Thompson (3.76-81). Other scholars, both in the British Museum and beyond, have been generous with specialist advice: Richard Abdy on Roman coins; Adelaide Adu-Amankwah on Ghanaian history; Philip Attwood on medals; Rosemary Baker on politics and satirical prints; John Berry on playing cards; Richard Blurton on the British in India; Sophie Carter on prostitution; Hugo Chapman on Canaletto; Tim Clayton on the print trade; Aileen Dawson on English porcelain and glass; Jeremy Evans on watchmaking; Delia Gaze on Deptford; Tony Gee on boxing; Clare Hall on equestrian matters; Jessica Harrison-Hall on Chinese export ware; Virginia Hewitt on banking; Ian Jenkins on Dr Richard Mead; J. H. Leopold on watchmaking; Jean Rankine on maritime subjects; Judy Rudoe on jewellery; and Laurence Worms on map- and printmakers and publishers. Others who have helped with advice and information include John Abbott, Janet Ambers, Diane Clements, Lucy Dixon, Diana Donald, Elizabeth Einberg, David Gaimster, Cheryl Wixon Gocken, Peter Jackson, Patrick Mannix, Heather McPherson, Robin Michaelson, Thorsten Opper, Bruce Robertson, Kim Sloan, David Solkin, Lindsay Stainton, Luke Syson, Matti Watton, Tim Wilcox and Martin Williams.

The exhibition has also made practical demands on many colleagues within the British Museum. There is not space to detail all their contributions, but the following deserve particular thanks: Simon Andreanoff, Dean Baylis, Lisa Baylis, Jenny Bescoby and her colleagues in the Department of Conservation, Martin Buttery, Richard Dunn, Geoffrey House, Ivor Kerslake, Janet Larkin, Sovati Louden-Smith, Kevin Lovelock, Nick Newbery, Jim Rossiter and John Williams. All the staff of the Department of Prints and Drawings have contributed in one way or another, but particular acknowledgement must go to Frances Carey, Charlie Collinson, Julia Nurse, Frank Potter and Janice Reading - as well as to those already mentioned.

The publication of the catalogue has been the responsibility of Nina Shandloff of British Museum Press. It was edited by John Banks, designed by James Shurmer and produced by Sarah Levesley. We thank them all for their care and attention.

Finally we must pay tribute to Roy Porter, a great eighteenth century scholar and lover of London, whose contribution to this catalogue was one of the last pieces of work that he produced before his sad and sudden death on 3 March 2002.

Neil MacGregor
Director, British Museum

Author's Note

In order to avoid repetitive footnotes, I have not cited standard reference works in catalogue entries. I have relied heavily on such works as the *Dictionary of National Biography* (in some cases authors have been kind enough to allow me access to entries in the forthcoming *New DNB*), the *London Encyclopedia* by Ben Weinreb and Christopher Hibbert and its predecessor, Wheatley and Cunningham's *London Past and Present*, Pevsner's volumes on London, and E. N. Williams's *Dictionary of English and European History 1485–1789*. Ambrose Heal's notes accompanying his collection of trade cards have also been a useful source of information. I have referred constantly to the London Topographical Society's publication of John Rocque's 1747 map, *The A–Z of Georgian London* – frequently consulted in conjunction with a recent edition of the Geographers' *London A–Z*. Full references to these and many other valuable publications will be found in the Bibliography.

Capitalization, punctuation and spelling of quotations have in some cases been modernized.

Measurements of prints and drawings are height by width. For most other objects only one dimension is given in order to give an indication of size.

Objects from British Museum Departments other than Prints and Drawings are indicated by initials: Coins and Medals (CM); Greek and Roman Antiquities (GR); Medieval and Modern Europe (MME); Oriental Antiquities (OA).

The majority of illustrations are made from photographs taken by the British Museum's Department of Photography and Imaging. Objects in collections other than the British Museum are reproduced by permission of their owners.

Prices translate into post-1971 decimal currency as follows:
1d = £0.004; 12d = 1s = £0.05; 20s = £1.00; one guinea = £1 1s = £1.05

THE WONDERFUL EXTENT AND VARIETY OF LONDON

ROY PORTER

When we came upon Highgate hill and had a view of London, I was all life and joy.

James Boswell

In London, everything is easy to him who has money and is not afraid of spending it.

Casanova

Writing soon after the Great Fire of 1666, John Dryden sang the praises of 'the most renowned and late flourishing City of London'. Phoenix-like, the capital rose again, to flourish once more during the following century.[1] 'New squares and new streets rising up every day to such a prodigy of buildings that nothing in the world does, or ever did equal it, except old Rome in Trajan's time', enthused Daniel Defoe in the 1720s,[2] while around 1750 Charles Jenner recast this tale of growth more earthily:

Where'er around I cast my wand'ring eyes
Long burning rows of fetid bricks arise.

As London expanded, the west/east divide became more marked, and the East End beyond the walls emerged as an exotic territory in its own right. Dr Johnson 'talked today a good deal of the wonderful extent and variety of London', recalled James Boswell: 'he in particular recommended us to explore *Wapping*'. The West End, for its part, became Quality Street, unique by European standards. Financed not by princes or popes but through aristocratic capitalism, it grew through the piecemeal development of aristocratic estates, and its squares acquired a character of their own: places not just to live, but to see and be seen in.[3] Let us survey this 'prodigy'.

Rebuilt after the Fire, the old City proper – the square mile contained within the walls – had its gems, notably the Wren churches[4] and the new Mansion House, completed by George Dance the Elder in 1753. Overall, however, it was architecturally disappointing; the critic James Ralph rightly lamented that it displayed little that was grand or gorgeous. Not the least of its drawbacks was its pall of smoke: the German visitor Lichtenberg complained of having to write 'by the light of a candle (at half-past ten in the morning)'.

Well-to-do City types increasingly chose to reside away from 'the shop', and aldermen opted for West End squares or country seats. 'Oh, how I long to be transported to the dear regions of Grosvenor-Square!', sighs Miss Sterling in George Colman's popular comedy *The Clandestine Marriage* (1766), 'far, far from the dull districts of Aldersgate, Cheap, Candlewick, and Farringdon Without and Within'.

Beyond the City, the metropolis as a whole grew and glittered. In 1700 its population was around 575,000, about the same as that of Paris. By 1750 it had hit 675,000, while by 1800 it was 900,000, a third as large again as Paris, and the western world's biggest city.

The City 'might, indeed, be viewed in a small compass', explained Defoe in the 1720s,

> but, when I speak of London, now in the modern acceptation, you expect I shall take in all that vast mass of buildings, reaching from Black-Wall in the east, to Tot-Hill Fields [Westminster] in the west; ... to Islington north ... to Cavendish Square, and all the new buildings by, and beyond, Hanover Square, by which the city of London, for so it is still to be called, is extended to Hide Park Corner in the Brentford Road, and almost to Marylebone in the Acton Road; and how much farther it may spread, who knows?[5]

Defoe guessed that London's perimeter stretched for 36 miles, to take in such villages as Deptford and Islington, though not as yet Chelsea, Knightsbridge, Marylebone, Poplar or Greenwich. Thirty years later, the green patches within his 'line of circumvallation' certainly had been infilled: to the east, Shadwell and Bethnal Green had dissolved into the sea of bricks; to the south, the Borough (Southwark) was spreading down to the Elephant and Castle; while to the west, Westminster was creeping towards Chelsea and Knightsbridge.

Better communications spurred development: new bridges opened up the area south of the river while the construction of the 'New Road' – today's Marylebone, Euston and Pentonville Roads – chalked out Marylebone and Bloomsbury for the developers.[6]

The rise of the West End as an elegant residential quarter had begun back in the 1630s with the building of the Covent Garden piazza.[7] St James's and Bloomsbury Squares had followed. Three great squares then arose in Mayfair. First came Hanover Square – topically patriotic name! – laid out from 1717 and blessed by the fashionable Church of St George. Berkeley Square emerged a little later from 1737, and Grosvenor Square sprang up adjacent, at 8 acres London's largest. Leading architects – the Adam brothers (Robert and James), Chambers, Soane, Wyatville, and James and Samuel Wyatt – continued to embellish the square over the next hundred years.[8]

Nearby, Bond Street became a classy mix of homes and shops. Laurence Sterne, author of *Tristram Shandy*, died in 1768 at number 41. James Boswell rented rooms around the same time at the Piccadilly end: 'A genteel lodging in a good part of the town is absolutely necessary', pronounced Dr Johnson's biographer.

To the north of Oxford Street, Cavendish Square was first to emerge, from 1717 onwards, the nucleus of the Harley-Cavendish Estate. After the Peace of Paris (1763) new developments were to spring up to the west, gradually filling the space defined by the New Road. Henry William Portman developed 200 acres of meadow, starting in 1764 with his square, which was to owe its popularity to Robert Adam, Wyatt and 'Athenian' Stewart.[9]

Many attractions lured high society into the West End: Parliament and politics, shops and the season, the marriage market and the availability of cheap mortgages. The Quality became convinced it was essential to own, or at least rent, a town house. This was something new, for cities had never enjoyed much of a reputation – think of Babel, Babylon, Sodom and Gomorrah, and Rome (in Protestant eyes, linked to the Beast). And while Mummerset hayseeds were ridiculed, critics could always condemn the 'Town' as loose and lecherous.[10]

A compromise was struck: urban living would be eligible so long as it had a solid rural touch. That is why, beyond St James's Palace, blazoned on the northern front of Buckingham House (later, Palace) were the words *Rus in Urbe*: the country in the city. Both Grosvenor Square and Portman Square were land-scaped with sylvan clumps, and sheep were imported into Cavendish Square, grazing picturesquely behind railings. That was going too far, judged *Critical Observations on the Buildings and Improvements of London* (1771), which pitied 'the poor things starting at every coach, and hurrying round their narrow bounds'.

Town living became confirmed as smart and classy. The new terraces may have been cramped compared to a Paris nobleman's *hôtel*, but this was a trivial sacrifice for grandees because they also had their country parks. 'Englishmen of rank', observed a foreigner, 'consider their houses in London as a kind of pied-à-terre. Many who have revenues of £20,000 and more live in London with hardly a dozen rooms.' A new art of urban living was choreographed. Public spaces – streets, squares, shops, the theatre and the club – were created where social life could blossom, while space was optimized at home.

Edward Gibbon was one of many who caught the West End bug. Trapped as a teenager in darkest Hampshire, he passed a year in Town in his early twenties, and was enchanted: 'The metropolis', he wrote, 'is itself an astonishing and perpetual

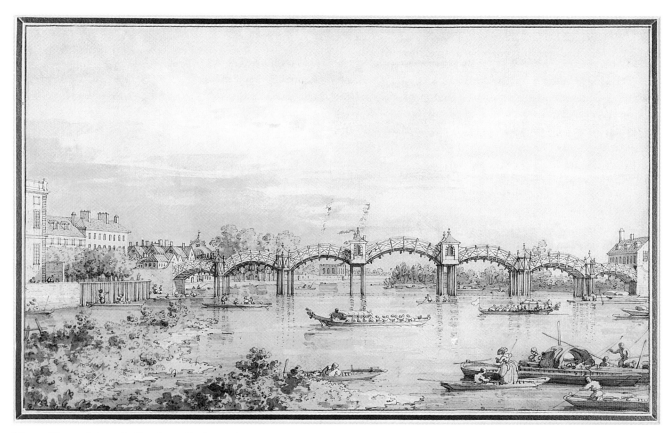

Fig. 1 Giovanni Antonio Canaletto, *Bridge at Hampton Court*, pen and ink and wash over black chalk.

spectacle to the curious eye.' That 'lord of irony' could on occasion feign disenchantment: 'the pleasures of a town life … are within the reach of every man who is regardless of his health, his money, and his company'. But the fact is that, on his father's death, he sold off the family estate and rented a bijou bachelor pad in Bentinck Street, drooling over the wallpaper he had chosen, light blue with a gold border, and purring at his good fortune. 'I had now attained the solid comforts of life', he wrote in his *Memoirs*,

> a convenient well-furnished house, a domestic table, half a dozen chosen servants, my own carriage, and all those decent luxuries whose value is the more sensibly felt the longer they are enjoyed … To a lover of books the shops and sales in London present irresistible temptations … By my own choice I passed in town the greatest part of the year.[11]

There, right by Cavendish Square, in the company of a lapdog and a parrot, his *Decline and Fall of the Roman Empire* was composed. What other history classic has ever been written in such stylish surroundings?

London did not expand only westwards. Beyond the walls to the east, development was fiercest on the waterfront, a strip half a mile wide extending from Wapping Wall and Ratcliff Highway to Limehouse and Blackwall.[12] A short way beyond those riverside slums, however, Hackney, Poplar, Old Ford, Clapton, Stratford and Leyton all remained attractive villages. Bow stretched over the Lea bridge towards Stratford; Bromley's main street hugged the River Lea; and the Isle of Dogs remained rough pasture. Closer in, however, things were changing rapidly. If Mile End was still somewhat genteel, Bethnal Green was growing crowded, its western end being packed by poor weavers, the Spitalfields overspill.

It was the riverside developments which really repelled, especially the jungle of courts beyond the wall in St Katharine's, east of the Tower. Ratcliff Highway was linked to Cable Street by mazes of alleys, notorious for brothels and seamen's lodgings; and Lower Ratcliff was a chaos of cramped courts twisting off the main streets – the very names said it all: Harebrain Court, Hog Yard, Black Dog and Black Boy Alleys, all occupied by sailors, lightermen, pawnshops, pothouse boys and porters.

Desirable residential areas began to sprout south of the river. As late as 1750, Camberwell was still a village of orchards and smallholdings, and the only settlements beyond it were clumps of houses at Peckham Rye, Goose Green, 'None Head' (Nunhead) and Dulwich Wells, whither citizens strolled on Sundays to take the air and the waters. Things changed with the building of Westminster Bridge (1750) and Blackfriars Bridge (1769), and soon a ribbon of developments was stretching down from Newington Butts to Camberwell Green and beyond.[13]

Nor was Camberwell alone. Defoe had noted back in 1724 how 'from Richmond to London, the river sides are full of villages … so full of beautiful buildings, charming gardens and rich habitations of gentlemen of quality that nothing in the world can imitate it' (Fig. 1). He singled out Richmond, Putney,

Hammersmith, Fulham and Chelsea for praise. Suburban living was a novelty, and the new commuters amused Robert Lloyd in 1757:

Some three or four miles out of town,
  (An hour's ride will bring you down),
    He fixes on his choice abode,
      Not half a furlong from the road:
    And so convenient does it lay,
      The stages pass it ev'ry day:
    And then so snugg, so mighty pretty,
      To have an house so near the city!

To the north, Hampstead bloomed as a fashionable village, thanks to its elevation and its iron-rich spring – the water gave a good purge! By 1750 it was assuming an arty, intellectual atmosphere, its first literary circle being run by the dramatist and poet Joanna Baillie. Highgate followed.[14]

Further east lay the first City suburb to be truly built up. On high ground, Islington had a well credited with health-giving properties (Sadler's Wells commemorates one of the 'spaws' so popular with the Georgians). High Street and Upper Street were house-lined by 1735, and Colebrooke Row was completed by 1768. It was 'a pretty neat town, mostly built of brick', noted Oliver Goldsmith, but, even then, it was also the butt of satire. George Colman mocked its denizens in *The Spleen; or, Islington Spa*, the tale of a tailor who retired there (the 'country') and found it deadly dull:

> Would not he Islington's fine air forego
> Could he again be choak'd in Butcher-Row?[15]

How was the metropolis judged? It came in for criticisms similar to the City. 'Unfortunately for the city and suburbs of London right lines have hardly ever been considered', grumbled the architect John Gwynn in his *London and Westminster Improved* (1766):

> Such a vast city as London ought to have had at least three capital streets which should have run through the whole, and at convenient distances have been intersected by other capital streets at right angles, by which means all the inferior streets would have an easy and convenient communication with them.

Architects are always whining, but Gwynn had a point. For all London's energy, there was little that was truly capital, and its public face remained disorganized. Unlike those at Baroque Turin, Dresden or St Petersburg, its public buildings were unimpressive, the royal palaces made a poor show and, with its tottering skyline, London Bridge was a medieval survival.

Many others groused about the unsafe alleys of old London and its ill-kept streets, rendered offensive by cattle markets and shambles. Refuse piled up at street corners; and ancient gates and narrow ways created bottlenecks, Charing Cross and Temple Bar being notoriously congested.

Improvements were afoot, however. Important was the first Westminster Paving Act of 1762, followed by other Acts for the

City and elsewhere. Hitherto it had been householders' duty to keep the street in front of their houses in good repair. Now paving commissioners were appointed with paid staffs. Gutters were built on either side of the road, the carriageway was made convex, and in main streets Purbeck paving stones replaced pebbles. This trend towards pavementing transformed streets for pedestrians, since they could now stroll along the sidewalks undisturbed by vehicles and animals. Such Acts also provided for scavenging and cleansing, and for the removal of obstructions – open coal-holes, sheds and projecting balconies.[16]

The old problem of the River Fleet, used as a sewer, was solved: in 1733 it was arched over between Holborn Bridge and Fleet Bridge at the foot of Ludgate Hill; about 1764 it was channelled underground as far as the Thames. In the 1760s the City pulled down its overhanging street signs. Repaired in 1757–9, London Bridge was stripped of its decaying houses and shops. In the 1760s the City gates – Aldgate, Moorgate, Ludgate and Bishopsgate – were taken down to improve traffic flow, though Temple Bar lasted longer – till 1878!

London thus became a wonder city, twenty times bigger than any of its provincial rivals, housing at mid-century about 11 per cent of England's population. This demographic expansion was wholly fuelled by migration. 'Not above one in twenty of shop and alehouse keepers, journeymen and labourers … were either born or served their apprenticeships in town', it was observed, with only some exaggeration.[17]

London was a magnet for the Scots – endlessly baited by Dr Johnson, himself from Lichfield.[18] An Irish colony ('little Dublin') grew in St Giles-in-the-Fields, another in the East End. Foreign communities included some twenty thousand Jews, resident chiefly in Whitechapel – the bearded Jewish old-clothes-man was a regular sight. In nearby Spitalfields congregated Huguenot migrants, French refugees fleeing religious persecution at the time of Louis XIV's revocation of the Edict of Nantes (1685). They formed the core of the East-End silkweaving community, other Huguenots settled in Soho and Covent Garden specializing in watchmaking, engraving and silversmithing. There were also a few thousand black people in mid-Georgian London; some were seamen, others had arrived as slaves or to satisfy the vogue for black servants.

Provincial consumers were sucked into London's season, from October to June, to spend their money on fashions and finery, *objets d'art* and the theatre. Landowners flocked in for pleasure or to draw on the services of doctors, architects, portrait-painters, barristers, bankers, brokers and other professionals. Few gentleman were without a satchel of lawsuits detaining them in town, often for weeks at a time. They might at the same time be looking after their money interests, as London emerged as the financial and credit capital where investments were negotiated and mortgages raised. Meanwhile, Parliament's increasing workload drew the ruling class to Westminster from autumn to Easter.

All such developments enhanced London's dominance. And if grumbletonians like Laurence Sterne's character Walter Shandy were sure that it was all a '*distemper*', threatening the nation's health, boosters stressed the benefits, particularly the role of the capital in fostering trade.

The heart of the overseas commercial empire which guaranteed England's economic success was the Port of London. Early in the eighteenth century its quays were handling a staggering 80 per cent of the country's imports, 69 per cent of its exports and 86 per cent of its re-exports, notably tobacco, sugar, silks and spices. But all manner of commodities passed through the port. Londoners routinely burnt coal for fuel – hence the fogs! By 1750 around 650,000 tons of it a year were being brought up the Thames from Newcastle.

The tripling of river-borne trade between 1720 and 1800 resulted in dire congestion, especially in the Upper Pool, where up to 1800 vessels crammed into mooring space for 500. The Thames grew log-jammed, 'almost hidden by merchant vessels from every country', gasped the Swiss visitor César de Saussure. The solution came in the nineteenth century with the building of the docks.

Riverside trade fuelled London's industries, not least shipbuilding itself. Prominent amongst East End industries were distilling, sugar-refining and brewing.[19] Booth's, Gordon's and other big distillers settled in Clerkenwell, to take advantage of the high-quality well-water. Joseph Truman had established himself around 1680 in Brick Lane, Spitalfields. Other major concerns included Meux, Perkins and Thrale's (in Southwark), and Whitbread's. 'The sight of a great London brewhouse exhibits a magnificence unspeakable', enthused the thirsty antiquarian Thomas Pennant.

London was proud of its quality trades. By 1750 there were five hundred master weavers in Spitalfields and fifty thousand locals dependent on a trade which, however, was fraught with industrial unrest, leading to serious rioting in the 1760s (cats 1.79–1.82). From the 1740s there were porcelain factories at Bow and Chelsea, inspired by the Chinese porcelain that the East India Company was importing. Another select trade was cabinet-making, boosted by the import of mahogany. Thomas Chippendale opened his workshops in Long Acre about 1745, later moving to St Martin's Lane.

The capital also had its share of dirty trades. Scattered through the East End and in the poorer south bank suburbs were bone-boilers, grease-makers, glue-makers, paint-makers and dye-works. Lime-burning kilns were established in Bethnal Green and Mile End, and brick-making gave Brick Lane its name. Across the river in Rotherhithe and Deptford, there were ropewalks, coopers' and boat-builders' yards, oil, colour and soap works.

London's supremacy was underlined by a revolution in retailing. Most goods had traditionally been sold by hawkers, with their time-honoured cries (cats 1.47–1.58), or vended in the established markets: Leadenhall for hardware, leather, cloth, poultry, meat and dairy produce, Billingsgate for fish,

Queenhithe for grain, Smithfield for cattle, Covent Garden for fruit and vegetables, and so forth.

High-grade retailing was now moving, however, to stylish shops in both the West End and the City: linen drapers, goldsmiths, instrument-makers, music publishers, tailors, milliners, perfumiers, jewellers, chemists, druggists, tea and coffee purveyors, wine and spirit merchants, pastrycooks, porcelain, china and glass shops – and scores more. Leading shopkeepers became household names: Mrs Chenevix at her toy-shop at Charing Cross (cats 3.47 and 3.48); Bartolommeo Valle at the Old Italian Warehouse, Haymarket (cats 5.88 and 5.89); John Dolland at the Golden Spectacles in the Strand.[20]

Mayfair sprouted chic shops, particularly around Bond Street. Lock the hatter was already flourishing by the 1760s: his chief suppliers were Thomas and William Bowler in Southwark Bridge Road. William Hamley founded in 1760 a toyshop in High Holborn called 'Noah's Ark'. Business booming, his descendants opened a Regent Street branch. In 1766 James Christie opened an auction hall. His Pall Mall sale rooms soon became *the* place for art dealing, thanks to his acquaintance with Reynolds and Gainsborough. Light, lofty and eye-catching, London's shops seduced the crowds.

'The City' (in modern parlance) had emerged as the financial centre after the Restoration. The huge growth in overseas trade spurred the rise of the marine insurance industry: Lloyd's originated in a coffee house kept by Edward Lloyd in Tower Street. Britain's world role in overseas trades demanded a rapid growth, an essayist noted in 1749, of 'agents, factors, brokers, insurers, bankers, negotiators, discounters, subscribers, contractors, remitters, ticket-mongers, stock-jobbers, and of a great Variety of other Dealers in Money'.

Fire insurance and life assurance developed at the same time. Meanwhile the banking sector developed in response to the need to transfer large sums of money safely and speedily around the country, and the money markets emerged. Until 1698 dealers in the trading companies met in the Royal Exchange. This growing 'vexatiously thronged', they moved to Jonathan's Coffee House in Change Alley, where the London Stock Exchange came into being. Stockbrokers later moved to Capel Court, by the side of the Bank of England, founded in 1694. The Baltic Exchange originated in 1744 at the Virginia and Baltick Coffee House, also in Threadneedle Street. Alongside the Bank of England, private banks developed too. Concentrated on Lombard Street, they numbered around forty in the 1760s.[21]

Headed by its aldermen and Lord Mayor, the City's government grew archaic. As in medieval and Tudor times, parishes and wards continued to supply its unpaid officers. The City's boundaries bore ever less relationship to the sprawling metropolis, some of which was barely governed at all, responsibility for poor relief and highways falling on the county justices.[22] Local government in Westminster, as also in the parishes of Marylebone and St Pancras, was in the hands of 'close' vestries, oligarchies of wealthy residents who had extensive powers over highways, poor relief and the rates.

As the metropolis thus approached a million inhabitants, its administration remained an incurably fragmented relic, divided between hundreds of bodies, often mutually distrustful or even antagonistic. It could not cope with crises such as the gin craze of the 1730s and 1740s, with its urban subculture exclusive to the poor – comparable to the drugs culture of inner-city ghettos nowadays.[23] Gin was cheap ('drunk for a penny, dead drunk for twopence, straw for nothing'), and it was consumed in staggering quantities – by the 1740s averaging two pints a week for every man, woman and child in London. Dram-shops multiplied – in some quarters, it was said in 1743, every eighth house sold spirits. The bodies of the paralytically drunk littered the streets of Bethnal Green and St Giles's, the rookery Hogarth chose for *Gin Lane*. The Westminster justices condemned it as 'the principal cause of the increase of the poor and of all the vice and debauchery among the inferior sort of people, as well as of the felonies and other disorders committed about this town'.

Partly for such reasons, fears rose about crime.[24] 'London is really dangerous at this time', reflected the poet William Shenstone at mid-century, 'the pickpockets, formerly contented with mere filching, make no scruple to knock people down with bludgeons in Fleet Street and the Strand, and that at no later hour than eight o'clock'. In his *Enquiry into the Causes of the late Increase of Robbers* (1751), Henry Fielding, a prominent magistrate as well as a novelist, explained that 'the Cities of London and Westminster, with … the great irregularity of their buildings [and] the immense number of lanes, alleys, courts and bye-places' seemed to have been designed 'for the very purpose of concealment … in which a thief may harbour with as great security, as wild beasts do in the desarts of Africa or Arabia'. Not for the last time, the media spread stories of a terrifying criminal underworld.

In truth, however, those committing felonies were less likely to be hardened professionals than the labouring poor, down on their luck or out of work, starving or just fatally tempted. Much crime arose out of the ambiguities of capitalism itself. Many were executed, and thousands more transported, for workplace crime, for making off with oddments of cloth from tailors, nails and plank-ends from shipyards, and pocketfuls of tea from Thames lighters.

Policing London long remained the job of beadles and constables, and the parish watch and ward – a total force, amateur and professional, of a little over three thousand unarmed men. They at least had the advantage of being locals. Any thought of imposing a metropolitan police, under central government, would have been resisted as a gross invasion of English liberties. The system's parochial character frustrated magistrates trying to track down offenders across administrative frontiers, including those separating the City from Westminster. It also proved quite incapable of dealing with major civil disorders, such as the Gordon Riots of 1780.[25]

Shortcomings in crime detection meant that the theatrical

symbols of justice assumed inordinate significance. Though relatively few were actually hanged – fewer than thirty a year – the gallows overshadowed all. Public executions were intended to act as a deterrent; but apprentices, allowed a 'Tyburn Fair' holiday, regarded convicts as heroes, especially when they made their exit with a swagger, dressed in finery (see cat. 5.96). The procession from Newgate Prison to Tyburn (now Marble Arch), would last about two hours; the carts stopped at taverns, and many were inebriated by the time they reached Tyburn Tree. The enormous crowds which gathered got drunk and disorderly. 'In real truth', commented Henry Fielding,

> the executions of criminals, as at present conducted, serve, I apprehend, a purpose diametrically opposite to that for which they were designed; and tend rather to inspire the vulgar with a contempt of the gallows rather than a fear of it.
>
> The day of execution is a holiday to the greatest part of the mob about town. On every such occasion they are sure to assemble in great numbers, and as sure to behave themselves with all kinds of disorder. All the avenues to Tyburn appear like those to a wake or festival, where idleness, wantonness, drunkenness, and every other species of debauchery are gratified.

Public hangings were thus clearly counterproductive. In recognition of this, Tyburn gallows were demolished in 1783 and executions moved to Newgate itself, while the last beheading on Tower Hill proved to be that of the Jacobite Lord Lovat – who had the last laugh as a stand collapsed, killing twelve.

Halting steps were taken to improve public order. Innovations in policing came with the Bow Street Office, founded by Henry Fielding in 1749. Together with his blind half-brother John, another Bow Street magistrate, Henry created a team of constables (the Bow Street Runners), paid one guinea a week and a share in the rewards for successful prosecutions.

Londoners were used to expressing their views and loyalties on the streets through processions, demonstrations and other forms of street theatre parading emotive icons such as the noose and Magna Carta. Popular power made itself felt in the 1760s when John Wilkes's supporters engaged in a highly effective legal battle against George III and his Prime Minister, Lord Bute (pp. 200–2). Crowds repeatedly took to the streets in powerful yet disciplined riots, demanding justice and constitutional rights, and carrying out menacing but restrained assaults on the property of opponents, smashing windows and the like.[26]

London exercised a powerful sway over national politics. A high proportion of City and Westminster male residents had the vote, and these constituencies often returned radical members. In the 1760s metropolitan M.P.s were strong supporters of William Pitt's expansionist foreign policies, and they became vocal members of the opposition after his replacement in 1763. In 1770 Pitt's ally Mayor Beckford, told the King that enemies of the City were enemies of the people – for which he was rewarded with a statue in the Guildhall. Four years later, City opposition culminated in the election as Mayor of the notorious radical Wilkes, plague of King and governments alike during the previous decade.

The capital had become a wonder, but, by a perverse logic, the greater the benefits metropolitan life conferred, the more it was vilified. Defoe had dubbed it 'the monstrous city', and a century later the radical William Cobbett anathematized the capital as the 'great wen'.

To many artists and intellectuals London was iniquity itself, the poisoned spring of fashion, the nursery of vice, crime, riot, and all the other enormities unmasked in Samuel Johnson's satirical poem, *London* (1738). In his novels Henry Fielding exposed its vanity, deceits and exploitation, and William Hogarth's capital was all disease and violence, filth, noise, falling buildings and fallen women, chaos, drunkenness, infidelity and insanity. In the moral contrasts drawn by his *Rake's Progress*, *Harlot's Progress*, *Marriage A-la-Mode* and *Industry and Idleness* series London's physical squalor was the embodiment of its moral bankruptcy.[27]

Despite such censures, contemporaries were energized by the urban experience. London's diversity thrilled Boswell, just down from Scotland in the early 1760s; he likened it to musical variations or an exhibition. He would plan such treats as perambulating it in a day, beginning at Hyde Park Corner and working up to Covent Garden – 'the variety that we met with as we went along is amazing', he marvelled: 'one end of London is like a different country from the other in look and manners'. Boswell searched out London's nooks and crannies: the rooms of the Sublime Society of Beefsteaks above the Bedford Coffee House, Mrs Salmon's waxworks, and even the St Mary-le-Bow publisher of children's stories he'd once enjoyed (see cats 1.76 and 1.77). The streets, crowds and sights inspired him, affording an inexhaustible theatre in which to perform or spectate.

During the Georgian century the Church's role in daily life in the city was on the wane. Hogarth's *Sleeping Congregation* captured a prevalent view of Establishment piety. Nonconformity, on the other hand, did not slumber, and Methodism was rooted in the metropolis. Together with George Whitefield, John Wesley addressed gatherings of thousands on Blackheath, and then preached in November 1739 at a disused foundry near Moorfields, which he purchased for £115. This remained his headquarters until 1778, when a new chapel was opened on the City Road.

Piety found practical expression in spirited philanthropy. Five great new London hospitals were founded through private charity. The Westminster was established in 1719 for the relief of the sick and needy. Guy's Hospital, on St Thomas's Street, Southwark, was founded in 1725 by the bookseller Thomas Guy, who had made his fortune by printing bibles and through astute South Sea stock investment. Guy's had accommodation for four hundred, including a wing for the insane. St George's Hospital at Hyde Park Corner was opened in 1733; the London Hospital, Whitechapel, was completed in 1759, with thirty-five wards and 439 beds; and the Middlesex was founded in 1745 in Windmill Street, in houses rented from Mr Goodge, with three beds set aside for women in labour. Some of the money was raised by Garrick and Handel, who gave performances gratis. The Foundling Hospital for abandoned babies achieved special prominence. Set up in 1739 by Captain Thomas Coram, it moved in 1745 to Lamb's Conduit Fields (cats 3.37–3.43).[28]

Despite all these expressions of piety, organized religion was becoming sidelined. A secular culture was emerging, with an accent on sociability and pleasure, contributing to 'the commercialization of leisure'.[29] Georgian public life increasingly revolved around the town itself, its streets, public spaces and entertainments. The urban environment set the scene for passing the time: sauntering, shopping, sitting, staring.

Certain zones, notably the Strand, Covent Garden and Leicester Square, delighted *flâneurs*. It was smart to stroll and sightsee: 'here you have the advantage of solitude without its disadvantage', reflected Henry Fielding, 'since you may be alone and in company at the same time; and while you sit or walk unobserved, noise, hurry, and a constant succession of objects entertain the mind'. London's streets seemed made for leisure.[30] Mid-Georgian London had a well-mapped pleasure topography. Once rather superior, the precincts around Fleet Street, the Strand, Covent Garden and Charing Cross had been overrun by inns and taverns, shows, street performers and shops (it was in Davies's bookshop in Russell Street, Covent Garden, that Boswell first met Johnson in 1763). As the chief corridor connecting Westminster and the City, 'Fleet Street has a very animated appearance', pronounced Johnson. It was associated with literary London, upmarket from Grub Street (Barbican), the classic haven of hacks. Off Fleet Street, the printer-novelist Samuel Richardson was to be found in Salisbury Square, while Johnson himself occupied ten successive addresses just off the Street.

Street life was lubricated by places of refreshment. The smart site for socializing remained the coffee house. These establishments, according to de Saussure in the 1730s, were 'not over clean or well furnished, owing to the quantity of people who resort to these places and because of the smoke'. A prime attraction lay in the newspapers kept there: 'All Englishmen are great newsmongers', he observed: 'workmen habitually begin the day by going to coffee-rooms in order to read the latest news'. Newspapers formed the daily mirror of London life. Small surprise that the Abbé Prévost hailed coffee houses – 'where you have the right to read all the papers for and against the government' – as the 'seats of English liberty'.[31]

From the coffee-house clubs emerged. White's in St James's Street established itself as the acme of fashion, though later rivalled by Boodle's and Crockford's, both in St James's Street, and by Almack's in Pall Mall, founded in 1762 by William Almack. In 1764 that club split into two, Boodle's and Brooks's, while a further two clubs met on Almack's premises, the Macaroni (for 'travelled young men with long curls and spying

glasses') and the Ladies' Coterie, a fashionable unisex club. Brooks's in St James's Street became the greatest gambling den of all, Lord Lauderdale speaking of £70,000 being lost in a single night. Alongside clubs were learned societies such as the Royal Society and the Society of Antiquaries.[32]

The craze for coffee did not lead to any decline in serious drinking – 'a man is never happy in the present', opined Johnson, 'unless he is drunk'. Johnson's London was reckoned to have 207 inns, 447 taverns, 5,875 beerhouses and 8,659 brandy shops. Upmarket taverns such as the Mitre in Fleet Street housed concerts, election dinners and clubs, and were used to entertain friends, hear the news or settle business. Johnson had a regular chair at the Turk's Head in Gerrard Street, where he presided over the 'Club' which he and Joshua Reynolds founded in 1764, but he was equally at home in the Devil, the Mitre and the Crown and Anchor in the Strand.[33]

Drinking aroused other male appetites. As Boswell's journals amply document,[34] the streets from Charing Cross to Drury Lane were the favourite haunt of street-walkers. Beds could be hired in the backrooms of taverns and 'bagnios' (we would now say 'saunas').[35]

Another scene of somewhat dissolute fun was the fair. Lasting two to six weeks, Southwark Fair, May Fair and Bartholomew Fair at Smithfield each featured sideshows, rope-dancers, wire-walkers, acrobats, puppets, freaks and sometimes wild animals – they were also heaven for pickpockets and prostitutes.

Pall Mall was popular as a promenade, and from there London's great parks were easily accessible – St James's Park, Green Park, Hyde Park and Kensington Gardens. Citizens also loved outings. Amongst the spas and watering places perfect for a Sunday jaunt were Sadler's Wells in Islington, Kilburn Wells, Bermondsey Spa (now marked by Spa Road), and Hockley-in-the-Hole (Clerkenwell).[36]

Leisure entrepreneurs also created more elaborate pleasure gardens. Spring Gardens, later known as Vauxhall, opened in 1660 up-river on the south bank (cats 5.54–5.67): access by boat created a romantic illusion. Laid out with walks, statues and tableaux, Vauxhall became a dazzling resort under the entrepreneur Jonathan Tyers. Orchestras played, the fireworks sparkled, there was dancing and one could sup in gaily decorated alcoves or flirt in the groves – and all for a shilling. The alcoves were hung with paintings by Francis Hayman and other leading artists, and Roubiliac's statue of Handel was put on show. Adjoining Chelsea Hospital, Ranelagh opened as a rival in 1742 (cats 5.31–5.37). Its chief attraction was a Rotonda, 150 feet in diameter, with an orchestra in the centre and tiers of boxes all round.[37]

Low-life entertainments included cockfighting (cats 5.21–5.25), bear-baiting and prize-fighting (cats 3.27–3.28). In 1747 John Broughton, self-styled boxing champion of England, opened an academy off Cockspur Street at which gloves were used for the first time. Boxing became commercialized, as did another traditional sport, cricket (Fig. 2). The top team was the White Conduit Cricket Club, led by the Earl of Winchelsea; they

Fig. 2 Antoine Benoist after Francis Hayman, *Cricket*, etching

played on a pitch superintended by Thomas Lord in what is now Dorset Square, Marylebone. In 1767 it changed its title to the Marylebone Cricket Club, and its ground eventually settled in 1814 in St John's Wood. Spectators paid 6*d* for admission, and large crowds gathered – as much for the betting as for the cricket. Then as now, there was money in sport.

More intellectual tastes were also catered for. Circulating libraries opened: by 1800, the capital sported some 122 of these 'evergreen trees of diabolical knowledge'. The Royal Academy, founded in 1768, staged art exhibitions. Mrs Salmon opened a waxworks in Fleet Street, long before Madame Tussaud arrived from Paris. The capital also possessed an effervescent musical life, orchestrated by composer/impresarios such as Handel (cat. 3.43) and with visiting performers such as the young Mozart (cat. 3.87).[38]

Theatre thrived. During the eighteenth century the playhouse developed a deep fore-stage, bringing the actor into close contact with the audience and aiding the rise of such stars as David Garrick, James Quin and Peg Woffington. Garrick, who spent his working life at Drury Lane, displaced the old formal rhetoric and developed a more emotional, naturalistic acting style (pp. 134–8). 'In London', commented the American Benjamin Franklin, 'you have plays performed by good actors. That, however, is, I think, the only advantage London has over Philadelphia.'[39]

In London's new world of leisure, a galaxy of entertainment was thus available – something for everyone. Around Leicester Square, down to the Strand or up through Soho to Piccadilly, there was a great archipelago of shows, galleries, theatres, cockpits and exhibitions. Visitors were surprised by the extraordinary degree of social mixing in a city presided over not by the Court or the Church but by cultural entrepreneurship and public taste. They were bowled over to find ordinary people – laundresses and lightermen – sitting in the gods at the theatre or tripping off to Vauxhall.

With its heady brew of the high and low, the serious and the sordid, London afforded a people's theatre. This fascinated Hogarth, who relished and reviled it at the same time. *A Rake's Progress*, *A Harlot's Progress*, and the careers of the industrious and idle apprentices are allegories but also literal journeys through the capital. Goodchild, the industrious apprentice, ends up heading the Lord Mayor's procession in Cheapside (cat. 1.27), whereas Tom Idle makes his Calvary-like way to Tyburn Tree (cats 5.95–5.96). Tom Rakewell likewise goes to the bad: from drinking at the Rose Tavern in Covent Garden he is arrested for debt in fashionable Piccadilly; after recouping himself by marrying an old maid, he loses his fortune gambling, and ends up successively an inmate of those two terrible institutions just beyond the City walls, the Fleet Prison and Bethlem Hospital.

Crown and Parliament did little to mould London's public culture. The commercial art-world thrived in mid-Georgian London, but there was no public collection to compare with those in Italy and France, and London had to wait till the nineteenth century for the National Gallery. Museums provide a similar story. London had various private museums and collections, but the British Museum – deriving from the will of Sir Hans Sloane and opened in 1759 – remained rather inaccessible and an underused resource.

Mid-century literary London was dominated by Samuel Johnson. Sometimes he maligned his adopted city:

Here Malice, Rapine, Accident, conspire,
And now a Rabble rages, now a Fire;
Their Ambush here relentless Ruffians lay,
And here the fell Attorney prowls for Prey;
Here falling Houses thunder on your Head,
And here a female Atheist talks you dead.[40]

But more often his mood was the reverse. 'I suggested a doubt', recalled Boswell, 'that if I were to reside in London, the exquisite zest with which I relished it in occasional visits might go off, and I might grow tired of it.' Johnson entertained no such reservations: 'Why, Sir, you find no man, at all intellectual, who is willing to leave London. No, Sir, when a man is tired of London, he is tired of life; for there is in London all that life can afford.'

1 Reddaway.
2 Lindsay.
3 For a masterly account see Summerson.
4 Summerson, Wren.
5 Defoe.
6 Thomson.
7 Stone.
8 Borer 1975.
9 Mackenzie.
10 Byrd.
11 Gibbon.
12 Palmer.
13 Dyos.
14 Thompson; Borer 1976; Shute, 1977 and 1981.
15 Harris; for Butcher Row, see cat. 3.72.
16 Sheppard 1958.
17. Earle 1976; 1994.
18 For Johnson and London see Schwartz 1983 and Pickard.
19 Schwarz 1992.
20 Davis.
21 Dickson.
22 A fine account is to be found in Rudé 1971.
23 Clark 1988.
24 Rumbelow 1971 and 1982. Linebaugh shows up Georgian callousness.
25 De Castro.
26 Rudé 1952 and 1962.
27 Paulson 1974.
28 Andrew; also see McClure.
29 Plumb.
30 Brewer.
31 Lillywhite 1963.
32 Clark 2000.
33 Clark 1983.
34 Pottle.
35 Wagner.
36 Boulton.
37 Southworth.
38 Weber.
39 Stone.
40 Johnson.

ART AND TRADE – FROM THE SOCIETY OF ARTS TO THE ROYAL ACADEMY OF ARTS

CELINA FOX

If any institution epitomized the thrusting materialism of mid-eighteenth-century London it was the Society for the Encouragement of Arts, Manufactures and Commerce, founded in 1754, a year after the British Museum. The Society of Arts, as it was generally called,[1] did not spring into being *sui generis* but was one of the most successful of a number of initiatives made throughout Europe in the eighteenth century to establish 'oeconomical' or 'patriotic' societies, offering incentives usually by way of cash premiums for improvements in agriculture, manufacture, trade and the arts. They were distinct from scientific societies in having an emphatically practical purpose.[2] They involved a broad range of classes, from tradesmen, craftsmen and manufacturers to the professions and even the gentry and aristocracy, although it was unusual for them to be dominated by the latter. As with so many of the voluntary societies and clubs formed in Georgian Britain, the opportunity the Society presented for group sociability, combining debate with conviviality, was symptomatic of a dynamic, increasingly urban society breaking through the traditional structures of corporate and community life which were slowly sinking into atrophy.[3]

The rich texture of the Society's activities is revealed in its manuscript records. The range of invention described therein gives the impression that the prospect of reward for ingenious machines and speculative inventions had struck a chord on every social level. A fascination with technical ingenuity and improvement, commercial innovation and enterprise was shared by an indiscriminate mix of talents and ranks. The applications poured into the Society, ranging from carefully written treatises of several pages to scribbled notes from artisans, sometimes accompanied by drawings and models. To read them is to discover the authentic voice of the mid-eighteenth-century city: from confident specialists with a fluent theoretical base to humble mechanics articulating in their own words and phonetic spelling projects and schemes, practical proposals and kites in the sky. And inevitably there were the chancers and losers, the desperate and downright disreputable, whose inventions in an age before professional boundaries had been set hovered on the fringes of legitimacy and teetered on the borders of madness, sent in 'on spec', not falling into any of the advertised premium categories.

During the first decades of its existence the Society of Arts was an extremely useful institution, a valuable bridge between earlier individual endeavours and later, state-sponsored schemes. It brought classes together, subverted the authority of gentlemen amateurs and substituted a degree of practical expertise. In encouraging independence from French models it boosted national confidence in British trade and manufactures; capitalizing upon free enterprise rather than restrictive privilege, it even became a source of envy to the French. It stimulated a plethora of inventions and improvements and, although they did not lead to revolutionary discoveries, it helped ensure among a wide spectrum of society that the potential of innovation gained acceptance and was seen as infinitely preferable to tradition and stagnation. It also contributed towards the development of a national school of fine art which came into its own in the 1760s, preparing the ground for the foundation of the Royal Academy of Arts in 1768. Nevertheless, there was nothing inevitable about this outcome. At the Society artists and tradesmen met on equal terms, not distinguished by an academic hierarchy of ascending value.

The meaning of 'Arts' in the context of the Society was ambiguous, symptomatic of an age when there was as yet no definitive characterization of its various disciplines and branches within the spectrum of knowledge. In the dictionaries and encyclopaedias of the day, the arts and sciences together were taken to refer to all knowledge, seen as an inclusive whole. But a general distinction was made between theory, observation or speculation, and practice, action or application: the former was thought of as 'science', the latter 'art'. Within art, a further distinction was made between the liberal professions (although significantly, if confusingly, sometimes the liberal arts were called liberal sciences) and the mechanical trades – between the liberal man who used his reason to pursue general principles and the vulgar mechanic whose narrow experience confined him to following particular instructions. From the start the Society of Arts attempted to improve both the liberal or 'polite' and the 'mechanical' arts; indeed, they were seen to be intimately connected.

In June 1753 William Shipley, a drawing master based in Northampton, produced a pamphlet outlining proposals for a Society ambitiously intended 'to embolden enterprise, to enlarge science, to refine art, to improve our manufactures, and extend our commerce; in a word, to render Great Britain the school of instruction, as it is already the centre of traffic to the greatest part of the known world'. Premiums or cash awards would be paid to whoever progressed 'any branch of beneficial knowledge', displayed 'the most complete performance in any species of mechanical skill', or executed 'any scheme or project calculated for the honour, the embellishment, the interest, the comfort (or in time of danger, for the defence) of this nation'. Thus Shipley, true to his times, saw his Society as a highly patriotic endeavour. In December 1753 he published the Society's draft constitution in London, promoting it as a means of 'introducing of such manufactures as may employ great numbers of the poor', yet adding that premiums should be given 'for the revival and advancement of those arts and sciences which are at a low ebb amongst us; as poetry, painting, tapestry, architecture etc.'. So he believed that it would bring benefits to the entire population, from the poor who could be employed in mechanical arts to the rich who might wish to patronize the liberal arts.

The founding meeting of the Society was held at Rawthmell's Coffee House, Covent Garden, on 22 March 1754. The nucleus of ten members from the 'Nobility, Clergy, Gentlemen and Merchants' included four Fellows of the Royal Society, but trade and manufacture were strongly represented and mercantilist policies of import substitution enthusiastically espoused. For example in 1756 Shipley's friend and fellow founder member, the energetic polymath Henry Baker F.R.S., wrote an anonymous promotional article in *The Gentleman's Magazine* entitled 'Advantages arising from the Society for encouraging Arts', itemizing the premiums on offer which would 'produce great advantages to this nation, by employing many hands, and saving annually large sums of money'. Alongside premiums for the home production of cobalt, madder, buff (oiled ox) leather and tinning with pure tin, Baker placed particular emphasis on the premiums introduced to encourage the commercial application of drawing: 'since drawing is necessary in so many trades, that the general knowledge of it must conduce greatly to the improvement of our manufactures, and give them an elegance of air and figure, which a rival nation (where drawing is much encouraged) has found, to its great advantage, capable of setting on even indifferent workmanship, and mean materials'.[4] The rival nation was of course France, against whom Britain was about to go to war yet again.

Baker's elaboration of the theme 'that drawing enlivens the conception, corrects the judgement, and supplies the fancy with a thousand varieties, which would never otherwise be thought of' was applied to the gamut of mechanical arts then practised in the metropolis. The Society would not be limited to increasing the number of painters; it was 'earnestly solicitous' of producing among the boys 'ingenious mechanics, such as carvers, joiners, upholsterers, cabinet-makers, coach-makers and coach painters, sign painters, weavers, curious workers in all sorts of metals, smiths, makers of toys, engravers, sculptors, chasers, calico-printers, &c. Sailors that can take the bearing of coasts or the plans of harbours, and soldiers better qualified for becoming engineers.' Nor did he forget the girls, proceeding to enumerate a range of characteristic female occupations: 'ingenious

milliners, mantua makers, embroiderers, pattern drawers, fan-painters, and good workwomen in many other sorts of business where fancy and variety are required'. It is clear that, unlike Shipley, Baker was not over concerned with encouraging the polite arts in their highest form. The focus of his interest was the training of artisans, as well as the naval and military engineers required to defend the country and promote its trading interests abroad.

The connection made between drawing – in effect designing – and high-quality manufacture was no more than an observation based on best workshop practice over the centuries.[5] But it acquired a particular force when it was identified as the key to satisfying consumer demand in the booming market for luxury goods, one in which France was seen to excel. Since the reign of Louis XIV the French had successfully promoted themselves as the leading power in the arts, fashion and manners, to be envied or even mocked, yet slavishly imitated. The careers advisory manual for metropolitan parents, Campbell's *The London Tradesman* (1747), went so far as to counsel that in order to be successful a budding mercer

> must have a great deal of the *French-man* in his manners, as well as a large parcel of *French* goods in his shop; he ought to keep close intelligence with the fashion-office at *Paris*, and supply himself with the newest patterns from that changeable people. Nothing that is mere *English* goes down with our modern ladies; from their shift to their topknots they must be equipped from dear *Paris*.[6]

Fancy, variety and ingenuity in design were welcomed as desirable attributes in the treatises on taste and beauty produced in the 1750s by aesthetic commentators from William Hogarth to Adam Smith.[7] These qualities were also extensively documented in a flood of prints depicting ornamental motifs, and in specialized books containing patterns for particular trades. They were almost wholly dedicated to the diffusion of the taste later referred to as 'Rococo', featuring a heady combination of extravagant asymmetrical forms, organic scrolls and naturalistic motifs – fruit, flowers, rocks and shells – on which changes could endlessly be rung, freed of the immutable rules which bound classicism. The lightness, informality and very caprice of the Rococo style enhanced its appeal to fashionable London consumers, ever demanding the latest novelty. It was even combined with fanciful motifs drawn from other anti-classical styles, notably chinoiserie and gothic.

The earliest ornament prints and pattern books were largely plagiarized from French sources, but leading London artisans soon realized the marketing potential for their own purposes. *The Gentleman and Cabinet-Maker's Director*, published in 1754 by Thomas Chippendale, 'being a New Book of Designs of Household Furniture in the Gothic, Chinese and Modern Taste as improved by the politest and most able artists', constituted the first comprehensive English furniture catalogue, comprising 161 designs engraved by Matthew Darly (Fig. 3). Skilled craftspeople such as the Spitalfields silk designer Anna Maria Garthwaite, the Swiss-born gold-chaser George Michael Moser

Fig. 3 Matthew Darly after Thomas Chippendale, *Pier Glass Frame*, from *The Gentleman and Cabinet Maker's Director*, Plate CXLIII. British Library, C.119.k.4.

tradesman to be a painter or connoisseur in designing; no, but I think it absolutely necessary, that every tradesman should have so much knowledge of that art as to draw the profile of most common things; especially to be able to delineate on paper a plan of every piece of work he intends to execute.'[10] In contrast, John Gwynn's *An Essay on Design* (1749) proposed a public academy 'for educating the British youth in drawing' primarily to emulate the Paris Académie Royale des Beaux-Arts, established by Colbert in 1664, which had conferred such honour and distinction on the liberal arts: 'We are apt enough to imitate the *French* in their fopperies and excesses: let an emulation of them in what is noble and praise-worthy at least keep pace with our pursuit of their fashions.'[11] Nevertheless, he acknowledged, 'there is scarce any mechanic, let his employment be ever so simple, who may not receive advantage from the knowledge of proportion, and more still from a little taste in design'.[12] Drawing, Gwynn concluded, was the 'animating Soul' of all other skills, as practised in the supreme inventive art of the painter, sculptor or architect and by the whole body of mechanics employed in fashioning or ornamenting the various utensils of life.

The plan for an academy of painting and sculpture which the sculptor Henry Cheere brought before the Society of Arts on 19 February 1755 encompassed both levels of artistic activity, albeit organized on a descending scale of value. Those who could not aspire to the highest forms would be taught ornamental design for manufactures:

> From architecture and all its ornaments external and internal, from painting and sculpture, graving and chasing, planting and gardening, and all the various performances, in which art and

Fig. 4 John Linnell, *Design for the Side of a Room*, watercolour. V&A Picture Library, E.263–1929.

or the furniture-maker John Linnell could draw on a variety of English and Continental sources to create their own distinctive designs (Fig. 4).[8] The process of imitation and ingenious adaptation by London artisans within the privacy of their workshops is revealed in the album composed by the carver and gilder Gideon Saint around 1760 (Fig. 5). Its 364 pages divided into twelve sections dealing with different types of furniture are pasted with his own drawings alongside their sources: cut-up prints culled from Matthias Lock, Thomas Johnson, assorted French artists and ornamental trade cards.[9]

The urgent need for London apprentices to acquire similar skills in drawing was widely recognized by mid-century, albeit with differences in emphasis. In *The London Tradesman* Campbell adopted a purely pragmatic stance, citing the example of the French king who had erected academies to teach drawing gratis in all the great cities of his dominions: 'By being learned to draw, I would not be understood, that it is necessary for every

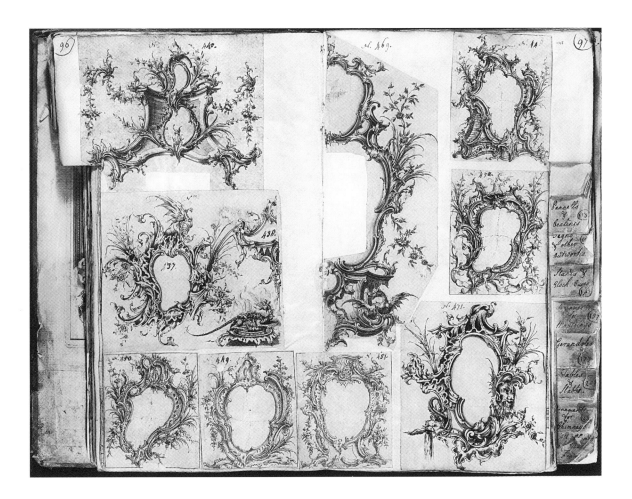

Fig. 5 Pages 96–7 from a scrapbook of designs compiled by
Gideon Saint. The Metropolitan Museum of Art, Haris Brisbane
Dick Fund, 1934, 34.90.1.

genius, elegancy of fancy, and accuracy of workmanship are
confessedly united, it will descend to the subordinate branches
of design, In utensils of all sorts, plate and cabinet work, patterns
of silks, jewelling, garniture, carriage building and equipage,
down to toys and trinkets, it will expect to find the same
manifestations of propriety and elegancy and will reject
whatsoever is apparently irreconcilable with the true standards
of use and beauty.[13]

Although Cheere's proposals were not progressed, it is clear
that in the 1750s and 1760s the Society of Arts did fulfil on an
informal basis many of the functions of an art academy and one
with a much wider remit than the Royal Academy that was to
upstage it in 1768. Take, for example, the motion proposed in
March 1757 by the wealthy Russia merchant Robert Dingley to
give a premium for modelling in wax and clay. As a successful
businessman as well as a talented amateur and member of
the Dilettante Society, his arguments were poised between the
pragmatic and the aesthetic, considering 'the benefit of modelling in a commercial national light' and as an 'art useful &
ornamental'. He argued the case for self-sufficiency in modelling

across a huge range of trades the results of which could also be
exported: china and earthenware; carving in wood such as
picture frames, joinery, coach and cart building, cabinet-making
and upholstery; glass manufacture; jewellery and toys; clocks,
watches and optical instruments; the improvement of machines
and cutting the dies for their manufacture; ironwork and
wrought plate; coins and medals; architecture and shipbuilding;
swords, snuff boxes, belt buckles, even plumes for turbans.
Premiums for modelling were duly endorsed.[14]

With so comprehensive and patriotic an agenda, it is not
surprising that the Society was successful in attracting a wide
membership. At a time when the government was still largely
reactive in promoting economic growth and employment, a
voluntary society whose express purpose was to further both was
highly attractive to the urban commercial classes, not to mention
the landed elite primarily concerned of course with agricultural
improvements, but also with achieving better returns on trade
and industrial enterprises undertaken on their property.[15]
By 1764 the Society had 2,136 members, of whom a tenth
(including women) had titles, ninety-nine were medical men,
sixty-six were clergymen and forty-eight of naval or military
background.[16] The remainder ranged from government officials
and merchants (twenty-eight Russia merchants alone) to tradespeople (with most of the City livery companies represented),

manufacturers and artisans, headed by eight watchmakers and seven printers. The membership list is studded with stars from the firmament of mid-Georgian London: artists, sculptors, architects, composers, writers and actors, admirals and generals, politicians, lawyers, bankers and leading city merchants, as well as the most renowned artisans of the day.[17] The Society also attracted an eminent network of foreign correspondents, from colonial America to Russia. As Smollett confirmed retrospectively in *Humphry Clinker* (1771), to be a member of the Society of Arts was all the rage. Melford, nephew of old Squire Bramble, writes to his friend and constant correspondent, Sir Watkin Phillips, regarding their London adventures:

> We are become members of the Society for the encouragement of the Arts, and have assisted at some of their deliberations, which were conducted with equal spirit and sagacity. My uncle is extremely fond of the institution, which will certainly be productive of great advantages to the public, if, from its democratical form, it does not degenerate into cabal and corruption.

Yet was the Society anything more than a fashionable diversion? To what extent was it representative of or even relevant to the economic realities of mid-eighteenth-century London? Did it improve manufactures, stimulate invention or raise standards in the fine arts? Surely the engine of progress in the city was driven by commercial profit, riding on the back of consumer demand over the booms and troughs of the trade cycle, not by a talking shop which awarded prizes on a seemingly serendipitous basis? Certainly the growth of wealth in London provided a mass of opportunities for the introduction of ever more specialized products and ingenious novelties. It is also true to say that in its first few years the workings of the Society appear little short of chaotic. Business was despatched by a small staff of officers, a growing number of committees set up *ad hoc* to deal with specific activities and increasingly large general meetings. But by the early 1760s the Committee of Premiums had been divided into six specialized standing committees dealing with the Polite Arts; Agriculture; Mechanics; Manufactures; Chemistry; the Colonies and Trade. Nor was its income and expenditure to be sniffed at. By the end of 1766 the Society had received over £33,000 and distributed nearly £7,000 in premiums for the Polite Arts alone, as well as around £2,000 apiece for Agriculture, Mechanics, Manufactures and the Colonies, and nearly £1,000 for Chemistry.[18]

The first volume of a work commissioned by the Society from the agriculturalist Robert Dossie, *Memoirs of Agriculture, and other Oeconomical Arts* (1768), provides a useful, if excessively rosy, summary of the Society's activities during the first dozen years of its existence. By the date of publication Shipley's core agenda had become even more relevant: to curtail the country's dependence on foreign imports by encouraging the cultivation of home substitutes, to provide employment for the poor and to raise standards of taste. After the protection to British manufacture afforded by the Seven Years War (1756–63) and despite the vast territorial gains of the Treaty of Paris, the country was

entering a period of political unrest and economic depression. For two days in 1765 the notoriously vulnerable and riotous Spitalfields silk weavers had picketed Bedford House, Bloomsbury Square, carrying black flags in protest against the Duke, who had defeated a bill designed to protect their livelihood by excluding French silks from the English market.[19] In May 1768 the mechanical sawmill erected by Charles Dingley (Robert's brother) in his Limehouse timber-yard, with the Society's full encouragement and approbation, was badly damaged by a mob of five hundred sawyers who feared for their livelihood.[20]

Dossie steered clear of making any direct mention of industrial troubles, but he constantly stressed the ways in which Society had helped to cut down dependence on imported French goods and reduce unemployment. Many premiums for 'Manufactures' were offered for improvements to textile industries. He cited the example of Turkey carpets made in imitation of those brought from the East and in general use 'from the increasing luxury of the age'. A large expense was saved by manufacturing them in Britain, which was also valuable because 'carding and spinning make a great part of the work: which, consequently, employ women and children; who are thus rendered profitable to the public, and moral in their conduct, instead of being burthensome, or loose in their way of life; as they otherwise would be.' A premium of £25 each was duly awarded in 1758 to Thomas Moore of Chiswell Street, who produced the best example with regard to pattern and colour, and Thomas Whitty of Axminster who produced the nearest approximation in staple.[21] On a more basic level, the Vicar and Overseers of the Parish of St Dunstan-in-the-West were among a number of parishes countrywide who applied in 1759 for the premium for spinning the best worsted yarn produced by women and children in their workhouse.[22]

The manufacture of different types of paper – for printing from copper-plates, made from silk rags, marbled or embossed – was encouraged to reduce the 'very considerable sum paid to foreigners, particularly the French'.[23] It was also of benefit to the polite arts which Dossie emphasized, not least those 'of a mixt nature, as being of the greatest consequence to commerce. This is, the drawing patterns and designs for ornaments: for several branches of which the Society have offered premiums.' To his disappointment, some premiums for manufactures had yet to be awarded, such as that for artificial flowers, imported from Italy and France at an incredible price and in large quantities. The publication of instructions would be helpful, he thought, 'as the want of this knowledge is the only means of accounting for the supineness of great numbers of women, who labour under difficulties in their circumstances, from trying to get, not only an easy, but even a genteel support, if they attained any degree of perfection in this art'.[24] Dossie was describing another 'mixt' art which potentially could combine both polite and mechanical features. Likewise, the procuring of cat-gut strings for musical instruments was deemed important in order to exclude frequently bad and exorbitantly priced foreign products, 'in a commercial light, and even for the improvement of music with us, which is not less a *polite* or *liberal art* than painting'.[25]

The Society's involvement in chemistry reveals a similar conjunction. It encompassed finding native raw materials for use in core dyeing and finishing processes such as verdigris, varnish, cobalt and saltpetre. It also encouraged the search for methods of purifying onyxes and cornelians, for making leaf metal and bronze for ormolu, or creating white or a true red for enamel painters. This concern with improving materials used for decorative or imitative finishes, although categorized by Dossie under 'Chemical Arts', was inextricably part of a broader spectrum of artful activity. The improved execution of the polite arts relied on better methods and materials, involving chemistry, manufactures and mechanics, as much as the mechanical arts required the designing and modelling skills associated with the polite arts. At the same time it was hoped that such improvements and inventions would help combat competition from abroad and unemployment at home.

Letters preserved in the Society's guard-books bring to life the individuals who responded to the Society's broad agenda. Here is John Pitt writing diffidently from a peruke-maker's in Long Acre in January 1761, regarding his assorted military inventions: 'Pardon my boldness in offering these proposals, to your Lordships inspection, having no friend to interduce me.'[26] Or the pushy Mrs Dorothy Holt who pestered the Society in 1757 with her samples of English point lace despite being told on two occasions that premiums were given only for articles advertised by their order. The Committee of Manufactures eventually succumbed in 1762, after a pair of her ruffles had been worn by George III at his coronation, and she received ten guineas 'in consideration of her frequent attendance hints & information'.[27] More poignant are those who accompanied their submissions with hard luck stories, such as John Giles, a silversmith until the trade had declined in the war of Austrian Succession, who was left with four guineas and a sickly wife and who volunteered an invention in 1754 to make any metal 'as fine a colour and lustre as standard silver'.[28] Such cases serve as reminders of the buffeting of the labour force in the mideighteenth-century city, largely unprotected from abrupt swings in the trade cycle and certainly from illness and disease spread by the dirty, unhealthy environment. In 1760 Daniel Pineau, a Southwark house, sign and floor-cloth painter, wrote in his finest calligraphic hand enclosing some patterns for wall hangings executed, 'without paper or canvas on walls or wainscoting which cannot harbour buggs as the paper &c does, & being painted in oil-colours will keep their colour much longer & are not liable to the accidents that paper often meet with; as damp walls which causes the paper to fall down &c'.[29]

Established craftsmen approached the Society with confidence and were often active members. The watchmaker Thomas Grignion joined in 1755 and was soon proposing that a premium be given to an apprentice in the watch trade, 'For the best plain watch movement' finished by hand. A clutch of London's finest clockmakers, including such luminaries as John Harrison and

John Ellicott, begged to differ, pointing out that the process of finishing watch wheels by hand had been superseded by machine which was more accurate and cost less.[30] The proposal was duly rejected but Grignion appeared to bear the Society no grudge, for in 1759 he presented it with a handsome timepiece (still in its possession) as a means of acquainting 'our worthy President, Vice President and members of our laudable Society … of my utmost esteem and regard'.[31] In 1764 the 'honour and happiness' felt by that indefatigable inventor Christopher Pinchbeck the younger at being a member induced him to demonstrate to the Committee of Mechanics 'divested of every pecuniary view' a model of a treadmill crane fitted with his invention of a self-acting pneumatic brake, designed to prevent the 'shocking and often fatal accidents' that frequently occurred in such machines. The model was displayed by gracious permission of the King, in whose royal cabinet it had been placed, but the Committee decided to commission another and to award Pinchbeck a gold medal. The Society also arranged for Pinchbeck's contrivance to be added to a crane at Dice's Quay, near Billingsgate, where it eventually rotted away through lack of maintenance and use.[32]

The Society was a place where the polite and mechanical classes could meet, where the traditional reserve of the gentleman removed from practical ends could break down and where the realm of polite arts extended inexorably into manufactures. But Baker was alert to the need to cater for the exclusively polite, who did not wish to be associated with profit. On 24 March 1756 he read a paper in which it was proposed to award medals as honorary premiums for those desirous of esteem rather than gain. Undoubtedly, money premiums gave 'the best encouragement to the mechanic, the manufacturer, and the planter, and to all the multitude in whom the desire of gain prevails; but may we not suppose that some honorary token of esteem would more effectually bring to your assistance the scholar, the philosopher, and the gentleman of estate?'[33]

His proposal was approved, and by 1758 gold and silver medals of a suitable design had been struck.[34] Not that the move created a rigid division along class lines, as there was no necessary correlation between class and financial security: some gentlemanly inventors such as the Reverend Humphrey Gainsborough opted for cash premiums[35] while leading craftsmen such as Christopher Pinchbeck the younger could be awarded medals. But more insidiously, the genteel could introduce a note of dilettantism. On 19 December 1763 Richard Lovell Edgeworth brought to the attention of the Society a portable camera obscura which, as it would fit in a pocket, was intended for 'travellers who by this means may obtain sketches of foreign curiosities, which their time nor skill could not otherwise permit them to take … true models of foreign fortifications and the situation of harbours &c, but above all in taking the proportions and exactest outline from antique statutes [*sic*]'.[36]

In his 1768 volume, having defined the polite arts as 'those which depend on design and taste; and are called by others the FINE ARTS', Dossie noted the amazingly successful effect of those premiums 'on the youth whose genius were turned to studies of this nature: and the incitement of emulation, arising thence, produced the most assiduous and spirited exertion of their talents'. Public exhibitions, due entirely to the example set by the Society, had completed what the premiums had begun: 'extending its effects to the oldest and most able artists, as well as the young, it has advanced, in a few years, almost every branch of these arts, to such an approach towards perfection as was scarcely to be expected'.[37] He was exaggerating of course. But, as Shipley had intended, a huge store was placed by the Society on improving the polite arts. His personal agenda as a drawing master with a school in the Strand happily accorded with the interests both of metropolitan artists who were keen to belong somewhere and of those polite members of the Society who wished to improve the higher arts.

The number of premiums offered for the polite arts grew rapidly, weaving a serpentine path between practical ends and high art ideals. After the successful experience of the first-year drawings premiums offered simply for the best drawings in two age categories – under fourteen and between the ages of fourteen and seventeen – it was decided that for the second year, 1755, premiums would be extended to the 'best fancied and most useful designs proper for weavers, embroiderers or calico printers, drawn by boys and girls under seventeen and of their own invention'. As first proposed, premiums offered for the third year, 1756/7, were to fall into the same categories, but they were by no means uncontested. The girls wished to have separate awards from the boys as they felt intimidated. Furthermore, on 28 January 1756, William Hogarth presented a paper which he had drawn up containing 'some hints relating to the premiums for drawings for the future'.

Although the paper he delivered to the Society has not been found and may never have existed in any formal sense, on his own admission it was not far removed from manuscript notes towards an 'Apology for Painters', dating from around 1760, which have survived.[38] From a comparison between the sentiments he expressed in retrospect and the actions of the Society in 1757 it is possible to surmise the reasons for Hogarth's resignation the same year. Firstly, he thought it a waste of time to entice young people with premiums into entering the fine arts, a field which was already crowded with history and landscape painters who barely made a living. He outlined an alternative career trajectory which paralleled that of the Industrious 'Prentice in his *Industry & Idleness* print series of 1747. What was the point of foregoing the pleasures of youth 'in a laborious study for empty fame when his next door neighbour perhaps a brewer or haberdasher of small wares shall accumulate a large fortune become Lord Mayor member of parliament and at length get a title for his heirs.'[39]

Secondly, Hogarth stood up for the country's commercial values, and even for its taste: 'it is proof rather of the good sense of this country that the encouragement has rather been to trade and mechanics than to the arts'. English manufactures were as good as if not better than those of the French, but prejudice would not allow it.[40] The reason the country did not produce

such goods was not for want of ability 'as some coxcombs would have it' but because, as a trading nation, we could buy 'curiositys' ready-made from abroad.[41] This brings us to the third problem he appears to have had with the ethos of the Society, which, although more obliquely expressed, probably loomed largest. He deplored the tendency of 'this great society', as he (sarcastically?) described it, to pander to 'people of leisure' who joined it because they were tired of public amusements and found themselves in good company and 'amused with the formal speeches of those who still had more pleasure in showing their talents for oratory'.[42] In particular, Hogarth was passionately opposed to the perceived superiority of the upper classes in matters of taste. Those who went to France or Italy for their studies were the worse for going, 'talking of the antiques in a kind of cant in half or whole Italian to the great surprise of the standers by and bring over wonderfull copies of bad originals ador'd for their names only'.[43]

Yet it was in just these fields that the premiums were multiplying. The fourth-year premiums announced on 13 April 1757 had markedly increased in number and revealed an ominous bias towards the polite arts. One or other or all precipitated Hogarth's resignation. They now included premiums for boys for drawings after prints and plaster casts, for the best models in wax, clay or any other composition and for medals. A further refinement might well have been the straw that broke Hogarth's back: 'As an honourable encouragement to young gentlemen or ladies of fortune or distinction, not exceeding sixteen years of age, who entertain or amuse themselves with drawing, the society propose to give a silver medal for the best performance in drawing of any kind; and also a silver medal for the second best.' Such provision for 'honorary drawings', as they were called, paralleled the award of honorary medals by the other committees. The young amateurs who practised the noble arts as a polite recreation would be happy, it was thought, to receive approbation rather than payment. It was further assumed that the effortless superiority of the children of the peerage with regard to matters of taste would rub off on less fortunate youth through emulation, while in later life the latter might look to the former as patrons.[44] Lady Louisa Augusta Greville, sister of the Earl of Warwick, duly won the first silver medal in 1758 for a drawing of a view of the priory of Warwick.[45]

Hogarth's antipathy to 'young people of fortune' who assumed the virtues of taste after the minimum of study was well documented in his 'Apology', and by the end of 1757 he had resigned from the Society, his name vigorously struck through in the membership book. The premiums took an even more pronounced turn towards academic art education. Taste as acquired on the Grand Tour was encouraged by premiums for drawings after the plaster casts of antique and old master sculpture displayed in the Duke of Richmond's gallery in his palatial Whitehall residence.[46] Furthermore, Joseph Wilton and Giovanni Battista Cipriani, who had been appointed keepers of the Duke's collection, offered tuition every Saturday to vetted boys over the age of twelve. Premiums were also awarded for drawings in chalk after living models at the academy of artists in St Martin's Lane (cats 3.44–3.46). By 1759 premiums for history and landscape paintings had been introduced for fully fledged professional artists.

The establishment by the early 1760s of separate standing committees confirmed the growth in Society business but also, perhaps, a desire by some to draw a line of demarcation between polite and mechanical arts. By 1764 there were fifty separate awards for different types of drawing and another fifty for different types of modelling and engraving. In 1765 there was even a proposal to establish a Rome scholarship for a young person under twenty-one who had obtained from the Society one or more premiums that indicated a 'genius for historical painting'. Such developments were of course one way of ensuring the continued support of the polite membership and, for a time, of professional artists keen to establish an academy. As Shipley commented in retrospect, 'Had we not patronised these very entertaining and extensive subjects [i.e. the Polite Arts] ... this Society had not now existed.'[47] Nevertheless, there was some grumbling, one member writing to a friend in 1759: 'Our Society has of late become a mere society of drawing, painting and sculpture, and attends to little else, as you may observe by a list of the premiums for this year which I shall send you.'[48]

During the period of Shipley's active association with the Society, polite arts premiums were by far the largest of those paid out.[49] Their effect is difficult to determine. The first prize-winner of £5 in the under-fourteen category, announced in January 1755, was Richard Cosway, who was twelve at the time. Shipley took young Cosway under his wing, and the boy was awarded a premium on four other occasions, an achievement which exploited to advantage the expanding range of premiums.[50] He was to become a fashionable portrait-painter working mainly in miniature, scarcely representative of the height of achievement of the British school in this period.[51] Nevertheless, in the years before the foundation of the Royal Academy in 1768, the Society offered step-by-step incentives to follow an art education of sorts, and the polite arts premium winners are by no means undistinguished.

Shipley's school groomed young artists for the Society's premiums, John Smart and William Pars – both of whom were to become portrait-painters, Pars later turning to landscape water-colours – alternating with Cosway in winning prizes. Thomas Banks, Joseph Nollekens and John Bacon the Elder, not to mention the Pingo family (pp. 189–91), more or less swept the board in the modelling classes. Lurking in the Society's register of premiums are others who were later to achieve considerable fame: John Russell, Michael Angelo Rooker, John Hamilton Mortimer, Francis Wheatley and William Hodges. Early winners of the valuable prizes for history painting included Robert Edge Pine, Mortimer and George Romney, while Anthony Devis, George Barret and Thomas Jones all won landscape premiums. Richard Earlom and William Sharp were later to become notable engravers.[52] So Hogarth's worst predictions do not appear to have been confirmed.

There are cases where Shipley and/or the Society encouraged boys bent on a career in trade to become fine artists. Ozias Humphry was destined to be a lace pattern designer, but having received training under Shipley (although he never won a premium), became another successful miniature- and portrait-painter.[53] John Bacon was originally apprenticed to a porcelain manufacturer yet was encouraged by his premium wins to turn to sculpture. But other premium winners, such as the watch-makers Thomas Grignion junior and Benjamin Vulliamy or the goldsmith William Wakelin, stuck to the family business. Most of the girls were the daughters or sisters of skilled artisans and artists and presumably also helped in family concerns. But scores of young hopefuls who applied for premiums remain elusive. Only a small selection of premium drawings – principally for 1757/8 – appear to have survived in the Society's archives for the period before 1800 and their quality is not outstanding. Some, being half-finished, were clearly executed in the Society's rooms as proof of competence. The watercolours are tinted drawings in the style of the period, the flower drawings executed by Mary Moser, George Michael Moser's only surviving child, being the most promising.[54] A number of drawings of Rococo ornament after the latest French prints were no doubt typical of the category of 'Fancy Designs' deemed proper for use by manufacturers.[55]

According to Dossie, the practice of holding exhibitions of premium winners in the polite arts, more than any other, kept the minds of young artists intent upon study, and made them strive to excel in preparing a 'new performance from which some additional honour and reputation was to be derived'.[56] The opportunity to display the premium-winning entries in enhanced surroundings came when in 1759 William Chambers supervised the conversion of the Society's premises in Denmark Court, opposite Beaufort Buildings in the Strand, creating an impressively large Great Room.[57] The same year a group of professional artists led by Robert Edge Pine and Francis Hayman also proposed hiring the new Great Room to exhibit their works, a request approved by the Society in 1760.

The 1760 landmark exhibition, comprising 130 works by sixty-nine professional artists and premium winners, drew twenty thousand visitors in the two weeks of its duration. The catalogue, priced at 6d, included portraits, landscapes and history pieces but also works representative of the Society's wider remit. Philip Mercier contributed 'A Sketch of the Distribution of the Premiums at the Society for the Encouragement of Arts, Manufactures, and Commerce', Miss Moser 'A Piece of Flowers in Water Colours' and Charles Catton two ornamental coach patterns. Richard Cosway showed a portrait of his mentor, William Shipley. There were sculptures, models and engravings, besides designs for bridges, monuments, medals and seals. But such a broad miscellany was not to everyone's taste. The problem was that the Society's premium history paintings got most of the publicity and were scattered among the other exhibits, leading many to believe from the labels that they were judged the best pictures overall. It was irritating to artists of the stature of Joshua Reynolds and Richard Wilson who not unnaturally wished to make alternative arrangements. In future they also wanted to restrict visitors to single admission by catalogue (*hoi polloi* had shared catalogues to crowd into the first exhibition), at double the price of a shilling. Their request was turned down by the Society which effectively put an end to its collaboration with Pine and Hayman's group. The majority of the professional artists severed their connection with the Society, exhibiting the following year at the Great Room in Spring Gardens as the newly established Society of Artists of Great Britain. In 1765 they were awarded a Royal Charter and became known as the Incorporated Society of Artists leading eventually, if acrimoniously, to the foundation of the Royal Academy.[58]

Some remained loyal to the Society of Arts, taking the name in 1763 of the Free Society of Artists, but their exhibitions were always second-rate. The 1761 exhibition is typical in that it included a number of flower and fruit pieces possibly intended as designs for manufactures, as well as drawings, engravings, sculpture, furniture, needlework and stained marble designs. It was the Free Society's mixed shows as much as the pretensions of those staged by the Society of Artists, not to mention the rivalry between them, that were mocked in Bonnell Thornton's spoof Sign Painters' Exhibition of 1762. Thornton was a hack journalist and supporter of Hogarth (who was probably the show's prime mover) against the pretensions of connoisseurs. London's elaborately painted street-signs were soon to be removed, but meanwhile they marked the juncture where fine and mechanical arts met (pp. 52–5). Often painted by skilled artists such as Charles Catton, they were nevertheless a demotic art form and, by their very nature as business or trade signs, connected with commerce.[59] Even though the Society of Arts stopped holding exhibitions in 1764 and curtailed its association with the Free Society after further quarrels, it retained a broad understanding as to what constituted polite arts, attracting fancy work and novelties frequently submitted by ladies whose ingenious endeavours hovered uneasily between genteel pursuits undertaken for pleasure and attempts to earn an honest crust.

Nevertheless, in retrospect the Society believed that it had been 'fortunately successful in rearing the infant arts in this kingdom, to such maturity as qualified them for royal favour'.[60] Dossie conceded in 1782 that the new institution of the Royal Academy gave 'an additional support to the superior and scientific parts, namely, to painting, sculpture, and architecture'. But he maintained that the 'united endeavours' of the Royal Academy and Society of Arts had produced a 'complete and permanent' establishment to the arts: 'The more eminent parts directed, rewarded, and openly commended by the Royal Academy, appeared to belong to that body; while the branches regarding fabrics and manufactures, original objects of the plan devised for promoting trade and commerce, remained to be shaped, fostered, and encouraged by the Society.'[61]

In his first *Discourse on Art*, delivered on 2 January 1769, the new President of the Royal Academy, Sir Joshua Reynolds, made explicit this fundamental difference in philosophy, nailing his colours to the mast of high art: 'An institution like this has often been recommended upon considerations merely mercantile; but an academy, founded upon such principles, can never effect even its own narrow purposes. If it has an origin no higher, no taste can ever be formed in manufactures; but if the higher arts of design flourish, these inferior ends will be answered of course.'[62] Reynolds's restatement of the supremacy of academic values was consciously pitched to exclude the low activities of commerce, for they were based on raw experience from which general ideas could not be abstracted. While the Society had viewed art as a utilitarian vehicle for patriotic endeavour and commercial profit, Reynolds saw such ends as elevating particular interests – even those of a particular nation, Britain – over universal values and thus corrupting influences on art. Painting was a liberal profession not a mechanical trade. Reynolds opposed 'mechanical felicity' in drawing as narrow, servile imitation, which he considered a 'fallacious mastery'. The drawing appropriate to a liberal art was dependent on general principles of truth and beauty, abstracting the intellectual from the sensual. The distinction between the liberal and the mechanical was the opposition between the mind and the hand, between principle and mere practice.

Reynolds's smooth cosmopolitan certainties, secured by the rules of international neo-classicism and a royal seal of approval, were to triumph over the national, commercial 'mixt' art which had been so vigorously endorsed by the Society of Arts and its membership. The metropolitan commercial classes who, as we have seen, had a vested interest in extending the polite realm to cover as many mechanical activities as possible, were to be marginalized. Taste was reserved not only for patrons and connoisseurs but now for an oligarchy of professional artists of reputation and distinction who sought to elevate themselves above the grubby, vibrant, trading world of the mid-eighteenth-century city.

1 In the eighteenth century it was also known as the Society of Arts and Sciences and the Premium Society. In 1908 it became the Royal Society of Arts (henceforth RSA).

2 McClellan III, pp. 37–9. For a useful overview of the role of patriotic societies in England see Colley, pp. 85–98.

3 Clark 2000, particularly pp. 141–93.

4 *The Gentleman's Magazine*, vol. 26 (1756), pp. 61–2. The original manuscript is in RSA Guard-book, 2: 83, dated 28 January 1756.

5 Snodin and Howard, pp. 18–56.

6 Campbell, pp. 197–8.

7 Hogarth, Smith 1759.

8 For Garthwaite see Rothstein, pp. 33–6, 41–52. For Moser see Edgcumbe, pp. 85–132. For Linnell see Hayward and Kirkham. See also Snodin and Howard, pp. 49, 141; Lambert, pp. 56, 68.

9 Snodin and Howard, pp. 46–7. Mason and Jackson-Stops cat. no. 17.

10 Campbell, pp. 20–1. In 1676 the French Crown did approve the establishment of schools of painting and sculpture in the provinces under the control of the Académie, but only two appear to have been founded – Reims in 1677 and Bordeaux in 1689 – and these soon closed. Campbell might have conflated them with the foundation of a school in

Rouen in 1741 by Jean-Baptiste Descamps, a second in Bordeaux in 1744 and the article written in 1745 by Antoine Ferrand de Monthelan entitled 'Projets pour l'établissement d'écoles gratuites de dessein' which was widely circulated and praised in 1746–8. Over forty drawing schools had been founded in French provincial cities before the Revolution, the majority intended to train artisans in basic design. Benhamou.

11 Gwynn, p. 43.

12 Gwynn, p. 22.

13 RSA Dr Templeman's Transactions, vol. 1, no. 5, 'A plan for an academy for sculpture and painting'. For a fuller commentary on the schizophrenic nature of the document see Brewer 1997, pp. 230–1.

14 RSA Guard-book, 18:85 and 87. For a résumé of Dingley's career see Appleby 1992, pp. 267–9.

15 For the importance of voluntary societies in Georgian London see Andrew, pp. 3–134. Also Davison *et al.*, pp. xxxix–xli. No doubt inspired by the example of the Foundling Hospital, Gwynn deliberately couched his proposal for an Academy in voluntary language, pending royal patronage: 'The Taste of Subscribing to Hospitals and Infirmaries is now very much in vogue. Suppose you make an Hospital for *Genius*, since she is so little able to provide for herself' pp. 78–9. For aristocratic investment in commerce see Stewart, and Emerson.

16 By far the most detailed analysis of the Society's membership in its early years is given in Allan, thesis, pp. 64–101.

17 For a short survey of famous early members see Hudson and Luckhurst, pp. 27–30.

18 Dossie, vol. 1, p. 27.

19 Rudé 1962, pp. 98–103. In 1766 a bill was passed once more banning the import of French silks.

20 Appleby 1995, pp. 54–6. He was awarded a gold medal by the Society in 1768.

21 RSA Dr Templeman's Transactions, vol. 2, pp. 168–9.

22 RSA Guard-book, 7: 40.

23 Dossie, vol. 1, pp. 91–3.

24 Dossie, vol. 1, pp. 148–50.

25 Dossie, vol. 1, pp. 132–5.

26 RSA Guard-book, 10: 137.

27 RSA Guard-book, 8: 131, 12: 130.

28 RSA Guard-book, 5: 3.

29 RSA Guard-book, 9: 6. According to Kalm, p. 51, bugs or 'wall-louse' were hardly known in England twenty years previously, 'but since that time they had travelled over here from foreign countries, so that there are now few houses in London in which these least welcome guests have not quartered themselves'.

30 RSA Dr Templeman's Transactions, vol. 2, pp. 139–48.

31 RSA Guard-book, 10: 90.

32 RSA Guard-book, 23: 2. Committee of Mechanics, 27 February 1766. For Pinchbeck's career see Altick, pp. 60–2. For the model of the crane see Morton and Wess, cat. E61. Pinchbeck presented the Society with a model plough in 1774 and a pair of his patent candle snuffers in 1778, an invention which exposed him to considerable ridicule.

33 RSA Dr Templeman's Transactions, vol. 1, no. 13.

34 See Eimer 1991, pp. 753–62 and, pp. 18–19. The model of the medal was chased in gold by Moser at a cost of £31 18s, to a design based in part on the ideas of Nicholas Crisp, the jeweller and porcelain manufacturer. However, the die-maker Richard Yeo discovered that it would require greater relief than had been envisaged and thus almost twice as much gold as the Society wished to expend. Consequently, a simpler, flatter and more classical design by James 'Athenian' Stuart was selected and the dies cut by Thomas Pingo. For Moser's fine design, incorporating on the obverse Minerva receiving a boy apprentice on the banks of the Thames and on the reverse a Newcomen steam engine, water mill and windmill above a profile of Newton, see Edgcumbe, pp. 108–10.

35 Gainsborough won a premium of £60 for a tide mill in 1761 and £30 for a drill-plough in 1766. £60 was equal to his annual stipend as pastor to the Independent Chapel at Henley on Thames. For Gainsborough's inventive career see Peters, and Belsey, pp. 22–3, 68–9.

36 RSA Guard-book, 14: 134. Edgeworth went on to win a silver medal in 1767 for an improved carriage design developed in collaboration with Erasmus Darwin and collected a gold medal for assorted mechanical inventions in 1769.

37 Dossie, vol. 1, pp. 32–3.

38 British Library, Add. ms. 27,993 reprinted with a commentary by Kitson, pp. 46–111.

39 Apology VIII, 270–6. See Wind, pp. 235–51, for the latest interpretation of this series. The Apology if anything confirms that Hogarth's depiction of the rise of the hardworking apprentice, Francis Goodchild, was not intended to be interpreted ironically.

40 Apology XIII, 484–90.

41 Apology IX, 307–13.

42 Apology II, 210–7. For further complaints regarding time-wasting and inconsiderate behaviour see Allan, thesis, pp. 51–2.

43 Apology XVIII, 600–9.

44 Dossie, vol. 3, pp. xxi–xxii.

45 An etching of the Priory at Warwick after her own drawing is in Richard Bull's album of *Etching and Engravings, by the Nobility and Gentry of England; or, by Persons not exercising the Art as a Trade*, in the British Museum Department of Prints and Drawings. Sloan, cat. 110.

46 The timing suggests that it was the Society of Arts who initiated the use of the gallery as an academy for the young, rather than the Society following on a ducal initiative as is proposed in Coutu, p. 176. For a description of drawing in the Richmond Gallery see the account given by Ozias Humphry reproduced in Brewer, p. 297.

47 Allan 1992, p. 103.

48 Reprinted Linnaeus, p. 459, quoted in Allan 1979, p. 149.

49 According to Allan, the number of premiums offered for the Polite Arts grew from 22 in 1758, out of a total of 122, to 106 out of 380 offered in 1764. They constituted during these early years by far the largest proportions of premiums awarded: 39 out of 51 in 1758 and 99 out of 147 in 1764. Allan 1992, p. 102.

50 In 1757 he won second prize in the under-seventeen category for the best design for use by weavers etc; in 1758 he came second to John Smart in the under-eighteen category for a drawing of a human figure in plaster; in 1759, he won fourth prize for his copy of a cast of *The Fighting Gladiator* in the Duke of Richmond's gallery; and in 1760 he won first prize, worth ten guineas, for the best drawing of a figure from life made at the St Martin's Lane Academy.

51 Lloyd, pp. 20–1.

52 *Register of the Premiums and Bounties Given by the Society Instituted at London for the Encouragement of Arts, Manufactures and Commerce* (1778). For a summary of Shipley's pupils and their premiums see Allan 1979, pp. 211–18.

53 For an extended account of Humphry's career see Brewer 1997, pp. 295–321.

54 Until her marriage she worked as a professional artist and became a founding member of the Royal Academy. Sloan, pp. 45, 75–6, cat. 50.

55 Snodin and Howard, p. 56. Snodin 1984, p. 73, cat. E20, E21.

56 Dossie, vol. 3, p. xxiii.

57 Unfortunately the building had structural problems and was in danger of collapse by 1762.

58 Allen 1991, pp. 265–9. For a recent short account of events leading up to the foundation of the Royal Academy see Brewer, pp. 228–38. For an interpretation in the context of 'Wilkes and Liberty' politics see Solkin, pp. 247–76.

59 Fox; Bindman, 124, 125.

60 *Register of the Premiums*, p. 54.

61 Dossie, vol. 3, p. xxvi.

62 Reynolds, p. 13. See also Barrell, pp. 69–82.

PORTRAYING LONDON
MID-CENTURY – JOHN ROCQUE
AND THE BROTHERS BUCK

RALPH HYDE

John Rocque's twenty-four-sheet wall-map of London was published in June 1747. Only two years later Samuel and Nathaniel Buck announced their equally remarkable five-sheet, 10-foot-long prospect of London and Westminster. How lucky we are! Rocque map and Buck prospect were the products of two quite separate and independent projects, but these two grand portraits of London complement each other, and provide us with a wealth of unique and invaluable topographical information. It makes a lot of sense, therefore, to study them together.

John Rocque's origins were obscure. The Rocques, it would seem, were a Huguenot family that fled from France after the revocation of the Edict of Nantes and settled in Geneva.[1] John, it is thought, was born in 1704 or 1705, and may have arrived in England as early as 1709 or more probably a bit later. He was certainly in England by 1734, for in that year he issued his first publication. This was a *Plan of the House, Gardens, Park & Hermitage of their Majesties at Richmond; and of their R. H. the Prince of Wales & the Princess Royal at Kew.*[2] Published by John Bowles at the Black Horse in Cornhill, it basically consisted of the plan of the gardens. It was greatly enlivened, however, by its inset views. These consisted of the King's house at Richmond and the Prince of Wales's House at Kew, two summerhouses, a hermitage, a greenhouse, and a dairy. Richmond would be typical of Rocque's early productions. Until 1743, and occasionally after that date too, he would produce a whole series of plans of royal and aristocratic gardens, describing himself from the start as a 'dessinateur de jardins.' The gardens included those of Wanstead House in Essex (1735); the Duke of Kent's seat at Wrest in Bedfordshire (1735); Lord Burlington's Chiswick House (1736); the plan of Hampton Court, which was dedicated to Frederick, Prince of Wales (1736); Kensington Palace and Gardens (1736; Fig. 6) Esher in Surrey (1737); South Dalton in Yorkshire (1737); Claremont in Surrey (1738); and Drumlangrig, the Duke of Queensbury's seat in Scotland (c.1740). From 1736 John Rocque gave his address as the Canister and Sugar Loaf in Great Windmill Street in Soho. This was on the edge of the French quarter, and very close to where Piccadilly Circus now is. Rocque's garden plans served to demonstrate his capabilities. They brought him to the attention of the high and the mighty – people with influence.

Conceivably it was as recipient of the Prince of Wales's patronage for the Hampton Court plan that Rocque came into contact with the engraver and antiquary George Vertue. Vertue

was the official engraver to the Society of Antiquaries. He had already dedicated his *Heads of the Kings of England* to Frederick, Prince of Wales, in 1736, and would later provide him with watercolours, act as copyist and draw up manuscript lists of works of art in the royal collections. Mapping London was one of his great interests. In 1723 he had copied and engraved a survey made immediately after the Great Fire of 1666 for the Corporation of London that established the extent of the devastation. Recently, at a meeting of the Society of Antiquaries, he had exhibited a plan that he had just engraved on pewter showing London in c.1560, copied in the main from a large, wood-cut map-view – the so-called 'Agas' map.[3] Making old maps available to fellow antiquaries was a useful and necessary exercise, but Vertue was also alive to the need for a completely new large-scale map of contemporary London. He discussed the matter with John Rocque.

George Vertue's concern was real. The need for a new survey had been under discussion for at least a decade. In the 1720s Delisle had provocatively calculated that Paris was larger than London. This rankled with Londoners. At the Royal Society, Peter Davall demonstrated that Delisle's calculations were hopelessly wrong and it was London that was the bigger. The RS minutes record, 'The 'President [Sir Hans Sloane], upon occasion of reading the Paper, made mention of a Design which is now on foot to make a more perfect and exact Survey and Plan of the City of London than has hitherto been made.'[4] Who was the surveyor? We do not know. What stage had he reached? We do not know that either. Evidently it was abandoned.

The most recent large-scale map on the market therefore was one first published back in 1682 by William Morgan, 'London &c. Actually Survey'd'.[5] This wall-map consisted of sixteen sheets and measured 1,120 × 2,360 mm (44 × 93 inches) overall. The product of an original survey, it was a spin-off from John Ogilby's ambitious *Britannia* project. It was a highly decorative map, displaying views of London's most important landmarks; and within luscious ornamentation the names of the royal family, the nobility, the Privy Council, the bishops, and the Oxford and Cambridge colleges. The map was supplemented by a long prospect of London and Westminster, which you could mount above the map or along the bottom according to taste. The copper-plates from which it was printed passed through several hands. According to George Vertue, there was an edition c.1692 published by Robert Morden and Philip Lea. Several

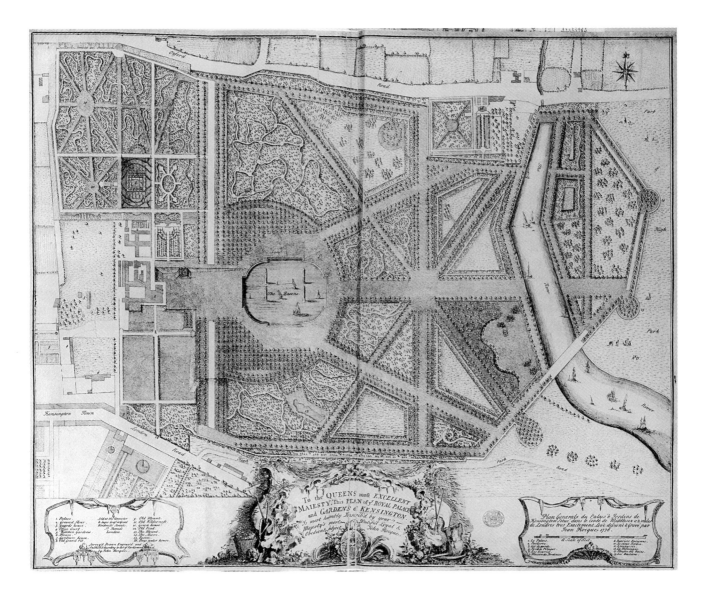

Fig. 6 John Rocque, *Plan of the Royal Palace and Gardens at Kensington*, etching, British Library, K. Top. 28.10.a.

copies of an edition updated to *c*.1720 survive, one of them Vertue's own copy. By this date the plates seem to have belonged to Anne Lea and Richard Glynne, though the imprint remained that of Morden and Lea. The plates were next acquired by George Willdey, who seems to have updated them to 1732. This is the edition that would have been available when Rocque and Vertue were having their discussion. Then the copper-plates were inherited by Thomas Willdey, who listed the map on his trade card. Eventually they would be acquired by the Charing Cross map-maker Thomas Jefferys, who would re-issue the map, seemingly without further revision, in *c*.1749–50.

It has to be said that the updating of Morgan had never been thorough, and the map had became progressively more unreliable. Moreover, for many potential users of a multi-sheet London map (estate owners and administrators, for

example), its scale – just over 17 inches to the mile – was woe-fully inadequate.

Morgan's great wall-map was not the only map you could buy, of course. The market demanded smaller, more manageable maps. In the 1730s these were being made and sold by such printmakers as Henry Overton at the White Horse without Newgate, Thomas Bowles, next to the Chapter House in St Paul's Churchyard, and George Willdey, who was at the Great Toy and Print Shop in St Paul's Churchyard on the corner of Ludgate Hill. The maps they produced were designed to decorate the walls of houses rather than palaces and livery halls. Unframed they could be easily consulted on a table. Even smaller maps were needed for illustrating topographies. To fulfil the decorative function, maps for the wall might carry inset views of London buildings or be embellished with the arms of the livery companies. To fulfil the practical function of maps that could be rolled out on a table, they often supplied the rates of watermen and hackney coachmen. Ventures into and around

London could thus be planned in advance. A new market for maps had recently been identified – 'strangers' (i.e. tourists) in London. For them Henry Overton, and Thomas Bowles's brother, John, produced the first London guidebooks, but also portable maps in slipcases that you could fit into your pocket. None of these maps was, or could be, the product of a new survey. All of them were ultimately derived from Morgan's. A new prototype for such maps was very overdue.

On 3 March 1738 George Vertue had a meeting in a house in Leicester Square with William Oldys, literary secretary to the Earl of Oxford, and with Joseph Ames, the Secretary of the Society of Antiquaries. At this meeting he revealed his 'grand design' for a new 'Ichnographical Survey or Map of London and all the suburbs.' He announced that he already had a surveyor in mind – John Rocque. But 'Mr Rocque and he are not yet come to an agreement', noted William Oldys darkly in his diary.[6]

Work on the survey began almost instantly. A Proposal for the map, issued in c.1740, states firmly that 'the survey was begun in March 1737' (i.e. 1738 new style).[7] The surveyor, promised the Proposal, would be John Rocque, and the engraver John Pine. Not George Vertue, be it noted. Evidently Rocque and he had failed to reach an agreement. Rocque and Pine would not only produce the map. They would also be its joint publishers.

Rocque's choice of John Pine to engrave his map was sensible and predictable. Pine moved in the right circles. A personal friend of William Hogarth, he features in *The Gate of Calais* as the fat friar (Fig. 7). In 1735 he and five other engravers had supported Hogarth in petitioning Parliament for copyright protection. Vertue had hoped to engrave the House of Lords tapestries of the Spanish Armada. His rival, Pine, got the job. Rocque's model for the decoration on the new London map was Louis Bretez's twenty-sheet map of Paris, just published. Pine would be more at home than Vertue with this French style. And the success of the House of Lords tapestry engravings and other ventures meant that Pine had capital to invest in Rocque's project.

Rocque's and Pine's ambitions for their map are set out in their Proposal. The map would be printed on twenty-four sheets of the best imperial paper. When mounted it would measure 6½ feet by almost 13 feet. The area covered would consist of ten thousand acres, with Tottenham Court in the north extending south to Kennington, and with Hyde Park in the west extending east to Mile End and Deptford. The scale would be 200 feet to the inch, large enough to admit 'an exact Description of all the Squares, Streets, Courts, and Alleys, in their true Proportions, but likewise of the Ground Plots of the several Churches, Halls, publick Buildings, and considerable Houses and Gardens'. The neighbouring country would be surveyed in detail too, 'with the

Fig. 7 William Hogarth and Charles Mosley, *The Gate of Calais*, etching.

several Roads and Foot-paths crossing it, and remarkable Objects contained in it'. This would fill up the vacant space 'more usefully, as well as more agreeably, than by crowding the Plan with unmeaning Ornaments'. In other words, Rocque's map would look very different to Morgan's – no inset views of London landmarks, and no long prospect of the city. The price would be three guineas, one to be paid at the time of subscribing, and the other two on the delivery of the work. The surveying would be completed 'in September next' (probably 1741), 'immediately after which the Engraving will be put in Hand, and finished with all possible Expedition'. Subscriptions would be taken in by John Pine at the Piccadilly end of Old Bond Street, and John Rocque at the Canister and Sugar Loaf in Great Windmill Street.

For his wall-map of Paris, Louis Bretez had received financial support from Louis XV. In less autocratic England it was to the Fathers of the City of London that Rocque and Pine turned, appealing to their civic pride. On 16 October 1739 the two men, armed with drawings that demonstrated how their map would look, attended a meeting of the Court of Aldermen at Guildhall. The Aldermen inspected the drawings, were impressed, and pronounced the project laudable. Since they represented wards they were anxious that ward boundaries should feature in the City section. They therefore ordered their Deputies and the Members of the Court of Common Council to instruct their beadles to supply the map-makers with detailed ward boundary information. They also called upon the citizens in general to give the map-makers every assistance.[8]

In addition to seeking the City's support, Rocque and Pine very wisely sought the support of the Royal Society. Martin Folkes, Vice-President of the Society, and Peter Davall, who was later its Secretary, were shown what had been done to date, and the surveying methods were explained to them. On occasions when important measurements were being taken and the principal angles were being verified, Rocque and Pine invited Folkes and Davall to join them. On 17 May 1740 Folkes and Davall provided Rocque and Pine with an enthusiastic Testimonial, declaring themselves satisfied, and recommending the survey as 'a Work of great Use, likely to be performed with Judgement and Exactness, and well deserving Encouragement'.[9]

The survey forged ahead, at first making good progress. Garden plans were relegated to second place. For the next few years Rocque's top priority would be town plans. Whilst working with Pine on the survey of built-up London, Rocque bravely, or foolhardily, embarked on a sixteen-sheet wall-map of London and 10 miles round on a scale of 5¼ inches to the mile. He also carried out surveys of Bristol and Exeter. For the four-sheet Bristol map it was Pine who was the engraver. Its publication was announced in the *Bristol Oracle* on 30 April 1743. Exeter appeared in the following year. Both plans received encouragement from the City Fathers of their respective cities. Both carried inset views. The scale bar of the Bristol map is smothered in putti confidently using surveying instruments.

In January 1744 the first of the sixteen sheets of Rocque's map of London and 10 miles round was announced, 'neatly engraved, price 2s.6d.'. The advertisement for it concludes: 'N.B. The original map, completely finished, may be seen at Mr. John Rocque's next to the sign of the Duke of Grafton's head in Hyde-Park-Road; where may be had the plans of the cities of Bristol and Exeter, from actual survey, taken by the said John Rocque.'[10]

Rocque, as this reveals, had moved from Soho to Hyde Park Road – the name then of the Hyde Park Corner end of Piccadilly. This stretch of the street was noted for dealers in statuary, fountains, and other garden ornaments, mocked by Hogarth in a plate in *The Analysis of Beauty* (1753). The Duke of Grafton's Head, next door to Rocque's premises, was the one of the best-known statuary yards, that of John Cheere.[11] Rocque was clearly loath to sever completely his connection with the world of gardens. And by now the twenty-four-sheet London map was giving him problems.

Rocque's decision to undertake the surveying of the largest city in Europe, if not the world, when so inexperienced was surely reckless. Had he bitten off more than he could chew? For a while it seemed so. He took the true bearings of a great number of church steeples from different positions, using an instrument of Jonathan Sissons, and trigonometrically computed the proportional distances of various points in the city. The operation can be seen in progress in one of the cartouches on the map of London and 10 miles round (Fig. 8). Unfortunately the distances that he measured trigonometrically differed from the same distances that had been arrived at earlier when he measured streets with his chain and theodolite. There was no alternative: the plan would have to be redrawn. It was a major setback.

In the meantime subscribers had to be reassured. Rocque and Pine asked Folkes and Davall to supply them with a second Testimonial. This they generously did. A new document from them, dated 24 July 1742, explained the delay.[12]

But it wasn't only surveying techniques that were the problem. Inevitably too, the collecting of place names proved a mammoth task. Rather than just copying them from existing

Fig. 8 Detail from John Rocque, *Map of London and Ten Miles Around*, etching. Guildhall Library.

sources, the surveyors carefully recorded them whilst in the field. Whenever they turned out to be different from the names as given in existing sources, the matter was conscientiously looked into 'and the Truth cleared up with as much Exactness as possible'.[13]

The draft for the twenty-four-sheet London map was completed in 1746, and the public was invited to come and inspect it. They were encouraged to point out mistakes. Each reported error would be examined on the spot and, wherever necessary, corrections would be made. By way of a final check-up, men were engaged to go through the town, 'each carrying with him that portion of the plan which related to his own division, and making a final Comparison between the real state and appearance of every place, and the representation of it upon paper'.[14]

The sixteen-sheet map of London and 10 miles round continued to appear one sheet at a time.[15] The twelfth sheet was announced on 20 May 1745. On 16 July, however, Rocque informed subscribers that he was 'indispensably oblig'd to go unto the country for a few months',[16] most likely to complete a survey of Shrewsbury. The engraving of the remaining four plates for the sixteen-sheet London and 10 miles round map would continue in his absence, but the correction and finishing of them would have to wait until he returned.

Rocque's visit to the country also held up the completion of the twenty-four-sheet London wall-map. Fresh Proposals were issued in May 1746.[17] Sensibly this time no date for publication was promised, but once again 'the curious' were invited to visit the publishers and look at the map and draw attention to errors and omissions. It would seem that Rocque had over-reached himself financially. The publishing duo is no longer given as Rocque and Pine, but as Pine (at a new address – the Golden Head opposite Burlington House in Piccadilly) and John Tinney, a print-seller at the Golden Lion in Fleet Street.[18]

On 21 October Pine and Tinney visited Guildhall to wait on the Court of Aldermen with what must have been proofs of the finished map. The Aldermen were well satisfied, instructed the Chamberlain to award Pine and Tinney a £50 gratuity and ordered that the plan be hung in the Justice Room.[19]

Advertisements in newspapers for the map were now appearing regularly, interspersed with advertisements for prints showing the scaffold and manner of executing the rebel lords on Tower Hill,[20] and Hogarth's portrait of Simon Lord Lovat.[21] One Pine and Tinney advertisement[22] explained the delay of publication on the continued receipt of corrections and omissions and the publisher's determination for perfection. The deadline for subscriptions was 9 May 1747.

On 27 June Pine and Tinney announced in the *General Advertiser* that the plan was at last ready to be delivered. Those who had subscribed with Pine should contact the Golden Head; and those who had subscribed through Rocque or Tinney, the Golden Lion. Five months later the map's availability to non-subscribers was announced.[23] An index volume with the subscribers' list was also available.[24]

The subscription list is interesting. It consists of 246 names, headed by those of Frederick, Prince of Wales (predictably), and the victor of the recently fought Battle of Culloden, the Duke of Cumberland (topically). There are eighteen more Dukes, ninety-six Lords, the Lord Mayor of London for 1745/6 (Sir Richard Hoare, the banker (cat.1.38)) and six other Aldermen. The other names include the Swiss architect Charles Labelye, whose Westminster Bridge was nearing completion and being regularly recorded by Samuel Scott and Canaletto; Peter Hudson, 'writing-master, accountant, and teacher of the French tongue'; and Hans Sloane.[25] The map's title is set in a Rococo cartouche, supported by a river god and goddess with oars, who recline on overturned urns. The cartouche is surmounted by the City's arms and the City regalia. The dedication, to Sir Richard Hoare and the members of the Court of Aldermen, is set in a cartouche consisting of putti cavorting amongst bales and barrels with skins and coins, to celebrate the City's triumphant role in trade and commerce. The border design is very much in the style of the border for Louis Bretez's 'Plan de Paris'.

In great contrast to Bretez's totally scenographical map of Paris, Rocque's London is sternly ichnographical. In other words it is not a map-view, but very much a plan. Anglican churches are shown with a bold line round the limits and the name within, non-conformist churches are shown with initials: AM Anabaptist Meeting, IM Independent Meeting, MethM Methodist Meeting, QM Quaker Meeting. Other significant buildings are shown with dark hatching. The imminent development of an area of Mayfair is shown by street outlines. The streets outlined would become Farm Street, Hill Street, Hays Mews and Charles Street. Various industries are indicated, especially along the banks of the Thames – brick kilns, timber yards, coal wharves, distilleries, whitening grounds, rope walks and so on. One suspects that less industry is shown than existed. The only pictorial elements are trees, the fields and gardens (note those in Lambeth in particular) and vessels on the Thames. Upstream from London Bridge are watermen's wherries galore, but none of the timber barges one might expect alongside the Lambeth timber wharves. Off Somerset House and the Temple we see the Lord Mayor's Day river procession with fifteen livery barges. In the Pool, downstream from London Bridge, are large numbers of seagoing vessels, many of them moored, but not on tiers as they would have been. Nothing is being towed, and there are few lighters. East of Wapping and Rotherhithe the centre of the river is occupied, as it would have been, by fully rigged merchant ships. Rocque, in other words, is content to convey a suggestion of a busy port and the importance to London of its river; he is not attempting to make a record of it.[26]

Following the publication of the London map, Rocque's business expanded. In 1749, when the Bucks were publishing their London and Westminster prospect, Rocque moved to what is now the north end of Whitehall, which was then called Charing Cross. His shop stood next to the Rumner Tavern which features in *Night* in Hogarth's *Times of the Day* series.

PROSPECT OF GREENWICH from the Observatory at the Top of the Hill. From this Place the eye commands a vast and most delightfull Prospect on every side of greenwich, What recomends is most is the distant Views of the City of London and the Course of the River Thames with its innumerable shipping from all parts of the World.

VEUE DE GREENWICH dessinée a coté de l'Observatoire au haut de la Colline. De cet endroit on aperçoit de tous les cotés de greenwich un vue et delicieux Prix, et la Ville de Londres dans l'Eloignement, avec le cours de la Tamise chargé d'une quantité étonante de Vaisseaux de toutes grandeurs, et de toutes les nations du monde, ce qui fait un aspect admirable.

Fig. 9 John Rocque, *Prospect of Greenwich*, etching. British Library, K.Top 17.1.3b

Early in his career he had published the occasional topographical print – Geneva (1736), Greenwich (1738; fig. 9), and a prospect of Greenwich Hospital from the river (1739). In 1750 he published a view of Constantinople. On 7 November 1750 a fire broke out in the premises, 'which burnt with great violence', the *General Advertiser* tells us, 'and in a short time consumed that house, together with the Rumner'. Having lost his stock Rocque took himself off to Paris to replenish it. By June 1751 his business was up and running again at new premises on the south side of the Strand at the corner with Buckingham Street. The advertisement in which he announces himself at the new address makes clear the present nature of his business.[27] A survey of Berkshire, Oxford and Buckinghamshire is under way, and the plates for a survey of Shropshire are being engraved. He undertakes land surveying and planning gentlemen's estates. He stocks 'a great choice of foreign maps, plans, battles, sieges, &c. newly imported; likewise plans of Nismes and Montpelier'. Prince Frederick had just died, his death precipitated, it was thought, by a bad cold caught when supervising workmen in his garden at Kew. Rocque describes himself as 'Chorographer and Topographer to their Royal Highnesses the late and present Prince of Wales'.

Later in the year Rocque moved to Southampton Street, north out of the Strand, and in 1753 he finally moved to a shop tucked away behind the north side of the Strand, two houses westward from Old Round Court. Though at this stage in his career county surveying was taking up a great deal of his time, Rocque continued to publish town plans – York, Paris and Rome, for example. In 1754 he opened up a branch in Dublin, and embarked on a very detailed four-sheet survey of that city.[28] In Ireland he also published town plans of Kilkenny and Cork, and county maps of County Dublin and County Armagh. In 1759 he concluded his work there with a four-sheet map of the Kingdom of Ireland, and returned to London. He died on 27 January 1762 and was succeeded by his widow, Mary Ann, who continued the business until *c*.1769.

The twenty-four-sheet London map was exploited to the full. It was re-issued by Pine and Tinney in 1748 and 1749; by Pine, Thomas Bowles and Tinney in 1753 and 1755; and by Tinney, Thomas Bowles and John Bowles in 1756. By 1775 the plates for it were in the hands of Thomas Jefferys and Sayer & Bennett.[29] At least five reduced versions of the map were published. Pine, Bowles, and Tinney brought out an eight-sheet reduction of the twenty-four-sheet map in 1755; the rest were single-sheet affairs.

Town plans, map-views, oblique (or bird's-eye) views, and profile views (often long) had traditionally been the territory of the same publishers. If you published any one of these species of town representation, the likelihood was that you published the others. These could be distinct publications, as when for example Jacob Millerd in Bristol in *c*.1673 produced both a plan and a prospect of his city. Alternatively the town plan might be inset on a town view, or the town view inset on a town plan. The Buck brothers were unique in confining themselves almost entirely to one species – long views or prospects, producing only

33

two town plans, and only on one occasion insetting a town plan on a prospect. They were also unique in the comprehensiveness of their work. In all they produced eighty-seven long views of towns throughout England and Wales. Their five-sheet London view was intended to be the climax of that series.

Like Rocque's, the Bucks' origins were obscure. It is almost certain that the brothers were born in Richmond in Yorkshire, or somewhere close by (Fig. 10).[30] Samuel first appears on the scene in 1719 as the artist for John Warburton's intended topographical account of Yorkshire. By the following year he was working on a long view of Leeds, and very soon he was issuing Proposals for the publication of long views not only of Leeds but of York and Wakefield, too. Each would consist of two sheets and measure approximately 400 by 900 mm (16 by 36 in.). Long views of Newcastle, Durham, Stockton on Tees, Maidstone (two views), and Sunderland followed. This, the First Series of Buck town views, was concluded with a long view of Lincoln – the one that carried the inset town plan.

By 1724 Samuel Buck had moved to London. The first address he gave for subscribers was the White Swan, Brownlow Street, off High Holborn. He associated himself closely with the recently formed Society of Antiquaries. The Society's engraver, George Vertue, engraved his views of Fountains Abbey. William Stukeley, the Society's Secretary, spent his summers exploring different parts of the country and recording antiquities. In 1722 he took John Pine with him, and in 1724 and 1725 Samuel Buck.

In 1724 Buck announced that he would be publishing a collection of twenty-four perspective views of ruins in Yorkshire.[31] Subscriptions would be taken in by himself in Brownlow Street, and by his brother Nathaniel at the Golden Buck in Warwick Street, Soho. These *Yorkshire Antiquities* appeared in 1726. A number of them were based on drawings he had made for Warburton. They were followed by ruins he had recorded when accompanying Stukeley in Lincolnshire and Nottinghamshire. By November 1726 he had resolved to record antiquities systematically throughout England.[32] In the summer of 1727 Samuel and Nathaniel Buck undertook a sketching peregrination of Lancashire, Cheshire and Debyshire. The plates were now signed 'S. B. delin. N. B. sculp.' or vice versa. From this point on, the brothers' regular practice was to undertake a sketching tour each summer in a different part of England and

Fig. 10 Richard Houston after Joseph Highmore, *Samuel Buck and Nathaniel Buck*, mezzotint.

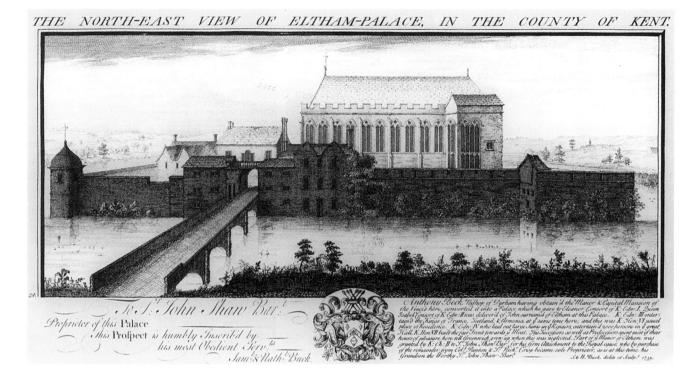

Fig. 11 Samuel Buck and Nathaniel Buck, *The North-east View of Eltham Palace*, from the Bucks' *Antiquities*, etching. Guildhall Library.

then Wales, engraving and printing during the winter months, and publishing in the spring (Fig. 11). From 1735 they operated from number. 1 Garden Court, Middle Temple, with a second address at the Green Canister, by the Crown and Anchor Tavern, opposite St Clement Danes in the Strand.

The Bucks now had two ambitious projects in progress – the Antiquities Series (Fig. 11), and a second series of town prospects, which for convenience let's call the Principal Series. These new town views were printed on single sheets and each measured approximately 303 × 775 mm (12½ × 30½ in.). The towns were sketched on the same tours as the Antiquities, starting with Lancashire and Cheshire. After the completion of the Antiquities in 1742 the brothers revisited the areas they had covered before the Principal Series of Town Prospects had been commenced. They also started work on their long view of London.

Buck's prospect of London would be sensationally superior to any long view of any British town before it. What did it replace?[33]

We have seen that William Morgan's very decorative wall-map of 1682, 'London &c. Actually Survey'd' was embellished with a long profile view of the capital. This followed an existing convention in showing the Thames as if stretched out straight. Unlike most seventeenth-century prospects, however, Morgan's was not copied from a copy of a distant prototype. It was an entirely fresh image. Also, unlike previous prospects, and indeed unlike quite a lot of later ones, it did not compress the detail. Instead it attempted to show all the riverside buildings, including insignificant wharves. The view extended from the Palace of Westminster in the west to Shadwell in the east. The imprint on the prospect was adjusted on two occasions, but the image itself was never updated. St Paul's, even after its completion in 1710, remained as Morgan had imagined it in 1682.

Curiously, Morgan's prospect had little influence on others. Long and thin, its proportions made it an unsuitable model for prospects that were independent of maps and intended for book illustration or wall decoration. In consequence, new profile views of London appearing in the first half of the eighteenth century reverted to the pre-Morgan convention of showing the significant Thames-side buildings but not too much in between. In c.1704 James Walker 'at the Star in Py-corner near West Smith-field', published a 'New Prospect of ye South-Side of ye City of London with the River Thames & London-Bridg [*sic*]'. It consisted of three sheets conjoined, and showed the scene on the north side of the river from the Temple to the Tower. Today it is a very rare print but in its day it must have been common. The copper-plates for it were acquired in due course by Henry Overton, and then by Robert Sayer. As late as 1775 it was still appearing in Sayer & Bennett's catalogue. Walker's print was the source for a more common, though anonymous, print, *The South Prospect of the City of London*, which first appeared in 1710 and was later published by Thomas Taylor and later still by John Bowles. It was also the source for a print that is not rare at all, *La Ville de Londres, Prospectus Londinensis*, which from 1714 appeared in the *Nouveau Théâtre de la Grand Britannia* (initially published by David Mortier and sometimes entitled *Britannia*

Illustrata). It was also issued as an independent print. The best-known London print of the period, it served as the source for several other London prospects and for inset prospects on maps. From 1720 *Prospectus Londoniensis* had a companion – *La Ville de Westmunster*. This was designed to be attached to the City of London prospect, extending it up-river as far as Peterborough House on Millbank. The idea of extending a London prospect was taken up by William Knight. His three-sheet *Prospect of London* (*c.*1715) could also be extended with supplementary sheets, eastwards to Shadwell, and westwards to the Palace of Westminster and St Mary's Lambeth.

Before 1700 almost all significant prospects of London were taken from Southwark looking north across the Thames. Walker broke the mould: his *New Prospect of ye South-Side of ye City of London* was one of a pair, its companion being *A New Prospect of ye North-Side of ye City of London*, described as 'very Ornamental over Chimneys or in Halls, Stair-Cases, or Entries.'[34] The 1710 *South Prospect of the City of London* was also given a companion – *The North Prospect of the City of London & Westminster* – which first appeared in 1712. Large prospects were also published looking up-river and down-river, and distant prospects appeared showing London from Greenwich. Most important of all, there was Jan Kip's twelve-sheet *Prospect of the City of London, Westminster and St. James's Park*, published in 1720, which consisted of the view looking east towards the City from Buckingham House.[35] Kip's view was an oddity, on account not only of its size and viewpoint but also its perspective. In common with works produced by his Dutch compatriots, much of Kip's work consisted of bird's-eye views, particularly of noblemen's and gentlemen's country seats. Apart from the City of London in the distance presented in profile, Kip's prospect is essentially a bird's-eye view. It was not a style to which English artists took naturally. Thomas Bakewell attempted the same technique with his *New and Exact Prospect of the North Side of the City of London taken from the Upper Pond near Islington* in 1730. There were few other examples.

By the 1740s, when the Buck brothers were embarking on their five-sheet view of London, virtually all the large views of London available in London's print shops were late editions of the prospects that had been issued in the first fifteen years of the century. Faulty from the start, they had been either very clumsily revised or not updated at all. They were certainly not sources to which one could turn for reliable topographical information. An attractive prospect that could fulfil that function was badly needed.

The Bucks' initial intention in 1746 was to produce a four-sheet view, issuing it with two prospects of Portsmouth to arrive at the usual set of six. The sheets for the London prospect, they warned, were going to 'take much more time on Performing them than any of the former sets.'[36] The price nevertheless would be the same: 5s on taking out the subscription, and 10s on delivery.

In November 1747, however, the plan was adjusted. The Bucks now announced in the press that they had taken five drawings of London. The set would consist of five engravings of London and just one of Portsmouth.[37] Proposals in the form of a broadside were also issued (Fig. 12), describing the new set and reminding the public of all the earlier sets of town prospects they had issued.[38] 'Subscription Money is taken in by the Authors, at their Chambers, No. 1 Garden-Court, Middle Temple; at the Green Canister, near the Crown and Anchor, opposite St Clement's Church in the Strand; and by Mrs Buck, at the Queen's Head, near Hatton Garden, in Holborn; where subscribers may have the above-said Prints.' On the reverse appear the names of 1,350 subscribers. They include John Rocque.

By the summer of 1749 those subscribers must have been getting restless. The Bucks begged them to pardon them 'as they are forced to delay publishing the Views of London and Portsmouth by the indisposition of Mr S. Buck, and their desire of rendering them as perfect as possible.'[39] They assured them they would be out by 1 September. On 28 August the Bucks were able to tell the subscribers that the plates of London and Portsmouth were printing off.[40] They would be ready to deliver on 11 September. After that date no more subscriptions would be accepted. The publication of the London and Portsmouth prospects was finally announced on 5 October.[41]

Three sets of drawings for Buck's London survive. A set in the Sutherland Collection at the Ashmolean consists of pen and wash drawings for the first and second plates. A second set, also consisting of pen and wash drawings for the first and second plates, is in a private collection. The topography in this set is almost identical to that on the engraved plates. Westminster Bridge, however, is clumsily drawn, and the lively activity on the Thames is entirely different though equally interesting. The third set of drawings is that in the British Museum's Department of Prints and Drawings (cat. 2.32). They are mounted to form one continuous strip. Edward Croft-Murray, sometime Keeper, attributed them to J. B. Chatelain.[42] (Other artists used by the Bucks at various times included Thomas Rosse, Samuel Scott, Peter Monamy and H. F. Gravelot.) An inscription on the back reads: 'Buck's original drawing of modern London finished in the reign of George II, Buck's widow had refused £70 for it. I bought it afterwards at Baker's in Covent Garden.' Who wrote this we do not know. Samuel Baker, the auctioneer, had his premises at what is now the junction of Tavistock Street and Wellington Street. In 1776, some years after his death, the business passed to his nephew John Sotheby. Sotheby's still flourish in New Bond Street, of course.

London, with Portsmouth, was supposed to be the climax to the Buck's Town Prospects series. In the event, with a final flourish, the Bucks published two exceptionally attractive prospects of what must have been their home town – Richmond, Yorkshire. Even that was not the end. Three years later they published new prospects of towns already represented in their series – Oxford and Birmingham.

In 1746 Nathaniel seems to have taken over the business of

Mrs Ann Buck. According to her trade card, the shop, the Queen's Head near Hatton Garden in Holborn bought and sold, 'Beds, Bedding, Buroes, Books Cases, Chairs, Glasses, Chine, and all sorts of Household Furniture, New & Old'. Ann Buck was, it has been suggested, the mother of Samuel and Nathaniel.[43] Nathaniel died some time between 1759 and 1774.

For many years Samuel continued to advertise and sell his Antiquities and Town Prospects. He instructed young ladies and gentlemen in their own houses in the art of drawing and painting in oil and watercolours; he made flower drawings; he sold drawings specially designed for young beginners to copy and improve their skills; he offered to clean and mend pictures; and he exhibited at the Royal Academy, the Free Society and the Society of Artists. Two years before he died he issued Proposals

for a set of four perspective views in Yorkshire from drawings made on the spot by himself.[44]

Buck's final years were spent in poverty. The antiquary Richard Gough supported him out of his own pocket and encouraged his friends to follow his example, publishing an appeal in *The Gentleman's Magazine* and elsewhere, and attempting to present it in the chamber of the Society of Antiquaries. It provoked a generous response, and Buck's last six months of life were spent free from financial worry. He died at the age of eighty-three on 17 August 1779, and was buried in the churchyard of St Clement Danes.

The copper-plates for the printing of the Antiquities and the Principal Series of Town Prospects were acquired by the Fleet Street publisher associated with the later editions of Rocque's

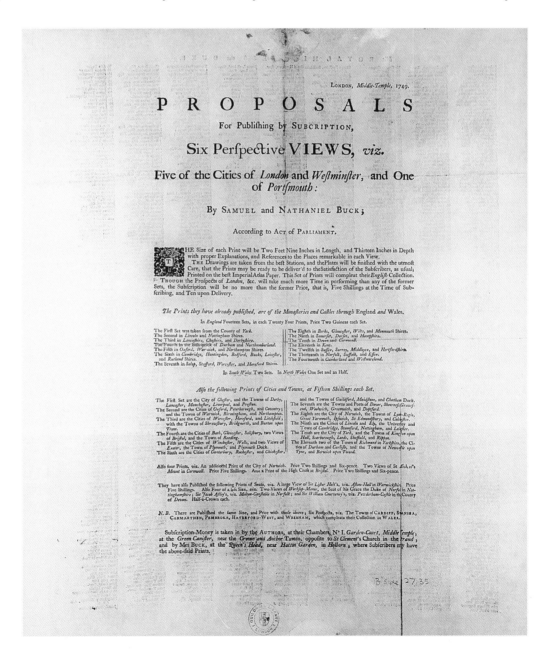

Fig. 12 Samuel Buck and Nathaniel Buck, *Proposals for Views of London and Portsmouth*, letterpress. The Bodleian Library, University of Oxford, North b.1 (20).

map, Robert Sayer. Sayer re-issued the prints in 1774, making them available in single sheets, or bound into three volumes with the comprehensive title, *Buck's Antiquities*. The prints continued to be listed in print publishers' catalogues at least until 1813. Only the London prospect was updated, though not thoroughly. Blackfriars Bridge, New Bridge Street, and the Adelphi were added, and the London Bridge detail was re-engraved to show it shorn of houses. Copies carrying the publication dates 1776, 1777 and 1778 have been recorded. The London Metropolitan Archives' revised version was looted in 1860 from the Summer Palace near Beijing during the Second Opium War. The Museum of London's revised version is covered with Persian inscriptions.

The Bucks' prospect of London and Westminster represents the final and best example of the genre. The convention of showing the north side of the Thames and stretching it out straight was abandoned. When the next multi-sheet London view appeared in 1792, it was taken from a single viewpoint and displayed the entire 360 degrees. It was not a prospect: it was a panorama. The word had been invented earlier in the year. That print was *London from the Roof of the Albion Mills*, and its maker was H. A. Barker, the son of Robert, the man who invented the panorama as a show. To see the show you went to the Panorama rotunda in Leicester Square where you would experience the giant painting from which the print had been reduced, and enjoy the illusion of actually being there in the scene depicted. Panoramic shows and panoramic prints were to enjoy a long and fruitful career in the nineteenth century.

Rocque's plan was also replaced by something more ambitious in the last decade of the century. In 1790 an obscure estate surveyor named Richard Horwood canvassed subscribers for a new London survey made, as his sample sheet put it, 'on a principle never before attempted'. Rocque's map had shown the principal buildings. Horwood's would show every building in London, or that was the aim. That it could be done on a plan of this scale had already been demonstrated by Rocque on his map of Dublin. Horwood, however, was dealing with a very much larger city, and showing every building was only part of it. His survey would supply street numbers. Sheets of Horwood's thirty-two-sheet map, extending further east than Rocque's, and drawn on a scale of 26 inches to the mile (i.e. the same as Rocque's), began to appear in 1792. The final sheets appeared in 1799.

1 Varley.
2 This and many of Rocque's other maps and plans are fully described on http://www.mapforum.com/05/rocqlist.htm.
3 Society of Antiquaries Minutes, 23 March 1737.
4 'Journal Book of the Royal Society' vol. 13 (1726–31), entry for 20 June 1728.
5 No. 33 in Howgego. The map was reproduced in facsimile by Harry Margary in association with Guildhall Library in 1976, with introductory notes by Ralph Hyde.
6 Oldys, p. 19.
7 Copy in Chetham Library, Manchester.
8 Preface to *An Alphabetical Index of the Streets, Squares, Lanes, Alleys,*

&c. Contained in the Plan of the Cities of London and Westminster and Borough of Southwark (London: John Pine and John Tinney 1747), p. v.
9 Transcribed in c.1740 Proposal.
10 *Daily Advertiser*, 13 January 1744.
11 Phillips 1952, pp. 12–13; Longstaffe-Gowan, pp. 127–8
12 Transcribed in *Alphabetical Index*, p. vi.
13 *Alphabetical Index*, p. vii.
14 *Alphabetical Index*, p. vii.
15 *Daily Advertiser*, 2 Jan 1745; 6 March 1745; 13 April 1745; 20 May 1745.
16 *Daily Advertiser*, 16 July 1745.
17 *General Advertiser*, 2 May 1746.
18 Tinney's interests were similar to Rocque's. In March he had published a *Plan of the Castle, Gardens, Plantations, &c. of Blair*, the seat of the Duke of Athol, advertising with it 'Eight Perspective Views of the most beautiful Parts of the Palace and Gardens of Hampton-Court and Kensington' (*General Advertiser*, 5 March 1746).
19 CLRO Rep. 150, 21 October 1846.
20 *General Advertiser*, 10 August 1746.
21 *General Advertiser*, 28 August 1746.
22 *General Advertiser*, 25 April 1747; *London Evening Post*, 30 April to May 1747.
23 *General Advertiser*, 13 November 1747. Several facsimiles of the map have been published including that by the London Topographical Society (LTS) in 1913–1918, and that by Harry Margary, with notes by James Howgego, in 1971. The map was also adapted to become Hyde 1982.
24 A facsimile of Rocque's index was published by Harry Margary and Phillimore & Co. in 1971.
25 Sloane's bound copy of the map is in the Department of Prints and Drawings.
26 I am grateful to Alex Werner of the Museum of London for comments on the shipping
27 *London Daily Advertiser*, 18 June 1751.
28 See Andrews 1967, pp. 275–92; Andrews 1977.
29 They re-emerged in 1825 at the sale of Robert Wilkinson's stock, being knocked down to a man called Smith for £25 4s (see Harley and Walters, p. 35).
30 For a discussion of the Bucks' origins see Hyde 1994, p. 35.
31 'Proposals for Publishing … Twenty Four Perspective Views of Ruins of Abbeys, Castles, and Religious Foundations in the County of York', by Samuel Buck, dated 8 January 1724 (copy in British Library Lansdowne Ms. 895, fol. 35).
32 Referred to in 'Proposals for Publishing … Twenty Four Views of Castles … in the Counties of Lincoln and Nottingham', by Samuel Buck, dated 1 November 1726 (copy in private collection).
33 All the following prospects are fully described in Hyde, *Prospects*. Several of them are described in the exhibition catalogue, Hyde 1985.
34 Henry Overton's catalogue, 1717.
35 Reproduced in facsimile by the London Topographical Society as publication No. 14 in 1903, and as publication No. 161 in 2003.
36 *London Evening Post*, 13–15 February 1746.
37 *London Evening Post*, 24–6 November 1747.
38 'Proposals for Publishing by Subscription, Six Perspective Views, viz. Five of the Cities of London and Westminster, and One of Portsmouth, by Samuel and Nathaniel Buck …', dated 1749 (copy in Bodleian Library).
39 *London Evening Post*, 17–20 June 1749.
40 *General Advertiser*, 2 September 1749.
41 *General Advertiser*, 5 October 1749.
42 ECM.
43 Phillips 1964, p. 196.
44 Copy in 'Collections for a Third Edition of Gough's *British Topography*' (Bodleian Library), vol. 4, p. 12.

CURIOUS AND ENTERTAINING – PRINTS OF LONDON AND LONDONERS

SHEILA O'CONNELL

The subject of this exhibition is mid-eighteenth-century London, but it is predominantly London as seen through the eyes of printmakers. Like any other artists, printmakers portrayed their subjects within certain constraints, conscious or otherwise. They were limited by the conventions of their time, and the London they showed depended on their perceptions of what was appropriate. More particularly they were limited by the market. This was the capital of what Adam Smith was to call 'a nation of shopkeepers',[1] and printmaking was largely a commercial enterprise: the aspects of London portrayed were those for which people were prepared to pay.

The majority of prints being made and sold in London fell broadly into three categories: topographical views, portraits and satires.[2]

So far as topography is concerned, we see prints of new buildings and major thoroughfares. The great new bridge at Westminster appears in prints that were published even before it was complete (pp. 127–9), but there are no new prints portraying St Paul's Cathedral except as a background feature (cats 1.39 or 2.31). St Paul's was an important subject for print-makers at the beginning of the century, and old plates survived from which sufficient prints could be reissued for the relatively limited market for a cathedral that was fifty or so years old. The medieval remains of London were of little interest – the taste for the picturesque had not yet developed. The eleventh-century Westminster Hall and sixteenth-century St James's Palace appear in prints only because they still performed important functions as the seats, respectively, of the House of Lords and the monarchy. The ancient Tower of London is only a background feature, shown in this exhibition as the setting for an execution and as a landmark identifying the location of a quayside where ships are unloading (cats 2.15 and 2.20). The other great Norman survival, St Bartholomew's church, is of less interest than the new buildings of the adjacent hospital (cat. 1.72).

If we were to judge from prints alone, we would assume that by 1750 little of pre-eighteenth-century London survived. But, beyond the bounds of the Great Fire of 1666 that destroyed the City from London Bridge to Smithfield, there were remnants dating back hundreds of years. At the end of the century J. T. Smith and others were to produce dozens of prints of tumbledown Tudor houses, many of which survived into the days of photography.[3] Even in a print whose purpose is satire

the printmaker has modernized the ancient houses of squalid Butchers' Row near Temple Bar (cat. 3.72).[4] This is all of a piece with a view of London that ignores the smoke that choked people, coated every surface with soot and brought regular fogs. We are not shown London in the rain – Anthony Walker's print of a sudden shower upsetting fashionable promenaders in the Mall (cat. 5.19) is a rare exception; no one shivers against a cold wind or slips on an icy pavement. London is an equable city, where the buildings are well constructed and in good order, the sun shines, and the poor may pick the odd pocket, but they do not threaten the state of things – even Hogarth's drunken soldiers at Tottenham Court (cat. 3.27) will be transformed into a disciplined military force by the time they begin their march to Finchley. There are no prints of silk-weavers besieging the Duke of Bedford in Bloomsbury Square, or of rioting coal-heavers in Wapping (pp. 95 and 101–2).

Portraits follow demand in an even more obvious way. A naive inspector of a collection of mid-eighteenth-century British portrait prints might gain the impression that the majority of Londoners were either members of the royal family or actors, that there were disproportionately few women and even fewer manual workers. The British Museum's arrangement of its collection of engraved portraits follows an eighteenth-century classification that corresponds with the predominant areas of the market. Members of the royal family constitute a class of their own. This is followed by six classes of male portraits: nobility; gentry; clergy; lawyers; military and naval; writers, artists and tradesmen. Women (nobility and others in two sub-sections) constitute a class on their own. Theatrical portraits include both men and women, as do those in the remaining classes 'Foreigners resident in England' and 'Phenomena, convicts, etc.'. This last is made up of the relatively small number of portrait prints of people below the level of polite society. Most were portrayed because they were seen as curiosities – the very tall, the very small, the very old and so on[5] – or because they were criminals, usually shown in their cells (a particular vogue of the mid-century, see cat. 5.94). Artists and actors – with notable exceptions – occupied a level of society below the polite, but were portrayed in disproportionate numbers because they realized the potential of prints for self-promotion. Theatrical portraits developed as a separate genre in the mid-century once David Garrick began to exploit the medium (see cats 3.5–3.10). As the celebrity status of actors rose, publishers cashed in on a growing market. Artists have a natural propensity to portray themselves and self-portraits of most of the well-known names appear in prints (see, for instance, cats 2.5, 3.44 and 3.46).

An exception to the commercial rule was the private plate: portraits were commissioned from printmakers for private distribution, normally by the sitter to family and friends (see cat. 5.7). There was a demand for impressions from private plates, but they were not for sale.[6]

The limited numbers of those whose portraits were painted leaves huge swathes of the population whose likenesses are lost. The faces of few of the artisan class are known, and only a tiny proportion of the thousands of London poor were recorded for posterity. The record of the appearance of individual women is even more limited than that of men. Men of the middling class appeared in portraits because their public roles – in politics, the army, the Church, the law or other professions – meant that there was a demand for their image. Their wives, sisters, daughters and mothers might be painted for private display, but few such portraits were reproduced in prints. Most of the individual women below the very highest rank who appear in the portraits in this exhibition had attained fame in ways that were beyond the conventions of society: the criminal Elizabeth Canning and Mary Squires who was perjured by her (cats 1.59 and 1.61–1.65), a woman who disguised herself as a soldier (cat. 2.13), actresses (cats 3.6, 3.9 and 3.10), courtesans (cats 3.11–3.17). The tiny image of the eminently respectable Dorothy Mercier behind her shop counter (cat. 3.66) may be the only portrait of a female print-seller in the mid-century, although many names are known.

Satires had been a feature of London print production for a hundred years.[7] They appeared in waves, responding to political scandals and crises – the Exclusion Crisis and the Popish Plot of 1678–81, the bursting of the South Sea Bubble in 1720, the Excise Crisis of 1733. In the mid-century the event that provoked satirical printmakers was the ministry of the Earl of Bute (see cat. 1.37 and p. 200). Between 1761 and 1763 more than four hundred satires were published attacking Bute.[8] Although relatively cheap – 6d was the usual price – such satires were not popular prints designed for a mass audience like the 'penny plain, twopence coloured' prints of the early nineteenth century.[9] They were often produced hurriedly and with little attention to aesthetic quality,[10] but they were aimed at an elite who would recognize the personalities and issues involved, and the position taken by the satirist in the current political in-fighting. This audience did not treat satires as ephemera; they were often collected and arranged in albums according to their subject. A particular feature of the 'paper war' against Bute was the annual publication of volumes of reduced versions of the anti-Bute prints that had appeared that year.[11]

Satirical prints were not intended merely for amusement. A comment by the Duke of Newcastle in a letter to Chancellor Hardwicke (cats 4.20 and 1.67) demonstrates how seriously they were taken by those concerned. On 30 September 1762, the Duke wrote: 'I own I don't understand any of those prints and burlesques. I am too dull to taste them, and if they are not deciphered for me, I could not in the least guess what they mean ... I detest the whole thing. But yet, they have their real consequences, and there is an amazing tameness in not daring to take any notice of them.'[12]

Satires could not be understood at a glance. They had to be deciphered element by element, and this depended on reading visual symbols – Bute's name fortuitously allowed him to be represented as a large riding boot, Henry Fox was depicted as a fox, the nation as the figure of Britannia; an election might be represented as a horse race (cat. 1.33) and attempts to end war, as a dove holding an olive branch or a team of firefighters at work (cat. 1.37). This emblematic means of expression was particularly strong in England, where it had developed in response to the suppression of naturalistic imagery at the Reformation. Religious prints throughout the seventeenth century used emblems to convey complex ideas – the image of the Broad and Narrow Way to hell or heaven is an example which became commonplace,[13] and the Spanish Armada of 1588 was immediately identifiable a hundred years later as a horseshoe-shaped arrangement of ships standing for the threat of Roman Catholic invasion.[14]

Throughout the eighteenth century such images were increasingly combined with everyday scenes, but they remained familiar to audiences and part of the visual language of prints. Paul Sandby produced a number of sophisticated, but vicious, attacks on Hogarth – in 1753–4 on the *Analysis of Beauty* and in 1762 on his support for Lord Bute – made up of complex groups of emblems and human figures.[15] The result can seem almost surreal to the modern viewer: *The Fire of Faction*, for instance,[16] shows a group of engravers clinging to a gigantic burin as they are propelled into a medieval hell-mouth; Hogarth, pumping bellows, fans the flames.

The artist who made the crucial shift away from emblematic towards pictorial story-telling was Hogarth himself. A close friend of Garrick, he understood the parallels between the visual language of theatre and that of painting and prints. He described how he saw his narratives as a 'dumb show' or mime. The clarity of his 'modern moral histories' had an immediacy that complex emblematic images lacked. Hogarth's stories could be read by almost any viewer without need for the speech balloons and lengthy texts that elucidated traditional satires. Hogarth's own prints were expensive and bought only by comparatively wealthy collectors, but they were avidly copied by the middle-range print publishers (especially the City firms of the Bowleses and Overtons) and so reached a huge audience at one or more removes. This copying – or piracy – naturally infuriated Hogarth, and in 1735 he succeeded in having an Act of Parliament passed that protected the copyright of print designers for fourteen years. This extraordinary achievement shows how great his influence was in powerful circles. His images were so marketable that after the expiry of thefourteen years publishers still found it worthwhile to have copies made.

It was not only Hogarth's compositions that were copied;

printmakers also grasped his new approach to subject matter. In the mid eighteenth century artists such as Louis Philippe Boitard and Charles Mosley produced prints that owe much to Hogarth: street scenes with stereotyped characters and humorous incidents set within convincing urban – often identifiably London – settings (see, for instance, cats 3.18 and 3.6). But, unlike Hogarth, neither artist manages entirely to abandon the written word in speech balloon or marginal text. John Collett, who was employed as a designer by Carington Bowles in the 1770s, also used Hogarthian characters and settings for milder social satires, and later generations of artists, notably David Wilkie, were influenced by Hogarth in creating scenes of everyday life that are full of narrative interest.

Hogarth moved towards greater naturalism in his images, but the other innovation of mid-century satire deliberately distorted the human figure. Caricature – in which one feature of the subject is exaggerated – was brought from Italy by the Grand Tourists (see cat. 4.17). Hogarth dismissed this new form of graphic wit as trivial. He showed his disdain in the subscription ticket for the *Marriage A-la-Mode* print series,[17] where he compares a various mass of heads of Londoners and the carefully characterized heads of biblical figures in Raphael's Sistine Chapel tapestry cartoons (acknowledged as the greatest works of art then in England) with the grotesque caricatures of Pier Leone Ghezzi, Annibale Carracci and Leonardo da Vinci (all well known in London through prints – the first two published recently by Arthur Pond, the latter by Wenceslaus Hollar). Hogarth's friend Henry Fielding shared his view of caricature as diminishing the subject to 'a nose, or any other feature of a preposterous size', and admired Hogarth's depiction of 'character': 'It has been thought a vast commendation of a painter, to say his figures seem to breathe; but surely, it is a much greater and nobler applause, that they appear to think'.[18]

In spite of such criticism, caricature quickly found a place in political satire – to such an extent that the genre as a whole is often referred to as 'Caricature'. As the emblematic tradition diminished, the habit of reading symbols was transferred to caricature. So Handel could be identified as a huge pig playing the organ (cat. 5.85), and in later years George III's bulbous eyes were exaggerated and Queen Charlotte's upturned nose became her identifying characteristic. The achievement of James Gillray, the great political satirist of the end of the century, was to combine emblem, caricature and Hogarthian pictorial narrative in complex images rich in meaning.

The two other major categories of prints also underwent crucial changes in the mid-century, under the influence of a major new artist in London: topographers had to rethink their approach once Canaletto had depicted the capital, and portrait prints followed the new approach to portraiture pioneered by Reynolds.

In the 1740s views of London were seen largely as useful records of the appearance of buildings. During his nine-year stay from 1746 to 1755 Canaletto evidently used such prints as reference material in creating his own compositions – most obviously in his view of London from the north (cat. 1.3); his radiant views of the Thames were undoubtedly informed by such unexceptional prints as those of J. Maurer or Thomas Bowles. Canaletto himself participated in the commercial print world with the drawings he provided for a dozen prints published by Robert Sayer in 1751 (see cat. 1.3). He was aware of the need to depict subjects which would interest his clients – a good proportion of his views of London showed the new bridge at Westminster. But he was not merely a recorder of topography: Canaletto's achievement was to introduce a new way of looking at London.

Topographical views had traditionally been closely bound up with the making of maps (see Ralph Hyde's discussion of John Rocque and the Buck brothers, pp. 33–4) and in consequence were dismissed as an inferior art form, at a low point in the hierarchy of artistic genres. Canaletto, however, approached views of identifiable locations with the same consideration that other artists might show to history paintings. Unlike previous artists who depicted London scenes from some indeterminate point in mid-air, his viewpoints were low so that foreground figures could add human scale and interest, and the sky took up a large part of the composition – London is a low-lying town and when there were few tall buildings the sky would indeed have dominated the observer's view. Canaletto drew his audience into the scene through arches (cat. 2.37) or arrangements of trees in the manner of Claude (cats 5.56–5.59); he showed well-known landmarks from the sort of odd angles from which Londoners might have seen them in everyday life, even bringing centre stage the backs of buildings whose grand façades were more familiar.[19] Above all Canaletto was concerned to depict – and to enhance – the light that illuminates the scene. This is most obvious in his paintings, and the same quality is achieved in his etchings of Venetian subjects[20] – which would have been well known in London. Canaletto did not himself etch views of London, and the printmakers who copied his drawings or paintings of London do not do him justice, but enough of his new vision was available to contemporaries for them to learn a new approach to the urban view.

Hogarth used the device of the view through an archway in his *Calais Gate* of 1749, and Samuel Scott drew more directly on Canaletto's view through an arch of Westminster Bridge for his views of the Thames around 1750 (see cat. 2.37), but nowhere was the influence of Canaletto more clearly seen than in the topographical views of Paul and Thomas Sandby. The brothers came from a background in functional draughtsmanship – ordnance surveying, architecture, map-making – but Paul, in particular, was determined to take his art beyond that level. The large prints that he designed to be etched by Edward Rooker in the 1760s were clearly influenced by Canaletto's work. We look through arches at buildings that are not fully visible – the corner of Covent Garden market (see cat. 3.4), or part of Horse Guards seen through an old gateway. The viewpoint is chosen for compositional reasons, and the building that is the subject of the print is seen beyond a great deal of foreground incidental interest. By the mid-1760s the conventional topographical views of the Bowleses, or even the Bucks, had lost their appeal to much of the market.[21]

Just as Canaletto applied new standards to the urban view, Joshua Reynolds changed the status of the portrait. He enlivened the genre with imaginative compositions based on his study of old master painting in Italy, and brought an intellectual approach that invested the genre with moral implications in the manner of painting of mythological or classical subjects. Sitters took on roles in Reynolds portraits: Lady Elizabeth Keppel is shown sacrificing to Hymen, god of marriage (cat. 5.16), Charles James Fox and Ladies Sarah Lennox and Susan Fox-Strangways act out a tableau at Holland House (cat. 5.17); the young Ladies Amabel and Mary Jemima Yorke are caught as if in a snapshot playing in their garden (cat. 5.4); the future Countess Spencer and her young daughter are portrayed like a proud Madonna presenting the Christ Child (cat. 5.6; Reynolds's sitters' book shows that in fact mother and child posed separately). Even in less elaborate compositions artists were, by 1760, giving added force to portraits by deliberately filling the picture plane, as shown in Gainsborough's brooding portrait of Robert Clive (cat. 4.14) and self-portraits by Thomas Frye (cat. 2.5) and James McArdell (cat. 3.46).

Portrait prints usually reproduced painted portraits, and in the mid eighteenth century their development went hand-in-hand. The preferred medium for reproducing paintings was mezzotint. The technique avoids line, using tone only, and lends itself to re-creating the rich variety of surface in painted portraits, especially those depicting wealthy sitters in luxurious silks (see cat. 5.31). A mezzotint is made by roughening a copper-plate uniformly with a fine-toothed tool called a rocker, and then scraping and burnishing certain areas to create an image that emerges in lighter tones against dark. The first few dozen impressions taken from a plate have a velvety texture, but the surface soon wears down and later impressions are dull and flat. The best mezzotinters did not sell their plates to print publishers but marketed impressions themselves. Their control of their plates meant that they could rework them when necessary.[22] Most print publishers would continue to print from worn plates for as long as impressions were marketable, and when the image had faded too badly they would strengthen the tones with some – often crude – extra work with the rocker. A mezzotinter's reputation could easily be ruined by prints made from old plates.

The most prolific mezzotinter of the period from the 1720s to the 1750s was John Faber – based for the last twenty years of his life in Bloomsbury Square. Faber published more than five hundred of his own portrait mezzotints. In 1742 George Vertue remarked that 'no sooner is a picture painted by any painter of any remarkable person but presently [Faber] has it out in print'.[23] His prints were generally of the standard 14 by 10 inches (about 350 by 250 mm), and could be framed as decoration in middle-class homes or in the lesser rooms of grand houses. Cheaper mezzotints were aimed at a wider public, and views of the Bowleses' shop windows and others of the period show the top rows of panes filled with mezzotint portraits.[24] These widely sold prints are often identifiable as portraits of popular preachers or victorious admirals and generals.

Faber's fame as a mezzotinter was eclipsed by James McArdell, the most talented of several young Irish mezzotinters who settled in London in the 1740s. McArdell's name was closely connected with Joshua Reynolds in the early days of the painter's career. Painters were aware of the value of publicizing their work through reproductive prints – Faber had made forty-two prints after Thomas Hudson's portraits and fifteen after Allan Ramsay – and Reynolds realized that his reputation as a painter depended to a large extent on the quality of those prints. In 1754 he commissioned McArdell to make a mezzotint after his portrait of Lady Charlotte Fitzwilliam, and published it himself. McArdell went on to make and publish around forty prints after Reynolds's portraits. The painter remarked that he would be 'immortalized' by McArdell, but as his career progressed he selected particular mezzotinters with skills to suit each portrait. The importance he attached to prints after his paintings is attested by a number of surviving proofs corrected by Reynolds himself.[25] As portraiture developed, so reproductive mezzotints grew in size and dramatic presence as well as in price. With the exception of the deliberately conservative private plate of Horace Walpole (cat. 5.7), the grand mezzotint portraits of aristocrats shown in Section V of this exhibition are all on a larger scale than those of a somewhat earlier date after painters such as William Hoare and Allan Ramsay that appear in earlier sections.

The innovations of Hogarth, Canaletto and Reynolds were a stimulus to other artists, but London printmakers learned also from their continental counterparts. Official figures of old master and newly published prints imported in the 1750s averaged around nine thousand,[26] and foreign printmakers – like other artists and artisans – were drawn to London by the growing market.

The numbers of prints coming into London meant not only that collectors saw work of a wide range and high quality, but that British printmakers were encouraged to emulate continental standards. Artists had always used prints as source material – the middle-range print publishers had a thriving trade in drawing books with models for artists to follow and pattern-books for the decorative arts (see cats 3.53 and 3.54). Hogarth owned a set of Salvator Rosa's *Figurine* and used one figure group as a model for Plate 3 of *Industry and Idleness*; he took a legless beggar from Bruegel for another print of a London street scene (cat. 1.13). But there is much evidence of a more fundamental type of influence than simply lifting groups from earlier works: Thomas Frye advertised his large mezzotint heads as being 'in the manner of [Giovanni Battista] Piazzetta' (see cat. 2.5); Samuel Scott owned Canaletto's etchings (as well as seeing his paintings) and clearly learned from them; Roubiliac saw prints of theatrical tomb sculpture in southern Germany and went on to introduce a new style to English funerary monuments. The influence of Rembrandt's etchings was particularly obvious. Arthur Pond and Thomas Worlidge both went so far as to depict themselves in the manner of Rembrandt in small etchings for limited circulation. Hogarth painted a brasher portrait of his friend the printmaker John Pine in flamboyant Rembrandtesque mode which was reproduced in mezzotint by McArdell.[27]

French prints both of the seventeenth century and by contemporary printmakers were universally admired as the best available. Hogarth aimed the prints of the *Marriage A-la-Mode* series at a discriminating market and employed French print-makers – Bernard Baron, Simon François Ravenet and Gérard Scotin – to make them. For *The March to Finchley*, 1750 (cat. 3.27), he employed the young Irish printmaker Luke Sullivan, who had trained under Baron in London. In the following year Vertue claimed that Sullivan had 'so far outdone his Master or any other, that his reputation must be above all engravers here or abroad – and to the honour of this nation'.[28]

In October 1748 the *Universal Magazine* – in patriotic mood, typical of Britain even as peace was being declared with France at Aix-la-Chapelle – claimed that 'no people ever more encouraged the artificers in this branch [of art], as might be exemplified by the great number of curious copper-plates daily published in this nation ... it must be acknowledged, even by those of other nations, that we are in a fair way to vie with, and, if possible, to exceed them in the improvement of this art'. This was an exaggeration. But by the mid-1760s London was well on the way to rivalling Paris as a centre for printmaking. Rising standards had boosted the market. A small audience of connoisseurs had always appreciated fine prints, and now a wider public was developing that wanted prints not just for their subject matter but as works of art. The frontispiece of Robert Sayer's catalogue of 1766 demonstrates the way that the market had changed: maps were described as 'new, useful and correct',[29] but prints, by contrast, were 'curious and entertaining'. Prints were no longer merely useful or correct, they were acquired for their own sake, a luxury commodity produced for an increasingly prosperous population.

In 1763 John Boydell began to issue *A Collection of Prints, Engraved from the most Capital Paintings in England* published serially over the next twenty years. The earliest prints of the series were by the French émigré Simon François Ravenet and by the best London printmakers Anthony Walker, Thomas Chambars and William Woollett. The quality was outstanding and the publication was a huge international success. The overseas market for British prints – and with them British painting – expanded under Boydell's entrepreneurial lead. By the end of the century London prints had come to dominate the European art world. They were no longer images of the city and its people produced for a domestic market, but works of art on the international stage.

1 Smith 1776.
2 The many old master and newly published foreign prints that were being imported into London fall outside the scope of this essay, as do the views of rural landscapes and the sporting prints which London printmakers were beginning to produce in the 1760s. For a comprehensive account of the developing London print trade in the mid-century see Clayton, pp. 104–206.
3 See, for instance, Smith 1791.
4 Hallett, p. 192. Malcolm (p.397) describes fifteenth-century Butchers' Row at the end of the eighteenth century: 'composed of those wretched fabrics overhanging their foundations, the receptacles of dirt in every corner of their projecting stories, the bane of ancient London'.
5 See O'Connell 1999, pp. 98–108 and 198–200.
6 When the vogue for portrait print collecting arose in the last decades of the eighteenth century, private plates were as eagerly sought after as those produced commercially. For the collecting of portrait prints see Pointon, pp. 53–78.
7 Griffiths 1998, pp. 144–61.
8 See Brewer 1973 for an account of the popular response to Bute.
9 See O'Connell, pp. 9–10, 91.
10 A number of political satires of this sort are reproduced in Langford 1986.
11 These collected volumes are described in BM Satire 3342; the volume for the years 1761–3 is entitled *A Political and Satirical History displaying the unhappy influence of Scotch Prevalency* (Press mark: 298.a.3).
12 British Library, Add. MSS 32,942, f. 429, quoted in Brewer 1973, p. 16, n.70.
13 See O'Connell, pp. 69–75.
14 Griffiths 1998, pp. 152–4, cat. 95.
15 Several of Sandby's satires are reproduced in Bindman, pp. 174–87.
16 BM Satire 3955.
17 Paulson 156.
18 Fielding, Preface.
19 Canaletto's remarkable paintings of Whitehall and the Privy Garden (at Goodwood and Bowhill) show the stables of Richmond House in the foreground with the back of Montagu House beyond and the brick-built side wall of the Banqueting House in the distance; the Bowhill version extends to include construction work in Whitehall.
20 Bromberg.
21 Ralph Hyde (pp. 36–8) describes how the Buck brothers' business fell off in the 1750s, although their extraordinary *Long View of London and Westminster* (cat. 2.31) continued to be updated and reissued for decades.
22 The first London mezzotinter to take systematic control of his copper-plates was John Smith (1652–1743); see Griffiths 1989.
23 Vertue, III, p. 109.
24 For the Bowleses' shop windows see BM Satires 3758, 5220 and 6352.
25 Penny, p. 36, and p. 42, n.160.
26 Pears, p. 212; in 1759 numbers were boosted to 17,908 by a massive importation of 8,124 prints from Italy. See Clayton, pp. 105–28, for an account of the thriving trade in prints in mid-century London.
27 White et al.; see nos 14, 149 and 155 for the prints mentioned here.
28 Vertue, VI, p. 204.
29 See pp. 28–9 for the reissuing of unreliable old maps in the earlier part of the century.

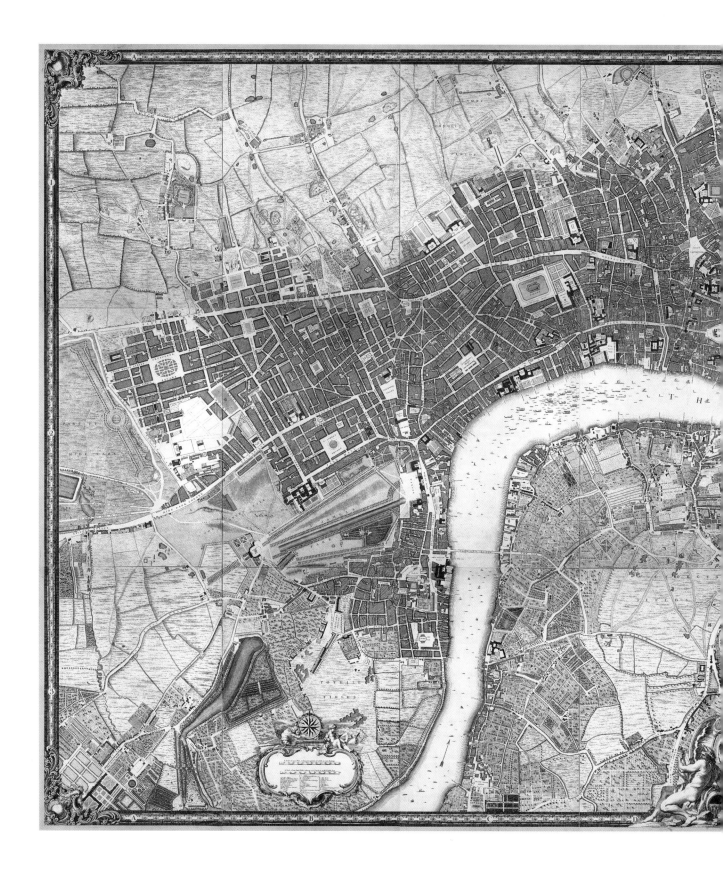

(*Previous page*)

John Pine (1690–1756) after John Rocque (fl. 1736–62)

A Plan of London and Westminster, and Borough of Southwark, 1747

Published by John Pine at the Golden Head against Burlington House, Piccadilly, and John Tinney at the Golden Lion, Fleet Street

Engraving and etching, with engraved lettering, 2,040 × 3,865 mm

Rocque's map defines the boundaries of London in the mid eighteenth century, from Hyde Park in the west to Deptford in the east, from Islington in the north to Chelsea and Vauxhall in the south. The major streets and the curve of the river remain familiar to modern Londoners; what surprises us are the open fields surrounding the great capital – fields on either side of Tottenham Court Road, in Bethnal Green and Stepney, behind what was still called Buckingham House – and acres of market gardens occupying the fertile land of Lambeth, Kennington and Bermondsey. The city that was the largest in the world covered less than 18 square miles.

See pp. 28–38 for an account of the making of this useful and beautifully produced map, and Hyde for a street index. The map reproduced here is not the copy from the British Library (Maps *3480 (293)) shown in the exhibition but a copy from a private collection reproduced by Motco Enterprises Limited (www.motco.com).

I

THE CITY

The City of London (the capital C is used here to distinguish the historic City from the metropolis as a whole) dates back to Roman Londinium founded on the north bank of the Thames around AD 50. The City boundary still follows very closely the line of the Roman and medieval walls encompassing an area slightly over one square mile, from the Tower of London in the east to Moorfields and Smithfield in the north, Holborn and Fleet Street in the west. These walls, and most of the gates, were demolished in the 1760s.

The key to the site of the City was the bridge across the Thames allowing goods carried by boat to be transferred to and from roads leading in all directions. The Roman routes are still major arteries: south to Canterbury; east via Aldgate to Colchester; north via Bishopsgate to Lincoln and York; west via Newgate and Holborn. The City was abandoned after the Romans left, but Viking raids in the ninth century led Alfred the Great to seek the safety of the old defensive walls and to restore the City. By 1066 the citizenry were sufficiently self-confident to demand and receive from William the Conqueror a charter granting them a certain amount of autonomy; William felt the need to throw up a large earth-work on the site of what was to be the Tower immediately outside the eastern wall. Successive monarchs remained wary of the power of London's popula-tion. Elizabeth I passed laws forbidding its expansion, and it was only in the seventeenth century that there was significant growth beyond the walls in what was then the county of Middlesex. Although the City was to become a tiny part of a vast conurbation, it has never

lost its distinct character: with its concentration on international trade and related financial services, its combination of workaday business life and ancient ceremonial, its medieval street pattern and tightly packed buildings, it remains proudly apart from the great capital that took its name.

From the twelfth century the City has been governed by its own mayor, sheriffs and aldermen, and has had its independent court of justice. In the eighteenth century freedom from royal and parliamentary interference was still jealously guarded: William Beckford, Lord Mayor in 1762/3 (as well as in 1769/70), caused horror but also much admiration when he broke protocol to challenge George III during an official audience. City merchants did not have the social status of the aristocrats who ran the country from Parliament, but their commercial power and wealth meant that City opinion had to be listened to. Hogarth's *The Times*, Plate 1 (cat. 1.37) illustrates the tension between the City which believed that international war would protect and extend trade, and the landed classes whose taxes largely funded the army and navy.

The enormous increase in British influence worldwide during the eighteenth century was based primarily on trade and commerce, and was centred on the City, still the country's major port. Manufacturing trades continued to thrive in the City on a more or less domestic scale, but they gave way in importance to new institutions such as the Bank of England (founded in 1694 and by the mid-1730s in a grand building in Threadneedle Street) and the mighty

East India Company which from the 1750s began to administer the British Empire in India from its headquarters in Leadenhall Street (see cat. 4.14). Merchants ran huge financial risks with ships at sea for months on end, and the business of managing risk and manipu-lating capital developed in the City as international trade grew: 'agents, factors, brokers, insurers, bankers, negotiators, discounters, subscribers, contractors, remitters, ticket-mongers, stock-jobbers, and … a great variety of other dealers in money, the names of whose employ-ments were wholly unknown to our forefathers' (*An Essay on the Increase and Decline of Trade*, 1749, p. 34, quoted in George, p. 313, n. 2).

Although there were fortunes to be made as trade expanded, new practices had their victims. In the industrial suburbs beyond City jurisdiction, factory systems and a wage economy took the place of paternalistic regimes where master, journeyman and apprentice knew their place. Philanthropic impulses led to the opening of hospitals and other institutions to help those who fell by the wayside. But social dislocation, rapid change, and massive migration to London inevitably brought periods of civil unrest – in the mid-century this was at its most violent in the East End where silk weavers and coal-heavers erupted into periodic riot (cats 1.79–1.82, 1.90).

A South View of Canonbury House, near Islington — *La Vue de l'Hotel de Canonbury près d'Islington du côté du Midi*

London, Printed for In? Boydell Engraver Cheapside

1.1

another and with occasional updating of fashionable clothing. This impression would have been taken from the plate after it had passed out of the hands of its original publisher: the date of publication has been erased and the name of the publisher, John Boydell, appears in clumsy lettering that contrasts with the refined script used for the title. The fact that the title is translated into French implies that the print was intended for export as well as domestic consumption, but the use of French was also a marketing tool for the British market: although Britain was at war with France for most of the period, French remained the language of fashion and its use lent a note of elegance to appeal to an aspiring audience.

The Approach to the City from the North

1.1–1.5

1.1

I. L. (unidentified)

A South view of Canonbury House, near Islington, 1750s

Published by John Boydell, Cheapside

Etching with engraved lettering, 260 × 414 mm (cropped)

Crace XXXII.163

1880-11-13-4972

The open country 2 miles north of the centre of the City is shown as an idyllic spot to which well-dressed citizens might stroll to take the air in fine weather. In the distance is the sixteenth-century manor house of Canonbury built just before the Reformation by the canons of St Bartholomew's, Smithfield; parts of the building survive, including the tower in the trees to the left. By the mid eighteenth century the house had been divided into lodgings. One of its most celebrated tenants was the poet Oliver Goldsmith, who lived there from 1762 to 1764.

Prints of this size, approximately 10 by 15 inches, were produced in huge numbers by the major commercial London publishers and would sell for 1s plain, or 2s coloured. They were intended for framing and hanging in series rather than to be collected in albums like old master prints in the collections of connoisseurs. Catalogues listed such prints by subject matter – designer and engraver were rarely of interest. They would continue to be offered for sale for decades, the plates often passing from one publisher to

1.2

Anonymous

A View of the New River Head, 1740s

Etching with engraved lettering, 189 × 257 mm (cropped)

Crace XXXII.56

1880-11-13-4865

A View of the New River Head.

1.2

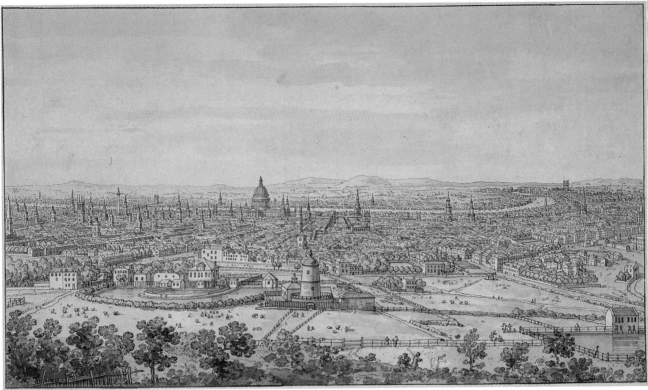

1.3

Closer to town than the suburban fields of Canonbury we see a more varied group of Londoners. There are well-dressed men and women and a child who pulls an expensive doll in a chariot, but an apple-woman is selling her wares from a wheelbarrow and a beggar on his knees holds out his hat to receive alms.

Early in the seventeenth century a channel nearly 40 miles long – the New River – was constructed by the entrepreneur Hugh Myddelton to bring water to London from springs at Chadwell and Amwell in Hertfordshire. At the head of the river on high ground in Clerkenwell, water was stored in four great reservoirs, one of which, the Round Pond, is shown here. Water was pumped up to the top of the circular tower so that there would be a sufficient pressure to carry water into the city; it flowed through wooden pipes along the main streets and small lead pipes supplied houses. Some fortunate Londoners were supplied with water from wells or springs; water was also provided directly from the Thames by waterworks at London Bridge, at York

Buildings near Charing Cross and at Chelsea (cat. 5.53). The curious buildings of the New River Head with their extraordinary view of the whole of London meant that they were favourite subjects for topographers from as early as 1665 when Wenceslaus Hollar made a set of six etchings of Islington.

The eighteenth-century City print publishers would frequently issue popular subjects in more than one size. As well as shilling prints, smaller copies such as this would be sold in sets of twelve for 1s 6d. Costume, notably the less exaggerated skirts of the women, suggests a date for this print in the 1740s.

1.3

Giovanni Antonio Canaletto (1697–1768)

A View of London from the North, 1751

Pen and brown ink and grey wash over black chalk, 231 × 397 mm

Constable 731

1862-12-13-51

This drawing shows a favourite eighteenth-century view of London from high ground to the north of the New River Head. St Paul's Cathedral dominates the skyline. The entire town can be seen, from the eccentric tower of Hawksmoor's St John's Horsleydown, south of the river to the east, to Westminster Abbey dominating the west. The Foundling Hospital with its walled forecourt (cats 3.37–3.43) appears in the middle ground on the right-hand edge of the sheet. These landmarks stand out from the mass of smaller buildings punctuated by the spires of dozens of parish churches.

When Canaletto returned to London in the middle of 1751 after some months in Venice, he was commissioned by Robert Sayer to produce drawings for a series of London subjects: this view of London from the north which was engraved by John Stevens, three views of Ranelagh Gardens (including cat. 5.36), two of St James's Park (including cat. 5.18) and four of Vauxhall Gardens (cats 5.56–5.59); a view of the Monument closely related to cat. 1.6 was engraved

49

by George Bickham and published in 1752. The prints remained popular for many years, appearing in the catalogue of Sayer's successors Laurie and Whittle in 1794.

The careful outlines and the somewhat laboured appearance of this drawing are explained by the fact that it served as a model for the engraver. Although Canaletto's characteristic penwork can be seen, especially in the freer drawing of the foreground foliage, the style is in clear contrast to the liveliness of his rapid sketches or drawings that were produced as finished works in their own right, like the views of the Thames and Westminster shown later in the exhibition. This view must itself have been based on a print, possibly one published by Thomas Bowles in 1730 (Crace XXXII.62), but Canaletto has adapted topographical details for compositional reasons: he has altered the arrangement of the pond and buildings at the New River Head and shifted the line of the road known as Black Mary's Hole, now King's Cross Road, running into town from the north-west.

See Constable, pp. 405–32 and 569–84, for a catalogue of Canaletto's work in England. Links, and Liversidge and Farrington, summarize recent research and provide good reproductions. Canaletto's work in the Royal collection is discussed in Millar with a note of the extensive bibliography of the artist up to 1980; J.G. Links notes more recent publications in his supplement to Constable.

1.4

Bewley Wynne Morrison
(fl. *c*.1750–*c*.1770)

Trade card of James Salmon, Cambridge, Carrier, 1750s

Etching with engraved lettering, 198 × 168 mm

Banks 31.15

D.2-2916 Sarah Banks collection, presented 1818

Trade cards (advertising hand-bills) were at their most ornamental in the mid eighteenth century, often with elaborate

Rococo decoration including the shop-sign and images connected with the trade. For a discussion of the production and styles of mid-eighteenth-century trade cards see Snodin 1986. This card announces the move of James Salmon's London terminus from the Four Swans Inn to the smaller Green Dragon Inn in Bishopsgate, one of the main roads out of the City. Both inns yards are shown on Rocque's map. Salmon carries goods by wagon to Cambridge, evidently transferring them there to boats on the Cam and Ouse for destinations in Norfolk. Goods dispatched from London on Thursday are promised for delivery to Downham's famous butter market by the following Monday. Carriers' wagons provided a cheap form of transport for people as well as goods, and a group of passengers can be seen at the back of Salmon's vehicle. Faster transport was available on stage coaches which in the 1750s would take passengers to Norwich in two and a half days, to Manchester or Chester in four and a half days, to Newcastle in nine days or to Edinburgh in ten to twelve days; journey times were

1.4

1.5

The Monument of LONDON in remembrance of the dreadfull Fire in 1666. Collone de LONDRES elevé pour une Perpetuelle Resouvenance de L'incendre
Its Haight is 202 feet. Printed for John Bowles at the Black Horse in Cornhill. Generalle de cette Ville en 1666. En Haut 202 Pieds.

1.6

reduced as roads were improved in successive decades.

The annotation '1799' at the foot of this sheet refers to the date when it was acquired by Sarah Banks; the style indicates that it dates from the middle of the century.

1.5
John Kirk (fl. 1725–61)
Trade card of the Bell Inn

Etched image with engraved cartouche and lettering, 198 × 158 mm (cropped)

Heal I.43 Bequeathed by Sir Ambrose Heal, 1959

The Bell Inn had a large yard in Friday Street south of Cheapside. Coaches left there on Saturdays for Abergavenny and on Thursdays for Gloucester; carriers left for towns in Dorset, Devon, Cornwall, Monmouth and south Wales. This card refers to a more stylish form of

transport, the chaise, a lightweight and therefore fast carriage carrying only two people, which was introduced in the 1740s.

It was normal practice for even wealthy Londoners to hire carriages and horses instead of, or in addition to, going to the expense of keeping their own stables and carriage-houses. Among Lord Winterton's bills in the Heal collection is one dated June 1766 from William Worthington of Oxford Road (Street) who advertised 'Neat post chaises to lett': Winterton has been charged a total of £1 18s 3d to hire three horses for two days and one horse for one day, including their keep overnight and the cost of a nightwatchman (Heal I.83).

The Streets of the City
1.6–1.12

1.6
Thomas Bowles (1712?–67)
The Monument of London in remembrance of the dreadful Fire in 1666, 1752

Published by John Bowles at the Black Horse in Cornhill

Etching with engraved lettering, 258 × 410 mm

Crace XXIV.16

1880-11-13-3872

The Monument to the Great Fire of London was a major landmark, the tallest building in the City except for St Paul's Cathedral, commemorating the Great Fire of 1666 that began here just to the north of London Bridge. The print shows Fish Street Hill leading south past

Monument Yard to St Magnus Martyr and the bridge which, until the opening of Westminster Bridge in 1750, was the only access to London from the south other than by boat.

Topographical prints published by the major London publishers showed a busy and well-organized town. Buildings are in good repair and the chimney smoke disappears into the sky; we see nothing of the fogs that visitors complained of. In Bowles's print the details of urban life are clearly delineated: the pedestrian area separated from the main roadway by a line of bollards; shop-signs hanging from every building; plant pots on a ledge. We are shown a range of traffic: a man pushes a wheelbarrow; others carry loads on their shoulders; a woman balances a basket on her head; genteel couples greet shopkeepers as they stroll past their doors; a chimney-sweep's boy rushes along with a sooty brush in his hand; sheep and cattle are being driven to market; a chaise and several coaches travel at a trot, while heavily laden carts make their way more slowly; a number of people on horseback include a lady riding side-saddle.

The print is one of a number of mid-eighteenth-century London views signed 'T. Bowles' and generally attributed to Thomas Bowles III who worked with his father, also Thomas, at the family business in St Paul's Churchyard. The prints were often published by, or in collaboration with, John Bowles, brother of Thomas II (see Hodson, I pp. 186–90).

Shop-signs

Until the 1760s there were no street numbers, and London trade premises were identified by signs hanging in the street like modern pub signs or the pawnbroker's three balls. Signs followed a traditional iconography usually indicating the trade carried on in the building: a trade card of the 1750s for John Fairchild & Son on London Bridge (Oxford, Bodleian Library, John Johnson trade cards 19.14a) lists 131 subjects from 'Adam and Eve' to

'Wheatsheaf'. Topographical views show how these signs dominated busy shopping streets; in narrow alleyways they blocked the light and from time to time falling signs caused injury. Furthermore, their lavish decoration had an air of vulgarity out of keeping with the aspirations of modernizing Londoners; signs were forbidden in the elegant streets of Paris in 1761. Acts of Parliament of 1762 and 1763 to improve the streets of Westminster by removing signs, as well as by paving, cleansing and lighting, were followed by Acts of 1766 and 1768 requiring the removal of signs and the introduction of street numbering in the City; the City had been empowered to levy a rate for street lighting since 1736. These Acts did much to make London safer and healthier.

The new numbering system did not immediately win the confidence of all shopkeepers, and many trade cards show the old signs as well as new street numbers. Regret for the passing of a demotic art form led William Hogarth and the campaigning journalist Bonnell Thornton to organize an exhibition of

painted signs in 1762. The exhibition also served to mock the pretensions of the Society of Arts.

The essential sources for the study of signs are Larwood and Hotten, Lillywhite, and Heal (1957). The latter lists some two thousand signs according to trade, with indexes of signs and shop-keepers' names and many illustrations taken from Ambrose Heal's collection of trade cards now at the British Museum and those in the Pepys Library, Magdalene College, Cambridge. The façade of Heal's furniture shop in Tottenham Court Road is decorated with 'the Sign of the Four-Poster' and other emblematic shop signs.

1.7

Anonymous

Sign of the Ape and Apple, c.1670

Painted stone, 590 × 485 × 205 mm

Museum of London 7134

This sign dates from the period of the rebuilding of the City after the Great Fire of 1666. It survived until the nine-

1.7

teenth century in Philip Lane, just inside the City wall near Cripplegate, set into the wall of what was probably originally a tavern.

1.8

Anonymous

Sign of the Leather Bottle, 18th century

Wood, covered with copper and leather
550 × 480 × approx. 310 mm
Museum of London 7150

This sign from Leather Lane, near Hatton Garden, is an example of the three-dimensional hanging sign, often reproducing goods for sale. Similar signs were the Tobacco Roll (Gowan, tobacconist, Rose Street, Covent Garen, *c*.1750), the Great Golden Spectacles and Quadrant (Joseph Linnell, optician, Ludgate Street, *c*.1763) and the Three Brushes (Nathan Smith, brushmaker, Snow Hill, *c*.1760). In the seventeenth century leather bottles were replaced in everyday use by bottles of pottery or glass, but they remained as pub signs until the late twentieth century.

Designs for Shop-signs

This group of drawings came from a volume of seventy-six lively designs for signs which were probably produced as patterns for prospective clients of a London sign workshop (see Fox 1984). They are attributed on stylistic grounds to Charles Catton, a tradesman-artist who was coach-painter to George III and also a founder-member of the Royal Academy.

1.9

Attributed to Charles Catton (1728–98)

*William Augustus, Duke of Cumberland, c.*1747

Watercolour and bodycolour over graphite, squared for transfer, 342 × 245 mm (painted surface)

Private collection; ex-collection Lord Clark of Saltwood

Cumberland became immensely popular throughout England after his defeat of the Jacobite rebels at Culloden in 1746. This design is based on a painting of 1744 by John Wootton and Thomas

Hudson; the direct source would have been John Faber's mezzotint published in 1744 (cat. 4.11). Similar images appeared everywhere as shop-signs as well as in cheap prints. Horace Walpole noted in April 1747 that Cumberland had taken the place of earlier military heroes, and gives evidence of the way that signs changed to keep up with current events: 'the Duke's head has succeeded almost universally to Admiral Vernon's, as his head had left few traces of the Duke of Ormond's. I pondered these things in my heart and said unto myself, surely all glory is but a sign.' In the early nineteenth century Thomas Bewick, the great Newcastle wood-engraver, remembered large woodcuts of 'Duke Willy' on the cottage walls of his childhood in the 1750s.

1.10

Attributed to Charles Catton (1728–98)

*The Black Boy and Hat, c.*1747

Bodycolour over graphite, 306 × 205 mm (painted surface)

Private collection; ex-collection Lord Clark of Saltwood

This is presumably a shop-sign for a hatter. About 1760 the hatter Charles Paget used the sign of the Black Boy and Hat at his shop in High Holborn (trade card, Heal 72.283), and in a print by John June (cat. 1.28) the same sign is clearly visible hanging from a building beside St Mary-le-Bow in Cheapside. The Black Boy had been a popular sign since the mid sixteenth century; there seems no obvious connection with the trade of the hatter, although another hatter, William Brackenbury, used the sign of the Black Boy at his shop in the Strand around 1760. In an apparently unashamed reference to slave labour in the West Indies, the Black Boy and Sugar Loaf was used by grocers – importers of sugar – in Leadenhall Street (Samuel Stone, 1754) and Wardour Street, Soho (Samuel Bowker, *c*.1755); the sign of the Blackamoor's Head was

1.8

1.9

1.10

1.11

used by grocers in Chancery Lane (Hugh James, 1764) and Fetter Lane (Thomas Jemmitt, 1737–48).

I.II

Attributed to Charles Catton (1728–98)

The Three Jolly Butchers, *c.*1747

Bodycolour over graphite, 220 × 333 mm (painted surface)

Private collection; ex-collection Lord Clark of Saltwood

This sign would clearly have been appropriate for a butcher's shop, but might also have been used by a tavern near to Smithfield or another cattle market. Butchers are frequently identified in views of London streets from the sharpening steels hanging from their waists. One of these men carries a cleaver, another is downing a pint of beer.

1.12

**Attributed to Charles Catton
(1728–98)**

The Three Mariners, c.1747

Bodycolour over graphite, squared for
transfer, 200 × 298 mm (painted surface)

Private collection; ex-collection Lord Clark
of Saltwood

This sign shows three levels of seafarers:
a seaman in his short wide trousers
holding a cross-staff to his eye (this was
a navigational instrument used for
measuring the height of the sun or a star
above the horizon); a bewigged navigator
measuring the lines of longitude on a
globe; an officer with a telescope.
Navigational accuracy was an obsession
of the eighteenth century when trade was
expanding across the world; the 1750s
saw John Harrison's invention of the
marine chronometer which allowed
longitude to be gauged accurately for the
first time (see cat. 3.79). This sign might
have been used by a maker of scientific
instruments, or at a riverside tavern.
Signs of the Three Mariners are
recorded in the middle of the eighteenth
century in Vauxhall and Spitalfields.

Living in the City

1.13–1.15

1.13

William Hogarth (1697–1764)

Industry and Idleness, Plate 6:
*The Industrious 'Prentice out of His
Time, & Married to his Master's
Daughter*, 30 September 1747

Published by William Hogarth

Engraving and etching with engraved
lettering, 262 × 345 mm

Paulson 173 (ii)

1868-8-22-1577 Bequeathed by Felix Slade

This print shows a prosperous middle-
class City home which, as was
customary, doubles as a place of
business; a shop-sign hangs outside.
The scene is situated in Fish Street Hill

1.12

1.13

(see cat. 1.6) identified by the base of the
Monument in the background with its
inscription attributing the Great Fire of
London in 1666 to Roman Catholic
enemies of the state. Fears of Catholic
invasion would not have seemed far-
fetched in 1747 when Britain was at war
with France and Spain and it was less
than two years since Prince Charles
Edward Stuart's army had marched as

far south as Derby. The anti-Catholic
inscription was removed from the
Monument only in 1830.

A newly wed couple sit at a window
open to the street, sipping tea from
porcelain bowls and wearing genteel
indoor 'undress' clothes – the young
man has removed his wig and wears a
cap and robe. The remains of the
wedding meal are shared with a poor

mother kneeling at the door, while a ballad-seller chants the song 'Jesse, or the Happy Pair'. The drummers and the butchers banging bones and cleavers seem to modern eyes to be joining in the celebrations of the happy day, but they are in fact subjecting the couple to 'rough music', a popular demonstration of disapproval at unequal marriages (see Alford). In this case an ambitious young man has finished his time as an apprentice, has married his master's daughter and has become a partner in the firm of what is now, according to the shop-sign, Goodchild and West; he is paying one of the drummers to ensure that their noisy playing does not get out of hand. Hogarth's story of the rise of Francis Goodchild is full of hints that his successful career does not always run as smoothly as it might appear.

Another aspect of the print that is not quite what it seems is the figure of the legless man balanced on a low trolley; what appears as a documentary glimpse of London street life is in fact based on a figure in Pieter Bruegel's *Justice* (Bastelaer 135). Hogarth lived at the centre of the international print trade and, like all artists of the period, wherever possible he turned to prints for source material rather than making studies from life.

1.14
William Hogarth (1697–1764)
Preliminary drawing for Plate 6 of Industry and Idleness, 1747

Graphite, pen and ink with indented perspective lines; verso coated with red chalk for transfer, 251 × 324 mm

Oppe 49; ECM 32*

1982-2-27-2; ex-collection Brownlow Cecil, 9th Earl of Exeter

This is one of two preliminary studies for the print shown as cat. 1.13. Hogarth's careful perspective construction gives a solid context for the life of the young man who will rise to the top of the City establishment; the scenes of his fellow apprentice's progress in the opposite direction are characterized by unstable environments and dilapidated structures. In a second study Hogarth replaces the woman with a wheelbarrow in the foreground with a little girl with a doll; she, in turn, is replaced by a legless ballad-seller in the finished print.

1.14

Invented Painted & Published by W.ᵐ Hogarth   Marriage A-la-Mode, (Plate VI)   *Engraved by G. Scotin*
According to Act of Parliaments April 1.ˢᵗ 1745

1.15

1.15

Louis Gérard Scotin (1698–*c*.1755)
after William Hogarth (1697–1764)

Marriage A-la-Mode, Plate VI,
1745

Published by William Hogarth

Etching and engraving with engraved
lettering, 384 × 458 mm

Paulson 163 (ii)

1868-8-22-1565 Bequeathed by Felix Slade

The merchant's daughter kills herself
after a disastrous marriage into the
aristocracy and the execution of her lover
– reported on the broadside at her feet.
The setting, identified by the view

through the window of London Bridge,
is a house in the City on one of the streets
running down to the river from Thames
Street. Hogarth's polemic against
marriages of convenience required the
distinction between the middle and
upper classes to be clearly made. He
aimed *Marriage A-la-Mode* at connoisseurs who would have read easily the
signs that what is being shown here is
the home of someone more concerned
with making money through trade than
with spending it, like the aristocrats in
the modish world where the merchant's
daughter had moved. Trade and
domestic life, even at the level of the
wealthiest citizens, were not separated.

Leading banking families, such as the
Hoares in Fleet Street and the Asgills in
Lombard Street, lived in the upper floors
above their banking halls.

Hogarth's merchant is a pillar of the
City community; his aldermanic gown
trimmed with bear fur hangs on the wall.
He is not concerned to hide the source of
his wealth, and business ledgers are left
on view in his dining room. Every detail
of the scene is carefully designed to
contrast with the sort of conspicuous
consumption demonstrated in grand
Mayfair interiors earlier in the series
(cats 5.72, 5.73). The window is a case-
ment with the arms of the City in stained
glass, though sashes with clear glass

panes had appeared in new buildings since the reign of Queen Anne; Dutch paintings of peasants in taverns and untidy still-lifes hang beside a cheap sheet almanac where aristocrats hung fashionable Italian old masters in elaborate frames. The fallen chair is heavy and four-square, upholstered in gilt-leather, while the chair that lies on the floor in the Mayfair house has graceful curving lines and silk damask upholstery. The merchant keeps time with a simple weight-driven wall-clock while the young aristocrats have an elaborate Rococo fantasy of ormolu and oriental porcelain; his floorboards are bare while the Mayfair houses have expensive imported carpets. The merchant entertains with pipes, tobacco, gin and a chipped punchbowl, a pig's head is the centrepiece of his meal; his daughter had played cards, employed musicians and drunk tea or chocolate (expensive luxuries) from Chinese porcelain. His servant is a dim-witted youth in an ill-fitting coat, she had had two black boys who could be dressed up in silken turbans.

City Government

1.16–1.19

From as early as Saxon times, groups of London artisans and merchants had grouped together to protect their interests, and these fraternities developed into the great Livery Companies that underpin the administration of the City. In the eighteenth century no trader could operate within the boundaries of the City unless he or she was a freeman of one of the seventy-seven Companies – though the old craft link was already broken and John Tinney, printmaker and publisher, was, for instance, a freeman of the Goldsmith's Company. Freedom (membership) was obtained either by serving an apprenticeship, by redemption (paying a fee) or by patrimony (inheritance). Women could obtain freedom and frequently ran businesses, but they could not progress

1.16

to the more senior rank of liveryman from which was elected the City's governing body, the Corporation of London.

In the middle of the eighteenth century the City was divided into twenty-six wards (one, Bridge Without, has since been abolished) with local responsibility for the preservation of the peace, supervision of trading, sanitation and so on. Citizens were required to take their turn in filling offices such as Scavenger, Constable or Collector for the Poor, or else to pay fines to avoid office. Ward beadles were employed to undertake day-to-day duties. Residents of each ward elected members of the Corporation from liverymen: between four and twelve Common Councilmen according to the size of the ward, and one Alderman who held office for life. Each year the Lord Mayor and at least one of the two Sheriffs were (and still are) elected from the Court of Aldermen by the Livery Companies.

1.16

William Hogarth (1697–1764)
Industry and Idleness, Plate 8:
The Industrious 'Prentice Grown Rich and Sheriff of London,
30 September 1747

Published by William Hogarth

Etching and engraving with engraved lettering, 266 × 350 mm

Paulson 175

1868-8-22-1579 Bequeathed by Felix Slade

A banquet of soup, joints of meat, poultry and huge pies is being enjoyed in Fishmonger's Hall beside London Bridge. The Hall is identifiable by the statue of Lord Mayor William Walworth, a Fishmonger, who killed Wat Tyler, one of the leaders of the Peasants' Revolt of 1381; the statue bears little resemblance to Edward Pierce's sculpture of *c.*1685 which – together with Walworth's dagger – is preserved in the modern Hall. Since its inception in the thirteenth century the Fismongers' Company has been responsible for the inspection of all fish sold in the City to ensure that it is fit for human consumption. The main London market for fish remained at Billingsate, just downstream of London Bridge, until 1982. The Hall portrayed by Hogarth was demolished in 1827 when London Bridge was reconstructed; the present Hall was completed in 1834.

Hogarth's industrious apprentice, Francis Goodchild, has been elected as one of the two Sheriffs of London, an essential step towards becoming Lord Mayor. He and his wife are guests of honour at a City banquet seated beneath a grand portrait of the King. A group of constituents present a petition at the door.

1.17

William Hogarth (1697–1764)

Preliminary drawing for Plate 8 of Industry and Idleness, 1747

ILLUSTRATED IN COLOUR, PLATE I

Graphite, pen and ink with grey and brown wash over indented perspective lines with pricking and traces of red chalk, 213 × 289 mm

Oppe 54; ECM 35

1896-7-10-18 ex-collection Horace Walpole

This drawing differs only in details from Hogarth's finished print (cat. 1.16): the female diner in the foreground is replaced by a man served by a black waiter, and one group of musicians has been omitted. Unlike most preliminary drawings, it is in the same direction as the print (not reversed left to right). This may be in order to ensure that knives and forks are held in the correct hands, but it may also be connected with the pains that Hogarth has taken, as in cat. 1.14, to place Francis Goodchild in a well-constructed environment. The perspective lines of the great room are indented and pricked so that chalk can be dusted through the tiny holes in order to transfer the design on to the copper-plate.

Ironmongers Hall with a View of Fenchurch Street.   L'Hotel des Ferronniers dans la Rue de Fenchurch a LONDRES.

1.18

1.18

Thomas Bowles (1712?–62) after John Donowell (fl. *c.*1750–86)

Ironmongers' Hall with a view of Fenchurch Street, *c.*1749

Etching with engraved lettering, 254 × 412 mm (cropped)

Crace XXIII.36

1880-11-13-3793

This print shows one of the grandest new City buildings of the mid-century. Ironmongers' Hall was rebuilt at the end of the 1740s and survived until damaged by bombing in the First World War. Fenchurch Street is a major City street and we see carts, carriages, riders and men carrying loads. The gutter down the middle of the roadway serves as a drain. As regulations (generally ignored) required, the wealthy Ironmongers have fixed lamps outside the Hall; much of the rest of the street would have been in darkness after nightfall and those walking the streets had to rely on link-boys with torches to guide them through the darkness (see cat. 3.3). The plaques, or firemarks, with symbols and numbers on a building on the right show that it was insured with two of the companies who employed firemen to protect buildings on which premiums had been paid. Buildings not clearly identified as under the protection of an insurance

company were left to the unreliable care of the parish fire service.

Donowell specialized in architectural subjects. He attended the St Martin's Lane Academy (cats 3.44–3.46) and exhibited at the Free Society of Artists (1761), the Society of Artists (1762–70) and the Royal Academy (1778–86). This print is cropped and the publication line has been removed, but it is probably one of the series of thirty-nine 'perspective views in and about London' listed in John Bowles's catalogue of 1749 (increasing to sixty-two by 1753).

1.19

Paul Fourdrinier (1695–1758) after Samuel Wale (1721?–86)

The Lord Mayor's Mansion House, 1751

Published by John Bowles at the Black Horse, Cornhill

Etching with engraved lettering, 261 × 413 mm

Crace XXI.104

1880-11-13-3619

The Mansion House and Horse Guards (cats 4.2–4.4) were the major London public buildings of the 1750s. Until 1753 Lord Mayors of the City had lived in their own houses, but it had long been thought proper for them to have a

The Lord Mayor's Mansion House / Le Palais du Lord Mayor ou premier Magistrat
Shewing the Front of the House & the West Side / de la Ville de Londres
Printed for John Bowles at the Black Horse in Cornhill.

1.19

designated building in keeping with the importance of their office and as a symbol of the status of the City. The site chosen was that of the thirteenth-century Stocks Market which was moved in 1737 to the Fleet Market (see cat. 1.68). The site is at the heart of the City, close to the Bank of England and the trade centre of the Royal Exchange (whose tower rises on the left above its entrance loggia in Cornhill) and linked to St Paul's by the broad thoroughfare of Cheapside. The architect was George Dance the Elder (1741–1825), and the fine Palladian building cost more than £70,000, raised from fines paid since 1730 by those declining to hold the office of Sheriff (these fines were later used to build Blackfriars Bridge). The two attic extrusions above the roofline provided extra height to the Egyptian Hall (banqueting room) and the Dancing Gallery (ballroom); they were removed in 1794 and 1842. Six lamp-posts are shown on the pavement at the front of the building; in the evenings their light would have had an impressive effect, illuminating the grand portico so that it dominated the darkness of the surrounding streets.

This print is designed with deliberately exaggerated perspective so that it could be used in a viewing apparatus that gave an effect of three-dimensionality (see cat. 1.21). Such prints are often

known by their French name as *vues d'optique*; they had an international market and were often published with bilingual titles. This print was published before the final completion of the Mansion House in 1753 and must have relied on plans supplied by the architect.

Cheapside

1.20–1.31

1.20

Thomas Bowles (1712?–67)

The Church of St Mary-le-Bow in Cheapside, London, 1762–3

Published by Carington Bowles in St Paul's Churchyard, John Bowles in Cornhill and Robert Sayer in Fleet Street

Etching with engraved lettering,
250 × 420 mm

Crace XXI.17

1880-11-13-3532

Cheapside was London's major shopping street from the twelfth century onwards; its name comes from the Old English word for market. By the eighteenth century its many shops concentrated on the sale of luxury goods.

This print is often reproduced as an illustration of a typical City street in the

days before the removal of shop-signs. It is not dated, but must have been published at about the time of Thomas Bowles III's death in 1762, when his cousin Carington Bowles took his place at the shop in St Paul's Churchyard. By the end of the decade, the shop-signs in Cheapside had disappeared.

1.21

Butler Clowes (*c.*1740–82)

Trade card of John Smith, Map and Printseller, 1750s

Etching with engraved lettering,
230 × 178 mm (cropped)

Banks 100.104

Bequeathed by Sir Augustus Wollaston Franks, 1897

Smith's shop in Cheapside was opposite that of the Wheatland sisters (cat. 1.22). His card indicates that he learned his trade by working with Robert Sayer, one of the largest print-sellers of the period. The card is a Rococo fantasy topped by the shop-sign of Hogarth's head, based on the self-portrait of the artist sketching the gate of Calais in *The Roast Beef of Old England* (Fig. 7). The print after Hogarth's painting (now Tate) was published in 1749, and Smith probably set up in business in that year or shortly afterwards. Hogarth's Head was also used as a sign in the 1750s by the booksellers Ryall and Withy in Fleet Street; Hogarth himself used Van Dyck's head as a sign at his house in Leicester Square.

The anti-French sentiment of Hogarth's *Roast Beef* would have chimed with that of most Londoners of the inter-war period, but French works of art were prized and Smith advertises that he sells fine French as well as English prints, illustrating a print of Cupid after Carle van Loo and a French print of a Dutch seventeenth-century painting. The range of Smith's activities tells a good deal about the print trade: he sold his own and other newly published prints, maps, drawing books (with figures and other subjects for students to copy), copy books (with examples of fine lettering),

The CHURCH of S.t Mary le Bow in Cheapside London   L'EGLISE de S.t Marie Le Bow dans Cheapside Londres.

1.20

1.21

1.22

books of ornament (with models for artisans), watch-papers (see cats 3.9–3.14) and coloured perspective views (cat. 1.39); he provided artists' materials such as watercolours, indian ink, black lead pencils and brushes ('hair pencils'); he catered for the storage of prints or drawings in portfolios (the term then referred to what would now be called albums), for their display by colouring, framing and glazing – all 'in the neatest manner' – or by backing large maps with linen or canvas and fitting them to rollers, and he sold the fashionable 'diagonal mirrors' with concave lenses, as shown at the left of the card, for use with perpective views (see Clayton, pp. 140–1); finally, Smith dealt in 'old prints and drawings' for the connoisseurs' market.

1.23

1.22

William Tringham (1723–66)

Trade card of Martha Wheatland and Sister, Milliners and Haberdashers, 1761

Etching with engraved lettering, 180 × 137 mm

Heal 86.87 Bequeathed by Sir Ambrose Heal, 1959

The Wheatlands' shop-sign shows the young Queen Charlotte as an emblem of fashionable taste. It is likely that the sisters took over the business of Joyce Mason who was trading as a milliner in 1745 at the sign·of Queen Caroline's Head at the corner of Wood Street, Cheapside. The decorative border of the card indicates that fashionable hats were still sold at the shop, as well as fans and jewellery including hair ornaments in the shape of floral sprays ('Italian flowers') and feathers ('aigrettes') as shown in cats 1.24–1.26. Women often ran businesses catering to other women, but they were involved in many other trades as well (see, for instance, cats 1.33 and 3.47).

1.23

Francis Poole (fl. 1760s)

A pair of women's shoes, 1760s

Blue green silk heavily trimmed with silver lace, lined with white kid, paper and cotton canvas, leather sole, length 254 mm (heel 82 mm high)

Museum of London A12570 and A12571; ex-collection Edwin Austin Abbey

The style of these shoes indicates that they date from the late 1760s. They must have been worn only indoors as there is very little wear, but the colour has faded.

1.25

1.24

1.26

The INDUSTRIOUS 'PRENTICE Lord-Mayor of London.

Proverbs CHAP: III. Ver: 10.
Length of days is in her right hand, and
in her left hand Riches and Honour.

1.27

Inside each shoe is the name of their owner, Miss Ellis, inscribed inside in ink, and a printed maker's label showing that they were made by Francis Poole, 'Woman's Shoemaker, in the Old Change, near Cheapside, London'. Old Change ran south from the west end of Cheapside.

The shoes would have been worn with buckles of silver set with paste or precious stones (see cat. 3.55).

1.24

Italian flower-spray hair ornament, mid 18th century

Gold and silver with diamonds and pearls, height 81 mm

HG 13

MME 1978,10–2,171 Presented by Professor and Mrs John Hull Grundy

1.25

English flower-spray hair ornament with butterfly trembler, mid 18th century

Gold, silver-gilt and silver with garnets, height 72 mm

HG 38

MME 1978,10–2,428 Presented by Professor and Mrs John Hull Grundy

1.26

English flower-spray hair ornament with bird trembler, mid 18th century

Gold, silver-gilt and silver with garnets, height 68 mm

HG 41

MME 1978,10–2,431 Presented by Professor and Mrs John Hull Grundy

1.27

William Hogarth (1697–1764)

Industry and Idleness, Plate 12: The Industrious 'Prentice Lord-Mayor of London, 30 September 1747

Published by William Hogarth

Etching with engraved lettering, 272 × 405 mm

Paulson 179 (ii)

1868-8-22-1583

The annual election of the Lord Mayor is celebrated with an elaborate procession and banquet at the Guildhall. The width of Cheapside meant that it was always the focus of public celebrations; four hundred years before Hogarth, Chaucer described a typical city apprentice who regarded such events as an excuse to abandon work for a day's rampage: 'Whenever any pageant or procession / Came down Cheapside, goodbye to his profession. / He'd leap out of the shop to see the sight / And join the dance and not come back that night' (*The Cook's Tale*).

Hogarth shows the Lord Mayor's procession entering Cheapside with the east end of St Paul's Cathedral visible on the right. The scene is riotous. Frederick, Prince of Wales, and Princess Augusta gaze down from a balcony on a drunken crowd that seems about to attack Francis Goodchild in the mayoral coach. The man in the beaver-fur hat defending the door is the official Swordbearer of the Lord Mayor.

See cat. 2.38 for the earlier part of the procession by barge to Westminster. Until 1751 the Lord Mayor's Show took place on 29 October; with the loss of eleven days at the reformation of the calendar in 1752 (see Preface) the date was changed to 9 November.

1.28

John June (fl. *c*.1747–70)

A View of Cheapside, as it appeared on Lord Mayor's Day Last, 16 November 1761

Published by John Smith at Hogarth's Head, Cheapside

Etching, 241 × 342 mm

BM Satire 3819

1867-10-12-780

The new King George III and Queen Charlotte are watching the Lord Mayor's procession of Sir Samuel Fludyer on 9 November 1761, just a week before this print was published. In the mid-eighteenth-century City, Fludyer's wealth was second only to that of the great sugar merchant William Beckford. At his death in 1768 Fludyer was deputy-governor of the Bank of England, but his

fortune – estimated at £900,000 – was based largely on government clothing contracts after he had broken the East India Company's monopoly of trade in scarlet cloth.

The Lord Mayor's coach is recognizable as the one still in use today and normally on display in the Museum of London. It was built in 1757 by Joseph Berry to designs by Robert Taylor and cost £1,065, a considerable sum, but one that does not compare with the £7,652 spent five years later on George III's gold state coach. The viewpoint is just to the west of St Mary-le-Bow; the bottom of the church tower can be seen on the right. Next to the church is a shop-sign of the Black Boy and Hat (see cat. 1.10). The printmaker John June is known for humorous views of London life, and he portrays the procession, perhaps deliberately echoing Hogarth, as an occasion for

A VIEW of CHEAPSIDE, *as it appeard on* LORD MAYOR'S DAY *last*.

1.28

the people of the City to let their hair down. Respectable Londoners stand decorously on balconies above the shopfronts fitted up as viewing stands – the royal family are recorded as having watched from the house of David Barclay opposite the church – while in contrast the crowd in the muddy street is full of excitement. Even professional musicians in the wind band on the left are drinking (Hogarth's print shows the back of their stage), the butchers with their bones and cleavers are making their own kind of rough music (see cat. 1.13), a soldier has stumbled into a woman whose basket of fruit falls to the ground and a fight is about to ensue, prostitutes are eyeing likely clients and, as ever, a pickpocket takes advantage of the distractions to relieve a gentleman of a watch or a handkerchief.

June must have anticipated the event when making this print in time to be sold on the day itself. In fact Lord Mayor's Day 1761 ended in riot. There was much opposition to the young King and his favourite minister Lord Bute; William Pitt – who was supported by the City (see cat. 4.22) – exploited the situation by appearing at the Guildhall banquet; the crowd turned on Bute, who survived unscathed only because he had taken the precaution of providing himself with a guard of butchers.

1.29

Attributed to Louis Philippe Boitard (fl. 1733–67)

The Lord Mayor's Procession, c.1747

ILLUSTRATED IN COLOUR, PLATE I

Brush drawing in grey wash over graphite, 267 × 368 mm

ECM 8

1978-5-20-9

The authorship of this vigorous drawing is uncertain but, like so many views of the Lord Mayor's procession, it owes a great deal to Hogarth's (cat. 1.27) with the central position of the coach and the tumble of figures in the foreground.

1.30

Attributed to John June (fl. c.1747–70)

Christmas Gambolls, 26 December 1747

Published by Peter Griffin, Fleet Street
Etching with engraved lettering, 223 × 305 mm
BM Satire 2876
1868-8-8-3838 Edward Hawkins collection

Cheapside is shown here from the west with a more or less accurate view of St Mary-le-Bow on the right. Humorous sixpenny prints of this sort found a ready market although they were far from the cheapest available – the carol singer's broadsides with woodcut illustrations would have sold for a penny. This print was published on Boxing Day when gifts of money were solicited by apprentices from their masters' customers and the contents of church collecting boxes were distributed. These small windfalls were, no doubt, eagerly spent on cheap consumer goods and publishers would have issued prints deliberately for the post-Christmas market. The presence of a number of London celebrities would have enhanced the print's appeal: Dr Rock, the famous quack-doctor, is

selling his medicine from a chaise; an anxious John Wesley preaches from the back of the crowd; the effeminate Fribble, on the left, and Captain Flash, on the right in a huge tricorne hat, are two characters from the popular play *Miss in Her Teens* first performed in January 1747 (see cat. 3.6). The fracas in the foreground includes some possible customers for such a print – a charity boy in his uniform, a sooty chimney-sweeper's boy and a barber's apprentice who has dropped a box containing an alderman's wig; they have evidently annoyed the beadle (the ward official responsible for law and good order) who overturns the orange-seller's barrow.

The publisher Peter Griffin had worked for Philip Overton at the Golden Buck, Fleet Street (later to become the famous print shop of Robert Sayer); he set up on his own in 1746 at the Three Crowns and Dial, Fleet Street, but died three years later. His widow Elizabeth carried on the business until 1753. She seems to have sold some at least of her husband's plates to John Bowles, who listed *Christmas Gambolls* in his catalogues of 1749 and 1753. In 1753 Michael Jackson took over the Griffin shop and reworked the trade card with the sign of Rembrandt's Head.

1.30

1.31

Anonymous

This is not the Thing: or, Molly Exalted, 1762

Published at the Bee-Hive, Strand

Etching and letterpress, with engraved lettering on plate, 368 × 203 mm (sheet), 129 × 170mm (etched plate, cropped)

BM Satire 3993

1868-8-8-4299 Edward Hawkins collection

As well as being the home of City festivities, Cheapside had also been the site of public punishments since the Middle Ages. The publication of this sixpenny broadside was announced in *The Public Advertiser* on 9 October 1762 by Thomas Ewart (fl. 1743–66) whose shop was at the Charing Cross end of the Strand opposite Northumberland House. It refers to an incident a week or so earlier when a man of about sixty was found guilty of sodomy and sentenced to stand in the Cheapside pillory; the crowd tore off his clothes (*Gentleman's Magazine*, 3 October 1762). The note in Edward Hawkins's handwriting refers to the death of another man who was killed by the crowd when standing in the Stratford pillory in April 1763 (*Gentleman's Magazine*, 3 April 1763).

Homosexuality was a capital offence until 1861 but, as with other capital crimes, in most cases a lesser sentence was imposed, especially as safe evidence of the act of sodomy was difficult to obtain. 'Mollies' were often depicted in satirical prints as figures of fun; but this broadsheet illustrates the cruelty that could underlie such portrayals. The figure in the pillory is diminutive and 'Of soft and effeminate sight'; most prosecutions for sodomy – by contrast – described robust, predatory men forcing themselves upon innocent parties.

Recent literature on homosexuality in eighteenth-century London, for instance Norton, describes a burgeoning homosexual milieu. A number of aristocrats, such as Lord Hervey and Stephen Fox, had well-known homosexual relationships, but were preserved a degree of immunity from persecution because of their positions in society. During the first half of the eighteenth century a distinctive homosexual subculture had emerged in London following moral crusades from the 1690s onwards. The Societies for Reformation of Manners used *agents provocateurs* to entrap sodomites and, ironically, in doing so helped to advertise cruising grounds such as Moorfields.

City Politics

1.32–1.37

1.32

Anonymous

The Jews Triumph, and England's Fears, Set Forth / The Circumcised Gentiles: or, a Journey to Jerusalem, 1753

Woodcut and letterpress, 453 × 568 mm (sheet), 305 × 235 mm (each woodcut)

BM Satire 3 206

1868-8-8-3938 Edward Hawkins collection

These two broadsides were produced as part of the campaign against the Jewish Naturalization Act that was passed in

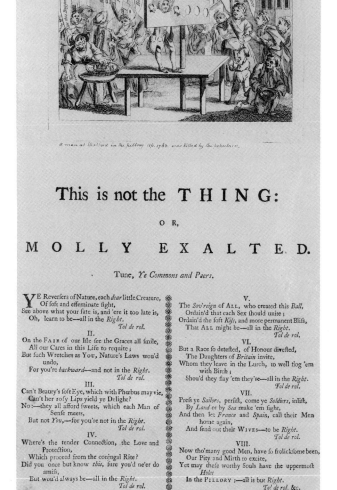

1.31

1.32

June 1753, and repealed six months later. Jews had been allowed to settle in Britain a hundred years earlier during the Commonwealth, but, like Roman Catholics and Protestant dissenters, they were precluded from voting or holding office. By the mid eighteenth century there were about eight hundred Jews living in England. Many were wealthy and public-spirited residents who wanted to contribute to political life – Samson Gideon (see cat. 1.35) was the most prominent example – but their emancipation was seen as a threat to local interests. Horace Walpole wryly remarked that 'in a few months the whole nation found itself inflamed with a Christian zeal' (Walpole, *Memoirs*, I, p. 238).

Xenophobia was a common element of popular imagery, but particularly anti-semitic prejudices are rehearsed here: Jews are shown as having bribed leading politicians – the Prime Minister, Henry Pelham, and his brother the Duke of Newcastle are shown as having taken £500,000, and Alderman Sir William Calvert, £100,000; one of the bishops who voted in favour of the Bill is shown clasping the Talmud; London is to become the 'New Jerusalem' with the introduction of compulsory circum-cision, or, conversely, there is a Jewish–Popish Plot to return Britain to Roman Catholicism.

'Woodcut Royals' of this size, selling wholesale at about a halfpenny each, enjoyed great popularity in the mid-century. Hundreds of thousands were sold, but only a few dozen survive because they did not attract the attention of collectors until decades later. Prints of this type were the speciality of three printshops in the City who distributed them throughout the country: Richard Marshall in Aldermary Churchyard, William and Cluer Dicey in nearby Bow Churchyard (these two firms some-times collaborating) and Henry Overton at the White Horse without Newgate (see O'Connell, pp. 187–90). The number '282' at the top right does not correspond with items in any of the surviving catalogues of these publishers (see Griffiths).

It was common practice at the bottom end of the market for two broadsides to be printed on one large sheet; they would be retailed separately. Cheap publishers frequently had woodcut copies made from more expensive prints, in these cases from two anonymous etchings (BM Satires 3204 and 3205).

1.33

Attributed to Anthony Walker (1726–65)

The Parliamentary Race, or The City Jockies, March 1754

Published by Mary Cooper at the Globe in Paternoster Row

Etching with engraved lettering, 202 × 375 mm

BM Satire 3268

1868-8-8-3963 Edward Hawkins collection

This and the following print (both priced at 6*d*) are related to the General Election of April 1754. The expected candidates for the four City seats are shown as if in a horse race – John Barnard; Slingsby Bethel; Richard Glyn; William Calvert; William Beckford; Robert Ladbroke; Crisp Gascoyne – of whom Barnard, Bethel, Ladbroke and Beckford were elected. Edward Hawkins, former owner of the print, has annotated it with the number of votes gained by each candidate. Calvert – shown here already fallen from his mount having collided with a stereotypical Jewish pedlar with his box – came last; his support of the so-called Jew Bill told heavily against him (see

cat. 1.32). Gascoyne chose not to enter the poll in the City, where he knew that his investigation of the Canning case (cats 1.59–1.66) would mean he had no chance of success; he stood instead in Southwark, but came bottom of the poll.

By the mid eighteenth century horse-racing had developed from an elite sport into a public enthusiasm. Its popularity was reflected in high sales of sporting prints and portraits of individual horses. As well as topical and political prints of this sort, the publisher Mary Cooper ran a network selling portraits of race-horses. The Jockey Club was founded in 1752 and still regulates the sport.

1.34

Attributed to Anthony Walker (1726–65)

A Stir in the City, or some folks at Guildhall, May 1754

Published by John Smith at Hogarth's Head, opposite Wood Street, Cheapside

Etching with engraved lettering, 208 × 381 mm

BM Satire 3266 (ii)

1868-8-8-3960 Edward Hawkins collection

Eighteenth-century elections were by open ballot, and candidates and voters gathered at the hustings – in this case at the Guildhall. In the counties, the vote was limited to male freeholders of property with a taxable value of 40*s* a year, but historic reasons gave boroughs different types of qualification. The City had a particularly democratic franchise which gave all freemen the vote; in Westminster and Southwark all inhabitant male householders paying the poor rate could vote. The City elected four members of Parliament, Westminster and Southwark two each.

Guildhall Yard is thronged with well-known characters including Dr Ward selling his quack medicines, Samson Gideon complaining that as a Jew he cannot vote, a clergyman en route to America on behalf of the Society for the Propagation of the Gospel. An opportunity is taken to mock Hogarth and his recently published treatise, *The Analysis of Beauty*, advocating the serpentine line. He is confronted by Mary Squires, the scrofulous Old Gypsy (cat. 1.63), who asks: 'Am I not a Beauty, Mr H-g-rth'. Hogarth (shown in a profile portrait like the one used for the

1.33

1.34

publisher John Smith's sign) replies: 'You was certainly form'd in a Crooked line, Madam'.

This print was first published in April 1754, and in May the second state, shown here, was published with the results of the election.

1.35
Samson Gideon (1699–1762)
Manuscript receipt

NOT ILLUSTRATED
Pen and ink, 100 × 190 mm
CM 1980-11-30-821

This receipt records the payment to Samson Gideon by Lord Vane on 24 December 1753 of £125, half of an annuity payable through the bankers Gosling and Bennett of Fleet Street (the bank was later taken over by Barclays). It is likely that the debtor was William Vane, 2nd Viscount Vane (1714–89), whose notoriously extravagant – and promiscuous – wife Lady Fanny Vane ran through his large fortune and drove him to the King's Bench debtors' prison;

Lady Fanny's scandalous *Memoirs of a Lady of Quality* appeared in Tobias Smollett's *Peregrine Pickle* (1751).

Gideon became one of the richest men of his generation through dealing in stocks and shares, marine insurance, lottery tickets and foreign currency. He was a leading light of Jonathan's Coffee House in Exchange Alley, Cornhill, the meeting place of stockbrokers from the 1690s until the Stock Exchange opened in the 1770s. He provided much government support for loans during the wars of the 1740s and 1750s, raising £1.7 million at the time of the 1745 Jacobite Rebellion, and paying bounties to aid recruitment at the start of the Seven Years War in 1756. He had a grand country seat at Belvedere, Kent, as well as other country estates, a collection of old master paintings, and a fortune valued at his death at £580,000, but because he was Jewish (though not practising from 1753 onwards) he was not offered the baronetcy he hoped for; this was instead conferred, in 1759, on his thirteen-year-old son who was brought up in the Church of England.

1.36
Anonymous
The Dog Killers of London & Westminster or Licenc'd Cruelty, August 1760

Published at the Acorn, Long Acre
Etching, 199 × 336 mm
BM Satire 3731
1868-8-8-4126 Edward Hawkins collection

This very coarse etching illustrates the response to a rabies scare in the City during the summer of 1760. On 26 August the Common Council of the City ordered that constables, beadles, watchmen and other officers should kill all dogs found in the streets; a reward of 2s was promised for every dog killed. The famous dog lover William Hogarth is shown in a state of distraction: 'Oh! my poor Pugg. Oh! my little Dog'; the blind magistrate John Fielding is portrayed as Justice Feel-um.

This print may have been published by Matthew and Mary Darly who used the sign of the Acorn at several addresses around 1760. See cat. 3.68.

1.36

1.37

1.37

William Hogarth (1697–1764)

The Times, Plate 1, 7 September 1762

Published by William Hogarth

Etching and engraving, 247 × 305 mm

Paulson 211 (i)

Cc.1-171 (1826-3-13-34)

The City strongly supported the Seven Years War which by the early 1760s had brought world wide trading opportunities under British control. But peace was urged by the new King George III and his minister John Stuart, 3rd Earl of Bute, backed by highly-taxed landed interests in Parliament whose concern was with the escalating cost of the army and navy. Hogarth has abandoned his usual naturalistic pictorial narrative, returning to a complex of emblems that echo his *South Sea Scheme* of 1721 which was the last occasion when he had ventured into overt political satire. Hogarth admitted that he made the print to 'stop a gap in my income', and the incoherence of the image suggests that he was not at ease with the subject. His recent appointment as Serjeant Painter to the King meant that he was open to accusations of being in the pay of the government. The King is represented by a fireman attempting to douse the conflagration from an engine marked with the words 'Union Office' in allusion to the Union between England and Scotland; Scots in kilts (standing for Bute and his countrymen) are prominent among the firefighting team. William Pitt, until recently Secretary of War, is shown as Henry VIII directing a pair of bellows towards a burning globe, cheered on by the ubiquitous City butchers and a crowd of aldermen in wigs and gowns. The faceless men pointing their hoses at the fireman are Pitt's allies, John Wilkes, Charles Churchill and Earl Temple. The banner lettered 'Alive from America' alludes to the three Cherokee chiefs who caused a stir when they were brought to London in the summer of 1762. Such banners were used to advertise shows at which curiosities – whether exotic

animals or people (see Altick) – were put on display, and the implication here is that wealthy City merchants in tobacco and sugar were to be equated with their curious, uncivilised transatlantic trading partners. Shop-signs allow for further detailed reading: on the left, the 'Norfolk Jig' painted by 'G T' refers to a manual on military discipline published by George, Viscount Townshend, also an amateur caricaturist (and as such despised by Hogarth), the sign of Newcastle falls (the Duke had been forced to resign in favour of Bute, see cat. 4.20) and is replaced by 'The Patriot Arms' (Pitt and his supporters had styled themselves as patriots in opposition to Robert Walpole in the 1730s); on the right, burning houses are identified by a sign with a Frenchman and a Spaniard joining hands, the fleur-de-lis of France, the two-headed eagle of Austria, and in the foreground, the globe.

For Wilkes's response to this print see cats 4.23, 4.24.

Banking and Money
1.38–1.46

1.38

John Faber (1684–1756) after Allan Ramsay (1713–84)

Sir Richard Hoare, 1746

Published by J. Faber at the Golden Head in Bloomsbury Square

Mezzotint, with scratched lines and engraved lettering, 354 × 252 mm

C.S. 190

1902-10-11-1522 Bequeathed by William Eaton, 2nd Baron Cheylesmore

Sir Richard Hoare (1709–54) was the grandson of the founder of the bank that still bears his name at the sign of the Golden Bottle in Fleet Street. He is shown here in the robes of office that he wore as Lord Mayor in the year 1745/6. During that year John Rocque published his map of London (pp. 44–5) and it is dedicated to Hoare, as Lord Mayor, and

to the Aldermen of the City. This print is, at 2s, unusually expensive for its size. It copies a painting by Allan Ramsay, a Scot who spent most of his career in London and was one of the most successful portraitists of the generation immediately preceding Joshua Reynolds. His elegant style and light touch echo French Rococo portraiture. For a full biography and catalogue see Smart 1992 and 1999.

English banking began in the sixteenth century when laws against usury were relaxed; previously only foreigners – mainly Jewish or Italian merchants – had been permitted to lend money. Gold was lodged for safekeeping with goldsmiths who would issue notes (the forerunners of modern banknotes) which could be exchanged for coin or traded; they also lent money at interest to individuals and to the government. Richard Hoare (1648–1718) began his career as a goldsmith, but turned his business entirely to banking and was a prominent participant in the financial revolution of the 1690s that set up the system of public credit. The Bank of England, founded in 1694 to administer the National Debt, was the pinnacle of a network of credit that supported trade right down to the lowest level.

1.39

Thomas Bowles (1712?–1767) after John Donowell (fl. c.1750–86)

St Brides, 1753

ILLUSTRATED IN COLOUR, PLATE 2

Hand-coloured etching with engraved lettering, 254 × 415 mm

1881-10-8-106 Presented by Charles William Fitzgerald, 4th Duke of Leinster

This is a *vue d'optique* made to be looked at through an apparatus with a concave lens, as shown in cat. 1.21. Such prints, usually showing views of London and other European cities, became immensely popular from the late 1740s. They were sold at 1s plain and 2s brightly coloured, together with the viewing apparatus priced at between 18s and

A. Ramsay Pinx.!   J. Faber Fec.!

The Right Honourable   S.r Richard Hoare

Lord MAYOR of the   City of LONDON. 1746.

PRIMA SALUS   Price 2.s. Sold by J. Faber at the Golden Head in Bloomsbury Square.

138

have been visible from much of London, towering above its surroundings, it scarcely appears in prints of the mid eighteenth century – completed in 1708, it belonged to a previous generation and was yet to achieve its iconic status.

1.40

Manuscript bill from Newsham & Ragg to Sir Richard Hoare, April 1749

NOT ILLUSTRATED

Pen and ink, 185 × 239 mm

Heal 58.20 Bequeathed by Sir Ambrose Heal, 1959

The risk of fire was a constant anxiety in London. Although new building regulations had been introduced after the Great Fire of 1666, the use of open flames for lighting, heating and cooking meant that the slightest carelessness could easily cause severe damage. See cat. 3.4 for the destruction by fire of the Little Piazza, Covent Garden, in 1769.

This bill for £24 17s is to pay for a fire engine for Hoare's Bank. Sir Richard evidently did not wish to rely on the parish fire-fighting system, nor on an insurance company. Newsham and Ragg, based in Cloth Fair near Smithfield, made a range of fire engines and sent their own teams out to fight fires. Water for fire-fighting was obtained by releasing a plug let into the wooden pipes that carried water under the streets from the Thames or one of its tributaries, or from the New River Head north of the City (cat. 1.2). Once the plug was opened, water would flood into the street so that fire-fighters could fill their engines. See cat. 1.37 for a fire engine at work.

£2 12s 6d. All the major printmakers of the City stocked these fashionable products and exported them in great numbers. In 1753 Robert Sayer published a catalogue of *Two Hundred and Six Perspective Views adapted to the Diagonal Mirror, or Optical Pillar Machine* which were sold with 'optical glasses on various principles after the newest inventions'. Printsellers were exploiting the developments in lens-making by opticians and scientific instrument-makers whose main purpose

was to improve navigational instruments. One of the most successful opticians was John Dollond (1706–61), founder of the firm that still bears his name, who was in business at the sign of the Golden Spectacles and Sea Quadrant in the Strand.

This print shows the foot of Fleet Street with St Bride's Church to the south and St Paul's Cathedral on the skyline. Buildings that would have blocked the view of St Bride's have been eliminated. Although St Paul's must

1.41

British Coins

GOLD COINS ILLUSTRATED IN COLOUR, PLATE 3

For most of the eighteenth century, after the Act of Union and effective closure of the Edinburgh mint in 1709, all of the official British national currency was manufactured at the single Royal Mint, still in its ancient home in Mint Street, about a third of a mile in length, between the inner and outer walls of the Tower of London, where were to be found the accommodations of the senior officers as well as the working premises of the mint.

In the mid eighteenth century the British currency should, in theory, have been in good condition. Fourteen denominations were in nominal production, four in gold, eight in silver and two in copper, giving a very broad range of coins. In practice, things were not so straightforward. The guinea provided the standard for the gold coinage. It was originally a £1 coin but, when increases in gold supplies in the late seventeenth century reduced the gold price, it was not replaced with a lighter coin but allowed to find its own value against the silver coinage. Eventually it stabilized at 21s, which was adopted as the formal value in 1718, and, effectively, a gold standard replaced the older silver one. Gold coin increasingly took the role of coinage of daily use, and was thus more subject to wear, clipping and abuse. This was encouraged by one of the consequences of the gold stabilisation, the relative undervaluing of silver, which meant that little came to the mint, leading to endemic shortages in the middle range of coinage. There were occasionally alleviations by windfall acquisitions, such as the one that produced the relatively plentiful 'Lima' coinage of 1745–9, struck from the silver in two captured French treasure ships. Nevertheless, silver coin all but disappeared after 1750. In the first half of the century copper coins were produced in reasonable quantities, and helped make up for the shortage of silver: it was reported in 1754 that poor people were paid almost wholly in copper. In fact the copper currency was virtually doubled by the huge numbers of counterfeits accumulating in circulation, and in 1754 official production was stopped. There would be only limited new issues until 1770, while the proportion of forgeries continued to rise. Finding and using good money in the towns and cities of Britain was not always an easy or straightforward business in the mid eighteenth century. For a further account see Challis, pp. 398–9, 431–6.

In some cases two examples of one coin are included below so that both sides can be shown.

Five guineas, 1748 and 1753

Gold, diameter 37 mm
CM 1748: E1929 and 1838-4-19-224

Two guineas, 1748

Gold, diameter 31 mm
CM G.III, p.148 and 1948-10-4-660 (Oldroyd Bequest)

Guinea, 1749 and 1750

Gold, diameter 24 mm
CM 1935-4-1-8281 (T.B. Clarke-Thornhill Bequest) and E1946

1.41

Half-guinea, 1752 and 1753

Gold, diameter 21 mm

CM 1935-4-1-8293 (T.B. Clarke-Thornhill Bequest) and E1960

Crown (5s), 1739 and 1743

Silver, 40 mm

CM 1918-9-18-433 and 1918-9-18-435 (T.H.B. Graham Bequest)

Half-crown, 'Lima' coinage, 1745 and 1746

Silver, diameter 33 mm

CM 1818-9-18-449 and 1918-9-18-450 (T.H.B. Graham Bequest)

In July 1745 two British privateers (contractors to the Royal Navy) captured two French treasure ships returning from Lima, Peru, and seized a million pounds' worth of gold and silver in coins and ingots, as well as 800 tons of cocoa. The booty was landed in Bristol three months later and carried in forty-five wagons to the Mint in the Tower of London. The bullion was melted down and silver coins produced in between 1745 and 1749 carried the word 'Lima' to celebrate the exploit; for further details see Apling.

Shilling, 1750

Silver, diameter 24 mm

CM 1935-4-1-8299 (T.B. Clarke-Thornhill Bequest)

Sixpence, 1743

Silver, diameter 20 mm

CM 1918-9-18-485 (T.H.B. Graham Bequest)

Groat (4d), 1743

Silver, diameter 19 mm

CM 1918-9-18-980 (T.H.B. Graham Bequest)

Threepence, 1743

Silver, diameter 17 mm

CM 1918-9-18-981 (T.H.B. Graham Bequest)

Half-groat (2d), 1746

Silver, diameter 14 mm

CM E4003

Penny, 1750

Silver, diameter 12 mm

CM E4009

Halfpenny, 1738

Copper, diameter 28 mm

CM 1926-8-17-290 (Presented by Miss Ruth Weightman) and 1870-5-7-136

Farthing, 1749

Copper, diameter 22 mm

CM 1918-9-18-1109 (T.H.B. Graham Bequest)

1.42
Foreign Coins

ILLUSTRATED IN COLOUR, PLATE 3

The gold mines of Minas Gerais in Brazil were discovered in 1692–4. Their output transformed Europe's gold supply in the eighteenth century, and Portuguese coins, made in the Lisbon or Brazilian mints, became widely familiar. Portuguese gold coin was in plentiful supply and regular use in Britain in the mid eighteenth century, encouraged by the Treaty of Methuen (1703) and favourable trade balances which took British goods to the Portuguese empire, in exchange for gold. Thus, when Sarah Malcolm was convicted of robbery in London in 1733 (see Hogarth's print (Paulson 129) and his painting of her, National Gallery of Scotland), she was in possession of 18 guineas and 20 Portuguese moidores (the common English name for the moeda). In Britain (unlike Ireland) Portuguese gold never became legal tender, but had a tolerated status alongside the native gold, which it

might often outnumber; it was described as 'in great measure, the current coin of the Kingdom', by a commentator in 1742. Portuguese gold coins existed in two series: the one based on the dobra (= 12,800 reis, and equal to the Spanish eight escudos), with the royal portrait, was the Portuguese national and international coin, while that based on the moeda (= 4,000 reis), with its design of the cross of Christ, a traditional Portuguese emblem, was intended for colonial and South American use. Both, however, were widespread internationally. By the late 1740s the tide began to turn: during the 1745 Jacobite Rebellion, many holders of foreign gold coin hastened to change it to guineas; the output of the Brazilian mines began to slacken in the 1760s, and the Portuguese began to curtail English trading privileges from the 1750s. For a further account see Kent.

Dobra of eight escudos ('joe') of João V, King of Portugal, Minas Gerais mint, Brazil, 1732

Gold, diameter 37 mm

CM Bank of England M397

Four escudos of João V, Rio de Janeiro mint, Brazil, 1739

Gold, diameter 32 mm

CM 1849-11-21-795

Two escudos of João V, Lisbon mint, Portugal, 1734

Gold, diameter 25 mm

CM Bank of England M399

Escudo of João V, Rio de Janeiro mint, 1727

Gold, diameter 21 mm

CM Bank of England M400

Half-escudo of João V, Lisbon mint, 1744

Gold, diameter 17 mm

CM 1872-3-5-4

Moeda (moidore) of João V, Rio de Janeiro mint, 1713 and 1719

Gold, diameter 29 mm

CM 1856-9-24-1 and 1924-9-8-1
(Presented by B. Vernon)

Half-moeda of João V, Rio de Janeiro mint, 1723 and 1725

Gold, diameter 25 mm

CM 1935-4-1-10937 (T.B. Clarke-Thornhill Bequest) and SSB. 152-84

Coin Balance and Weights

It has always been customary to check the weight of precious metal coin, especially the high-value gold ones, to guard against receiving underweight or forged coin. It was particularly important to check older or foreign coin. Special weights designed to match particular coins have also been widespread. The fashion for using purpose-made sets of weights and balances arose in Europe in the sixteenth century, and remained widespread into the nineteenth century. The engraver John Kirk was by far the dominant figure in British coin weight production in the mid eighteenth century, producing several series of weights for the main currency coins, typically for the guinea and half-guinea and the two series of Portuguese coins commonly encountered. He kept up to date with these, changing the portrait and name along with the change of monarch in 1750, when José I succeeded João V, even anticipating a denomination for José (the dobra) which was never in fact produced (the weight could still have been used for the old dobras of João, of course). His weights generally copy the coin on the obverse, very skilfully engraved, and spell out the value in sterling on the reverse. His dominance was such that his weights might be counterfeited by other manufacturers. The standard account of British coin weights is Withers.

1.43

1.43
James Kirk (1733–91)
Advertisement for John Kirk, engraver, about 1760

Etching with engraved lettering,
64 × 135 mm
Heal 103.8 Bequeathed by Sir Ambrose Heal, 1959

John Kirk advertised in the *London Evening Post* for 3–5 September 1747 'a most useful and curious set of weights to prevent the unknowing from being imposed upon by false and counterfeit guineas and foreign coins'. This small sheet, which was probably intended to be pasted in a box containing a coin balance and weights, describes the uses of the weights and scales. The patriotic value of Kirk's product is emphasized by the fact that the scales are held by the figure of Britannia, with the cap of liberty in her other hand; beyond is a view of the north side of St Paul's Cathedral as it would have appeared from Kirk's shop in the churchyard. A similar view of the cathedral appears on one of Kirk's tokens (cat. 1.46) and on the 7 of diamonds in a pack of playing cards with figures of street criers in London settings that he published *c.*1754 (Guildhall Library).

The advertisement was engraved by James Kirk, John Kirk's son. He was to carry on the business after his father's death, trading in the 1770s as Kirk and Savage and in 1785 as James Kirk & Co. from 52 St Paul's Churchyard.

1.44
John Kirk (1701?–61)
Coin balance, box and weights

Balance and box, 1746–7

Box: wood, 200 mm × 89 mm × 30 mm
Balance: brass, iron and string,
177 mm × 200 mm
CM Weight Box II.3

Coin weight for guinea of George II, 1748

Brass, diameter 25 mm
Withers 1462
CM W112 and 1906-11-3-4601 (Parkes Weber Gift)

Coin weight for half-guinea of George II

Copper or bronze, diameter 21 mm
Withers 1468
CM W118 and W119

Coin weight for eight escudos ('joe', or 'Portugal piece') of José I, King of Portugal, *c.*1750, valued in Britain at £3 12s

Brass, diameter 29 mm
Withers 1565
CM 1980-12-25-200 and W325

Coin weight for four escudos of João V, King of Portugal, 1747, valued at 36s

Copper and brass, diameter 28 mm

Withers 1526

CM W622 and 1966-11-3-4602

Coin weight for two escudos of João V, 1746, valued at 18s

Copper, diameter 20 mm

Withers 1522

CM W339 and W660

Coin weight for escudo of João V, 1746, valued at 9s

Copper, diameter 20 mm

Withers 1523

CM W352 and W699

Coin weight for half-escudo of João V, undated, valued at 4s 6d

Brass, diameter 17 mm

Withers 1556

CM W362 and W739

Coin weight for moeda (moidore) of Portugal, 1748, valued at 27s

Brass, diameter 26mm

Withers 1486

CM 1935-11-2-141 and W277

Coin weight for half-moidore, Portugal, 1747, valued at 13s 6d

Copper, diameter 21 mm

Withers 1492

CM W290 and W291

Coin weight for quarter-moidore, Portugal, 1753, valued at 6s 9d

Brass, 17 mm

Withers 1506

CM W3006

1.45

John Kirk (1701?–61)

Trade card of John Kirk, Engraver, about 1760

Etching with engraved lettering, 171 × 139 mm

Banks 59.104

Bequeathed by Sir Augustus Wollaston Franks, 1897

Kirk's trade extended far beyond the manufacture of coin weights, and this card demonstrates some of the types of decorative engraving that he undertook. The drapery hanging above his name gives examples of his work: an elaborate

1.44

1.45

monogram for a seal, buttons, a key, a medal and an admission ticket. See cats 4.7 and 4.8 for Kirk's medals; he also engraved prints and trade cards.

Kirk's three sons followed him into the same trade (information from Laurence Worms): Alexander (1726–50), John (1728–78), who had set up on his own in Covent Garden by 1760, and James who continued the St Paul's Churchyard business (see cat 1.43).

1.46
Kirk's tokens

The best known trade tokens are those issued as currency substitutes at times of shortage between 1648 and 1679 and in the late eighteenth and early nineteenth centuries. This group was, on the contrary, issued by Kirk in the 1750s as advertisements and they provide appealing glimpses of the interior of his shop.

1.46

Token, 1750s

Obverse: Interior of shop

Reverse: Inscribed 'Dutch and English Toys, Fans, &c. sold by I. Kirk in St Paul's Churchyard'

Copper alloy, diameter 30 mm

SSB 192–2 Sarah Banks collection, presented 1818

Token, 1750s

Obverse: Interior of shop

Reverse: Inscribed 'Dutch and English Toys, Fans, &c. sold by I. Kirk in St Paul's Churchyard'

Copper alloy, diameter 25 mm

CM 1870-5-7-4511 Freudenthal collection

Token, 1750s

Obverse: Cartouche with putto, inscribed 'Seals Dies Stamps Silver & Copper Plate'

Reverse: Cartouche inscribed 'Engraved by I. Kirk in St. Pauls Church Yard'

Copper alloy, height 34 mm

SSB 192–1 Sarah Banks collection, presented 1818

Token, 1750s

Obverse: Britannia holding a pair of scales with a distant view of St Paul's Cathedral, inscribed 'I. Kirk'

Reverse: Inscribed 'Scales aand Weights for Gold Coins made and sold by I. Kirk in St. Pauls Church Yard'

Copper alloy, diameter 25 mm

SSB 192–3 Sarah Banks collection, presented 1818

Street Criers

1.47–58
Paul Sandby (1731–1809)

Twelve London Cries Done from the Life, Part 1st, 1760

Published by Paul Sandby

Etching, average 213 × 156 mm (all sheets cropped)

1904-8-19-560 to 571 Bequeathed by William Sandby

Series of prints of street vendors with their characteristic cries appeared from the sixteenth century onwards in all European countries. See Beall for a catalogue of all known prints, and Shesgreen for a discussion of Marcellus Laroon's influential series first published in 1688. Sandby's *Cries* are a particularly stylish series, etched with a freedom that is new to English printmaking. These impressions are particularly fine. Sandby's use of bilingual English and French titles suggests that he saw a potential export market, or at least wished to make it clear that his intended audience was one that appreciated the current fashion for all things French. Despite their elegance, the prints present convincingly realistic images of the poor of the streets of mid-eighteenth-century London with their ragged clothes and – with the exception of the very youngest – care-worn faces.

The set contains twelve prints, but further sets were evidently planned: a group of seventy-six drawings related to the *Cries* was sold at Christie's on 27 April 1965; they are now distributed between the Museum of London, Yale Center for British Art, Nottingham Castle Museum and the Huntington Art Gallery in San Marino, California; another drawing is in the Ashmolean Museum; another (for cat. 1.51) was on the London art market in 1952; a man who appears in a drawing in the Royal collection is identical with the pudding-seller (cat. 1.53). The Yale drawings are discussed by Robertson (pp. 46–52, with illustrations), who points out that a number of the criers were used by Sandby and his pupils for other drawings.

For a note on Sandby's career see cat. 2.35.

1.48

1.49

1.47

ILLUSTRATED AS FRONTISPIECE, PAGE 2

Sandby follows the convention of introducing a series of prints with a peep-show: a pretty young woman makes a ragged living from children who peer through a lens to look at prints of interesting scenes. A porter carries boxes with the titles of some of the prints in the series.

1.48

The sticks sold here are intended for beating clothes and carpets to remove dust, but in the background we see a popular world-turned-upside-down scene where a tailor's wife is beating her husband. The cry 'My pretty little Gimy Tarters …' is obscure, but is translated into French as 'baguettes' (sticks).

A large and very grand carpet is being beaten with similar sticks

outside a house at the end of Downing Street in Canaletto's drawing of Horse Guards.

1.49

The offal seller pushes a basket of tripe, neats' (cattle) feet, pigs' trotters, hearts, liver and lights (lungs) in a heavy wheel-barrow supported by straps over his shoulders. The sharpening steel hanging from his waist is the usual badge of the butcher, but this man must represent a very low level of what could be a lucrative trade.

1.50

A better-dressed young woman than the peep-show girl in cat. 1.47 wears a robe of what is probably printed calico. Her breasts are almost bare and she is selling nosegays or memorandum books to male customers: 'your honour' / 'Messieurs'. Prints of street traders often hint that

their bodies as well as their goods might be available to customers; court reports and execution broadsides – rare biographies of the poor – show that young women often moved between street trading and prostitution (see Linebaugh).

1.51

A mother and daughter are selling pottery for everyday use. Prices – 3*d* for a plate or 2*d* for a washbasin – are a fraction of what, for instance, the future Earl Winterton's household spent even on basic ware: four white enamel beakers at at 1*s* 6*d* each and a large brown teapot and cover at 2*s* purchased from a shop near Leicester Square. Only comparatively wealthy Londoners used shops: the mass of the population bought what they needed from street sellers.

Will your Honour buy a Sweet Nosegay
or a Memorandum Book

Messieurs, achetter des Bouquets pour rejour
votre odorat

1.50

All Sorts of Earthen ware, Plates three ha'pence
a piece. Washhands Basons two pence a piece
A white stone Mug or a Tea pot

Toute forte de Potterie a un sol et demi par
assiette; des Bassins a deux sols piece.
Des cruches de grais ou des pots a Thé.

1.51

The Walking Stationer   **Le Libraire ambulant.**   6

Memorandum books a penny a piece of the Poor blind.
God bless you pity the Blind.

Ayez pitié du pauvre Aveugle, achetter
ses petits Livrets et que bon Dieu vous bénisse.

1.52

A pudding, a pudding a hot pudding
The Grand Machine from Italy Bake as I go

La Grande Machine d'Italie qui cuit des
Gateaux en Marchant.   7

1.53

79

Rare Mackarel Three a Groat
Or Four for Sixpence

Maquereaux, Maquereaux Monsieur,
Madame en voulez vous des Maquereaux.

1.54

All fire and no smoke, a very Good Flint or a very
Good Steel, do you want a Good Flint and Steel.

Feu sans fumée, ou excellentes
pierres à Fusil

1.55

1.52

A blind 'walking stationer' carries a
basket of memorandum books for sale at a
penny. His stick must have helped him find
his way, but on this occasion he is led by a
ubiquitous street boy.

1.53

This man pushes a 'machine from Italy' in
which hot puddings are cooking. It is supported
– like the offal-seller's barrow – by straps from
his shoulders, leaving his hands free to sprinkle
sugar on the pudding before selling it. A hungry
dog looks on.

1.54

In this print Sandby brings an unashamed
hoyden face to face with a respectable woman at
her (or her master's) front door. The seller of
mackerel was the lowest of the street trading
hierarchy: a person with no change of clothing
or facilities for bathing would have smelt
permanently of fish. Her confrontation with the

Rare Melch Oysters, rare Newing Oysters

Excellentes Huitres et Bonnes Huitres à clever.

1.56

Do you want any Spoons any Hardmettle spoons.
Have you any Old Brass or Pewter to sell or change?

Des cuillairs de metal. Avez vous de vieux
Cuivre, ou de vieux Etain a troquier?

1.57

Fun upon Fun, or the first and second part of Miss Kitty Fisher
Merry thought. No Joke like a True Joke. Come, who'l Fish in my Fishpond?

1.58

woman behind the door chained against
just such an intrusion is echoed in the
snarls of the dog and terrified cat. In the
background is the shop or tavern sign of
'A man loaded with mischief' showing a
man carrying a drunken wife and a pet
monkey on his shoulders (see O'Connell,
fig. 4.48); Larwood and Hotten record a
tavern with this sign in Oxford Street.
The mysterious shadow in the foreground suggests that two men are
watching the scene.

Hogarth's *Shrimp Girl* (National
Gallery) shows a more affectionate view
of a similar young Billingsgate trader.

1.55

This weatherbeaten man is offering flints
and steels for creating sparks to light fires
or pipes. Sandby experimented to vary
his etched surfaces and in this and other
prints in the series he used a tool with
two or three prongs to suggest rough
texture.

1.56

This mother and daughter appear to be
setting out from the fish dock at
Billingsgate to sell oysters. Oysters were
a cheap source of protein for the poor
until nineteenth-century dredging
almost wiped out the natural beds.

1.57

This comparatively well-dressed woman
is selling spoons from her basket, while
her companion hammers on a metal pan
to draw attention to their call for scrap
brass and pewter that he can recycle: he
carries a pair of bellows – the tools of
the metalworker's trade – on his back.
St Paul's is in the distance.

1.58

A poor family is selling a ballad about a
notorious courtesan (see cat. 3.11): 'Miss
Kitty Fisher's Merry Thought / No
Joke, like a true joke / Who'll fish in my

fish pond'. The father holds a mock
fishing rod, while the mother chants the
verses with her hand to her ear. Street
sellers drew attention to their wares with
characteristic cries; the raucous voices of
ballad-sellers were a feature of London
streets until well into the twentieth
century.

The Old Bailey and the case of Elizabeth Canning

1.59–1.66

The Old Bailey Sessions House, built in
1539, was part of the series of prison
buildings attached to the medieval
Newgate. Conditions in the prison were
appalling, and outbreaks of gaol fever (a
form of typhus) were so commonplace
that the Justice Hall was open to the air
on one side in an attempt to prevent
infection passing from prisoners to
others in the court. Nevertheless in 1750
gaol fever killed fifty people including

the Lord Mayor, two judges, an alderman and an under-sheriff. Lawyers carried posies of sweet-smelling flowers and medicinal herbs to ward off the fever. The prison and sessions house were rebuilt in 1770–8.

The case of Elizabeth Canning was the *cause célèbre* of 1753 (see Treherne for a full account). On 1 January, Canning, an eighteen-year-old scullery maid living in Aldermanbury postern, disappeared on the way home from visiting relations in the East End. A month later she turned up at her mother's house in a dishevelled state saying that she had been kidnapped by a brothel-keeper. A neighbour suggested that the house where she had been held was that of Susannah Wells in Enfield, a poor parish some 8 miles north of the City. Canning was taken to Enfield and there identified Wells, a disreputable old woman, and her friend Mary Squires, who was to become famous as 'the old gypsy'. Canning repeated her story to Henry Fielding, the novelist and chief magistrate for Middlesex, who had the two old women arrested. At the subsequent Old Bailey trial Wells was found guilty, branded on the thumb and sentenced to serve six months in Newgate prison; Squires was found guilty of the capital offence of stealing Canning's stays valued at 10s and was sentenced to be hanged. Although the jury believed Canning's story, the judge, Lord Mayor Crisp Gascoyne, was suspicious. Squires claimed to have been in Abbotsbury, Dorset, at the time of Canning's disappearance and to have walked back with her son and daughter, not arriving in Enfield until late January. Gascoyne wrote to the vicar of Abbotsbury who was able to confirm the alibi. Other respectable witnesses were found who had encountered the family during their 120-mile walk. The King granted Squires a free pardon.

London divided over the case: at least £300 was collected for Canning by well-wishers; she was invited to White's Chocolate House in St James's and given thirty guineas; the mob pelted Gascoyne's coach. A pamphlet war broke out between Henry Fielding and the

journalist and botanist Dr John Hill, known as 'The Inspector' (see cat. 5.37); the painter Allan Ramsay published an anonymous letter suggesting that Canning's absence was in order to conceal pregnancy; news even spread abroad and Voltaire wrote an essay on the case. The prints below include some of the cheap publications that followed the ramifications of the case, as well as two more expensive etchings made by Thomas Worlidge, one based on a study of the old gypsy made by a member of the aristocracy. Canning was eventually found guilty of perjury and sentenced to be transported to America. She ended her days in Weathersfield, Connecticut, married into a respectable local family and the mother of five children. The truth of where she spent January 1753 has never been discovered.

1.59

Anonymous

Elizabeth Canning at the house of Mother Wells at Enfield Wash, 3 March 1753

Published by William Herbert, London Bridge

Etching with engraved lettering, 346 × 244 mm

1851-3-8-166

This print was published during the first of the Canning trials, evidently without time being taken to check facts. Mary Squires is mistakenly called Elizabeth Squires – she is shown holding the stays, the alleged theft of which was to bring her a sentence of death – and Canning's mother is described as living in Rosemary Lane, whereas this was the address of the aunt and uncle whom the girl had visited on 1 January. In spite of

1.59

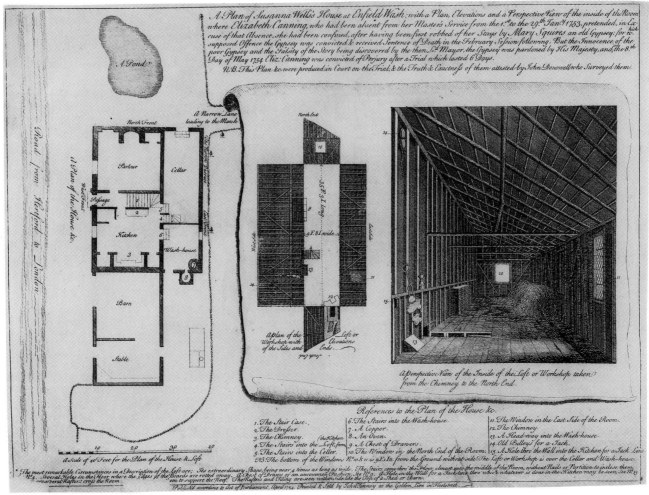

1.60

the annotation 'Drawn from the Life', Squires's appearance bears no relation to that of the scrofulous woman whose image was to become so familiar to Londoners over the following months.

1.60

After John Donowell
(fl. *c.* 1750–86)

A Plan of Susanna Wells's House at Enfield Wash, April 1754

Published by John Tinney at the Golden Lion in Fleet Street

Etching with engraved lettering,
309 × 416 mm

1851-3-8-169

This print was published during Canning's trial for perjury. We are here

shown a plan of Susannah Wells's house – a rare view of the living arrangements of the suburban poor. The print would have been based on the plans, elevation and model of the house made according to a survey by John Donowell and produced at the trial to demonstrate the conflict between Canning's description of the small, square upstairs room where she said she had been imprisoned, and the large loft of Wells's house.

Publishers exploited the notoriety of the case with images to be collected by those pursuing its development. Tinney is better known for high-quality prints and seven years earlier had been joint publisher of Rocque's map of London (pp. 44–5). This sheet evidently went into more than one edition: it is dated April 1754, but refers to Canning's conviction in May.

1.61

Thomas Worlidge (1700–66)

Elizabeth Canning in the witness box, 1754

Graphite, 215 × 158 mm

ECM 3

1851-3-8-163

This drawing – inscribed 'Betty Canning' – is the preliminary study for cat. 1.62. It appears to have been drawn from life, with the face carefully delineated and the remainder rapidly sketched.

1.61

1.62

1.62

Thomas Worlidge (1700–66)

Elizabeth Canning, 1754

Etching, 186 × 152 mm

1859-8-6-15

Worlidge had pretensions as an artist and made copies of Rembrandt's etchings. He clearly did not intend this print of Canning – sold at 3s – to be seen as part of the popular genre of prints of criminals (see O'Connell, pp. 93–6) and portrayed the scullery maid with unusual gravitas. He doubtless also saw that there was status to be gained from producing the print as a pair to the portrait of the old gypsy after an aristocratic amateur (cat. 1.63).

1.63

Thomas Worlidge (1700–66) after the Hon. Richard E … d

Mary Squires, 1754

Etching, 209 × 170 mm

1859-8-6-16

This print is based on a drawing by an unidentified aristocrat who would have passed it to Worlidge to make into a print. It was common practice for amateurs to commission satirical prints from roughly sketched ideas and at the end of the century James Gillray regularly worked up compositions from such drawings. The fact that the 'Old Gypsy' was drawn by someone from the highest level of society indicates how widespread was interest in the Canning case.

Worlidge has had the plate lettered with a note describing himself as a painter (painters had a higher status than printmakers) and giving his address in the Little Piazza, Covent Garden.

1.64

Anonymous

Elizabeth Canning, Drawn from the Life … at the Bar, 16 August 1754

Etching with engraved lettering and letterpress, 405 × 248 mm (sheet), 236 × 248 mm (etched plate)

1851-3-8-162

This broadside was published at the time of Canning's transportation, three months after her trial, and sold for 6d plain and 1s coloured. The publisher (almost certainly T. Fox; see cat 5.93) has saved time and money by recycling a copper-plate used for a broadside of another popular trial, that of James Maclaine in 1751. The figure of the highwayman in the dock has been burnished out and the servant girl etched in its place; some of Maclaine's female admirers have been replaced by gentlemen, but others remain on the furthest benches. It was by no means unusual for cheap print publishers to re-use copper-plates and wood-blocks to serve new purposes (see, for instance, O'Connell, fig. 1.5).

1.65

John June (fl. 1747–70)

A Sceene of Sceenes: Elizabeth Canning's Dream [with] a Letter from a Merchant in Boston, 1755

Published by T. Fox

Etching with engraved lettering and letterpress, 331 × 245 mm (sheet), 175 × 245 mm (etched plate)

1851-3-8-167

This sixpenny sequel (1s coloured) to Canning's transportation is an attempt to cash

Mary Squires the Gypsy, who was Condemned for Stripping Eliz.th Canning, at Endsfield Wash; and has since obtain'd his Majesty's most gracious Pardon. Drawn from the Life by the Honourable R__d E__d and Etch'd by Tho.s Worlidge, Printer, in the Little Piazza, Covent Garden.

1.63

ELIZABETH CANNING,

Drawn from the Life, as she stood at the Bar to receive her Sentence, in the Session's-House, in the *Old-Bailey*.

1.64

A SCEENE of SCEENES.

Elizabeth Canning's Dream for y.e good of her Native country which she Dreamt soon after her arival in america.

Extract of a Letter from a Merchant in Boston, to his Correspondent in London, dated Nov. 5. 1754.

1.65

in on her selling power, but the publisher has introduced further
appeal to a wide market in the form of Mother Shipton; the sixteenth-century prophetess was first recorded in a pamphlet of 1641 and remained a stalwart of cheap literature until the Victorian era. The message of the 'Letter' is violently anti-French, serving as patriotic propaganda in the preliminary stages of what was to become the Seven Years War. Canning dreams that Mother Shipton has told her to follow the example of Joan of Arc and dress as a soldier to fight her country's enemy; St Joan's status as a popular heroine was clearly strong enough to gloss over the fact that she fought for France against England.

The location of the scene in America is identified by the view through the window of soldiers marching to war against the French in the Ohio country

and black slaves carrying bundles on their shoulders. Transported convicts and indentured servants (emigrants whose transatlantic passage was provided in return for a period of service) were normally treated little differently from slaves (see George, pp. 147–54), but Canning's influential supporters arranged for her to be taken care of by a respectable New England family.

1.66

James McArdell (1729–65) after William Keable (?1714–74)

Sir Crisp Gascoyne, 1753

Mezzotint, 507 × 350 mm

Goodwin 30 (ii), C.S. 81(ii)

1886-6-17-31

Gascoyne, a wealthy brewer with premises in Houndsditch, served as Lord

Mayor in the year 1752/3 and he is shown here with the sword and mace of office, wearing his fur-lined aldermanic robe over a richly laced coat and fringed satin waistcoat. He was the first Lord Mayor to live in the Mansion House (cat. 1.19). Lord Mayors were ex-officio Chief Justices for the City and their formal role in adminstering the law was an important one, but in this case the statue of blind Justice has a particular resonance and must refer to Gascoyne's scrupulous pursuit of the Canning case. Popular support for Canning cost Gascoyne the seat in the House of Commons that he was expected to win in the 1754 election (see cats 1.33 and 1.34).

Keable was a member of the St Martin's Lane Academy; in the early 1760s he travelled to Italy and settled in Bologna.

The Fleet prison and the Marriage Act of 1753

1.67–1.70

'Hardwicke's' Marriage Act of 1753 required marriages to take place in prescribed Church of England churches and chapels (Jews and Quakers were allowed their own arrangements); banns were to be read and minors could not be married without parental consent. The intention was to bring to an end the problems resulting from clandestine marriages that took place under the previous unregulated system whereby a couple could become man and wife simply by exchanging vows before witnesses. George describes (pp. 305–6) how heiresses were particularly vulnerable at a time when husbands took possession of their wives' property, how women married insolvent debtors in order to rid themselves of their debts, and how parish overseers arranged marriages so that a pauper and her children would become the responsibility of another parish (see cats 3.21–3.26 for poor laws); more frivolously, the ease with which marriages could be made encouraged

1.66

bigamy, seduction and 'marriage as the result of a drunken frolic'. Disreputable clergymen set up a trade in instant marriages, most notoriously in the area under the jurisdiction of the Fleet prison ('in the Rules of the Fleet'). Thomas Pennant, writing in 1790, recalled the area before the passing of the Marriage Act: 'in walking along the street in my youth … I have often been tempted by the question, "Sir, will you be pleased to walk in and be married?" … The parson was seen walking before his shop, a squalid profligate fellow clad in a tattered plaid night-gown, with a fiery face and ready to couple you for a dram of gin or a roll of tobacco.'

Despite such obvious abuses, Hardwicke's bill met fierce opposition as an infringement of personal liberty, as unwarranted interference by the state in private matters. One of the most vociferous opponents in Parliament was

Henry Fox, Secretary at War, whose own long and happy marriage with Caroline Lennox, daughter of the Duke of Richmond, began in 1744 with an elopement (see Tillyard). Marriages by declaration remained legal in Scotland until 1940, and Gretna Green, just north of the border, became famous for weddings of eloping English couples.

1.67

John Faber (1684–1756) after Thomas Hudson (1701–79)

Philip Yorke, Lord Hardwicke, 1751

Published by John Faber

Mezzotint with engraved lettering, 500 × 353 mm

C.S. 178 (i); Miles 49

1902-10-11-1509 Bequeathed by William Eaton, 2nd Baron Cheylesmore

1.67

Philip Yorke (1690–1764) was an immensely powerful politician at the centre of government from the age of twenty-nine when he became solicitor-general within a year of being elected to Parliament. In 1733 he was elevated to the House of Lords as Baron Hardwicke, at first holding the office of Lord Chief Justice (at a salary of £4,000 a year), and from 1737 to 1756 as Lord Chancellor. He was also a governor of the Foundling Hospital (cats 3.37–3.43) and ex-officio trustee of the British Museum. In 1754 he was created 1st Earl of Hardwicke. Hardwicke's young granddaughters, Ladies Amabel and Jemima Yorke, are shown in cat. 5.4.

Faber was the leading London mezzotinter of his generation, and he produced more than five hundred prints, including forty-two after Hudson's portraits. This print was published as a pair to a mezzotint after Hudson's portrait of another great national figure, Thomas Herring, Archbishop of Canterbury; each portrait is dedicated to the other sitter. Hudson was the most fashionable portraitist of the 1740s and early 1750s, until the rise of his former pupil Joshua Reynolds. In the late 1740s he set his prices at forty-eight guineas for a full-length portrait, twenty-four for a half-length – like the present example – and twelve for a head-and-shoulders portrait; in 1759 he raised his prices to those currently charged by Reynolds: sixty, thirty and fifteen guineas. His career is outlined and sixty of his portraits, or mezzotints after them, are reproduced in Miles.

1.68

John June (fl. 1747–70)

A Fleet Wedding, 20 October 1747

Etching with engraved lettering, 228 × 305 mm

BM Satire 2874

1868-8-8-3836 Edward Hawkins collection

This sixpenny print was advertised in the *General Advertiser* on 20 October 1747. It represents the arrival in the

ILEWORTH FROM STOCKSMARKET

Between a brisk young Sailor & his Landlady's Daughter at Rederiff.

Scarce had the Coach discharg'd its trusty Fare,	Pray step this way—just to the Pen in Hand	Th'alarmed Parsons quickly hear the Din!	Till slow advancing from the Coache's Side,
But gaping Crowds surround th'amorous Pair:	The Doctor's ready there at your Command:	And haste with soothing Words t'invite'em in!	Th'experienc'd Matron came (an artful Guide)
The busy Plyers make a mighty Stir!	This way (another cries) Sir I declare	In this Confusion jostled to and fro,	She led the way without regarding either,
And whisp'ring cry, d'ye want the Parson, Sir?	The true and ancient Register is Here:	Th'inamour'd Couple know not where to go;	And the first Parson spliced 'em both together.

Publish'd according to Act of Parliament October ye 20th 1747.

Price 6d

Oct. 1747

1.68

Rules of the Fleet of a naive sailor and his bride, the daughter of a Rederiff (Rotherhithe) landlady (see cat. 2.14). The sailor may well be intended as one of the crew of the fourteen ships under Admiral Anson that had defeated two French squadrons off Cape Finisterre the previous May; booty worth £300,000 had been brought back to London, and there would have been many sailors with unwonted amounts of money in their pockets vulnerable to the depredations of landladies and their daughters. It was normal practice for loot to be distributed to all ranks, in a proportion that reflected their status: after the fall of Havana in 1762 prize money ranged from over £100,000 for the most senior officers to £3 for ordinary seamen.

The location of the scene is made clear from the view of the Fleet Market building, erected in 1737 between Holborn Bridge and the Fleet Bridge

where the filthy Fleet River had recently been channelled underground; the market replaced the old Stocks Market that had been closed down in order to build the Mansion House. A series of shop-signs with the legalistic Hand and Pen indicate the presence of marriage 'chapels'. The scene is inhabited by a cast of characters typical of prints of London street life, but they carry with them signals of impending disaster: a herb-seller offers bunches of rue, hinting that the sailor will rue – regret – his marriage; a chimney-sweep's boy is dipping a piece of bread into a pail of milk – his sooty hand will cost the milk-maid dearly.

The publisher's name does not appear on this print, but it is likely to have been published by Mary Cooper, who was responsible for its sequel (cat. 1.69).

1.69

John June (fl. 1747–70)

The Sailor's Fleet Wedding Entertainment, 10 November 1747

Published by Mary Cooper

Etching with engraved lettering, 230 × 309 mm

BM Satire 2875

1868-8-8-3837 Edward Hawkins collection

This sixpenny print is a sequel to cat. 1.68 and issued a month later. It is not signed by the engraver, but the style is so close to the earlier print that it must also be by John June. The entertainment after the wedding takes place in a well-appointed tavern, but the forebodings of the earlier print are about to be fulfilled with the arrival of the bailiff accompanying a diminutive mercer

THE SAILORS FLEET WEDDING ENTERTAINMENT.

Jack, rich in Prizes, now the Knot is ty'd, | The Bawd, now from her Daughter's charge | The Lawyer grins, & Peg with wanton Glance | The Skimmington Observe. Mirth to provoke
Sits pleas'd by her he thinks his maiden Bride | With pleasure smiles to think how he's deceiv'd; | Seems much delighted by Tom's antic Dance. | Sam points the Horns, with many a bawdy Joke.
But tho a modest Look by Molly's shown, | Experienc'd in the Trade, and void of Shame, | Kit kisses Kate, vows she shall be his Wife. | For Spouse's Cloaths the Baily's Crew are seen.
She only longs for what she oft has known. | To her the Man in Crape imparts his Flame. | While Cat & Dog resemble nuptial Strife. | And change, oh sad Mishap! the jovial Scene.

Publish'd according to Act of Parliament; November ÿ 10, 1747. Price 6d, by M. Cooper

Nov. 1747

1.69

bearing an unpaid bill of £70 for the bride's fine clothes.

Like many prints of London low life from this period and for the following hundred years, this print owes a good deal to Hogarth: the overall composition is based on Plate 3 of *A Rake's Progress* published in 1735; the painting of the Skimmington (a raucous public parade of effigies of an adulterous couple, or henpecked husband and shrewish wife, with horns and petticoats held aloft) is close to the same subject in Hogarth's *Hudibras* of 1726, with the addition of ships' masts to identify the unhappy pair as a sailor and his wife; the old woman whose candle sets fire to the turban of the black man as he lunges forward to kiss her echoes the drunken man setting his own sleeve alight in *A Midnight Modern Conversation* (1733); the sparring cat and dog come from Plate 4 of *Industry and Idleness* published two months earlier.

1.70

John Bowles's catalogues from 1749 to 1764 list two sixpenny prints with the same titles as cats 1.68 and 1.69. They may be copies, but it is also possible that Cooper sold the plates to Bowles, who was always keen to acquire saleable stock.

1.70

Fleet marriage certificate, 1748

Engraved lettering, 99 × 115 mm

D.3-180 Sarah Banks collection

This certificate records the marriage of John Brittain, a carman (a carrier or carter), and Elizabeth Spindelour. The informal ceremony was performed by a Mr Wyatt, Minister of the Fleet, on 12 June 1748. Few Fleet marriage certificates survive, but there are register books in the Public Record Office.

1.71

Hospitals and Medicine

1.71–1.78

Eighteenth-century hospitals treated the poor – anyone with a comfortable home would be treated there rather run the risk of infection in a public ward. Hospitals were a focus of philanthropy, and wealthy individuals and groups contributed towards building and running them. Donors of substantial sums were normally appointed governors with the right to nominate patients. Between 1720 and 1759 six new general hospitals were built on open ground at the edge of London: St Luke's (cat. 1.71) and the London (cat. 1.73) near the City; the Middlesex, the Westminster and St George's to the west; Guy's in Southwark. Three lying-in (maternity) hospitals were opened between 1739 and 1751. Existing hospitals were also improved: ancient buildings were replaced at St Bartholomew's (cat. 1.72), and the physician Richard Mead did much to enhance facilities at St Thomas's.

1.71

Robert Pranker (fl. *c.*1750–74) after John Griffiths (fl. *c.*1750–74?)

Enthusiasm Displayed, 1753

Published by John Griffiths, Chief Porter of the Middle Temple, opposite the General Post Office

Etching with engraving and engraved lettering, 410 × 502 mm

BM Satire 3339

1868-8-8-3619 Edward Hawkins collection

St Luke's Hospital 'for Lunatics' was opened in 1751 when the seventeenth-century Bedlam Hospital ran out of space. Its policy was that, if treated with humanity, lunacy was no less curable than any other disease.

The parish of St Luke, with its fine church designed by Nicholas Hawksmoor and John James, had been created in 1733 in an area of increasing population to the north of the City. The hospital is seen from the grounds of the parish workhouse to the south of Old Street where a motley crowd appears to have gathered to witness a marriage of the sort that is about to be

outlawed by Hardwicke's Act (see cats 1.67–70): a young man and woman are making their vows in the open air before a Methodist preacher. This area was – and remains – associated with alternative forms of Protestantism: a Methodist Meeting House was marked on Rocque's map (pp. 44–5) only a few hundred yards to the east (in 1778 John Wesley was to open his chapel even closer in City Road), and the nonconformist burying ground of Bunhill Fields was immediately to the south; the tavern sign of the Fox may be an ironic reference to George Fox, founder of the Society of Friends, who was buried there in 1691.

The print owes something to the paintings mocking Quaker meetings which were a speciality of Egbert van Heemskerk (*c.*1635–1704) and were well known through reproductive prints (see Raines). Several figures in the informal congregation are so individualized as to appear to be portraits, but only the woman on the far right has so far been identified – she is Mary Squires, the old gypsy who featured in many cheap prints published around 1753–4 (see cats 1.59–1.64 and 1.34).

John Griffiths, the designer and publisher of this print, describes himself as Chief Porter at the Middle Temple. The anecdotal conglomeration of incidents and somewhat unbalanced composition suggests that he was a self-taught enthusiast who was prepared to risk the considerable cost of publishing a large print. He showed a painting entitled *Enthusiasm Displayed in the Character of a Methodist Preacher and his Congregation in Moorfields* at the exhibition of the Free Society of Artists in 1765; this may be the painting on which this print was based or perhaps a version based near Bedlam Hospital. He continued to exhibit with the Free Society until 1774.

1.72

1.72

Anonymous

The East Prospect of St Bartholomew's Hospital, 12 March 1752

Published by Thomas Jefferys

Etching with engraved lettering, 264 × 413 mm

Crace XXVI.47

Unlike the new hospitals built on the edge of town, the medieval St Bartholomew's was surrounded by cramped City streets. It took decades – from 1729 to 1769 – for four elegant new buildings designed by James Gibbs to be erected to house more than five hundred patients. In 1747 Rocque's map showed two buildings complete and the third in outline, but the site of the fourth building and the wide central square were still covered by buildings in King Street and Well Yard. The building nearest to Smithfield was built to house administrative offices and a Great Hall; on its staircase are Hogarth's paintings of the Pool of Bethesda and the Good Samaritan (1734–7). Neither Gibbs nor Hogarth took a fee for his work. This print suggests that the fine new buildings and the airy quadrangle not only contributed to the health of patients but also served as a promenade for the

wealthy visitors who were essential to an institution that relied on charitable contributions.

A small committee of governors – the treasurer and almoners – dealt with the management of the hospital. The daily care of the patients was the responsibility of the matron and nursing staff, and there were normally three surgeons whose work consisted of bone-setting, treating burns and other wounds, draining boils, administering purges and enemas, bleeding (see cat. 1.74) and tooth-pulling. Surgical operations were a treatment of last resort in the days before anaesthetics, and only about fifty a year were performed, the most common being amputations (two one-legged men appear in this print) and removal of bladder stones. Percival Pott (1715–88), surgeon at the hospital between 1749 and 1787, was a scholar who helped raise the status of surgeons at a period when they were seen as mere tradesmen required to defer to university-trained physicians.

1.73

Jean Baptist Claude Chatelain (1710–58) and William Henry Toms (*c*.1700–50) after William Bellers (fl. 1734–63)

View of the London Hospital in White Chapel Road, 1 May 1753

Published by William Bellers in Poppins Court, Fleet Street

Etching with engraved lettering, 401 × 540 mm

1871-12-9-4677

The London Hospital had been founded in 1740. Its first cramped quarters were in Featherstone Street, Moorfields; in 1741 it moved to Prescott Street, near Goodman's Fields. The spacious new building completed in 1759 on the eastern edge of town held up to two hundred patients. Beyond are open fields with views towards St George in the East (1714–26) and a forest of ships' masts in the river at Wapping. The Mile End Road is busy with sheep and cattle being herded into town, a heavy wagon and light chaises. Incidental interest is created in the foreground by a contretemps between men on horseback and on foot carrying long sticks for herding animals; this may be intended to show the beginning of a 'bull hank' when an animal on the way to market

To his Grace William Duke of Devonshire, President, & the rest of the Governors, this View of the LONDON HOSPITAL in White Chapel Road, with the Ground & Country adjacent, is humbly Inscrib'd by their most Obedient, & Oblig'd humble Servant Will.m Bellers.

1.73

was driven out of the herd and chased through the streets – youths from Spitalfields and Whitechapel armed with long ash sticks were notorious for this trick.

This print is based on Boulton Mainwaring's design for the London Hospital. It was published four years before building began in 1757, and Bellers was undoubtedly aware that he would make sales in the market for views of London's proud new philanthropic developments. But this is by no means a run-of-the-mill topographical print and should be seen in the context of Bellers's pioneering picturesque views of land-scape, often – as in this case – made after his own paintings (see Clayton, pp. 159–61). The trees on the left of the view are clearly a Claudian compositional device (Rocque's map shows that the

north side of Mile End Road was already built up by the late 1740s). They are balanced by the hillock on the right which represents Chapel Mount, the remains of Civil War fortifications that gave their name to Mount Field, the site of the Hospital; Mount Terrace survives today beside the Hospital.

1.74

Anonymous

Trade card of Samuel Darkin the Younger, Bleeder and Operator of the Teeth

Etching with engraved lettering, 192 × 125 mm

Heal 54.5 Bequeathed by Sir Ambrose Heal, 1959

In the eighteenth century the health of the human body was still believed to depend on a balance of the 'humours' – phlegm, blood, choler and black bile. Bleeding was a regular medical treatment designed to correct what was diagnosed as an excess of blood. This image shows bleeding in process, but what must have been a messy operation is presented in a manner intended to calm the anxieties of potential patients: we are shown a genteel interior, a fashionable black page holding the bleeding bowl and a woman attending with smelling salts. Darkin's house in Church Lane, just off Whitechapel High Street, was a few hundred yards west of the London Hospital. He was at least the third member of his family to follow the trade at the same premises: trade cards were issued earlier in the eighteenth century by Richard Darkin and by Samuel Darkin the Elder; J. Toplis issued a later card in which he described himself as 'Successor to the late Mr Darkin Junr., Apothecary & Operator for the Teeth'.

Dental problems were a serious matter in the eighteenth century, and abscesses resulting from gum infections were a common cause of death.

1.75
Thomas Kitchin (1719–84)

Trade card of Dr James's Powder sold by John Newbery, about 1760

Etching with engraved lettering, 375 × 240 mm

Banks 35.46

D.2-3512 Sarah Banks collection, presented 1818

John Newbery (1713–67), whose shop was in St Paul's Churchyard, published a whole range of books and periodicals, but he is chiefly remembered as the first publisher to develop the children's book market as a major part of his business (see Roscoe). Like many other cheap publishers Newbery sold medicines as a sideline – presumably in order to exploit the network of small retailers and pedlars travelling from town to town with packs of relatively lightweight goods. In his edition of *Little Goody Two Shoes* Newbery used one aspect of his business to support the other: he describes how the heroine's father 'died miserably seized with a violent fever where Dr James's powder was not to be had'. A more convincing endorsement of the Powder came from Horace Walpole, who wrote to George Montague in February

1765 that he was taking it for a bad cold. Along with Bateman's Pectoral Drops and Daffy's Elixir (see cat. 1.76), Dr James's Powder pioneered the sale of mass-market brand-name medicines. Newbery is said to have sold over one and a half million sachets of the powder in a twenty-year period (see Crellin). Isaacs discusses the close connection of the publishing trade with proprietary medicines from the mid seventeenth century onwards; he quotes a contributor to *The Morning Post* in 1752 complaining that in walking the half-mile from St Paul's to Temple Bar, he had a dozen different quack handbills thrust on him.

The image of the Good Samaritan on this fine advertisement is loosely based on the painting made by Hogarth for St Bartholomew's Hospital in 1737. The engraver Thomas Kitchin is among the

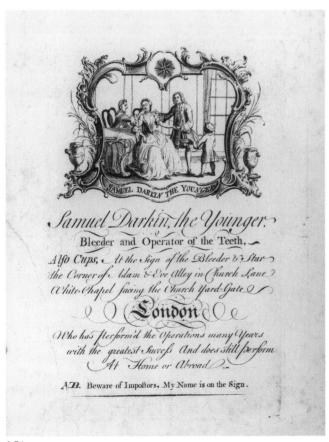

1.74

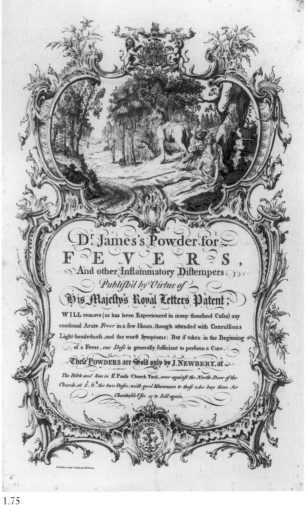

1.75

best known of all British map engravers, responsible with Emanuel Bowen for a cartographic landmark of the period, the *Large English Atlas*, but he also produced a huge range of other useful and decorative prints (see Worms).

1.76

Medicine bottle supplied by Dicey & Co. for 'True Daffy's Elixir', 1760s

Glass, height 115 mm
Museum of London A 2/3 7197

The Dicey firm flourished both in Bow Churchyard, off Cheapside, and in Northampton from about 1720 until the late nineteenth century. Its main activity was the publication of the *Northampton Mercury* and of cheap ballads, pictorial prints and chapbooks which were sold nationwide, but it also enjoyed a large trade in medicines; the two best-known brands were Daffy's Elixir and Dr Bateman's Pectoral Drops (see O'Connell, pp. 55–6).

Bow Churchyard had been associated with patent remedies since at least the early part of the century when the Diceys' predecessor John Cluer had advertised 'Daffy's Elixir Warehouse and the French Hungary Water Warehouse

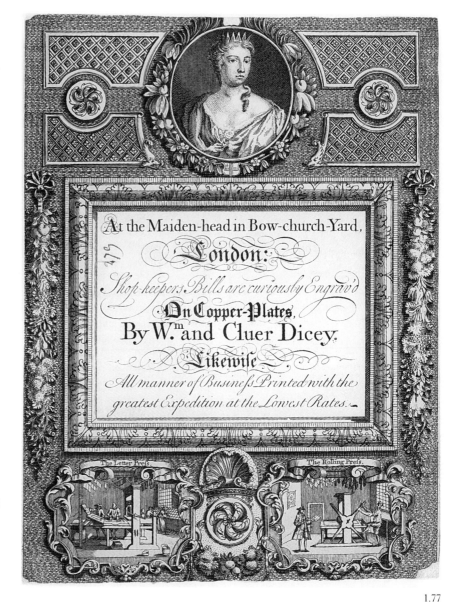

1.77

1.76

at Cluer's Printing Office'. Dr Bateman's Pectoral Drops had been invented by Benjamin Okell whose widow owned the adjacent premises. Another close neighbour – perhaps a tenant – was the surgeon G. West, at the Golden Ball in Goose Alley which ran down the side of the Diceys' premises: among a number of other announcements of cures for all ills on the back page of the *General London Evening Mercury* on 13 September 1746, West advertised that he 'cureth all the symptoms of the French Distemper, whether fresh contracted, or of long continuance, by a new, speedy and sure method: and a recent Clap in a few days,

without confinement, hindrance of business, or the knowledge of a bed-fellow, and as for such unfortunate persons who by neglect of themselves, or for want of the timely use of my never failing remedies, lie under the miserable circumstances of virulent runnings, old gleets, heat of urine, cordees, buboes, shankers, tumifyed testicles, ulcers in the nose and throat, daily or nocturnal pains, or any other filthy symptoms attending this distemper, I cure according to the best approved method now in practice.'

This bottle bearing the address 10 Bow Churchyard must postdate street numbering in the 1760s.

1.77

Anonymous

Trade card of William and Cluer Dicey, printers, 1736–56

Etching and engraving with engraved lettering, 204 × 152 mm

Heal 59.56 Bequeathed by Sir Ambrose Heal, 1959

This card is an unusually elaborate publication from the Dicey firm. Even at the beginning of the father-and-son partnership in 1736 it would have been old-fashioned in style and it may well have been used originally by their predecessor John Cluer. The shop was well known for wood-cuts (of the type described at cat. 1.32) and other cheap publications. The vignettes at the bottom of the sheet show a letterpress used for printing woodcuts as well as type, and a rolling press for copper-plates.

1.78

Anonymous

Bill head of Ambrose Godfrey Hanckwitz, Chemist, at the Phoenix in Southampton Street, Covent Garden, 1749

NOT ILLUSTRATED

Etching with engraved lettering, 206 × 156 mm

Heal 35.34 Bequeathed by Sir Ambrose Heal, 1959

This bill, made out to the banker Sir Richard Hoare (cat. 1.38) and receipted by William Stephenson, lists 4 ounces of sal volatile at 1s 6d, 6 ounces of spirit of hartshorn at 2s 3d and smelling salts with essence at 2s 6d. All are ammonium-based preparations used as restoratives in faintness. Two bottles with glass stoppers are priced at 1s 5d; it was usual for containers for goods purchased to be charged separately.

Ambrose Godfrey the elder (the first surname was usually used alone) had learnt his trade as assistant to the great experimental scientist Robert Boyle (1627–91) and established the laboratory in Southampton Street before 1721. At his death in 1741 it passed to his two sons Ambrose (d. 1756) and John (d. 1747/9), while a third son, Boyle (d. 1756?), turned to alchemy and then to medicine; Boyle Godfrey's son, a third Ambrose Godfrey, continued the laboratory and it survived until the late nineteenth century making patent medicines under the name Godfrey & Cooke.

Spitalfields and the Silk Trade

1.79–1.82

Protestant Huguenot refugees from France settled in London as religious toleration came to an end with the revocation of the Edict of Nantes in 1685; they developed the silk industry into one of major international importance. Like other manufacturing trades, silk weaving involved a series of specialist processes. The raw material, imported from Italy, Turkey, China and Bengal, had first to be wound or 'thrown' to form yarn that could be woven. It was then dyed, and sold to a master weaver who would 'put out' the weaving to journeymen, paid by the piece. The finished piece would be sold on to a mercer for retail.

Some operations were on a large scale – in 1750 Lewis Chauvet, a master weaver in Spitalfields, employed 450 people; in 1755, Thomas Pearson, a throwster in Goodman's Fields, employed about eight hundred people, though many of them worked in their own homes. Silk winders, earning about 3s a week, were among the most poorly paid of London workers, often undercut by workhouses, whose inmates would be forced to wind silk for next to no pay. The most highly skilled journeymen weavers could earn as much as a guinea a week, but they normally worked from home and would have to rent looms at a shilling a week and pay unskilled assistants, or employ members of their families. The trade was an uncertain one, dependent both on the vagaries of fashion and on supplies of silk from across the world. Since much of the trade was centred outside the City boundary and therefore beyond the jurisdiction of the Company of Weavers, there was little control over unscrupulous employers. In 1762 weavers compiled a Book of Prices, and the next decade saw a series of violent riots over rates of payment: looms were destroyed, woven silk was cut. In 1765 a bill laying additional customs duties on imported silks was supported by demonstrations and processions by weavers who attacked the house of the Duke of Bedford in Bloomsbury Square because he had voted against the bill. In 1773 matters were finally settled with the Spitalfields Act by which local magistrates were empowered to regulate pay. But by then the less-skilled branches of the trade had moved to the Midlands, where new factory processes were being developed. For accounts of the trade see George, pp. 178–96, and Linebaugh, pp. 256–87.

1.79

Anonymous

A Draught of the Silk Windles, or the Method of Winding and Twisting Silk for the Weavers, August 1747

Published by John Hinton in *The Universal Magazine* at the King's Arms in St Paul's Church Yard

Etching with engraved lettering, 157 × 259 mm

Y.4-14 Sarah Banks collection, presented 1818

The Universal Magazine was one of the most successful of the early magazines published from 1747 to 1799 with articles on subjects from electricity to the political state of Europe; a gardening calendar, recipes for roast duck, eel pie and pickled vegetables; lists of births, marriages, deaths and so on. This illustration accompanies what purports to be a letter from two Spitalfields silk winders describing the complicated process of winding silk and twisting threads into yarn for weaving.

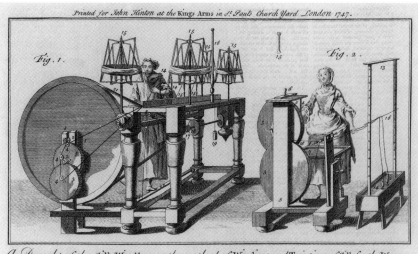

Printed for John Hinton at the Kings Arms in St Pauls Church Yard London 1747.

Fig. 1.   *Fig. 2.*

A Draught of the Silk-Windles *or the method of* Winding *and* Twisting *of* Silk *for the* Weavers

1.79

himself conscientiously, eyes on his work as he passes the shuttle carrying the thread of the weft between the threads of the warp on his loom; Tom Idle is asleep having drunk a copious amount of beer. Their master enters the room with his stick ready to strike the lazy worker.

The broadsides and ballads stuck on the wall show the context in which the cheapest prints would have been familiar to even the poorest Londoners. In Hogarth's finished print, Goodchild works below ballads of Dick Whittington and the legendary Valiant London 'Prentice (who fought off two lions when thrown into their den by the Sultan of Turkey), while Idle sleeps beneath a sheet bearing the name of Defoe's notorious Moll Flanders.

1.80

Anonymous

Trade card of Samuel Spragg, Thomas Hopkins & Co, Silk Throwers and Silk-men

Etching with engraved lettering, 165 × 125 mm

Heal 127.23 Bequeathed by Sir Ambrose Heal, 1959

Spragg and Hopkins would have been employers of women like those shown in cat. 1.79. Their 'house' in Mason's Court, off Brick Lane, was presumably the factory, filled with the noise and dust of machines; customers were encouraged to place orders for yarn at the premises at the sign of the Ship, in Bishopsgate.

1.81

William Hogarth (1697–1764)

Preliminary drawing for Plate I of Industry and Idleness, 1747

ILLUSTRATED IN COLOUR, PLATE 2

Pen and brown ink, with grey wash over black chalk, 261 x 328 mm

Oppe 41; ECM 25

1896-7-10-2 ex-collection Horace Walpole

Hogarth shows the interior of a weaving workroom identified from the lettering on a tankard as being in Spitalfields.

The – somewhat simplified – equipment consists of two looms, a windle wound with silk thread and a spinning wheel.

This is the more finished of two preliminary drawings for the first plate. It is already clear which apprentice weaver is destined for success and which for failure: Francis Goodchild applies

1.82

Panel from a dress, 1740s

Woven silk brocaded with silver thread, approximately 750 × 520 mm

Museum of London 87.162

Sam.ˡ Spragg, Tho.ˢ Hopkins, & Cᵒ
SILK-THROWERS and SILK-MEN,
At the Ship, opposite the Bull Inn, within Bishops-gate,
London.
Or at their House (Late Mr. Adam Dennes)
In Masons Court, Spital-Fields.
Sell all Sorts of Raw and Dy'd Belladine Silks,
China 3 Cord, Blond & Lace Silks, Silver Silks,
Stay Watch & Purse Twist, Naples-Floss, Legee,
Bologna, Spun, Knittings and Sleave.
NB. Orders taken in at Bishops-gate Street.

1.80

1.82

1.83

This silk with its vividly coloured plants brocaded on an acid-green patterned ground is typical of the luxuriant Spitalfields designs of the 1740s. English dyes were excellent and bright colours were favoured rather than the pastels preferred in France. Natalie Rothstein describes the development of English textile design of the period in Snodin 1984 (pp. 210–34). Naturalistic botanical motifs, like those used here, appeared in 1742, and in the following year the influence of Hogarth's advocacy of the serpentine line (published in his *Analysis of Beauty* in 1753) becomes apparent.

The panel shown here is the full width of the woven piece (520 mm). Four pieces, each about 50 m, were usually woven, enough for sixteen dresses. These were expensive textiles made for a fashionable market where tastes soon changed. By the end of the 1740s the brocaded elements of the design had given way to the self-coloured pattern of the background and the stems of flowers were cut short.

The leading textile designer of the period was Anna Maria Garthwaite (1690–1763), a Yorkshirewoman who settled in Spitalfields about 1730. Over a thousand of her designs (she produced about eighty a year) survive in the Victoria and Albert Museum, bound in volumes with an index giving the names of the weavers who had commissioned them.

Some City Trades
1.83–1.91

The following group of prints and trade cards has been chosen to illustrate people at work in the City.

1.83

George Bickham (*c*.1706–71)

*A Tailor, c.*1750

Published by George Bickham
Etching with engraved lettering,
320 × 190 mm

This sixpenny print is one of a series of six that follow the tradition of showing tradespeople in the form of a collection of the tools of their trades: Apothecary, Barber, Butcher, Maid, Tailor, Victualler (see BM Satires 2469–72).

The cabbage which stands for the tailor's head refers to the slang term for the tailor's perquisite of offcuts of the fabric with which he would have been provided to make an item of clothing. Such perquisites were a tradition of early modern urban life, but they were

This Flourishing Company is of great Antiquity & Honour: I find that Edmond Creping Anno 1331. Sold his House whereon their Hall now Stands to John Yakley Pavillion Maker to King Edward I.ˢᵗ 28 of His Reign confirmed their Guild by ÿ name of Taylors & Lennen Armourers their Arms were granted in the 21.ˢᵗ of Edward 4.ᵗʰ 1481. Incorporated in ÿ Reign of Hen.7.ᵗʰ they have been dignified with Persons of ÿ greatest Quality viz Kings 11, Princes 3, Bishops 27, Dukes 26. Earles 47, Lords 81 & Lord Mayors above 80, (of which last) was that famous liberal Gent.ˢⁱʳ Tho: White Mayor in the 1.ˢᵗ year of ÿ Mary, 1553, whose great Example most worthyly recommends it self to ÿ World for its Bounteous Immitation. Their Mansion Dill Situated in Threadneedle Street. LONDON.

1.84

---

disappearing in the process of the modernization of employment practices. In the second half of the eighteenth century the 'putting-out' system, where artisans were provided with raw materials and were paid for their finished work, was replaced with a factory-based wage economy (see Linebaugh for a discussion of the difficult transition from one system to another).

1.84
George Bickham (*c*.1706–71) after Louis Philippe Boitard (fl. 1733–67)

The Merchant Taylors, 29 June 1749

Published by George Bickham, May Building, Covent Garden

Etching and engraving with engraved lettering, 250 × 335 mm

G.12-111 Bequeathed by John Charles Crowle, 1811

This ambitious print shows a workshop with tailors sitting cross-legged beside the sort of long window which was inserted into many attic workshops where good light was essential. Customers are being measured for coats while patterns hang from nails. A small boy brings a hot flat iron to the tailors, while a young woman carries a large jug.

The print represents the Merchant Taylors' Company, one of the leading Livery Companies. It has had little connection with the trade of tailoring since the seventeenth century and its activities are largely philanthropic. The Hall remains in Threadneedle Street, but little survives of the original building after damage both in the Great Fire and in the Second World War.

It is instructive to compare the Rococo scrolling framework of this print with that of cat. 1.83, a cheaper print where Bickham has been much more summary in his efforts.

1.85
John Faber (1684–1756) after Francis Kyte (1710–45)

William Caslon, *c*.1740

Mezzotint with engraved lettering, 350 × 248 mm

C.S. 70

1902-10-11-1286 Bequeathed by William Eaton, 2nd Baron Cheylesmore

William Caslon (1692–1766) was one of the greatest type-founders, and his clear and elegant type is still in use. He learned the trade of metal engraving in Worcestershire but moved to London in 1716. In 1720 he was commissioned by the Society for Promoting Christian Knowledge to cut the font for its Arabic version of the New Testament. He went on to produce some of the most admired roman, italic and Hebrew types. In 1735 he settled in Chiswell Street on the northern edge of the City near Moorfields. A view of his foundry was published in the *Universal Magazine* in 1750 as an illustration of 'the art of cutting and preparing letters for printing'. Caslon is shown here as a modest tradesman wearing an unpretentious coat and simple, rather old-fashioned wig and holding a specimen sheet of his types, but the Latinization of his name and trade ('Typorum Librariorum Artifex Londinensis', London maker of type for books) indicate his status for an educated audience. The business was continued by Caslon's son and grandsons.

1.86

Attributed to Francis Garden
(*c*.1710–68)

Trade card of Phillips Garden, Working Goldsmith and Jeweller, 1750s

Etching and engraving with engraved lettering, 275 × 213 mm

Heal 67.156 Bequeathed by Sir Ambrose Heal, 1959

This charming view of a shop interior is in the newly fashionable gothic style. The shop window on the left is shown filled with a tempting display of silver of the type that impressed visitors to London. The door on the right may lead to workshops behind the shop as implied by the last line on the card. The large scales behind the counter are a reminder that objects made of precious metals were sold by weight (see cat. 3.48).

There are records for Phillips Garden, goldsmith, between 1739 and 1773 though these may be to different members of the same family; three different marks were entered at Goldsmith's Hall and there are several addresses. A goldsmith of that name was living and working at the Golden Lion, St Paul's Churchyard, from 1751 – when he bought patterns and tools left by the great Huguenot goldsmith Paul de Lamerie – to 1762, when the business was taken over by John Townsend, perhaps as a result of Garden's bankruptcy.

Francis Garden made another trade card for Phillips Garden and the figures in this view may be attributed to him (Snodin 1986, p. 99).

1.85

1.86

1.87

1.88

John Kirk (1701–61)

Trade card of Robert Peircy, Pewterer, 1750s

Etching with engraved lettering, 196 × 145 mm

Heal 95.27 Bequeathed by Sir Ambrose Heal, 1959

Robert Peircy of Whitecross Street was elected to the Yeomanry of Pewterers' Company in 1722; he attained the Livery in 1749 and was Steward in 1760. His 'touch' (registered mark) was a dial with his initials each side of the hour hand

1.87

Anonymous

Trade card of Henry Parkinson, Tallow Chandler, 1760s

Etching with engraved lettering, 81 × 102 mm (cropped)

Heal 33.77 Bequeathed by Sir Ambrose Heal, 1959

This charming night-time interior shows a humble shop selling tallow candles made of sheep or cattle fat. The smell of burning tallow candles caused them to be avoided in grander settings. They were thought to give less light than more expensive beeswax candles, but Parkinson counters this reputation by showing that only two candles could illuminate his entire shop, and having a customer claim that 'They burn like wax'. Another customer brings in an order for candles from the famous London Tavern in nearby Bishopsgate Street.

Parkinson gives his new street number (see p. 52) but also gives a detailed description of the whereabouts of his shop in the warren of small streets, alleys and courts to the east of Moorfields.

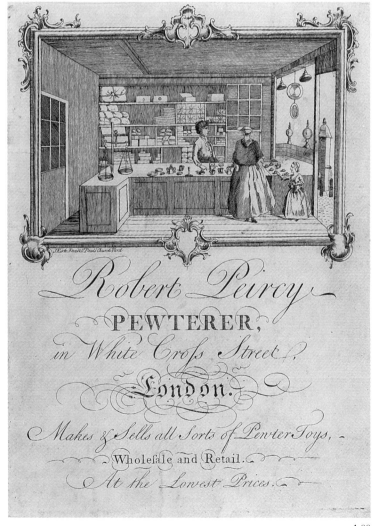

1.88

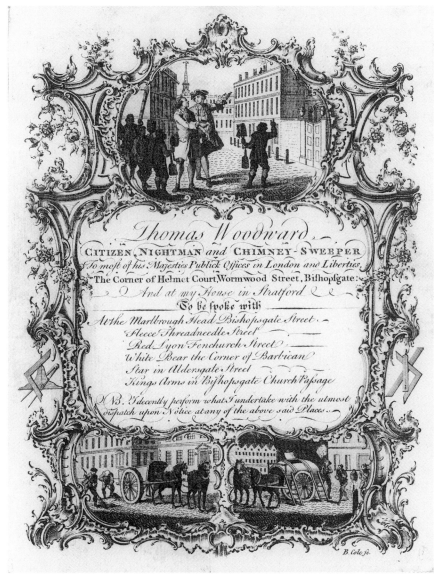

1.89

half-clothed, bruised and injured in the course of their work, forced to beg for a living during the summer months, and susceptible to 'sooty warts' or chimney-sweepers' cancer from constant contact with soot. In 1760 Jonas Hanway (cat. 3.26) began a campaign to improve their lot, but it was only at the end of the century that a more humane spirit led to the founding of the Society for Superseding the Necessity of Climbing Boys whose members advocated the use of brushes with extended handles rather than small boys for cleaning chimneys. An Act of 1840 finally banned the use of climbing boys. See Heal's notes.

1.90

Anonymous

Trade card of Richard Fruchard, Coal Merchant

Etching with engraved lettering, 70 × 117 mm

Heal 44.15 Bequeathed by Sir Ambrose Heal, 1959

Coal was essential for domestic heating and cooking, and for industrial furnaces. It was the cause of London's smoky air and of the black grime that coated every surface. Most coal was shipped from Newcastle – by 1750, 675,000 tons a year – and coal-heavers working in gangs of sixteen or eighteen unloaded colliery ships into barges like the one shown here and in cat. 2.39.

In the 1690s de-regulation took away the monopoly of the Fellowship Porters and Billingsgate Porters. By the 1750s most coal-heavers were Irishmen working in gangs assembled by contractors who undertook to unload ships. In response to a petition from the coal-heavers against exploitative undertakers, an Act of 1758 gave responsibility for unloading coal to the alderman of Billingsgate Ward (until 1770 William Beckford). But abuse continued and resentment was increased by the introduction of new equipment requiring fewer workers: the 'coal-whipping' system using a system of

1.89

Benjamin Cole (*c.*1697–1783)

Trade card of Thomas Woodward, Nightman and chimney sweeper, 1760s

Etching with engraved lettering, 220 × 170 mm (cropped)

Heal 36.52 Bequeathed by Sir Ambrose Heal, 1959

The business of keeping London clean relied, like much else, on individual enterprise. Waste was stored in cesspits that were emptied by nightmen into carts and huge barrels, as shown in this incongruously elegant card. 'Nightsoil' served to manure the market gardens on the edge of town, transported by boat from Dung Wharf near Puddle Dock. Trade cards of Robert Stone of Golden Lane (Heal 36.38 and 36.39) indicate that the price for removal of nightsoil was 4s a ton.

Soot was also used as fertilizer, and nightmen cleaned chimneys with the aid of small climbing boys – a boy is shown here waving from a chimney-top at his fellows and their master. Boys as young as four or five were sold to sweeps for a pound or so by callous parents or parish authorities. They were left barefoot and ropes and pulleys. In 1768 Wapping and Shadwell coal-heavers led a violent withdrawal of labour among river workers. Ships' sails were struck so that they could not leave port, and the word 'strike' was introduced to the language (see Linebaugh, pp. 304–7).

1.91

John Kirk (1701?–61)

Trade card of William Lem, Broker

Etching with engraved lettering,
198 × 156 mm

Banks 5.27

1897-12-31 Bequeathed by Sir Augustus Wollaston Franks, 1897

Lem is an example of one of the new types of businessman thrown up by commercial expansion. He has an office in Exchange Alley – home of financial services since the late seventeenth century – which is open from nine until eight, but also does business at home in Lime Street. He sells ships, or parts of ships (there was always a good chance that ships would never return, and investors would often risk only a share of a ship – the Duke of Bedford, for instance, frequently invested in one-eighth or one-sixteenth of a ship, whether a whaler setting off for Greenland or an East Indiaman, see Thomson, pp. 314–19). Lem acts as a shipping agent, letting out ships to carry cargo, dealing with Customs clearance, and arranging insurance.

1.90

1.91

II

THE RIVER

The River Thames is the reason for London's existence, for its commercial importance and thus for its political power. From Roman times the river has allowed goods to be shipped to and from a base 40 miles inland. In 1751, 1,682 ships from foreign ports entered London; many more coasters brought foodstuffs, manufactured products and raw materials from other parts of the country – sea transport, dependent on wind and tides, was usually preferred to the hazards of the roads. The immense task of administering the nation's largest port was in the hands of the Corporation of London. Regulation was applied by the long-established method of allowing monopoly rights to commercial interests who would police matters to their own advantage: only members of the Watermen and Lightermen's Company were allowed to carry passengers and goods; the Fishmongers' Company controlled the fish market at Billingsgate – and successfully opposed the rival market opened at the north end of Westminster Bridge in 1750. With the exception of the large ships of the East India Company which could not come so far upstream, international trade had been restricted since 1558 to the so-called Legal Quays between the Tower and London Bridge where they were overseen by officials of the Custom House (cat. 2.18). As the increase in trade led to greater congestion, a number of 'sufferance' wharves were tolerated to the east of the Tower and on the south bank; they were eventually legalized in 1789. London's great system of commercial docks was not built until the beginning of the nineteenth century – when the demands of war overcame

vested interests – but wet and dry docks were used for shipbuilding and repair from the sixteenth century.

From Deptford to Vauxhall the south bank was almost entirely given over to industry and commerce – Lambeth Palace (cat. 2.39) stood out as an exception: Rocque's map shows the Lambeth riverside lined with timber yards servicing the expansion of west London (see Section V). The north bank opposite had a more leisured aspect. Open prospects were highly prized, and Somerset House, situated on a bend in the river, boasted the finest views in London looking towards St Paul's in one direction and the towers of Westminster and Lambeth Palace in the other. A line of mansions built since the Whitehall Palace fire of 1698 edged the river between Westminster Hall and Charing Cross, their peaceful appearance belying the fact that their residents were embroiled in the government of an expanding world power.

It was at this fashionable end of London's river that the work of Giovanni Antonio Canaletto found its natural subject matter. The great Venetian painter came to London in 1746, seeking British patrons who had curtailed their Grand Tours when the War of Austrian Succession reached Italy. Apart from a visit to Venice of a few months in 1750–1, Canaletto remained in Britain until 1755. His drawings of Westminster Bridge, the Thames and Horse Guards (shown here and in the Westminster section of the exhibition) combine elegance with workaday description in a way that is especially evocative of London of the period.

Downriver

2.1–2.14

2.1

John Wood (1720–1780?) after Peter Tillemans (1684–1734)

The View from One-Tree Hill in Greenwich Park, 10 August 1744

Published by Arthur Pond

Etching with engraved lettering, 419 × 677 mm

Crace XXXVI.28

1880-11-13-5525

The view of Greenwich with the Thames and London beyond was a favourite one. The middle ground is dominated by Greenwich Hospital – arguably the grandest building in London, and not a royal palace (though it was begun as such in the 1660s on the site of a fifteenth-century royal residence) but a home for old sailors. The second stage of building, to the designs of Christopher Wren, was begun in the 1690s as a pair to the Chelsea Hospital for old soldiers. Work was not completed until the mid eighteenth century but the Hospital began to take pensioners in 1705, and by 1755 there were fifteen hundred in residence. The Park on rising ground behind the Hospital allowed a clear prospect across low-lying land to the east and south of the City, with the busy river threading its way from St Paul's – its dome standing out against the horizon. One-Tree Hill – then, as now, a place of recreation for Londoners seeking respite from over-crowded city life, and often depicted as such (see, for instance,

The View from One-Tree Hill in Greenwich Park
From an original Picture of Pr Tillemans in the Collection of the R.^t Honble the Earl of Radnor.

2.1

a view of the Greenwich Easter Fair, 1750, reproduced in Weinreb, p. 336) – is shown here inhabited by gentry returning from the hunt.

Arthur Pond, most genteel of print publishers (see Lippincott 1983 and 1988), has presented a topographical view in a style that refers ultimately to the landscapes of Claude, but more immediately to the depictions of the country estates of the landed classes for which the painter Peter Tillemans was well known; the painting on which the print is based was owned by John Robartes, 4th Earl of Radnor (Raines 1980, 52). It is significant that the lettering below the image refers to the size of the painting and to its noble owner, rather than providing a key to the buildings depicted. This was one of a series of large prints after paintings published by Pond between 1744 and 1751 (see Lippincott 1983, p. 189, n. 45 for a complete list). The view from Greenwich was sold at 3s 6d plain or

coloured and framed for as much as one and a half guineas. It sold well, even as far afield as Boston, Massachusetts, where it was imported together with others of Pond's prints by the artist and dealer John Smibert. John Wood was also employed by Pond and his partner Charles Knapton to work on a series of prints after Claude and Gaspar Poussin published between 1741 and 1746, and by Pond to engrave some of the plates to illustrate Anson's account of his circumnavigation of the world (see cat. 4.12), published in 1748. He and Pond also attempted, in 1745, to cash in on the craze for Garrick (cats 3.5–3.8) by publishing Wood's engraved portrait of the actor after a painting by Pond (see Lippincott 1983, pp. 50–2).

2.2

Pierre Charles Canot (1710–77) after Thomas Milton (fl. c.1753)

His Majesty's Dockyard at Deptford, 30 July 1753

Published by Thomas Milton

Etching with engraved lettering, 469 × 648 mm

Crace VIII.127

1880-11-13-1732

This decorative print, evidently intended for framing and hanging on a wall, gives a clear description of Deptford dockyard, showing both plan and elevation with a detailed key. It is one of a series of views of the naval dockyards – Woolwich, Chatham, Sheerness, Portsmouth and Plymouth as well as Deptford – published by Milton 1753–6. These yards were the greatest industrial establishments in the country until the nineteenth century. Deptford's proximity to the Navy Board in the City

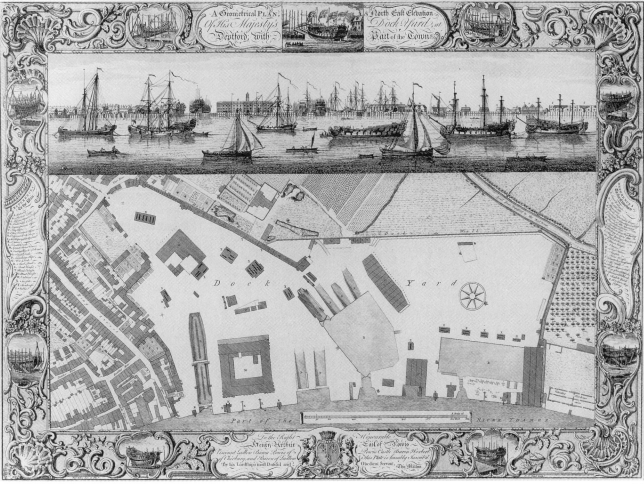

2.2

and the Admiralty in Whitehall meant that it was there that innovations in shipbuilding were introduced. The dockyard was founded by Henry VIII in 1513 and by 1700 it supported a town with a population of more than ten thousand people – larger than most English cities. It was an early example of a community of wage-earners rather than independent small businessmen of the type who still made up the middle ranks of society elsewhere. In the 1740s the Master Shipwright who ran Deptford Dockyard earned a salary of £200 a year while other employees' wages ranged from 1s a day for labourers to 3s for master craftsmen. In 1754 the workforce totalled 801, and with the outbreak of the Seven Years War in 1756 it rose to 1,236.

By the late eighteenth century the dockyard was in decline owing to silting of the Thames and the need for larger docks for building larger ships. Deptford saw only piecemeal development thereafter, and a fair number of the small houses of dockyard employees survive; they demonstrate a type of eighteenth-century urban vernacular building which is otherwise largely unknown (see Guillery and Herman for a historical summary and detailed survey).

2.3
William Hogarth (1697–1764)
Preliminary drawing for Plate 5 of Industry and Idleness, 1747

Wash drawing indented for transfer, 214 × 290 mm

Oppe 48; ECM 32

1896-7-10-12

This drawing for a print in Hogarth's *Industry and Idleness* series shows a likely fate for a ne'er-do-well boy: he is sent to sea. Tom Idle is not the victim of a press gang; he sets off with a chest of possessions, and it appears that his mother has bought his place on a ship in a last hope that he will learn a trade. Her tearful role is clearly to elicit sympathy which might have been less forthcoming as far as the boy himself was concerned; Hogarth's finished print carries the biblical verse, 'A foolish son is the heaviness of his mother' (Proverbs, 10.1). While Jonas Hanway saw naval life as salvation for street children (cat. 3.26), Samuel Johnson's view was more commonly held: 'No man will be a sailor who has contrivance enough to get himself into a gaol; for being in a ship is being in a gaol, with the chance of being drowned … A

2.3

man in a gaol has more room, better food and commonly better company'.

The location of the scene has been disputed (see for instance, Phillips 1951, p. 25, where a position opposite Greenwich Hospital is suggested), but the mills appear to be those of Millwall – to be seen in cat. 2.1 – suggesting that the boat is in Limehouse Reach; Idle makes the cuckold's sign (imitating horns with his index and little fingers) not only to indicate his bravado in the face of his mocking companions but also as an allusion to Cuckold's Point on the other side of the river; the gallows on the shore that Hogarth has added as an after-thought stood opposite Greenwich on the tip of the Isle of Dogs. The river bank was not as devoid of habitation as Hogarth suggests, but he has doubtless exaggerated the bleak landscape to add to the sense of foreboding. Hogarth's concern is not topographical accuracy, but to emphasize the grim future ahead of Tom Idle: the boatman has a skeletal look as if he is rowing Idle to his death (this touch of melodrama is amended in the finished print) and a sailor swings a rope end as a reminder of the cruel cat-o'-nine-tails.

2.4

John Boydell (1719–1804)

Limehouse, 1751

Published by John Boydell
Etching with engraved lettering,
257 × 429 mm
Crace VIII.94
1880-11-13-1699

The village of Limehouse grew up during the Middle Ages, taking its name

from the lime-burning industry which was established by the fourteenth century, but also subsisting on farming, fishing and shipbuilding. In the mid eighteenth century reclaimed land on the so-called Isle of Dogs to the south of Limehouse was still used for holding and fattening sheep and cattle brought to market in London.

This view is taken from the bridge spanning the dock in the middle of Narrow Street; some of the early eighteenth-century houses backing on to the river survive today, and this is one of the few views of the working Thames that can still be recognized. Boydell was aiming here at an audience that wanted visual infomation rather than works of art. He shows a range of craft: heavy barges on or near the foreshore waiting for high tide; a sailing barge with furled sails; a naval cutter taking passengers downstream; two men, each with an oar, standing to manoeuvre a wherry which is probably servicing the seagoing ship to the right; in the distance can be seen the tall masts of a large ship under repair in Lime Kiln Dock.

This is one of a series of shilling views of London and the river that Boydell produced at the beginning of his career. They evidently sold well enough to establish his business, but the enormous success he was to achieve was based on publishing prints by others – at first by

A View taken near Limehouse Bridge, looking down the Thames

2.4

buying up old plates (cat. 1.1 is evidently one such) and later by employing the best available printmakers to engrave prints of the highest quality reproducing paintings. Boydell's achievement was as a businessman, in his ability to recognize the potential market for fine printmaking and to exploit it both at home and abroad. His identification with trade is made clear by the fact that he associated himself firmly with the City – his shop was in Cheapside and he was to become an Alderman and eventually Lord Mayor; most artist/print-publishers, by contrast, lived as near as possible to fashionable clients in the western parts of London – Hogarth in Leicester Fields, Vandergucht in Mayfair, Faber in Bloomsbury Square and McArdell in Covent Garden.

For other London views published by Boydell see index; for the development of his career see Clayton.

Bow

In 1747 a consortium of City tradesmen set up a factory at Bow – then a rural suburb on the Middlesex–Essex border about 2 miles north-east of Limehouse – in order to make porcelain on a commercial scale. The factory was named New Canton in recognition of its debt to Chinese porcelain (see cat. 5.75). Translucent porcelain was first made in China in the Tang dynasty, AD 618–907; it was exported to Europe by the fourteenth century and shipments arrived regularly from the seventeenth century. In 1709 Johann Friedrich Böttger succeeded in making hard-paste porcelain at the court of Augustus III of Saxony at Meissen, near Dresden, but the method was kept a close secret. The development of porcelain in England was – by contrast – not an aristocratic venture but a commercial one. In 1744, the painter and printmaker Thomas Frye and the clothier Edward Heylyn took out the first English patent using a type of clay called unaker thought to have been introduced to England by an enterprising American colonist named

Andrew Duché, who had purchased an area of Cherokee land in Virginia rich in the material. In 1749 Frye took out in his own name a second patent including bone ash.

The Bow factory relied on watermills powered by streams running into the River Lea which joined the Thames at Blackwall. The same streams allowed raw materials to be carried to the factory and finished wares to be shipped to warehouses in the City and beyond; other London potteries tended to be close to the river for the same reasons – Woolwich, Limehouse, Wapping, Thames Street in the City, Southwark, Lambeth, Chelsea, Vauxhall, Fulham and, upstream, Mortlake and Isleworth. Purchases of Bow china are recorded by the Duchess of Newcastle, and the Earls of Egremont and Bute, but – unlike the rival factory in Chelsea (cats 5.38–5.50) – Bow concentrated on a middle-class market and specialized in table ware. In 1762 Samuel Richardson wrote in the sixth edition of Defoe's *Tour of Great Britain* – in the tone of a patriotic tradesman typical of the period: 'the first village we come to is Bow, where a large manufactory of porcelain is carried on. They have already made large quantities of tea cups, saucers, plates, dishes, tureens, and most other sorts of useful porcelain; which, though not so fine as some made at Chelsea, or as that brought from Dresden, is much stronger than either, and therefore better for common use; and, being much cheaper than any other china, there is a greater demand for it. The proprietors of this manufactory have also procured some very good artists in painting, who are employed in painting some of their finest sort of porcelain, and is so well performed, as to equal most of that from Dresden in this respect. If they can work this, so as to undersell the foreign porcelain, it may become a very profitable business to the undertakers, and save great sums to the public, which are annually sent abroad for this commodity.'

Thomas Craft, who worked as a decorator at Bow, describes a factory with three hundred workers, ninety of

whom were painters and two hundred turners (manuscript note, British Museum, MME Porc. Cat. I.62). Skilled staff were sought far afield: an advertisement was placed in *Aris's Birmingham Gazette* in November 1753 for 'painters in the blue and white potting way, and enamellers in china ware … painters brought up in the snuff-box way, japanning, fan-painting, etc. … a person is wanted who can model small figures neatly.' In 1755 the firm's assets including the factory, the warehouse in Cornhill and their contents were insured for £8,650. The early years, under Frye's management, were extremely successful, and Bow china was sold throughout the country and abroad: in November 1754 Philip Breaching of Fifth Street, Boston, Massachusetts, advertised 'variety of Bow china, cup and saucers, bowls, etc.' Bow declined in the later 1760s, and in 1776 the stock was sold to William Duesbury, proprietor of Derby China Works; he transferred the business to Derby. Frye's recipe for porcelain using bone ash was the precursor of 'bone china' which was the basis for all future developments in British porcelain.

The British Museum's collection of Bow porcelain is described in Tait. The standard work on Bow remains Adams and Redstone, but Gabszewicz should be referred to for recent discoveries.

2.5

Thomas Frye (1710–62)
Thomas Frye, 1760

Published by Thomas Frye, Hatton Garden

Mezzotint, 505 × 350 mm

C.S. 6

1845-7-24-99 Smith Collection

Thomas Frye epitomized the artist-tradesman of the type encouraged by the Society of Arts in its earliest days (see pp. 18–27), before the drive to raise the status of painters and sculptors estranged them from practitioners of other visual arts. Frye began his career as a portrait-

2.5

2.6

painter in Ireland and came to London in the mid-1730s, living for ten years with his wife Sarah Kirk in the parish of St Olave's in the City; in the 1740s he turned to porcelain manufacture and ran the Bow China factory until ill-health forced him to retire in 1759. After a year's rest in Wales, he returned to London, settled in Hatton Garden and took up mezzotint. He made a series of large heads, distinctive in their lifesize scale, intensity of expression and dramatic contrasts of light and shade, which he described (advertisement in the *London Chronicle*, 3–5 June 1760) as being 'in the manner of Piazzetta'; two sets of prints after Giovanni Battista Piazzetta's heads had been published by Giovanni Battista Pasquali in Venice in the 1750s and these would have been Frye's immediate inspiration. This self-portrait shows the artist at work holding a pencil holder with black and white chalks.

Frye was to die of tuberculosis a

2.7

year after this portrait was made. His daughters, Sarah and Mary, worked as painters at Bow and married men in the same trade. In 1773 Sarah and her husband Ralph Willcock worked on Wedgwood's famous Frog service for Catherine the Great of Russia. See cat. 5.14 for Frye's portrait of the young Queen Charlotte.

2.6

Inkpot inscribed with the name 'Edward Bermingham', 1752

Soft-paste porcelain painted in underglaze blue, height 50 mm

MME 1938,3-14,40 Bequeathed by Wallace Elliot; ex-collection W. Sydney Smith

This is one of four similar inkpots made at Bow in the early 1750s when the paste still had what has been described as 'the appearance of sodden snow'; by the 1760s the factory had developed a coarser, granular body of a brighter white (see Gabszewicz, pp. 19–21).

2.7

Bowl decorated with a ship, 1762

Soft-paste porcelain painted in underglaze-blue and overglaze colours, height 92 mm, diameter 224 mm

MME 1996,1-5,1

The outside of this bowl is decorated with flowers in several colours, but its most striking feature is the interior painted in underglaze-blue with a sailing ship and the inscription 'Success to Trade and Navigation / 1762'. It is the earliest of a number of ship bowls of this type and the only one known to have been made at the Bow factory.

2.8

Figure of John Manners, Marquis of Granby (1721–70), c.1760

Soft-paste porcelain painted in overglaze colours and gilded, height 358 mm

Hobson I.19

MME Porc. Cat. I.19 Presented by Sir Augustus Wollaston Franks

The Marquis of Granby, eldest son of the 3rd Duke of Rutland, was colonel of the Royal Horse Guards at the battles of Minden (1759) and Warburg (1760). The unusual depiction of a gentleman with neither hat nor wig must refer to the expression 'to go at it bald-headed' which came into use after Granby's hat and wig blew off in a charge at Warburg; but Granby was known for disliking wigs and was shown bare-headed as early as 1745 in a portrait by Allan Ramsay (Smart 204). He was greeted with a hero's welcome when he returned to London in 1763, and in 1766 was made commander-in-chief of the army. The large number of public houses named after the Marquis of Granby is said to reflect his generosity to his troops.

This figure is stamped with the monogram 'To' which is a mark used by a modeller or repairer who worked at

Bow and also at Worcester and Bristol (possibly John Toulouse or otherwise a man named Tebo). The Bow factory produced a matching figure of another great Seven Years War hero, General James Wolfe, who had been killed at the siege of Quebec in 1759.

2.9

Figure of a ratcatcher, 1755–60

Soft-paste porcelain, painted in overglaze colours, height 510 mm

MME 1938,3-14,70 Bequeathed by Wallace Elliot

This old woman carries a pack on her back and a box hanging from her neck that contains bottles of poisons for vermin; in her hand is a scroll lettered 'Powder to kill'. The sort of characters who appear in prints of street cries (cats 1.47–1.58) were popular subjects for decorative porcelain throughout

2.8

2.9

Europe, together with *commedia dell'arte* figures, shepherds, shepherdesses and other country types. These were by no means realistic portrayals of the poor and the vivid colouring of the old woman's clothing is typical of the glamorization of such subjects.

2.10

Plate, 1750s

Soft-paste porcelain, transfer printed, diameter 193 mm

Hobson I.65

MME Porc. Cat. I.65 Presented by Sir Augustus Wollaston Franks

The plate is decorated with two transfer prints combined to show a scene in the Rococo taste with a genteel couple taking tea in a garden and a child in a push-chair. The prints are by Robert Hancock (1730–1817) whose prints were used principally by the Worcester porcelain factory. Hancock developed the technique of using prints to transfer designs to porcelain or enamel ware – a crucial stage in the move towards mass production. The copper-plate was not inked in the usual way, but instead with a mixture of glaze and pigment, and the resulting printed image was transferred

2.11

from paper to the ceramic surface by rubbing with turpentine. The same copper-plate could be used to produce thousands of identical decorations.

2.11

Air: white-glazed group of Chinese figures

Porcelain, height 199 mm

MME 1938,3–14,80 Presented by Wallace Elliot

This group of Chinese figures is a reminder of the source of inspiration for the Bow factory at New Canton. The element Air is symbolized by birds, whether escaping from a cage or resting on the hand of the man who is dressed in feathers. The design is based on a print

2.10

by Pierre Aveline after François Boucher from a series of *chinoiseries* much used by jewellers, goldsmiths and other craftsmen producing objects in the fashionable chinoiserie style.

2.12

Anonymous

The Treat at Stepney

Etching and engraving with engraved lettering, 338 × 374 mm

Crace XXXIII.80

1880-11-13-5104

Stepney, a short walk from the riverside at Limehouse and Shadwell, was still a rural suburb in the mid eighteenth century, with market gardens clustered around St Dunstan's Church. This print shows a downmarket version of the pleasure gardens at Vauxhall and Ranelagh (cats 5.31–5.37 and 5.54–5.67): Spring Gardens in Stepney flourished from 1702 to 1764. The revellers are sailors home from the sea with cash in their pockets. The verse points out that one man, Frank, lies beneath the table in order to peer beneath the skirts of his 'venal Frow', while Kit has impetuously married his 'trollop' in an informal ceremony of the type abolished by Hardwicke's Act of 1753 (see cats 1.67–70).

2.13

John Faber (1684–1756) after Richard Phelps (1718/19–85)

Hannah Snell, 1750

Mezzotint with some scratched lines and engraved lettering, 328 × 225 mm

C.S. 334

1902-10-11-1885 Bequeathed by William Eaton, 2nd Baron Cheylesmore

In the 1750s Hannah Snell (1723–92) ran a tavern in Wapping less than a mile downstream of the City, but her fame rested on her earlier life. She was born in Worcester, but at the age of seventeen went to live with a married sister in

2.12

2.13

Wapping. Three years later she was married to a Dutch sailor by a Fleet parson (see cats 1.67–1.70); when he abandoned her after a few months, she waited only to give birth to their child before adopting man's clothing and setting off in pursuit. Her search lasted almost five years and included a spell in the army raised against the Jacobite Rebellion and another as a marine in Admiral Boscawen's expedition to India (cat. 4.13); her gender was not discovered despite her receiving a flogging and serious wounds. Hearing that her husband had been executed, she returned to London and the story of her adventures was published in June 1750 under the title *The Female Soldier: or the Surprising Adventures of Hannah Snell.* She exploited her fame by making appearances on stage in uniform at the Royalty Theatre in Wellclose Square, Stepney, and at Sadler's Wells, and by using the sign of the Female Warrior for her tavern in Wapping. Snell married again in 1759 and for a third time in 1772. In 1789 she was committed to Bedlam Hospital and died there three years later. There are proven instances of women disguised as men serving in the army or the navy during the eighteenth century; contemporaries clearly believed Snell and she was granted an annuity in compensation for the wounds she received in India and, in the end, a burial place at the military hospital in Chelsea.

This print is based on one of three painted portraits of Snell dating from 1750. Its high quality and relatively high price of 1s 6d – this is by no means a 'popular print' – indicate that she was known well beyond the East End. It is not clear how she came to sit to Richard Phelps for her portrait. Phelps was a Somerset painter who trained with Thomas Hudson as a fellow pupil with Joshua Reynolds. He remained primarily a local tradesman, working as an interior decorator as well as producing portraits of local families and restoring old master paintings, but he may have made occasional visits to London. Apart from the portrait of Hannah Snell, his best-known work is a portrait of Bampfylde

More Carew, the 'King of the Gypsies' (National Portrait Gallery), which was also published as a mezzotint by Faber in 1750. An album of drawings by Phelps was presented to the British Museum by a descendant in 1918, and they represent the greater part of his surviving work.

2.14

Samuel Scott (1702–72)

A distant view of Rotherhithe, c.1750

ILLUSTRATED IN COLOUR, PLATE 4

Wash drawing with watercolour and pen and ink over graphite, 341 × 522 mm

ECM 7; Kingzett D99; Stainton 8

Oo.5-8 Bequeathed by Richard Payne Knight, 1824

Rotherhithe is on the south bank of the river opposite Wapping. Scott's even tones and spacious compositions give an air of tranquillity to his river views, but Rotherhithe was in reality a busy maritime village with a reputation for rowdy sailors and bawdy taverns. It was linked to Bermondsey, further west, by continuous development, and the road continued with intermittent wharves for a further 2 miles downstream as far as the Greenland Dock where whalers landed their cargo just north of Deptford. The ship shown here has anchored about a quarter of a mile east of Rotherhithe near where a mill stream entered the Thames. The church tower in the distance is that of the newly rebuilt St Mary's, Rotherhithe (completed 1747).

Scott appears to have made at least the preliminary sketch of the ship on the spot – there are a few pencilled notes in the area of the mast and rigging (only the word 'Boom' is legible) – but the colour washes were probably added in the studio as was usual practice at this period. He used the drawing in 1756 for the background of a painting of shipping on the Thames off Rotherhithe (Kingzett, p. 41)

Scott was the most well respected painter of marine subjects of the period, and almost all his views of London focus on the river. Although a professional

painter – he sold his largest canvases (2 m wide) for between sixty and seventy guineas and took apprentices including Sawrey Gilpin and William Marlow – Scott had a post in the Stamp Duty Office that earned him £100 a year. This was evidently little more than a sinecure which required only two or three hours' attendance a week; Scott is said to have purchased the post for the sum of £1,000. He and his wife Ann hosted a small club at their house in Henrietta Street, Covent Garden, where members included fellow artists, tax officials and Sir Edward Walpole, elder brother of Horace. From 1749 Scott had a suburban villa in fashionable Twickenham where he spent weekends. In 1765 he moved to Ludlow, Shropshire, and in 1769 to Bath, where he died in 1772. See Kingzett for a catalogue of Scott's paintings and drawings, transcriptions of the sales of his collection and biographical information.

The Tower to London Bridge

2.15–2.30

2.15

Pierre Charles Canot (1710–77) after George Budd (fl. 1745–56)

Tower Hill with the execution of Lords Balmerino and Kilmarnock on 18 August 1746, 1747 (this impression 1760s)

Published at 2 Maiden Lane, Cheapside

Etching with engraved lettering, 378 × 603 mm

Crace XX.136

1880-11-13-3457

The Tower of London was built in the late eleventh century at the crucial point where the eastern end of the City wall met the Thames. Its looming presence was designed to remind recalcitrant citizens of the power of the monarchy and it is here shown continuing to

A True Representation of TOWER-HILL, as it Appear'd from a rais'd point of View on the North side, Aug.ᵗ ỹ 18ᵗʰ 1746. when the Earl of Kilmarnock and the Lord Balmerino were Beheaded.

2.15

perform this primary function, although by the mid eighteenth century the Tower was also home to the Mint (see cat. 1.41), the Record Office, a menagerie (four lions, two bears, three tigers and a leopard) and an armoury that attracted tourists to see elaborate displays of weapons and a line of equestrian figures in historic armour. The focus here is the open space to the west of the Tower where an enormous crowd is assembled on temporary stands and on every rooftop and balcony as well as on the ground. They have come to watch the beheading of Lords Balmerino and Kilmarnock, two of the 'Rebel Lords' who supported the Young Pretender in 1745–6. For other executions of Jacobites see cat. 3.73.

The print is based on a painting by George Budd, a hosier turned drawing master who taught at Dr Newcome's School in Hackney and produced a number of paintings of topical subjects (see Saur). It is possible that, like John

Griffiths (cat. 1.71), he published the print himself, expecting to find a market for a topical subject of great interest (the address given in the publication line has not been identified and in any case must indicate a late impression dating from the 1760s after street numbering was introduced). His semi-amateur approach is demonstrated in the uncertainty of his composition where newsworthy and topographical elements are reduced to the background and the foreground is taken up with an undifferentiated mass of spectators. A comparison with Hogarth's execution of Tom Idle (cats 5.95, 5.96) shows how a master of narrative might also place the scaffold beyond the crowd, but only in order to focus on the incidental interest of those enjoying a day out at an execution and to increase the pathos of the small figure about to meet his fate.

2.16

Anonymous

Ticket to the trials of Lords Balmerino, Cromerty and Kilmarnock, 1746

Etching with engraved lettering, 159 × 120 mm

C.2-1752 Sarah Banks Collection, presented 1818

Trials of noblemen were held before the House of Lords in Westminster Hall, and a large number of seats were available for peeresses and their daughters, for members of the House of Commons and for others holding tickets available through peers. This ticket, numbered 753, allowed admission to the trial on 29–30 July 1746 of three of the Scottish nobles who had supported the 1745 Jacobite Rebellion: Arthur Elphinstone, 6th Baron Balmerino, George Mackenzie, 3rd Earl of Cromarty, and William Boyd,

4th Earl of Kilmarnock. Lords Kilmarnock and Balmerino were beheaded at Tower Hill on 18 August 1746, but Cromarty was reprieved possibly because, although he had declared for the Pretender, he never fought with the Jacobites.

The trial was presided over by Lord Hardwicke (cat. 1.67), but administration was the responsibility of the Great Chamberlain, Peregrine Bertie, 3rd Duke of Ancaster, whose coat of arms and seal appear on tickets. In 1750 Ancaster was to marry Mary Panton (cat. 5.31); his brother Albermarle Bertie appears in cat. 5.21.

2.17

James Cole (c.1696–1749)

Ticket to the trial of Lord Lovat, 1747

Etching with engraved lettering, 163 × 188 mm

C.2-1751 Sarah Banks collection, presented 1818

This elaborate ticket is numbered 1148. The trial of the eighty-year-old Simon Fraser, 12th Baron Lovat, lasted from 9 to 19 March 1747; he was executed on 9 April – the last person to be judicially beheaded in Britain. Hogarth exploited Lovat's notoriety with a shilling print based on a drawing he made at St Albans when Lovat was being brought to London for trial; five thousand impressions were said to have been sold.

2.18

Thomas Bowles (1712?–67) after J. Maurer (fl. c.1713–61)

A view of the Custom House, 1753

Published by Thomas Bowles in St Paul's Churchyard, John Bowles and Son in Cornhill, Robert Sayer in Fleet Street, and Henry Overton without Newgate

Etching with engraved lettering, 262 × 403 mm

Crace VIII.20

1880-11-13-1625

2.16

2.17

A View of the Custom House, with part of the Tower, taken from ÿ River.   Vüe de la Douane et une partie de la Tour, prise de la Riviere
Thames London.   Thamise a Londres.
London Printed for J. Bowles in St Pauls Church Yard. John Bowles and Son in Cornhill. Rob.t Sayer in Fleet Street: and Hen.y Overton without Newgate.

2.18

Large ships could not pass through the narrow arches of London Bridge, and so the port of London developed along the stretch of the north bank of the Thames between the Bridge and the eastern border of the City at the Tower. In 1275 a Custom House was built there to collect duty and in 1559 it was forbidden to land dutiable goods elsewhere than at these so-called Legal Quays; the huge ships of the East India Company were later exempted and customs men met them further downstream before their goods were transferred to secure ware-houses in the City. After the Great Fire of 1666 warehouses were set back from the water's edge to allow an open space 40 feet wide which can be seen in this print. The Custom House shown here was built to the designs of Thomas Ripley between 1717 and 1725; fees and duties were paid in the grand Long Room. The building was destroyed by fire in 1814.

This print appears in Sayer's 1753 catalogue as one of 206 perspective views sold at 1s plain and 2s coloured.

2.19

Louis Philippe Boitard
(fl. 1733–67)

Preliminary drawing for The Imports of Great Britain from France, 1757

ILLUSTRATED IN COLOUR, PLATE 4

Pen and ink and wash over graphite, indented for transfer, 203 × 344 mm

ECM 3

1908-8-22-1 Presented by Michael H. Salaman

Boitard was the son of the French draughtsman François Boitard, and his free-ranging penwork owes something to that of his father, but his subject matter and the solid coherence of his composi-tions echo Hogarth. Although he was

of French descent, his style was not strongly influenced by the elegant Rococo line introduced by Gravelot; Boitard is not recorded as a member of the St Martin's Lane Academy (cats 3.44–3.46) where most ambitious artists of his generation congregated. He seems to have contented himself with working for publishers, making book illustrations and mildly satirical prints for a general market. Boydell, who worked with him in William Henry Toms's workshop when they were both young men, describes him as more concerned with taking snuff than with applying himself to his work. Most of Boitard's known drawings come from an album that was kept together until the 1950s (see cat. 3.23) and is now widely distributed in public and private collections.

The IMPORTS of GREAT BRITAIN from FRANCE.

Humbly Address'd to the Laudable Associations of Anti-Gallicans, and the generous promoters of the British Arts & Manufactories;
by their sincere Well-wisher, and truly devoted humble Servant, L.P. Boitard

Plate 1st

2.20

2.20

Louis Philippe Boitard
(fl. 1733–67)

The Imports of Great Britain from France, 7 March 1757

Published by John Bowles and Son at the Black Horse, Cornhill

Etching with engraved lettering,
247 × 350 mm

BM Satire 3653

1871-12-9-981

Boitard's composition is unusually elaborate for a sixpenny print. It is also surprising to find a satire on the British taste for all things French made by a Frenchman. The dedicatees of this print are the associations of Anti-Gallicans (see cat. 2.21) and the promoters of British arts and manufactures who saw trade as a patriotic duty.

Britain was at war with France, but fashionable London still yearned for French styles. Boitard shows a ship unloading stereotypical French immigrants and imports: an effeminate man with a huge muff, a hairdresser with a long queue and a pair of curling tongs, a doctor carrying a clyster, a peasant wearing clogs, a Roman Catholic milliner with a crucifix around her neck, a tailor with a large pair of scissors, a dancing master with a tiny violin, disguised Jesuits, a cook received eagerly by what the text calls 'emaciated epicures', an abbé who is to take care of the education of two wealthy children, a dancer who is embraced eagerly by an elaborately dressed English lady. There are crates of perfumes for Monsieur Pomade and millinery for Mademoiselle Chicane. Men taste the contents of wine barrels,

a boy holds his nose over a cask of Normandy cheese.

Although the purpose of the print is satire, it also serves as a description of Custom House Quay with the Tower in the distance: beyond the lively foreground are detailed views of huge scales, cranes and their cabins and a forest of masts; we are shown various methods of packing and carrying goods – barrels, crates, bundles stamped with traders' marks, and tackle-porters carrying a weighty chest slung between two long poles. These men would have been licensed porters paid by the recipient of the load. The pay of others working at the Quay was recorded by Maitland (quoted in Phillips 1951, pp. 42–3): weighing porters who operated the scales were paid £33 a year; clerks, between £20 and £60; wine tasters, £80; the Inspectors General (each of whom dealt

116

with a specific commodity), between £250 and £500; the fourteen Commissioners responsible to government for the operation of the Custom House were each paid £1,000 a year. The Inspector of Prosecutions was not paid a salary, but retained a commission on all moneys paid to the Exchequer.

This print belongs to a genre of satire which, though political, was not aimed at a sophisticated audience that would insist on topicality. Long after the Peace of Paris in 1763 there was still a market for anti-French sentiment, and the print appears in John Bowles's catalogue of 1768 (pp. 85–7), together with another sixpenny satire entitled *British Resentment, or the French coopt up at Louisbourg*, celebrating an event of 1755.

The same catalogue includes *The funeral procession of Madam Geneva, on occasion of the act to prohibit retailing spirituous liquors* – the Gin Act of 1751.

2.21

Anti-Gallican Society President's badge, 1750–5

Painted enamel, gold, silver, glass and rock-crystal, height 139 mm

Hull Grundy 335

MME 1978,10–2,161 Presented by Professor and Mrs John Hull Grundy

The Anti-Gallican Society was founded in 1745 'to oppose the insidious arts of the French nation' and continued to be active for fifty years. It met at Lebeck's Head in the Strand, and there were branches throughout the country. The Society's arms show St George on a white horse spearing a shield with the fleur-de-lis of France, supported by the British lion and a double-headed eagle representing Austria, then an ally against the French but fighting with the French in the Seven Years War (1756–63); the motto is 'For Our Country' and Britannia usually appears as the crest. The arms on this badge are in enamel (made either in Battersea or in Birmingham) surrounded by rock-crystals set in silver; the figure of Britannia, reverse-painted on glass, hangs as a pendant. The arms appear again on a silver-gilt plaque on the

2.21

2.22

reverse. The badge is surmounted by a
crown incorporating five sails, which
may indicate that it belonged to Admiral
Vernon, who was president of the
Society.

See cat. 2.28 for an anti-Gallican
brush-maker, and Snodin, p. 48, no.
C23, and p. 176, no. L44, for the
elaborate Rococo dedication to the
Anti-Gallican Society in Thomas
Johnson's set of furniture designs
(1756–61). The Society is discussed by
Colley, pp. 88–90.

2.23

2.22

Anti-Gallican Society badge, mid
18th century

Gilt-metal, with pastes set in silver, height
107 mm

MME 1890,8–7,7 Presented by Lady
Charlotte Schreiber

This badge was made for William
Plumer of Blakesware, Member of
Parliament for Hertfordshire (d. 1767)

2.23

*Famille rose teacup with the arms of
the Anti-Gallican Society,* 1750s
(Qing dynasty)

Enamelled porcelain, height 42 mm,
diameter 77 mm

Krahl and Harrison-Hall 43

OA Franks 1415 Presented by Sir
Augustus Wollaston Franks

A number of Chinese export pieces were
commissioned with the arms of the Anti-
Gallican Society. For the European taste
for Chinese porcelain see cat. 5.75.

2.24

2.24

*Famille rose plate with the arms of
the Anti-Gallican Society,* 1750s
(Qing dynasty)

Enamelled porcelain, diameter 222 mm

Krahl and Harrison-Hall 44

OA Franks 1414 Presented by Sir
Augustus Wollaston Franks

The motto used here is different from
the usual Anti-Gallican 'For our
Country'; it is intended to read
'St George and Old England', but a
Chinese decorator has substituted an N
for the R in 'St George'. It was not
unusual for Chinese export commissions
to be painted with misunderstood
versions of English inscriptions.

2.25

Giovanni Antonio Canaletto
(1697–1768)

London Bridge, 1750s

ILLUSTRATED IN COLOUR, PLATE 5

Pen and ink and wash, 307 × 539 mm

Constable 738

1909-4-6-4

The first London Bridge was built by the Romans. Several bridges were built and destroyed in the early Middle Ages, but the one built between 1176 and 1209 stood until the 1820s. It was constructed on nineteen narrow arches with a drawbridge in the centre that was lifted occasionally to allow tall ships to pass through, and houses lined its sides like any City street. The piers and their foundations took up eighty per cent of the width of the river bed and the bridge acted like a dam to hold water back; when the tide was going out the water level on the downstream side of the bridge could be several feet lower than that on the other side.

Canaletto's view has a Venetian feel with graceful boats floating on the tranquil water, workers about their business on the south bank, teetering houses on the bridge itself and, on the north bank, grand buildings and towers – Fishmongers' Hall, the Monument, the Water Tower and the church of St Magnus Martyr. The picturesque appearance of the bridge evokes memories of a historic past with triumphal processions and traitors'

heads on the gate, but the mid-eighteenth-century City was a modernizing one and this major route – the only route from the south – had to be brought up to date. Between 1758 and 1762 the bridge was overhauled by George Dance and Robert Taylor: the houses were removed, the roadway widened and several of the spans enlarged to allow greater access for shipping.

A painting of London Bridge by Canaletto was recorded in 1801 (since untraced) and this drawing may be related, but it is a finished work in its own right and may have been conceived as an independent project. Canaletto's drawings were certainly collected during his lifetime and a drawing of London Bridge was sold in 1766 for £3 3s.

2.26

Anonymous

Pin wrapper of George Worrall, Thomas Weaver, John Woodward and John Jefferis, Pinmakers and Citizens, [of] the Company of Pinmakers, c.1756

Woodcut, 170 × 101 mm
Heal 97.14 Bequeathed by Sir Ambrose Heal, 1959

This partnership of pin-makers trading on London Bridge used the sign of the Maidenhead (see also cat. 1.77). The sheet has evidently been used as scrap paper: on the verso are columns of figures, the date 1756 and, in careful script, the name 'William Angell'.

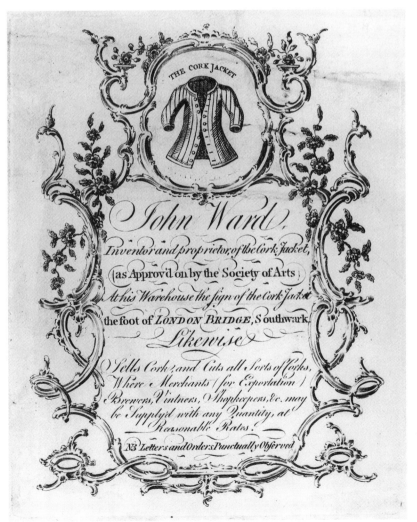

2.26

2.27

2.27

Anonymous

*Trade card of John Ward,
cork-maker*

Etching with engraved lettering,
190 × 151 mm (cropped)

Heal 50.11 Bequeathed by Sir Ambrose
Heal, 1959

Ward boasts that his cork life-jacket has
the approval of the Society of Arts.

2.28

Anonymous

*Trade card of John Grant,
brush-maker*

Etching with engraved lettering,
185 × 143 mm

Heal 24.7 Bequeathed by Sir Ambrose
Heal, 1959

Grant gives his address as at the corner
of the Square, a gap in the houses
towards the northern end of the London
Bridge. His was one of ten new houses
built in the 1740s, and when it was
demolished in 1760 it was recorded as
having had a rental value of £12 a year;
Grant subsequently moved to
Leadenhall Street. His card indicates
that he was both a freemason (emblems
hanging on either side) and an anti-
Gallican (the badge at the bottom).

2.28

2.29

Anonymous

*Trade card of William Herbert,
map- and print-seller, 1749*

Etching with engraved lettering,
193 × 156 mm

Banks 100.56*

1862-10-11-598 John Fillinham collection

Herbert moved to his shop at the sign of
the Golden Globe on London Bridge in
1747. He was a neighbour of John Grant
in one of the new houses on the bridge;
he paid £18 rent a year. He also moved to
Leadenhall Street when the houses were

demolished, and later moved again to
Gulston Square, Whitechapel. In 1758
Herbert published a broadside showing
the damage caused by a fire during work
to widen an arch (see Clayton, p. 109,
fig. 123)

2.30

Anonymous

*Trade card of Basil Denn Junior,
goldsmith and jeweller*

Etching with engraved lettering,
164 × 127 mm (cropped)

Heal 67.118 Bequeathed by Sir Ambrose
Heal, 1959

Denn traded at the Gold Ring on
London Bridge from 1743 to 1754; he is
recorded in Tooley Street, Southwark, in
1771. This charming Rococo card shows
a range of jewellery and silver ware: a
miniature portrait in an elaborate frame,
jewellery, seals, silver teapots and jugs; at
the bottom is a masonic emblem.

2.29

2.30

London Bridge to Lambeth

2.31–2.41

2.31

Samuel Buck (1696–1779) and
Nathaniel Buck (c.1700–after 1753)

*Long view of London and
Westminster*, 11 September 1749

Published by Samuel and Nathaniel Buck,
No. 1 Garden Court, Middle Temple

Etching with engraved lettering,
314 × 3990 mm (cropped)

Crace III.89

1880-11-13-1197

The print, nearly 4 m long and covering
five sheets of paper, shows the north
bank of the Thames from the new bridge
at Westminster (opened in 1750) to old
London Bridge. It was the first long view
of London for over thirty years and
fulfilled a need for an accurate record of

recent building developments on the
northern bank of the Thames. It was sold
to subscribers, with a single-sheet view
of Portsmouth, for 15s. Ralph Hyde
describes the making of the print and its
place in the Bucks' oeuvre on pp. 34–38;
a detailed account of the riverside shown
in the print is given in Phillips 1951, pp.
47–142, with further identifications in
Hyde 1994, pp. 47–8.

The print is reproduced here in six
sections in parallel with the preliminary
drawing (cat. 2.32).

2.32

Samuel Buck (1696–1779),
Nathaniel Buck (c.1700–after 1753)
and Jean-Baptiste-Claude
Chatelain (c.1710–58)

*Long view of London and
Westminster*, c.1746

Pen and ink with grey wash,
309 × 4049 mm

1886-4-10-24

The Bucks always began the process of
creating prints for their series of town
views (there were 87 in all, see Hyde
1994) by making preliminary studies on
the spot. In this case their initial viewpoints on the south bank of the Thames
are noted in the lower margin of the
print (which also carries a key to major
buildings on the north bank): 'Mr
Scheve's Sugar House, opposite to York
House', 'Mr Watson's Summer House,
opposite to Somerset House', 'Mr
Everard's Summer House opposite to
St Bride's Churchyard', 'the west part
of the leads of St Mary Overy's Church
[now Southwark Cathedral]'; the last
viewpoint is repeated twice and takes in
most of the view of the City.

Early sketches would be developed by
one or both brothers into a detailed
topographical 'portrait' of the town.
Assistants would then add picturesque
detail and foreground figures to enliven
the view, and grey wash would be added
to the outline drawing to pull the

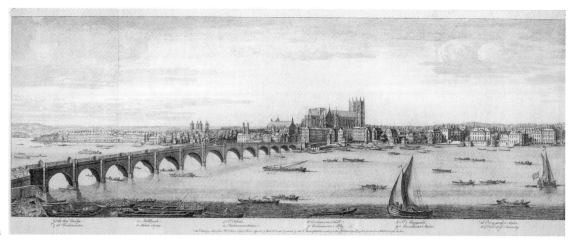

2.31a

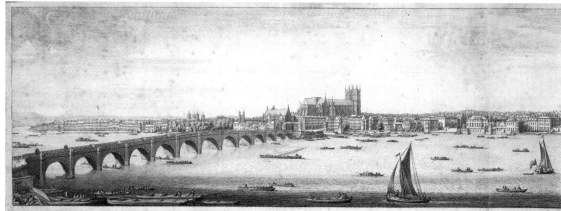

2.32a

composition together. The Bucks employed a number of assistants, but their role was not acknowledged in lettering on the prints and they have been identified only on the basis of their drawing style. In this case the working-up of the Bucks' study has been attributed to Jean-Baptiste-Claude Chatelain, a Huguenot artist resident in London, whose characteristic style is evident in a number of the Bucks' town views (see particularly drawings in the British Museum for views of Cardiff and Wrexham, both of which were advertised in the *London Evening Post* of 24–6 November 1747 as being available for viewing at the same time as the present drawing). The ambitious view of London was a much more complicated production than the single-sheet prints of smaller towns, and there were three and a half years between its inception and publication. It is likely that many more preliminary drawings than usual were made as part of the planning process: there are two sets of studies for

2.31c

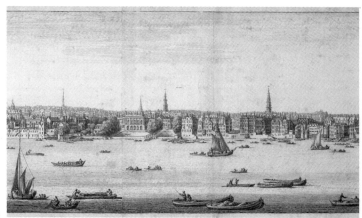

2.32c

2.31b

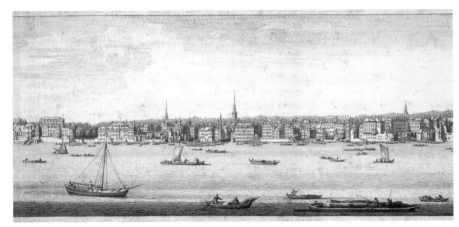

2.32b

2.31d

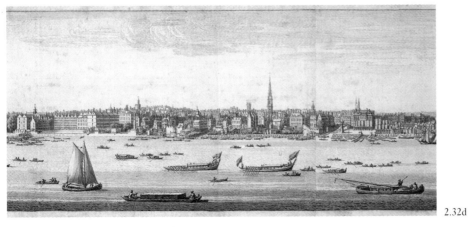

2.32d

2.31e

2.32e

2.31f

2.32f

A·VIEW·OF·PART·OF·THE·INTENDED BRIDGE·AT·BLACKFRIARS·LONDON
IN·AVGVST MDCCLXIIII
BY·ROBERT·MYLNE·ARCHITECT ENGRAVED·BY·PIRANESI·AT·ROME

the left-hand part of the print (one in the Ashmolean Museum, Oxford, and one in a private collection) and it is clear that the drawing of the as yet incomplete Westminster Bridge was problematic.

2.33

Giovanni Battista Piranesi (1720–78) after Robert Mylne (1734–1811)

Blackfriars Bridge under construction, 10 March 1766

Etching with engraved lettering, 409 × 614 mm

Crace VI.254; Wilton-Ely G.III.1014

1880-11-13-1474

The Corporation of London had objected strongly to the building of Westminster Bridge (opened 1750) and Parliament gave the Corporation permission for a new bridge at the point where the Fleet River emptied into the Thames near the western boundary of the City. The lower part of the Fleet was covered over and the bridge was built

between 1760 and 1769; its cost – £230,000 – was found from fines paid by those avoiding serving as Sheriff and a toll was introduced to cover maintenance. The architect was Robert Mylne who had known Giovanni Battista Piranesi in Rome (1755–8) and must have sent him a drawing of the bridge as it appeared in August 1764 to use as the basis for this print. Mylne admired Piranesi's studies of ancient Roman building and engineering in the *Antichità Romane* and must have been glad to see his bridge treated in a similar style, glorying in the mighty scale of a techno-logical marvel with tiny figures exaggerating the size of the huge arches. A less dynamic view of the bridge as it appeared in 1766 was engraved after Mylne by Edward Rooker (reproduced in Weinreb and Hibbert, p. 68).

2.34

Paul Sandby (1731–1809)

View to the west from the gardens of Somerset House

ILLUSTRATED IN COLOUR, PLATE 5

Watercolour with grey wash and pen and ink over graphite, 467 × 1924 mm

Stainton 21a

G.13-30 Bequeathed by John Charles Crowle, 1811

2.35

Paul Sandby (1731–1809)

View to the east from the gardens of Somerset House

ILLUSTRATED IN COLOUR, PLATE 5

Watercolour with grey wash and pen and ink over graphite, 514 × 1893 mm

Stainton 21b

G.13-31 Bequeathed by John Charles Crowle, 1811

Half a mile upstream from the mouth of the Fleet, Somerset House had stood since 1550: the first renaissance palace in

England. It had been built for Edward Seymour, Duke of Somerset, Lord Protector during the reign of Edward VI. When Somerset was beheaded in 1552 the House passed to the Crown. It was used as the official home of the future Elizabeth I, and later of the Stuart queens; by the mid eighteenth century it was an old-fashioned complex of courts, yards and gardens providing grace-and-favour residences and accommodation for eminent visitors. In 1776 the buildings were demolished and the present Somerset House was erected to the designs of William Chambers.

This pair of impressively extensive views from the gardens of Somerset House has been variously attributed either to Paul or to Thomas Sandby. The present attribution follows that of J.T. Smith, Keeper of Prints and Drawings at the British Museum from 1816 to 1833, who knew both brothers.

Thomas Sandby (1723–98) came to London from Nottingham at the age of nineteen and joined the Board of Ordnance at the Tower of London as military draughtsmen; his brother Paul followed four years later at the age of fifteen. Both were to work for the Board in Scotland, Paul playing an important part in the survey of the Highlands made after the defeat of the Jacobite Rebellion. By 1750 Thomas had been appointed official draughtsman to the Duke of Cumberland; he eventually rose to the position of Deputy Ranger of Windsor Forest. By 1759 Thomas was describing himself as an architect, and in 1777 he became one of the two architects to the Board of Works, and Professor of Architecture at the Royal Academy. Paul has enjoyed greater posthumous fame as the 'father of British watercolour' and as the first British printmaker to use aquatint systematically, but his career was not smooth. He was an ambitious young man – talented and inventive – but his personality was perhaps abrasive; his involvement in the campaign for the founding of a royal academy led him, in 1753 and 1754, to publish a series of etched satires against William Hogarth who preferred the less formal style of the

St Martin's Lane Academy (cats 3.44–3.46); in the early 1760s Sandby's further cruel attacks in response to Hogarth's print *The Times*, Plate I (cat. 1.37) which called for an end to the Seven Years War, were also by implication criticisms of Lord Bute and the King (for Sandby's satires see Bindman, pp. 174–80, 185, 186 and 193). Paul never achieved the sort of secure post that allowed his brother to live comfortably; he was appointed drawing master to the Royal Military Academy at Woolwich in 1768, but ten years later was passed over for the post of Surveyor of the King's Pictures.

It is notoriously difficult to distinguish the hand of one brother from another in their watercolours, and they frequently worked together, Paul adding figures to Thomas's topographical or architectural drawings; such co-operation was by no means unusual at the period (see, for instance, cat. 4.11. where Thomas Hudson supplied the head and shoulders in an equestrian portrait of the Duke of Cumberland by John Wootton). Several of the figures in the present pair of watercolours appear elsewhere (see Stainton, no. 21, where a number of other related drawings are also listed). For the large collection of Sandby drawings in the Royal collection see Oppe 1947; see Robertson, Ball and Herrmann for accounts of the careers of both brothers.

It is tempting to compare this pair of drawings with Canaletto's paintings of the views from Somerset House. At the very least the Sandbys would have known the prints after the paintings by Canaletto belonging to Thomas West (now at the Yale Center for British Art) which had been engraved by Edward Rooker and J. S. Müller and published by Sayer in August 1751. The largest and most impressive of Canaletto's views from Somerset House are the pair in the Royal collection. They were painted for Consul Smith in Venice in 1750 or 1751 from drawings made by the artist during his first years in London (and perhaps with reference to prints) and were sold to George III in 1763 as part of Smith's

collection. Thomas Sandby, as a senior employee of the Duke of Cumberland, the King's uncle, must have been able to contrive some means whereby he and his brother could see such important paintings. Smith's collection also included two drawings by Canaletto of the views from Somerset House and four of Westminster Bridge.

Although the Sandbys would have admired Canaletto's magnificent panoramas, and Paul may well have been inspired by them to try his own hand at long views along the Thames, it appears very likely that the immediate source for the view to the west was a commonplace topographical print by the obscure J. Maurer published in 1742. So many details of this print are repeated in Sandby's watercolour that it is hard to dismiss it as a model. Canaletto himself used prints as the basis for urban views (see, for instance, cat. 1.3) and there is no reason to suppose that artists – other than the most assiduous topographers such as the Bucks or surveyors such as Rocque – would have seen any virtue in spending time making accurate drawings of complex cityscapes when there were prints available to follow. The value of Sandby's views from Somerset House does not depend on originality, or on accuracy, but in an apparently effortless control of perspective over a huge area, and in the use of elegant line and delicate application of transparent colour to convey an impression of light and atmosphere.

The drawings have been removed from an extra-illustrated volume of Thomas Pennant's *London* bequeathed to the Museum by John Charles Crowle. Both are unfinished, damaged and reworked (the view to the west is drawn on a patchwork of five sheets of paper) but they remain evocative views of London in the mid eighteenth century, demonstrating the dominance of the river in what was a small-scale urban landscape in comparison with the one with which we are familiar. Since the building of the Embankment, the nearest approach to these views is seen from Waterloo Bridge.

2.36

Samuel Scott (1702–72)

Montagu House, Westminster, 1749

ILLUSTRATED IN COLOUR, PLATE 6

Wash drawing with watercolour and pen
and ink over graphite, 317 × 568 mm

Crace XVI.59

1880-11-13-1320

This drawing relates to a painting made
by Scott in 1749 for John Montagu, 2nd
Duke of Montagu, who died in that year
(Kingzett, pp. 52–3). His house is the
imposing seven-bay building that
dominates the scene. It was this house
that the Montagus preferred to the old-
fashioned mansion in Bloomsbury that
was to become the British Museum
(cat. 3.32). The riverside at Westminster
was lined with fine houses built on the
site of old Whitehall Palace after the fire
of 1698; for a plan of the new buildings,
c.1750, see Phillips 1951, p. 211. The old
stone wall of the Palace with its circular
bastions survived along the water's edge.
Shown here to the left is the terrace of
the house of Charles Lennox, 2nd Duke
of Richmond, for whom Canaletto had
painted two magnificent views of the
Thames in 1747. To the right of
Montagu House are the houses of Joshua
Smith (with a summerhouse built into
the riverside bastion), William
Cavendish, 2nd Duke of Portland,
Andrew Stone, Under Secretary of
State, Jane, Countess of Portland, and
Henry Herbert, 9th Earl of Pembroke,
the 'architect' earl who promoted the
building of Westminster Bridge. In the
distance is the octagonal tower of the
York Buildings Waterworks, a London
landmark of the period, standing to the
east of York Water Gate (still in situ).
The company was set up in the late
seventeenth century to supply Thames
water to the new developments that were
replacing the riverside mansions along
the Strand, but it eventually pumped
water as far as a reservoir in Marylebone
Fields (the site of the present Mansfield
Street) from where it supplied the area
around Hanover Square; water was taken
from a pipe 600 feet out in the river in

order to avoid contamination by sewage
near the bank.

Kingzett did not include this drawing
in his catalogue of Scott's work; he
followed the old inscription attributing
it to Thomas Sandby, but the style is
identical with that of other drawings by
Scott (for instance, cat. 4.27) relying
almost entirely on grey wash with only
minimal addition of watercolour and
some strengthening in pen and ink.

Westminster Bridge

Until 1750 there was no bridge across the
Thames in London other than London
Bridge. From the seventeenth century
there had been demands for another
bridge to serve the growing western part
of town, but opposition from watermen,
ferry operators and the Corporation of
London – which feared damage to City
trade – prevailed until the new bridge
was approved by an Act of Parliament in
1736. The building of a bridge to span
1,200 feet of river was by far the most
ambitious engineering project attempted
in the country to date, and the Swiss
expert on land-drainage, river and
harbour works Charles Labelye was
selected as designer. Labelye was a
Huguenot who first came to England in
1720 and evidently worked as an assistant
to the scientist John Theophilus
Desaguliers, curator to the Royal Society
(see Murdoch, pp. 134–7). In January
1739 the first stone of the new bridge was
laid by Henry Herbert, 9th Earl of
Pembroke, an enthusiastic amateur
architect who had done much to push the
scheme through. Work was more or less
completed in the autumn of 1746, but
the following spring the fifth pier from
the Westminster side began to sink.
Enquiries were held and a great deal of
controversy ensued (English architects
eagerly blaming the foreign designer)
before a solution was agreed on. The pier
and two arches were rebuilt and the
bridge finally opened on 17 November
1750. The total cost was nearly
£400,000, about half of which was
raised by a lottery, the remainder from

government grants. The bridge was a
spectacular structure of white Portland
stone with fifteen semicircular arches,
the widest measuring 76 feet. It had an
immediate effect on the adjacent part of
the south bank – Lambeth – where
approach roads were built and development followed. The area on the north
bank was already built up, and expansion
was blocked by St James's Park to the
west and the marshy ground of what later
became Pimlico to the south.

Some of the finest views of
Westminster Bridge are by Canaletto,
but it is not easy to date his English work
as he often made replicas or developed
compositions from earlier studies. As
Westminster Bridge was still under
construction during the early years of his
visit it is tempting to assume that his
drawings and paintings can be dated
according to the progress of the building
work (described in detail in Walker), but
this is not the case. Like other artists,
Canaletto often anticipated planned
architectural work. Matters are further
complicated by the rebuilding of the
sinking pier which meant that scaffolding
removed from the bridge in 1747 was
replaced within a year; views with work
in progress may, therefore, be based on
its appearance when Canaletto arrived in
London in 1746, or refer to the period
when it was under repair.

See cats 4.25–4.27 for other views of
Westminster Bridge.

2.37

Richard Parr (c.1707– after 1754)
and Samuel Wale (1721?–86) after
Giovanni Antonio Canaletto
(1697–1768)

*View of London through one of the
arches of Westminster Bridge*, 1747

Published by J. Brindley, New Bond Street

Etching with engraved lettering,
439 × 597 mm

Crace V.91

1880-11-13-1311

The print is based on one of two
paintings (Constable 412) made by

To Sir Hugh Smithson Bart. Taken through one of the Centers of the Arches of from a Painting of Canaletti, is most humbly Dedicated

This VIEW of the City of London the New Bridge at Westminster and Engrav'd by his most Obliged Humble Servant. John Brindley.

2.37

Canaletto shortly after his arrival in London in 1746 for Hugh Smithson, later Duke of Northumberland, one of the commissioners of Westminster Bridge; both paintings remain in the family collection. The framing of scaffolding supporting the arch under construction emphasizes that this is a working city, and there is a detailed view of the timber yards on the south bank.

The publisher John Brindley (who was primarily a bookseller rather than a print–seller) was quick to exploit Canaletto's presence in London, and to take advantage of the marketing opportunity of a new bridge. In March 1747 he had published a print based on Canaletto's painting of the bridge from the north (now at the Yale Center for British Art). The present print followed within three months. Both are after

drawings by Samuel Wale and engraved by 'R. Parr' who has been identified variously as Remy (or Remigius) Parr or, as convincingly suggested by Laurence Worms ('Society and Maps', unpublished lecture, Warburg Institute, London, January 1998), Richard Parr, an engraver who, like Wale, undertook work for the map-maker John Rocque.

The inscription refers to Canaletto and his patron, but also includes a useful key to notable buildings for those whose main interest was the print's subject matter. An advertisement issued by Brindley (*General Advertiser*, 2 June 1747) follows a standard formula, making it clear that the print was intended to be framed and used as decoration 'for the ornament of gentlemen and ladies apartments, nobleman's halls, &c., in the country'.

Views through framing arches were familiar devices in Canaletto's work: see, for instance, his etching *Portico with a Lantern* (Bromberg 10), where the hanging lantern is a precursor of the bucket dangling below the arch of Westminster Bridge. In the present composition, the fact that the arch is slightly off-centre enlivens the view; the eye is led in from the left by the naturalistic grouping of large and small boats, and eventually rests at the spire of St Clement Danes on the horizon. In the hands of Wale and Parr much of the atmosphere of the painting is lost. Whereas Canaletto has created an image of a broad, peaceful river under a luminous sky, Parr and Wale have concentrated on topographical accuracy. The proportion has been altered to a squarer format, the space allowed for the river view is reduced and so it has become more crowded with boats, and the church spires are enlarged so that Canaletto's sense of the river stretching into a hazy distance is lost.

Other artists adopted more successfully the dramatic view through the arch. The earliest to pick up this compositional device appears to have been Hogarth in his *Calais Gate*, 1749 (see fig. 7). Around 1750 Samuel Scott painted several views of the Thames seen through Westminster Bridge (Kingzett, pp. 62–4), and by the mid-1760s Paul Sandby routinely chose viewpoints through arches and gateways (see cat. 3.4). Smithson's painting would have been known to Scott, who worked for him at Northumberland House, Charing Cross. Scott's sale catalogues of 1765 and 1773 show that he made copies after Canaletto and that he owned impressions of his etchings (transcribed Kingzett, pp. 108–29). Artists might occasionally have seen paintings in aristocratic collections – and would have taken advantage of the two studio viewings that Canaletto advertised in 1749 and 1751 – but it would have been his etchings that did most to transmit his innovations within artistic circles.

Canaletto's work had enormous influence on British artists. While they learned, especially at St Martin's Lane Academy from Gravelot (see cats 3.44–3.46), to draw graceful figures in a French Rococo style and to combine them in light-hearted subjects, Canaletto's compositions showed how everyday urban topography could be turned into works of art.

2.38

Giovanni Antonio Canaletto (1697–1768)

Westminster Bridge with the Lord Mayor's Procession

ILLUSTRATED IN COLOUR, PLATE 6

Pen and ink with grey wash, 307 × 517 mm

Constable 750

1857-5-20-61

As in his view of London Bridge (cat. 2.25), Canaletto contrasts the apparently unstructured workaday world of the south bank with the formality of grand buildings on the north – in this case the scruffy waterfront is a foil to the elegant bridge itself. The landmarks beyond the new bridge are the four towers of the church of St John the Evangelist finished in 1728 and survivals of medieval royal Westminster: the House of Commons (formerly St Stephen's Chapel), Westminster Hall and Westminster Abbey, with its western towers completed by Nicholas Hawksmoor in 1745.

The river is thronged not only with busy little craft but also with a number of grand shallops or passenger barges rowed by teams of watermen. The spacious expanse of the Thames was a more fitting setting for ostentatious processions than the crowded streets of London and a note in Canaletto's hand on the verso of the drawing explains that what is shown is a 'Foncion de Lord Mayor of London'. The annually elected Lord Mayor of the City of London is required to swear allegiance to the monarch, and until 1856 this was the occasion of a magnificent river-borne progress to Westminster Hall; see cats 1.27–1.29 for views of the later part of the procession along Cheapside.

Canaletto included the Lord Mayor's procession in two paintings of the Thames (National Gallery, Prague, and Yale Center for British Art), but they are not related to this drawing. There is another version of the present drawing in the Royal collection; several versions (both drawings and paintings) also exist of the view of Westminster Bridge described at cat. 4.25, some of which also show the procession. The question of which particular event – if any – Canaletto was recording in these views has not been clarified. The painting at Yale was published as a print in March 1747, which would suggest that the procession was that of Sir Richard Hoare (Lord Mayor 1746/7), but Canaletto shows the bridge complete and without scaffolding although it was still not completely finished at the time of Hoare's procession. Walker has identified the arms of the Goldsmith's Company on the barge in one version and suggests that the procession must be that of John Blatchford (Lord Mayor 1750/1), who was a goldsmith. Canaletto's predeliction for making several versions of the same subject, with or without minor modifications, suggests that a number of different Lord Mayors' processions may be intended and that none should be taken as faithful representations of the event. There must have been a ready market, and Canaletto may well have adapted details to suit particular occasions as the need arose.

The drawing has some old damage: to the left where Canaletto has drawn clouds in grey wash is a large area of brown tone which is the result of old staining; what appears somewhat like diagonal rainfall in the top left-hand corner is another old mark left by brushing paste on the verso.

2.39

J Maurer (fl. *c*.1713–61)

Lambeth Palace from Milbank, c.1750

Pen and ink and wash over graphite with touches of coloured chalks, 224 × 414 mm

ECM 13

1976-6-19-4

Lambeth is the London home of the Archbishop of Canterbury, primate of England; it is the only survivor of the great ecclesiastical palaces that lined the Thames before the Reformation. Archbishops in the middle years of the eighteenth century were Thomas Herring (1747–57), William Hutton (1757–8) and Thomas Secker (1758–68).

This is a preliminary drawing for a print engraved by Pierre Charles Canot, published by John Bowles at the Black Horse in Cornhill on 28 July 1745. The as yet unfinished Westminster Bridge appears in a somewhat fanciful version. At lower left is a coal boat (see cat. 1.90) unloading at Millbank.

2.39

2.40

Paul Sandby (1731–1809)

The Lambeth Drug Mill

ILLUSTRATED IN COLOUR, PLATE 7

Watercolour and pen and ink over graphite,
210 × 287 mm

1978-5-20-8

The mill shown in this drawing was in
Grays Walk, off Three Coney Walk (now
Lambeth Walk) half a mile or so south-
east of Lambeth Palace. A number of
contemporary references (see Short,
pp. 42–3) identify the uses to which the
mill was put. On 10 January 1730 an
advertisement in *The Country Journal,
or, The Craftsman* offered to let 'at
Lambeth in Surrey, a potter's windmill,
together with a small house and garden
thereunto belonging, and also two acres
and a half of [market] garden ground.
Enquire at Lambeth Wells, or at Mr
Dry's lodgings at Mr Bray's house in
Pearl Court in Whitefriars.' In 1759
records of a court case reveal that the
Reverend John Dry of Thames Ditton,
Surrey, was letting the mill to the
druggist George Rutt of Friday Street in
the City at a rent of 6*d* a year. Rutt died

in 1778, but another court case suggests
that the mill continued to be used for
grinding materials for drugs; it passed
into the joint trusteeship of Rutt's
widow, a hosier named Samuel
Etheridge of Lewisham, and John
Howell and John Field both of Newgate
Street in the City, the latter being
described as an apothecary.

Sandby made at least three other views
of the mill (two in the Guildhall Library
and one belonging to Lambeth Public
Libraries) and made a print after one of
them. The print is dated 1780 but, given
Sandby's propensity for re-using images,
that date is no indication of when his
drawing was made and the crisp style fits
well with his work of the 1750s and
1760s.

2.41

William Hoare (1706–92)

Christian Frederick Zincke, 1752

ILLUSTRATED IN COLOUR, PLATE 7

Black and red chalk, 416 × 320 mm

ECM 1

1860-7-28-167

This is a rare informal image of an artist
at work. Most portraits show the sitter as
he or she wishes to be seen by society at
large, and artists' portraits tend to stress
their gentility rather than dwelling on
the details of their craft. In cats 3.44 and
3.45, for instance, Hogarth is shown as
painting the Comic Muse, a classical
abstraction far away from his actual
subject matter taken from the streets of
London, while Roubiliac is adding
delicate finishing touches to a model for
his statue of Shakespeare; he is elegantly
dressed and there is no evidence of the
heavy physical work of the sculptor. It is
perhaps because Zincke – approaching
seventy years of age – was already retired
from active pursuit of his career that
he allowed himself to be drawn in an
informal indoor cap working at a portrait
of his daughter with all his enamellist's
paraphernalia laid out in front of him.
Zincke (1683/4–1767) was born in
Dresden but settled in London in 1706.
He lived in Tavistock Street, Covent
Garden, until he retired to Lambeth in
1746.

III

COVENT GARDEN AND BLOOMSBURY

The earliest-known settlement in the area immediately to the west of the City of London was the Saxon town of Lundenwic, developed where the shore, or strand, sloped gently and boats could be beached for unloading at low tide. Remains of Saxon timber buildings have been excavated in recent years as far north as the old Roman road now known as Holborn and Oxford Street. This was the London described by Bede in the eighth century as 'the market of many peoples coming by land and sea'. In the late ninth century Viking raids drove citizens back to the protection of the the walled City, and the Saxon town disappeared, remembered only in the names of Wych Street and later Aldwych.

By the twelfth century the north bank of the river from the City to Westminster was lined with grand houses convenient for the royal Court, mainly in the hands of powerful bishops and abbots. The same area became the site of the growth of the legal profession. Schools of law were forbidden in the City – the monarchy was wary of an alliance between wealthy merchants and the law – and in the late thirteenth century legal training began at the Lord Chancellor's office in what was to become Chancery Lane. Four Inns of Court (Lincoln's Inn, Gray's Inn, Inner and Middle Temple) developed as residences and training institutions, with ten satellite Chancery Inns. The area immediately west of the City is still the centre of the legal profession.

The Reformation saw most of the ecclesiastical palaces pass to the nobility; by the mid eighteenth century the powerful and fashionable world had in turn moved on to Westminster, St James's and Mayfair. Only Somerset and Northumberland Houses and the ruined Palace of Savoy survived of the riverside mansions along the Strand, the remainder replaced by developments bearing their aristocratic owners' names: Essex, Arundel, Norfolk, Howard, Surrey, Cecil, Salisbury, George, Villiers, Duke and Buckingham Streets; Durham Yard stood on the site of the Bishop of Durham's house; Beaufort Buildings (cat. 3.70) replaced the Duke of Beaufort's house.

The area immediately to the north of the Strand took its name from the former convent garden developed in the 1630s by Francis Russell, 4th Earl of Bedford, who had employed Inigo Jones to create an elegant square – the first of the London squares – surrounded by an arcade on the model of the Place des Vosges in Paris and the Piazza at Livorno. A hundred years later the residents of Covent Garden were, like those of neighbouring Charing Cross, Leicester Fields and Soho, artisans, shopkeepers and artists rather than aristocrats. The entertainment industry was centred there on Covent Garden and Drury Lane theatres, and on the informal world of coffee houses, taverns, turkish baths and brothels.

The northern border of London ran along Oxford Street and Great Russell Street, taking in the square and surrounding streets of Bloomsbury developed by Thomas Wriothesley, 4th Earl of Southampton, in the 1660s. Bloomsbury passed to the highly political Russells of Bedford with the marriage of the Earl's daughter, and in the mid eighteenth century the great house on the north side of Bloomsbury Square was the London home of John Russell, 4th Duke of Bedford. Along the edge of town were new institutions reflecting the period's developing sense of public responsibility: the Middlesex Hospital, George Whitefield's Methodist chapel, the Foundling Hospital and – in a mansion deserted by the Dukes of Montagu – the British Museum.

North of them in 1756 the New Road (now Marylebone, Euston and Pentonville Roads) was built in open fields. This was a fine road, 40 feet wide with building forbidden within 50 feet on either side; the City Road was opened as an eastern extension in 1761. The main purpose of the road was to allow cattle to be driven to market without blocking the streets of rapidly developing west London. Some idea of the urgent need for such a road can be inferred from records of animal traffic coming from the north through Islington down to St John Street and Smithfield: in 1757, cattle amounted to 30,952 and sheep to 200,180; in 1758, 28,602 cattle and 267,567 sheep.

Covent Garden

3.1–3.20

3.1

Thomas Bowles (1712?–67)

A View of Covent Garden, 20 August 1751

Published by Robert Sayer at the Golden Buck, opposite Fetter Lane, Fleet Street

Etching with engraved lettering, 260 × 403 mm

Crace XVIII.62

1880 11-13-3048

This view of Covent Garden market from the south is still recognizable although the surrounding buildings have all been replaced, the central square is now filled with the market building of the 1820s and even Inigo Jones's St Paul's was restored after a fire of 1795. The print represents a collaboration between the Bowles family and Robert Sayer, the two most prominent middle-market print publishers in London: the print is by Thomas Bowles and published by Sayer. It was not unusual for the two firms to share the cost of publication, sometimes including Henry Overton, John Tinney or other publishers in the arrangement, but in this case Sayer was evidently the sole publisher.

3.2

J. Maurer (fl. *c.*1713–61)

A Perspective View of Covent Garden, *c.*1749 (this edition after 1768)

Published by Robert Wilkinson in Cornhill and Carington Bowles in St Paul's Churchyard

Etching with engraved lettering, 252 × 422 mm

Crace XVIII.60

1880-11-13-3046

This view of Covent Garden market from the east is a late impression of a print that was originally a joint publication of John and Thomas Bowles in the late 1740s. It appears in John Bowles's catalogue of 1749 among thirty-nine 'perspective views in and about London', and again in the 1753 catalogue, by which time the number of views had risen to sixty-two. Robert Wilkinson took over John Bowles's stock after his death in 1768; Carington Bowles took over the St Paul's Churchyard shop in 1763.

3.3

Louis Philippe Boitard (fl. 1733–67)

The Covent Garden Morning Frolick, 9 October 1747

Etching with engraved lettering, 238 × 320 mm (cropped)

BM Sat 2877

1860-6-23-29

The frolic of the title is that enjoyed by two well-dressed gentlemen, one of whom holds a large artichoke that he has evidently acquired from a market woman, while the other sprawls drunkenly on the roof of a sedan-chair in which sleeps a woman whose breasts fall out of her bodice. One of the young men has evidently struck a bellman (nightwatchman) on the head, and compensated him with a few coins that the old man holds in his hat. The supposed names of the drunken trio have been added to the print by a later hand: Captain Laroon, Captain Montague and Bet Careless. The sedan-chair is carried by two exhausted men and has clearly been led through the dark early morning streets by a barefoot link-boy (recognizable as Little Cazey, cat. 3.23) carrying a torch made of burning flax and pitch; another street-boy plays a hurdy-gurdy. J. T. Smith, Keeper of Prints and Drawings and writer of anecdotes of London life, recalled that 'whenever Captain [Marcellus] Laroon was named by Henry Fielding [novelist and Bow Street magistrate], he said, "I consider him and his friend Captain Montague, and their constant companion, Little Cazey, the Link-boy, as the three most troublesome and difficult to manage of all my Bow-street visitors". Cazey was transported for stealing a gentleman's gold watch' (Smith, p. 272–3).

There was clearly a market for mildly humorous street scenes set in identifiable locations. This is no moralizing satire, the only hint of criticism of the rowdy young gentlemen is the motto 'Sic Transit Gloria Mundi' ('Thus passes earthly glory') beneath the clock in the pediment of St Paul's Church.

3.4

Thomas Sandby (1723–98) and Paul Sandby (1731–1809)

The Piazza, Covent Garden, *c.*1770

ILLUSTRATED IN COLOUR, PLATE 8

Watercolour and pen and ink over graphite, 510 × 675 mm

Stainton 24

G.6-25 Bequeathed by John Charles Crowle, 1811

This boldly composed view of Covent Garden is seen through the arcade in the north-east corner; the arcade, rather than the square itself, was commonly referred to as the Piazza. The overall design corresponds with a print of 1768 by Edward Rooker after Thomas Sandby, and with a watercolour in the Guildhall Library, but there are many differences both in the figures and in architectural details – the oil lamps suspended between the arches do not appear in the print, and the row of buildings shown on the right is quite different. The houses at the southern end of the east side of the square were replaced after a fire in 1769 and these new houses are represented here. The watercolour is clearly a reworking of the composition used in Rooker's print.

As was their frequent practice, the Sandby brothers seem to have collaborated on this drawing and some of the figures appear elsewhere in studies by Paul Sandby; for instance the woman selling cherries in the market area

A View of Covent Garden LONDON. Vûe du Couvent Jardin à LONDRES.

3.1

A Perspective View of Covent Garden Vûe de Covent Garden.

3.2

The Cov: Garden Morning Frolick

Invented & Engrav'd by L.P. Boitard Publish'd According to Act of Parliam! Oct. 9. 1747 Price one Shilling.

3.4

appears in a drawing at the Yale Center for British Art.

A sheet on one of the arches announces a benefit performance for Mrs Yates of *The Earl of Warwick* at the Theatre Royal, Covent Garden; benefit performances where profits went to particular individuals were regular features of eighteenth-century theatre, and tickets and notices such as this one were specially produced for them. The actress Mary Ann Graham (1728–87) married Richard Yates, a well-known comedian, in 1756. She was renowned for her performance as Margaret of Anjou in Thomas Francklin's *Earl of Warwick*, a part she created at Drury Lane Theatre in 1766. The benefit at Covent Garden took place on 22 March 1770 and she made £218. 3s (Stone, p. 1463).

The Theatre – David Garrick

In 1737 Robert Walpole – enraged by Henry Fielding's satires on his administration – had cracked down on theatres with the Licensing Act, closing all but the two so-called patent theatres, Covent Garden and Drury Lane, and introducing censorship by the Lord Chamberlain. Small theatres continued in the guise of chocolate houses, concert halls and the like, giving performances as incidental entertainment, but in 1752 the loophole that allowed such evasions of the law was closed and performances of any kind were required to be licensed by a magistrate. Nevertheless theatre played an extremely important part in the social life of London at all levels. There was no Court theatre like those in on the Continent (for instance the magnificent

theatres at Drottningholm, Stockholm, or in the Munich Residenz) and the royal family were frequently to be seen in the public playhouses. All classes and both sexes met in the confined auditoriums: Drury Lane Theatre held an audience of about nine hundred in the mid-century, the upper classes occupying boxes, while cheaper tickets were available in the pit. An evening's entertainment was designed to please a range of tastes and might include a Shakesperian tragedy with an interval display of tightrope walking, followed by a pantomime or a comedy as an afterpiece.

In contrast with the spectacles of Continental Court theatre, or the limelit London stage of Victorian times, contact between audience and performers was intimate. The stage – at Drury Lane about 30 feet wide and 20 feet deep – was surrounded on three side by boxes, and further benches might even be placed at the back of the stage on benefit nights; light levels were the same throughout the theatre. The focus was on the actor. Facial expression was a vital part of a performance, and the ability to transform his face from one part to another was one of David Garrick's claims to fame.

Prints of Garrick (1717–79) are used here to epitomize the London theatre of the mid eighteenth century. Garrick became Britain's leading actor in the 1740s, establishing a naturalistic style in contrast to the declamatory performances of previous generations. In 1747 he bought, for £8,000, a half-share in the Drury Lane Theatre, which he ran for the next thirty years. Garrick's importance as a public figure went far beyond the stage and his personal reputation did much to raise that of the theatre as a whole; for a collection of 1,362 letters with many of the most distinguished figures of the day see Little and Kahrl. There are portraits of Garrick in every medium from oil on canvas to Wedgwood Jasperware. He was the first actor to exploit the publicity potential of prints: hundreds of thousands of impressions of his portraits would have been sold in the print shops, and his face – in many guises – would have been familiar throughout London and beyond. O'Donoghue lists 176 engraved portraits of Garrick, ninety-six in character, eighty in private dress; the only contemporary who approaches such a number of portraits is George III with 162. Largely thanks to Garrick, theatrical portraits became a commercial proposition for print publishers at a time – before the late eighteenth-century vogue for portrait collecting – when engraved portraits rarely enjoyed large sales.

The Georgian theatre is discussed and well illustrated in Mackintosh and Lennox-Boyd. Standard reference works are Stone, and Highfill et al. and for Garrick, Stone and Kahrl; see also MacIntyre.

3.5

3.5
William Hogarth (1697–1764) and Charles Grignion (1721–1810) after William Hogarth

Garrick as Richard III, 20 June 1746

Published by William Hogarth

Etching and engraving with engraved lettering, 413 × 510 mm

Paulson 165

Ee.3-121 Charles Burney collection

Garrick came to London from Lichfield in 1737 with his former teacher Samuel Johnson, intending to train in the law, but theatre soon claimed him. He made his London stage debut as Richard III at the theatre in Goodman's Fields, Whitechapel, in 1741. His performances in this play and others in the season were a roaring success, bringing carriages full of West End audiences to the other end of town: Thomas Gray wrote to John Chute that 'There are a dozen dukes of a night at Goodman's Fields'.

Garrick was particularly admired for his acting of Richard III's dream before the final battle and it is this moment that Hogarth has chosen to depict. He based the design on the *Tent of Darius* by Charles Le Brun (1619–90), known through a print by Gérard Edelinck. Garrick's anxious grimace also owes something to Le Brun, the illustrations to whose treatise on the expression of the passions were to remain a source for artists for another century: Hogarth refers to an English copy in his *Analysis of Beauty* (p. 127) as 'the common drawing-book, called Le Brun's passions of the mind; selected from that great master's works for the use of learners; where you may have a compendious view of all the common expressions at once'. It is likely that Garrick studied Le Brun himself when developing his much-lauded facial expressions.

Although theatrical subjects had appeared in prints before, Hogarth showed with this print and the large painting that it was based on (Liverpool, Walker Art Gallery), measuring two by two and a half metres, that the stage could provide material of a stature approaching that of history painting. Shakespearian tragedies, in particular, lent themselves to ambitious portrayal,

3.6

3.7

appealing both to the patriotic Briton and to the lover of the stage. Hogarth used theatrical conventions to tell his stories as if his characters were on a stage, as he put it in a 'dumb-shew': his 'Progresses' need none of the speech balloons that were the norm in satirical prints. Garrick's performances, too, were said to be understood in purely visual terms, even by those who were deaf.

In 1757 Hogarth painted Garrick again with his wife Eva-Maria Veigel (Royal collection). They were firm friends, and the actor wrote the epitaph that appears on Hogarth's tomb at Chiswick.

3.6

Charles Mosley (fl. 1737–56)

The Modern Duel, 29 January 1747

Etching and engraving with engraved lettering, 218 × 383 mm

BM Satire 2855

1868-8-8-3823 Edward Hawkins collection

This sixpenny print is one of several made of the popular farce *Miss in her Teens*, written by Garrick (he wrote more than forty dramatic pieces) and first performed as an afterpiece at Covent Garden in January 1747. It was one of the successes of Garrick's only season there. He is shown here as the feeble Fribble, performing with three of London's leading actors: the great comedian Henry Woodward (1714–77) as the flamboyant Captain Flash; Jane Hippisley (1719–91) – who, as Mrs Green, was later that year to create the part of Mrs Malaprop – as Biddy Bellair; and Hannah Pritchard (1711–68) as Mrs Tag. Flash and Fribble rapidly became household names; see cats 1.30 and 3.72.

The print is the earliest-known view of a performance at Covent Garden and shows members of the audience in boxes on either side of the stage, as well as giving a clear view of the rows of spikes protecting actors. In the coming years there were to be two major theatrical disturbances involving stage invasions:

the 1755 Chinese Festival riots objecting to the engagement of a troupe of French dancers at Drury Lane during the build-up to the Seven Years War, and the 1763 Half-Price riots at both theatres in response to an attempt to discontinue the tradition of half-price tickets after 9 p.m. See BM Satire 3834 4004 for a view of the rioting audience at Covent Garden in 1763.

3.7
Gabriel Smith (1724– c.1783)

Mr Garrick in the Character of Lord Chalkstone in the Farce of Lethe, c.1760

Published by Mary Dickinson at the corner of Belle Savage Inn, Ludgate Hill

Etching with engraved lettering, 345 × 252 mm (cropped)

Ee.3-128 Charles Burney collection

Lethe, or Esop in the Shade, was written by Garrick and first produced on 15 April 1740, before his acting debut. The farce concerns a group of characters – a fine gentleman, a poet, a female writer, a dissolute old nobleman – who meet in the Underworld where they have come to forget their troubles and start afresh. It was extremely popular and was frequently performed. Garrick is shown here – in one of many prints related to *Lethe* – as Lord Chalkstone quizzing young women with his glass; his stockings are padded to suggest gout-swollen ankles. The character of Mrs Riot was added for Kitty Clive in 1749 (see cat. 3.10).

This impression has been cut, probably to fit an album page, and

Mary Dickinson's publication line is lost. She was the widow of Bispham Dickinson and continued the business after his death in 1754. She developed a line in theatrical subjects to exploit the market built up by Garrick's assiduous self-promotion.

3.8
Edward Fisher (1722–82) after Joshua Reynolds (1723–92)

Garrick between Tragedy and Comedy, 1762

Published by Edward Fisher at the Golden Head the south side of Leicester Square, John Boydell, Engraver, at the Unicorn, Cheapside, and E. Bakewell and H. Parker, Printsellers in Cornhill, opposite Birchin Lane, London (publication line in finished state)

3.8

Mezzotint with some scratched lines,
400 × 502 mm

C.S.20(i)

1868-8-22-2099 Felix Slade Bequest

Garrick was renowned for his ability to
switch with equal brilliance between
tragic and comic roles, and here he
shrugs his shoulders, unable to chose
which muse to follow. Reynolds has
followed the precepts of Lord
Shaftesbury in his instructions to Paolo
de Matteis in his painting of the
Judgement of Hercules (now Ashmolean
Museum) where the difficulty of the
choice – traditionally that between virtue
and pleasure – is represented by having
Hercules/Garrick turning his body in
one direction and his head in the other.
But this is no earnest moralizing image,
and Reynolds treats the subject with wit
worthy of Garrick, whose evident good-
nature suggests that while he cannot
resist the charming muse of Comedy his
arms are equally open to embrace
Tragedy.

The painting (private collection,
Mannings 700) was reproduced in at
least fourteen different mezzotints; this
remarkably fine example is by Edward
Fisher, one of the group of mezzotinters
who came to London from Dublin in
the 1740s and brought new life to the
technique. It is shown here in a proof
impression, but the lettering on the
finished state showed that Fisher shared
the costs of publication with John
Boydell and the partnership of Elizabeth
Bakewell and Henry Parker; Boydell
continued to sell impressions into the
nineteenth century. The print was
originally sold at 10s 6d, but cheaper
versions proliferated: Garrick's friend
the playwright George Colman wrote to
him from Paris in 1766, 'There hangs out
here in every street, pirated prints of
Reynolds' picture of you, which are
underwritten, L'Homme entre le Vice
et la Vertu'.

Watch-papers

Circles of fine fabric or paper were
inserted into watch-cases to protect
against dust. Print publishers saw an
opportunity for sales and issued
watch-papers printed with portraits of
celebrities. In Robert Sayer's catalogue
of 1766 is a list of sixty-one 'Designs in
miniature for watchcases' engraved by
Louis Philippe Boitard at 3*d* plain and
6*d* coloured. The following group of
watch-papers includes two of actors and
actresses and four of famous courtesans.

3.9

Louis Philippe Boitard
(fl. 1733–67)

*Mr Beard and Miss Brent in Thomas
and Sally*, *c.*1760

Etching with engraved lettering, diameter
48 mm

1902-10-18-65

John Beard (1716?–1791) was a leading
actor and a singer of such stature that
Handel composed some of his greatest
tenor parts with Beard in mind. He was
married for the second time to Charlotte
Rich, daughter of John Rich, whom he
succeeded as manager of Covent Garden
Theatre in 1761. Charlotte Brent
(d. 1802) was also a fine singer – the
favourite pupil of Thomas Arne. Her
first success was playing opposite Beard
as Polly Peachum in *The Beggar's Opera*
at Covent Garden; the production had

what was for the period an unusually
long run of thirty-seven consecutive
nights from 10 October 1759. *Thomas
and Sally* opened a year later.

3.10

Anonymous

*Mrs Clive in the character of the
Mrs Riot in Lethe*, 1750s

Etching with engraved lettering, diameter
48 mm

1902-10-18-71

Kitty Clive (1711–85) was the most
successful comic actress of her
generation; she was also renowned as a
singer and performed regularly in
Handel's oratorios. She first played at
Drury Lane at the age of seventeen and
except for a short period in the early
1740s spent most of her career there.
Here she is shown in one of the leading
roles in Garrick's farce *Lethe*. The
watch-paper is based on a print by
Charles Mosely after Thomas Worlidge
which was also used as the model for a
Bow porcelain figure; a matching figure
was made after James McArdell's
mezzotint of Francis Hayman's portrayal
of Henry Woodward as the Fine
Gentleman in *Lethe* (see Allen, p. 127).

In retirement Mrs Clive lived in a
house called Little Strawberry Hill on
the Twickenham estate of her friend
Horace Walpole and she became one of
his closest companions.

3.9

3.10

3.11

3.11

John June (fl. *c*.1747–70) after
Joshua Reynolds (1723–92)

*Miss Kitty Fischer, c.*1759

Published by Robert Sayer, opposite Fetter
Lane, Fleet Street

Etching with engraved lettering, diameter
58 mm

1902-10-18-67

Kitty Fisher, or Fischer (1738–67), was
one of the most notorious courtesans
of the mid eighteenth century. This
watch-paper, after a portrait by Joshua
Reynolds (Mannings 611), refers coyly to
her way of life with its frame of hearts
and cupid's bows and arrows. Fisher's
fame was such that she was the subject of
a ballad sold in the streets (see cat. 1.58)
as well as a number of cheap pamphlets
(see *DNB*); on 30 March 1759 a notice in
The Public Advertiser signed C. Fisher
complained of 'the baseness of little
scribblers and scurvy malevolence'
which had caused her to be 'abused in
public papers [and] exposed in print
shops'. Her extravagance was legendary,
and Casanova recorded the story that she
had once placed a promissory note for
£20 between two slices of bread and
eaten it: Reynolds alluded to this in his
portrait of Fisher as Cleopatra dissolving
a pearl in a glass of wine (Mannings 612).
He painted her portrait ten times in all,
but the record of his sitters' book makes
it clear that he was careful to make her
appointments at his studio in Leicester
Square at times when respectable ladies

would not meet her. Fisher's career
ended with a marriage to John Norris,
M.P. for Rye in Sussex.

3.12

John June (fl. *c*.1747–70) after
Henry Morland (1716–97)

Miss Fanny Murray

Published by John Smith at Hogarth's
Head, Cheapside

Etching with engraved lettering, diameter
51 mm

1902-10-18-68

For Fanny Murray see cats 3.16–3.17.
This portrait is based on James
McArdell's mezzotint after Henry
Morland (Goodwin 184). As with the
watch-paper of Kitty Fisher, June has
surrounded the portrait with hearts, this
time burning ardently.

3.12

3.13

3.13

Louis Philippe Boitard
(fl. 1733–67) after Joshua Reynolds
(1723–92)

*Miss Nelly O'Brien, c.*1764

Published by Robert Sayer, 53 Fleet St

Etching with engraved lettering, diameter
50 mm

1902-10-18-69

For Nelly O'Brien see cat. 3.15. The
watch-paper is based on one of three
portraits of the famous courtesan by
Joshua Reynolds (Mannings 1354).

3.14

John June (fl. *c*.1747–70) after
Joshua Reynolds (1723–92)

*Miss Day, c.*1760

Published by John Smith, at Hogarth's
Head, Cheapside

Etching with engraaved lettering, diameter
46 mm

1902-10-18-70

Ann Day was the mistress and mother of
four children of Richard Edgcumbe, 2nd
Baron Edgcumbe. After his death in
1761 she married Sir Peter Fenhoulet, an
officer of the Yeomen of the Royal
Guard, but afterwards lived apart from
him in Calais. Her presence on this
watch-paper suggests that she was well
known and regarded in somewhat the
same light as the notorious courtesans
Kitty Fisher, Fanny Murray and Nelly
O'Brien. This print is based on a portrait

3.14

by Joshua Reynolds (Mannings 498), but was probably copied directly from James McArdell's mezzotint of 1760 (Goodwin 80). Her hat is of the type known as a 'Woffington' after the famous actress Peg Woffington (c.1714–60).

Prostitution

The best-known references to prostitution in mid-eighteenth-century London are in pornographic novels – most notoriously John Cleland's *Fanny Hill, or the Memoirs of a Woman of Pleasure* (1749) – and the diaries of James Boswell (1762–3) and Giacomo Casanova (in London 1763–4). Such sources are inevitably unreliable and can be read as no more than suggestions of what might have seemed believable to a contemporary readership; recent studies, attempting a more accurate view by examining literary and visual sources in the light of court records and other documentary evidence, reveal a less attractive view of the life of young women supporting themselves by selling sexual favours (see Carter and Henderson).

According to an anonymous writer in 1758, there was a 'gradation of whores in the metropolis: women of fashion who intrigue, demi-reps, good-natured girls, kept mistresses, ladies of pleasure, whores, park-walkers, street-walkers, bunters, bulk-mongers' (*A Congratulatory Epistle from a Reformed Rake to John Fielding, Esq., upon the New Scheme of Reclaiming Prostitutes*, quoted in Carter, Chapter 1). John Fielding (brother of the novelist and his successor as magistrate at Bow Street), Jonas Hanway (see cat. 3.26) and others were moving towards reform rather than punishment of prostitutes – in 1758 the Magdalen Hospital was established in the building vacated by the London Hospital in Goodman's Fields, Whitechapel (see Ogborn, pp. 39–74). Prints do not reflect such changes in attitude. Prostitutes are portrayed in a manner that blends prurience with blame: they are shown as provocatively

attractive, but also as the bringers of disease, destroyers of family life and parasites on their clients.

3.15
Samuel Okey (fl. c.1748–71) after Sir Joshua Reynolds (1723–92)
Nelly O'Brien, c.1764

Published by Ryland and Bryer at the King's Arms in Cornhill (publication line in finished state)

Mezzotint with engraved lettering, 329 × 246 mm

C.S.7 (i)

1902-10-11-3559 Bequeathed by William Eaton, 2nd Baron Cheylesmore

This print is based on a painting by Joshua Reynolds now in the Wallace Collection (Mannings 1353). Reynolds's three paintings are the prime record of O'Brien's life although she appears as a footnote in the biographies of a number of prominent men. In 1764 she bore a son, Alfred, to Frederick St John, 2nd Viscount Bolingbroke. She died in March 1768.

The status of courtesan has been given to a number of glamorous women of low birth who maintained expensive and

3.15

highly visible lifestyles with funds
provided by lovers and admirers.
Although not accepted in polite society,
they were extremely well known and
appeared regularly in the press. They
might even set trends in fashionable
dress: Tillyard (p. 155) describes how
the young Lady Susan Fox-Strangways
(cat. 5.17) aped what her aunt disapprov-
ingly called 'the Kitty Fisher style'.

3.16

Thomas Johnson (fl. c.1763–70) after Page (fl. 1750s)

Mrs Murray

Mezzotint with etching, 351 × 249 mm

C.S. 3

1934-7-6-1 Purchased with funds
bequeathed by Henry Louis Florence

Fanny Murray (1729–78) wears a
popular masquerade costume known as
'Van Dyck dress', a grander version of
which is worn by the Duchess of
Ancaster in cat. 5.31. Commercial
masquerades were introduced to London
in the first decade of the eighteenth
century, and the opportunity that they
allowed for illicit sexual encounters and
for transgressing class boundaries was
both the basis of their success and the
cause of much moralistic anxiety. The
parallel between the costumes illustrates
the frequent complaint that well-dressed
prostitutes could too easily be taken for
respectable ladies; masquerade costume,
intended to disguise, exploited such
confusion. A contemporary audience
would, however, have been able to read
signs that are less obvious today: for
instance, the strands of hair falling across
Murray's brow would have suggested
loose morals. In cat. 5.72 Hogarth
deliberately showed the young bride's
hair falling from her cap as an indication
of her waywardness; her downfall comes
with an assignation at a masquerade,
followed by an encounter in a bagnio
(see cat. 3.18).

Fanny Murray herself married the
actor David Ross in 1756 and remained a
faithful wife for over twenty years.

3.16

3.17

Anonymous

The Morning Tast: or Fanny M_'s Maid Washing her Toes, 1751

Etching with engraved lettering,
193 × 319 mm (cropped)

BM Satire 3180

1868-8-8-3579 Edward Hawkins collection

We are shown here a sordid version of
the fashionable morning levée of cat. 00.
The room is grandly panelled, but the
picture of copulating dogs is one that no
respectable household would hang.
Fanny Murray has a maid to dry her feet
and a hairdresser attends to her coiffure,
but her reading matter is limited to a
penny execution broadside. Rather
than offering expensive chocolate from
porcelain cups like Hogarth's Countess,
she provides a barrel of oysters – cheap
food sold by street-criers. She displays
her legs to a seedy young gentleman and
a leering lawyer who brings a deed of
settlement, from a wealthy lover.

The Morning Taft; or Fanny M—'s Maid Washing her Toes.

3.17

One piece of evidence suggests that Fanny Murray actually furnished her home quite conventionally: Arthur Pond's account book (transcribed in Lippincott 1988) records that on 15 July 1748 he sold Fanny Murray three framed and glazed prints from his series *Roman Antiquities*. The prints by Johann Sebastian Müller were large (about 450 × 600 mm) capriccios of well-known Roman buildings and sculpture after paintings by Giovanni Paolo Pannini, a favourite artist with aristocratic Grand Tourists. Fanny Murray paid 2s 3d each for the prints and 8s each for the frames. It is significant that Pond – who was very careful about methods of address – refers to her as 'Fanny Murray' while all his other women clients, even fellow print-sellers, are given the courtesy of 'Mrs', if not a more elevated title; christian names alone are used for domestic servants, and christian names and surnames for engravers employed to make prints – John Wood, James Mason and so on.

3.18

Louis Philippe Boitard (c.1733–67)

The Sailor's Revenge or The Strand in an Uproar, 1749

Etching with engraved lettering, 232 × 300 mm

BM Satire 3035

1868-8-8-3895 Edward Hawkins collection

This sixpenny print records a riot in a brothel in the Strand on 2 July 1749. A group of sailors had been robbed and returned the next day to wreck the premises. The riot was blamed on a young sailor named Bosavern Penlez who was subsequently hanged. The street is thronged with bystanders, most of whom rejoice to see the destruction either because they have been ruined by prostitutes ('The jades have reduced me to a shadow'), because they hope it means they will see more of their husbands ('Now shall I have family duty performed again') or because they are taking advantage of the property hurled

from the window ('A gown for my wife without a robbery'); one woman picks up a box of letters that might provide material for blackmail. Prostitutes and bawds make their escape – one girl *en déshabille* seeks the protection of the sailors' captain, who takes advantage of the situation to fondle her naked breast.

The brothel in question was run by one Peter Wood (*Select Trials at the Sessions House of the Old Bailey*, 1764, vol. 1, p. 271, cited by Carter, Chapter 4). Alex Werner has provided a glimpse of two other London brothels in his study of the probate inventory of Elizabeth Haddock (d. 1752) who, with her husband Richard (d. 1748) and another woman named Sophia Lemoy, ran the New Bagnio, or Turk's Head, at Charing Cross from the early 1720s, and Haddock's Bagnio in Covent Garden from the mid-1740s. The words 'bagnio', from the Italian for bath-house, and 'hummum', from the Turkish, were synonymous with brothel. The Haddocks ran establishments with some

The Sailor's Revenge or the Strand in an Uproar
a Tragi Comical Farce exhibited before a numerous Audience of ye Nobility & others July ye 1st & 2d
NB the Speeches adapted to the Characters
The Scene where the unfortunate Penlez lost his life. Gent Mag. 1749. 228 &c.

Boitard Invt et Sculp.

1749

Price Six-Pence

3.18

pretensions: clients from the nobility and gentry are listed in the inventory as owing sums from a few shillings up to £5. There were up to twenty-five well-appointed rooms available at the Turk's Head and ten at Covent Garden. Furniture was of fashionable mahogany, there were paintings and prints on the walls, and clients were served refreshments on silver and porcelain. The total value of silver at the New Bagnio was £401 and the contents of just one of the best rooms were valued at £52 8s. As well as their London properties, the Haddocks had a luxuriously furnished country retreat at Wotton, near Isleworth, to the west of London.

3.19

Charles Mosley (fl. 1737–56)

The Tar's Triumph, or Bawdy-House Battery, 1749

Etching with engraved lettering,
245 × 334 mm
BM Sat 3036
1868-8-8-3896 Edward Hawkins collection

In another sixpenny print of the so-called Penlez riot, Charles Mosley focuses on just a few figures: a sailor and a prostitute in the foreground tussle for a bedsheet, behind them a girl in her underwear (stays and a long shift) carrying a birch escorts an old gentleman who holds on to his open breeches, a large bare-breasted woman – probably

a bawd – is about to be soaked by the contents of a chamber pot, a figure swathed in sheets is probably intended as a victim of venereal disease; an advertisement for Dr Rock's remedy is attached to the wall (see also cat. 3.27). A bonfire has been made of the brothel's fashionable furniture as well as a box of 'machines' (prophylactic sheaths), an execution broadside and a disparate group of pamphlets: Bernard de Mandeville's *Defence of Public Stews*, the anonymous *Onania or the Heinous Sin of Self-Pollution*, Dr Edward Cobden's *Persuasive to Chastity* and George Whitefield's *Memoirs*. The objects thrown from upstairs windows include the supposed tools of the prostitute's trade: a drawer with more prophylactic

3.19

sheaths, a portable bidet, a birch, boxes of pills and patches, a medicine bottle, a fan decorated with a print of naked woman and an unfortunate cat (open fans symbolized the female genitals and 'cat' was one of many slang terms for a prostitute), a watch that would have been stolen from a customer, and an array of cosmetic aids – false hair, false teeth and a false eye. The latter recall the first lines of Swift's *Beautiful Young Nymph going to Bed* (1731):

Corinna, pride of Drury Lane,
For whom no shepherd sighed in vain;
… Takes off her artificial hair:
Now, picking out a crystal eye,
She wipes it clean, and lays it by
Her eyebrows from a mouse's hide,
Stuck on with art on either side,
Pulls off with care, and first displays 'em,
Then in a play-book smoothly lays 'em.
Now dexterously her plumpers draws,
That serve to fill her hollow jaws.
Untwist a wire; and from her gums
A set of teeth completely comes.

3.20

Two prophylactic sheaths, c.1790

NOT ILLUSTRATED

Animal membrane, one with a silk ribbon, length 208 mm and 190 mm

MME 1953-2-6-1 Presented by Eric J. Dingwall

The condoms shown here are of the type – made from animal gut, re-usable and secured with a ribbon – which James Boswell describes using with 'dull satisfaction' in an encounter with a prostitute in January 1763 (see cat. 5.20) and which can be seen flying from the window of a brothel in cat. 3.19. These contexts illustrate the main purpose of the condom as prophylactic rather than contraceptive.

Condoms were developed in the late sixteenth century, their name traditionally derived from that of Dr Condom, physician to Charles II. By the eighteenth century they were readily available in London.

Poverty

3.21–3.26

A huge proportion of the mid-eighteenth century-population of London lived in poverty, but the poor leave little evidence of their lives. Material remains are few, and most information comes at second hand, through reports written by philanthropists or by the legal authorities. In comparison with the intimate details that are recorded of some famous lives very little is known about poor individuals, and biographies of the poor are almost entirely restricted to those who ended their lives on the gallows, court records and execution broadsides constituting what Linebaugh calls the 'Tyburnography'.

After the dissolution of the monasteries in the mid sixteenth century, responsibility for those who could not take care of themselves was taken over by local parishes and charities. The Poor Law Act of 1601 required every parish to

1.17

1.29

PLATE I

A Perspective View of the North West Front of ye Parish Church of St. Brides, w. the beautiful Spire &c. The Height from the Cross above the Vain to the Ground. is 242 feet. | Vue de L'Eglise Paroissiale de St. Bride dont Son Cloche est de 242 Pieds.

1.39

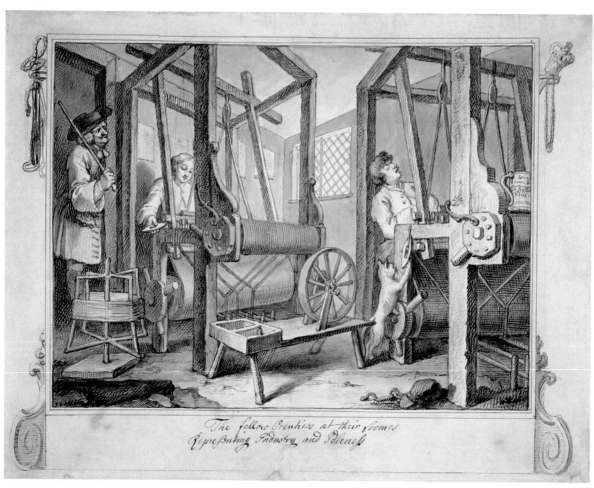

The fellow Prentices at their Looms Representing Industry and Idleness

1.81

PLATE 2

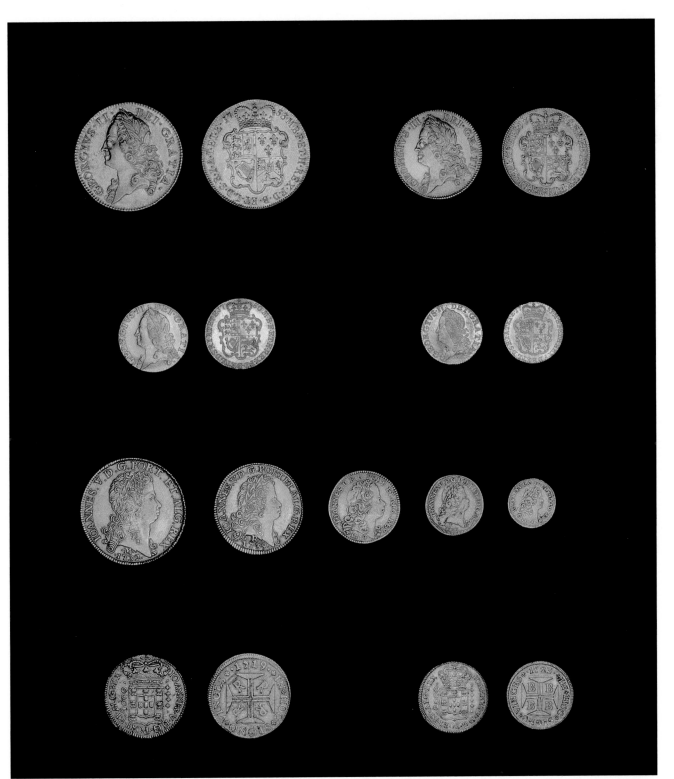

1.41, 1.42

PLATE 3

2.14

2.19

PLATE 4

2.25

2.34

2.35

PLATE 5

2.36

2.38

PLATE 6

2.40

Frederick Zink Painter in Enamel
drawn by William Hoare from his Love
and Friendship as well as many Obligations
to him in the year 1752, Mr Zink being at
that time retired from Business & amusing himself
in painting His own Daughters Picture

2.41

PLATE 7

3.4

3.23

3.35

PLATE 8

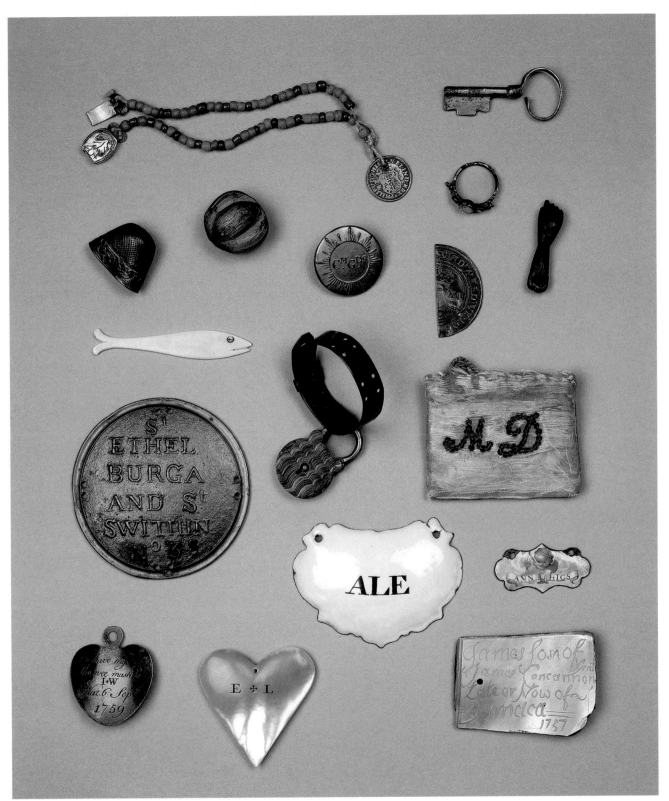

3.38

PLATE 9

3.70

PLATE 10

3.87

PLATE 11

4.2

4.15

PLATE 12

4.25

4.26

PLATE 13

4.27

J. Wale delin.

H. Roberts Sculp.

The Inside of the Elegant Music Room in VAUX HALL GARDENS.

Le dedans du Concert Elegant aux Jardins du VAUX HALL.

Printed for John Bowles at the Black Horse in Cornhil. & Carrington Bowles in St Pauls Church Yard, London.

5

5.55

PLATE 14

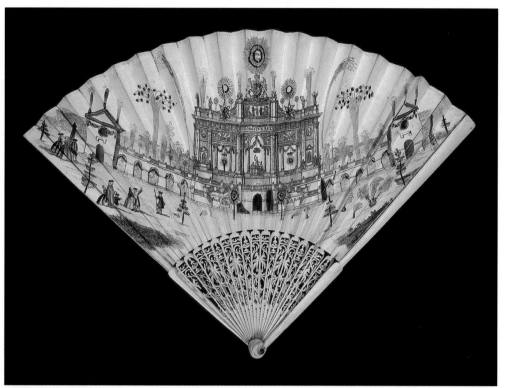

5.28

5.77

PLATE 15

5.95

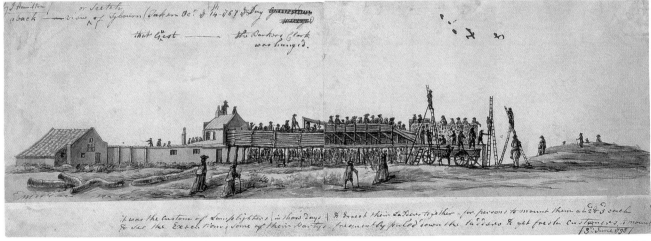

5.97

PLATE 16

levy a poor rate from which to relieve the aged and infirm, to ensure that the able-bodied poor were provided with work, and to care for, educate and in due course to apprentice the children of paupers. By the eighteenth century most urban parishes ran workhouses and charity schools in order to fulfil their obligations, though practical support of other sorts was still provided. In the 1750s public expenditure on the relief of the poor amounted to almost £700,000 a year, and parishes were concerned to provide only for those to whom they had an obligation – those who could genuinely claim rights of settlement by birth, marriage or long residence. Drastic measures were taken to avoid a drain on parish funds, among the worst being the treatment of orphaned children put out to wet-nurses for a flat fee; Thomas Coram's campaign for the Foundling Hospital (cats 3.37–3.43) was largely a reaction to the inadequacies of the parish system of childcare.

Dorothy George's *London Life in the Eighteenth Century* remains the most compelling and most detailed account of the life of the mass of Londoners of the period.

GIN LANE.

3.21

3.21

William Hogarth (1697–1764)

Gin Lane, 1 February 1751

Published by William Hogarth

Etching and engraving with engraved lettering, 385 × 320 mm

Paulson 186 (iii)

S.2-122

Hogarth's most famous image, *Gin Lane*, is set in the poverty-stricken area to the north of Covent Garden, identifiable by the tower of St George's, Bloomsbury in the background. Gin was the plague of London in the first half of the eighteenth century; a series of acts of Parliament in the 1690s had encouraged gin production and stills proliferated, with the result that by 1750 more than one in six houses in this part of London sold gin. Gin was said to be responsible for a lowering of

the birth rate and an increase in infant mortality; despite immigration to London the population began to fall. Acts of 1736 and 1743 were ineffective, but the campaign launched in 1750 – of which *Gin Lane* was a part – led to the Gin Act of 1751 which introduced licensing of retail premises and finally reduced consumption. See Dillon for a detailed account of the eighteenth-century gin trade and its effects.

Gin Lane is a pair to *Beer Street* where healthy working people – butchers, builders, fishwives – are shown consuming flagons of the national brew in contrast to the emaciated drinkers of liquor of foreign origin that has reduced the population to frenzied inebriates.

Hogarth inverts the conventional mother and child image – symbolic of domestic security and good order – with a half-naked drunken woman who fails to notice that her child is falling to certain death. In the foreground a skeletal ballad singer recalls the medieval figure of Death; beyond, a craftsman pawns his tools and a woman her cooking pots, a boy sleeps while a snail crawls on to his shoulder, another shares a bone with a dog, a baby is impaled (a standard image of atrocity), the lame and the blind fight each other and gin is drunk by everyone from babies to young charity girls (identifiable by their uniform caps and aprons and the badges on their sleeves) to an old woman confined to a wheelbarrow. Hogarth's acute observation of the effects of alcoholism is clear in his alteration of the face of the baby falling from his mother's lap in the foreground (as shown here) to show the large eyes, pointed chin and sunken cheeks of what is now described as foetal alcohol syndrome; the child of a gin-drinking mother in cat. 3.27 displays the same symptoms.

Hogarth's friend Henry Fielding (1707–54), novelist and magistrate for Middlesex (that is, the area of London north of the river, excluding the City), was a fellow campaigner for the Gin Act. In January 1750 he published a pamphlet entitled *An Inquiry into the Causes of the Late Increase of Robbers*, blaming gin for the street crime that was causing Londoners much anxiety.

3.22

William Hogarth (1697–1764)

First Stage of Cruelty, 1 February 1751

Etching and engraving with engraved lettering, 385 × 320 mm

Published by William Hogarth

Paulson 187

Cc.2-166

This is the first in a series of four prints telling a story that leads from childhood cruelty to animals, to murder and the gallows (cats. 5.95, 5.96). The distinctive cap (see cat. 3.25) and the badge lettered 'St. G' worn by the protagonist Tom Nero identify him as a child in the care of the parish of St Giles-in-the-Fields, just to the west of Bloomsbury, one of the poorest and most notorious districts.

The *Four Stages of Cruelty*, like *Beer Street* and *Gin Lane*, are often described as popular prints, and Hogarth himself claimed that they were 'calculated to reform some reigning vices peculiar to the lower class of people', but they were priced at 1s each and would have been too expensive for many Londoners. Impressions on better-quality paper – like this one – were aimed at the collectors' market and overstamped

FIRST STAGE OF CRUELTY.

While various Scenes of sportive Woe
The Infant Race employ,
And tortur'd Victims bleeding shew
The Tyrant in the Boy.

Behold a Youth of gentler Heart,
To spare the Creature's pain,
O take, he cries—take all my Tart.
But Tears and Tart are vain.

Learn from this fair Example—You
Whom savage Sports delight,
How Cruelty disgusts the view
While Pity charms the sight.

Designd by W. Hogarth   *Published according to Act of Parliament Feb. 1. 1751.*   *Price 1s.*

3.22

'1s 6d'. Even though these series are more simply executed than Hogarth's more ambitious prints, they are are still far more complex than the sort of sixpenny prints that, for instance, Boitard or Mosley engraved and the Bowleses or Sayer published as run-of-the-mill productions. Dicey's penny prints (cat. 1.32) were the true popular prints of the day and Hogarth's work reached the widest market only through cheap pirated copies (which he, naturally, deplored). In the case of the *Cruelty* series he made a serious attempt to produce accessible copies by commissioning a proficient wood-cutter, J. Bell (see O'Connell, p. 65), to copy his own prints, but in the event only the last two prints in the series seem to have been

copied and they were not published until long after Hogarth's death when John Boydell issued them as collectors' items.

3.23

Louis Philippe Boitard (c.1733–67)

Little Cazey, c.1747

ILLUSTRATED IN COLOUR, PLATE 8

Pen and brown ink with grey wash and watercolour, 187 × 105 mm

1962-7-14-11 Bequeathed by Iolo Williams; ex-collection Leonard Duke

This small boy – evidently known as Little Cazey – was drawn in Bridewell, the former royal palace given to the City by Edward VI to serve both as a short-term prison for petty offenders and disorderly women, and as a school for destitute children. Children normally wore a blue uniform which was renewed annually, but this boy is barefoot and ragged. He is recognizable by his cross-eyes and the same torn coat as the link-boy in cat. 3.3. Such street children were frequently associated with dubious night-time activities and are often depicted suggestively. Reynolds portrayed Cupid as a link-boy (Mannings 1607, 1774) and a shoe-black is described as a willing young prostitute in *The Ladies Whim-Wham*, a bawdy ballad in James Boswell's collection (Harvard University, Houghton Library) full of double-entendres about a game of catcher and ball: 'two frolick-some gentlemen' meet a shoe-black and offer to play him for a bet of a guinea to sixpence, 'And so with his catcher they both went to play / The Boy who was master indeed of the game / He tossed it, and catched it without any pain'.

This sketch, and another in a private collection showing the same boy in a different pose, came from an album of sixty-five drawings by Boitard that remained intact until the 1950s.

3.24
Stock catalogue of John Coles, Stationer, 1750s

Letterpress with woodcut ornaments, 268 × 185 mm

Heal 111.36 Bequeathed by Sir Ambrose Heal, 1959

The commonplace list of forms for the use of Justices of the Peace gives a glimpse of the day-to-day struggle of unfortunate Londoners: warrants for good behaviour, to search for stolen goods, to keep the peace, against drunkeness, to appoint overseers of the poor, to distrain for the poor rate, to 'examine touching the place of settlement', to 'remove such as are returned from the place they were removed to', to summon parish officers 'to show cause why a poor person should not be relieved', to search for stolen wood, to punish wood-stealers, to apprehend vagrants and 'wandering persons', for overseers of the poor to bring in their accounts; mittimuses (warrants for commitment) for gaol or house of correction; passes for vagrants or for poor travellers; hue and cries after highwaymen or house-robbers; summonses for not paying servants' wages; indentures for binding out parish children; examinations of the mother of a bastard child and warrants to apprehend the reputed father, before or after birth; bonds to indemnify a parish from a bastard child, before or after birth.

The stationer John Coles is recorded at the Sun and Mitre, Fleet Street, from 1745 to about 1772.

3.25
Price list of John Hall and John Lodge of the Charity School Warehouse, 1765

Letterpress, 258 × 211 mm

Heal 40.52 Bequeathed by Sir Ambrose Heal, 1959

Most records of eighteenth-century dress relate to the wealthy, but this double-sided list indicates what was seen as the minimum of decent clothing. A man or woman housed in a parish work-house could be clothed for £1 6s 8d, a boy for 18s 5d and a girl for 18s 4d or 18s 6d, presumably according to size. Children wore the sort of uniform head-gear shown in cats 3.21 and 3.22; for boys, 'a knit cap, with tuft and string' at 9d, and for girls, 'a coif and band of fine ghenting [linen]'; boys also had three-penny neck bands. Several pairs of eighteenth-century sculptures of 'parish children' in uniforms of this type survive, outside, for instance, the church of St Andrew Holborn, Peter Hill's School in Rotherhithe and the Greycoat School in Westminster.

The list carries a manuscript receipt

3.24

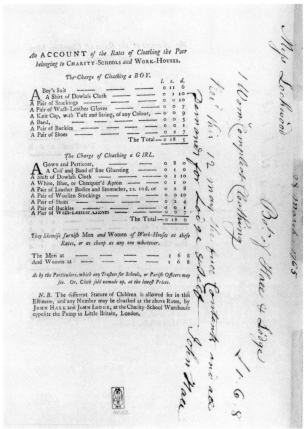

J.B. Cipriani delineavit∙piæque institutioni dicavit.

3.25

3.26

made out by John Hall to a Miss Lockwood, presumably a charitable lady, on 28 March 1765 for a set of clothing costing £1 6s 8d for a woman named A. Alcock.

3.26

After Giovanni Battista Cipriani (1727–85)

Frontispiece to Jonas Hanway, Three Letters on the subject of the Marine Society, 1758

Published by Jonas Hanway

Etching and engraving, 224 × 175 mm

1872-10-12-5145

The Marine Society, founded in 1756, was one of a number of philanthropic initiatives undertaken by Jonas Hanway (1712–86). He was a governor of the Foundling Hospital and founder of the Magdalen Hospital for reformed prostitutes (1758); among the numerous

causes for which he campaigned were improved parish care of poor children and the ending of the use of chimney-sweeping boys (finally banned in 1840) – the *DNB* lists seventy-four books and pamphlets by Hanway. As was the case with the Foundling Hospital (cats 3.37–3.43), the Marine Society's aims combined charity towards individuals with practical benefits for the nation; boys were to be saved from a life of abject poverty by being trained to serve at sea, and in doing so would solve the difficulties of recruitment at a time when the British navy was crucial to national trade and power. Within a year 1,200 boys and 249 men had been recruited by the Society at a total cost of £8,000 for clothing, housing and feeding. Cipriani's design shows kindly gentlemen transforming barefoot urchins into upright young sailors neatly dressed in wide trousers and broad-brimmed hats. The Society, now based in Lambeth, is still active in training for careers at sea.

Tottenham Court Road

3.27–3.31

3.27

Luke Sullivan (c. 1725–71) after William Hogarth (1697–1764)

The March to Finchley, 30 December 1750

Published by William Hogarth

Etching and engraving with engraved lettering, 431 × 553 mm

Paulson 237

1858-6-26-369

On 10 December 1745 three regiments of infantry and one of Horse Guards were ordered to Finchley where William, Duke of Cumberland, had set up camp intending to proceed to Northampton to engage Prince Charles Edward Stuart's Jacobite army. Charles had landed in the Hebrides five months

3.27

earlier, raised a force of five thousand Highlanders and marched south, reaching Derby on 4 December. Fortunately for London, the expected French support failed to arrive and the Jacobites turned north; on 16 April 1746 they were defeated by Cumberland's army at Culloden.

Hogarth's view of the British force assembling at Tottenham Court turnpike – painted after Culloden – gives no sense that this is a power to be reckoned with. George II was supposed to have refused to allow the print to be dedicated to him (hence the dedication to the great military leader and patron of the arts, Frederick the Great of Prussia – who was George's nephew and rival) with the comment: 'I hate painting and poetry

too. Neither the one nor the other ever did any good. Does the fellow mean to laugh at my guards?' The drunken soldiers are surrounded by a mêlée comprising the usual stock of street characters: ballad- and newspaper-sellers, a shoe-black, milkmaid and pieman, a gin-sodden mother. A prize-fighting ring has been set up at the Adam and Eve pleasure garden, and prostitutes lean from the windows of a brothel at the sign of the profligate King Charles II, great-uncle of the Young Pretender; across the way a syphilitic soldier is urinating painfully while eyeing an advertisement for Dr Rock's remedy for venereal disease (see also cat. 3.19).

Hogarth usually employed specialist engravers to make prints after his most

complex compositions, and this print was made by Luke Sullivan, reputedly for a fee of £100. Whereas Hogarth's prints combine etching and engraving, Sullivan has worked almost entirely in etching – a tour-de-force of technical skill learnt from the leading French engraver, Bernard Baron. A squared drawing by Sullivan of the entire composition and a number of tracings by Hogarth of the heads of the principal figures (British Museum) would have been made as preliminary studies. By the late 1740s Sullivan was reputed the best engraver in London. In the 1760s he exhibited with the Society of Artists giving addresses near the Haymarket, but he is said to have died in poverty at the White Bear in Piccadilly; he was

Sold by Andrew Miller at the Coffin, the upper end of Wytch Street, near the New Church in the Strand.

3.28

buried at St James's, Piccadilly, on
27 March 1771.

Hogarth offered the painting of *The March to Finchley* as a prize in a draw of tickets distributed to subscribers to the print; a number of unsold tickets were given to the Foundling Hospital and one of those was drawn – the painting remains in the collection.

3.28

Andrew Miller (d. 1763)

George Taylor, late 1740s

Published by Andrew Miller at the Coffin, the upper end of Wytch Street, near the New Church in the Strand

Mezzotint, 350 × 248 mm

C.S.54 (i)

1902-10-11-3522 Bequeathed by William Eaton, 2nd Baron Cheylesmore

George Taylor (fl. 1737–after 1750) was reckoned as a boxer second only to the great Jack Broughton, who was unbeaten for twenty-four years (*General Advertiser*, 9 April 1750). He was associated with the Great Booth at Tottenham Court, but in 1743 Broughton, who had wealthy backers, erected his Amphitheatre nearby in Oxford Road (Street) and Taylor ended up fighting there. He would have followed the rules laid down by Broughton which were the first to set a framework for fair play in boxing, but fights were still bare-knuckle and lasted until one man could carry on no longer.

An advertisement for a fight at the Amphitheatre between Taylor and James Field appears in Hogarth's print *The Second Stage of Cruelty* (February 1751). Taylor and Field are recorded as having fought at least once, in December 1743 (Gee 1998, p. 20). The inclusion of Field was topical for he was, in fact, hanged within days of the publication of Hogarth's series; his name appears above one of the skeletons displayed in cat. 5.98.

Newspapers were inclined to record erroneously the demise of boxers, and Taylor suffered from such misreporting when the *Daily Advertiser* announced his death on 21 February 1750. On 6 February of the following year, however, he fought and beat the Norwich butcher Jack Slack (Gee 1999, p. 28). By then he was landlord of the Fountain tavern in Deptford. Drawings by Hogarth show Death giving Taylor a cross-buttock (the move for which the boxer was famous) and Taylor triumphing over Death (Tate and Yale Center for British Art). These are thought to be designs for Taylor's tombstone at St Paul's Deptford, but no stone remains. Later sources state that he died in December 1758.

Tony Gee's extensive research in archives and newspapers of the period (see Bibliography) has corrected much misinformation published in nineteenth-century histories of the early days of boxing. A contemporary view of Taylor's reputation is given by Godfrey;

Egan is the best known, but not always reliable, general account of the eighteenth-century prize-ring.

3.29
John Faber (1684–1756) after John Wollaston (fl. 1738–75)
George Whitefield, 1742

Mezzotint, 344 × 251 mm

C.S.382 (i)

1950-5-20-215 Presented by F.W.B. Maufe and Mrs G.B. Lane

George Whitefield (1714–70) was a leader of the evangelical revival that grew in power from the 1730s onwards. He had joined John Wesley's Holy Club at Oxford and developed the practice of highly emotional preaching. The Methodists – as they came to be called – had their greatest impact in Wales, Cornwall and the Midlands as well as in the new colony of Georgia, but Wesley and Whitefield famously preached in open spaces around London such as Moorfields, Kennington Common and Marylebone Fields, and in the prisons of Newgate and the Marshalsea. In cat. 5.96 Hogarth shows Wesley accompanying Tom Idle to his execution at Tyburn. Methodism was most effective among the poor, especially where the established church gave little support, but there was also a strong movement to evangelize the rich, who were most subject to temptation to sin – see cat. 5.72, where the Squanderfields' steward, attempting in vain to mend the ways of his master and mistress, has in his pocket a copy of a book entitled 'Regeneration' (Whitefield's *The nature and necessity of our new birth in Christ Jesus*, a sermon published in three editions, 1737–8). Adherents of the Countess of Huntingdon's Connection – to which Whitefield was chaplain – included a number of members of the aristocracy, but there was also wide suspicion of Methodist denial of the riches of the world – a doctrine which was seen as contemptuous of the values of a

3.29

3.30

commercial society and suspected as a revival of seventeenth-century Puritanism. Hogarth was far from alone in satirizing Methodism: Samuel Foote's play *The Minor* (1760) caricatured Whitefield as Dr Squintum and gave rise to many imitations.

By the 1760s there was a strong movement towards separation from the Church of England whose role at the centre of the national state inevitably threw up conflict with the moral and spiritual tenets of strict Methodism. Secession finally came in 1795, four years after Wesley's death. For an account of the eighteenth-century evangelical revival, with further references, see Langford, pp. 235–87; for the wide range of religious groups of the period see Rudé 1971, pp. 100–17.

Wollaston's painting on which this print is based is in the National Portrait Gallery. The adoring woman in the foreground is said to be Whitefield's future wife, Elizabeth James.

3.30
Anonymous
Whitefield's Chapel, 11 April 1764

Published by J. Jones at the Bible in Fetter Lane, the corner of Clifford's Inn, near Fleet Street

Etching with engraved lettering, 313 × 331 mm

Crace XXXI.14

1880-11-13-4733

Whitefield's Chapel, or Tabernacle, in Tottenham Court Road was the world's largest nonconformist place of worship, seating between seven and eight thousand people. It was built in 1756, and extended in 1760; the American Church now stands on the site, its architecture echoing that of the original building.

The print is larger than the usual sixpenny print and was doubtless intended to encourage attendance at the chapel.

3.31

3.31
William Hogarth (1697–1764)
Enthusiasm Delineated, c.1761

Etching and engraving, 376 × 326 mm (cropped)

Paulson 210

1858-4-17-582

Hogarth demonstrates here a view of Methodism – Enthusiasm – that was widespread. Zealous piety and emotional forms of worship were likened to the excesses of Roman Catholicism – so the preacher has monkish tonsure beneath his wig, figures of saints and Old

Testament characters are displayed (albeit as puppets) around the pulpit, a woman swoons in ecstatic frenzy and, in a reference to the doctrine of transubstantiation, the congregation chew on figures of Christ.

This is one of two proofs of a print (the other is in the Aschenbach Foundation, San Francisco) that Hogarth evidently decided was too offensive for publication. He issued a much-modified version in 1762 under the title *Credulity, Superstition and Fanaticism*.

The British Museum

3.32–3.35

The eminent physician Sir Hans Sloane died on 11 January 1753. His magnificent library and collections of works of art, antiquities and specimens of natural history, valued at £80,000, were left to the nation in return for payment of £20,000 to his daughters. Parliament set up a distinguished board of trustees to take responsibility, not only for the Sloane bequest but also for manuscripts from the collection of Robert Harley, 1st Earl of Oxford, and his son Edward, 2nd Earl, which were passed to the nation, in the same year, by their heir, Margaret Cavendish, Duchess of Portland, for the sum of £10,000. The trustees also took over the care of the extraordinary library of historical manuscripts put together by Sir Robert Cotton (1571-1631) which had been in public hands since 1702 and had been in serious need of rehousing since being damaged in a fire in 1731. In 1757 George II donated to the Museum the Royal Library of 10,500 volumes collected by British monarchs from Henry VIII to Charles II.

Sloane had displayed the collection in eighteen rooms in the manor house at Chelsea, where he had lived in the latter years of his life; he had lived in a house near Bloomsbury Square from 1695 to 1745. It was deemed impracticable to maintain the collection in Chelsea and in April 1754 the trustees decided to purchase Montagu House in Bloomsbury, a seventeenth-century mansion abandoned by John Montagu, 2nd Duke of Montagu, in favour of more fashionable Westminster. A year later the house was handed over to trustees, and repairs to the house and alterations to the garden were put in hand. In 1756 Dr Gowin Knight was appointed as Principal Librarian, Charles Morton as Keeper of Manuscripts Andrew Gifford as Assistant Keeper, and Henry Rimms as Keeper of Natural History. Robert Bramley of Kentish Town was given a gardening contract at £85 a year inclusive of all expenses, although the trustees would pay for all new plants. The first servants were Joseph Markland, porter, Jane Waddell, head maid, and Dorothy Markland, Elizabeth Chaplin and Judith Stanley, maids. The first visitors were admitted on 12 January 1759.

The early years of the Museum's history are discussed in Wilson; for Sloane and his collection see MacGregor.

3.32

Sutton Nicholls (?1668–c.1730)

Montagu House, 1731, this impression published 1754

Published by John Bowles, Print and Mapseller over against Stocks Market

Etching, 331 × 456 mm (cropped)

Crace XXVIII.74

1880-11-13-4411

By 1753 the French taste of 1680s Montagu House had been overtaken by Palladianism. The fifth edition of Stow, published in that year, quoted the *Critical Review of Public Buildings of London* (1734): 'Montagu House has been long, but very ridiculously, esteemed one of the most beautiful lodgings about town. I must own it is grand and expensive, will admit of very noble ranges of apartments within, and fully answers all the dignity of a British nobleman of the first rank. But after I have allowed this, I must add that … the whole front is defective both in beauty and variety.'

This print was first published in 1731 in John Bowles's *London Described* (Adams 29), but was one of thirty-two prints from that volume that were reused (together with more than ninety from other sources) in the 1754 edition of Stow (Adams 37).

3.33

Head of Sophocles, 300–100 BC

Bronze, height 293 mm

Bronze Cat. 847

GR 1760-9-19-1 Presented by Brownlow Cecil, 9th Earl of Exeter; ex-collections Thomas Howard, 2nd Earl of Arundel, and Dr Richard Mead

This magnificent head impressed an otherwise critical early visitor to the Museum: 'I am sorry to acquaint you that the collection of these antiquities is far short of what I hoped to find. Among them, however, there is of brass, a noble bust of Homer' (Anonymous, *Letters on the British Museum*, 1767, pp. 28–9).

3.32

Michael Lort had been less complimentary in a letter to Horace Walpole of 14 March 1762: 'Notwithstanding it bears so great a resemblance to the head in Hollar's print of Lord and Lady Arundel, there are some people pretend to say it is a modern piece, which Sir A[ndrew] Fountayne procured and passed off as a modern copy.'

There are now no doubts as to the antiquity of the head, but it is identified as Sophocles rather than Homer. It would have been originally part of a full-length statue and was probably excavated in Turkey. What is evidently intended to be the same head appears in a print by Wenceslaus Hollar with an allegory on the death of Thomas Howard, 2nd Earl of Arundel (1585–1646), and dedicated to his widow (Pennington 466). Part of Arundel's extraordinary collection of aniquities was sold by his descendants in 1720 and the

head was bought by the great physician and collector Richard Mead. At the posthumous sale of Mead's sculpture at Langford's, Covent Garden, in March 1755, the head was purchased by Brownlow Cecil, 9th Earl of Exeter.

3.34

3·34

Lewis Pingo (1743–1830)

Medal with the head of Richard Mead and, on the reverse, the infant Hercules strangling a pair of snakes, 1775

Silver, diameter 40 mm

MI, i, 72; Eimer 51

Richard Mead (1673–1754) was the leading physician of his day, serving both George I and George II. His international reputation brought, among others, the great French painter Jean

Antoine Watteau to London seeking a cure for consumption. Mead was a pioneer of inoculation against smallpox, laid the foundations of a public health system with proposals for quarantine as a preventative measure against bubonic plague, and was a governor of and honorary physician to the Foundling Hospital (cats 3.37–3.43). His practice earned him between £5,000 and £6,000 a year. In 1720 he settled in Great Ormond Street, where he built a gallery to hold his collections. Friends who joined him at his regular Wednesday-afternoon dining club were painters, sculptors, poets, antiquaries and scientists, many of whom are represented in this exhibition: Richard Bentley, Thomas Coram, Martin Folkes, Edmund Halley, William Hogarth, Alexander Pope, Allan Ramsay, Jonathan Richardson, John Michael Rysbrack, George Vertue.

The image on the reverse of the medal refers to Mead's treatise on poisons (1702) for which he was elected a fellow of the Royal Society; it is based on a bronze group by Alessandro Algardi in Mead's collection (now in the Exeter collection, Burghley House). The medal was designed for the centenary of Mead's birth in 1773 and struck in 1775.

For an account of Mead's collecting see Jenkins.

3.33

3.35
Maria Sibylla Merian (1647–1717)
Passionflower

ILLUSTRATED IN COLOUR, PLATE 8

Watercolour on vellum, 422 × 295 mm

Sloane 5276-87

Two albums from Hans Sloane's collection containing 160 drawings by Maria Sibylla Merian were among the highlights of early visits to the Museum. The trustees insisted that they should not normally be taken off public display in order to be examined by students in the Reading Room: 'Dr Templeman [superintendent of the reading room] is to observe that the miniature paintings of Merian, [Nicolas] Robert and others are not … to be carried into the Reading Room without particular leave; they being in continual use for the amusement of persons coming to see the Museum.'

This drawing is typical of Merian's carefully observed and beautifully composed drawings of insects and plants in watercolour on vellum. They appeared in her two publications: *Der Raupen wunderbare Verwandlung und sonderbare Blumennahrung* (1679) and *Metamorphosis insectorum Surinamensium* (1705). The second volume was based on studies made on a visit to Surinam where Merian did important entomological fieldwork. She corresponded with Sloane and he would have acquired the drawings directly from her.

3.36
Jacques Antoine Dassier (1715–59)
Medal with the head of Hans Sloane, 1744

Bronze, diameter 55 mm

MI, p.589, 234

Private collection

Dassier was a member of a distinguished Swiss family of medallists. From 1740 to 1757 he worked as assistant engraver at the Royal Mint in the Tower of London. In 1741 he published proposals for a series of

3.36

medals of famous men living in England at four guineas for the series or 7*s* 6*d* each. The project was possible only because Dassier was able to strike the medals at the Mint. Concern had long been expressed within Sloane's circle about the lack both of medals of great Englishmen and of the necessary skills to produce them; these concerns were to be specifically addressed by the Society of Arts (see cats 4.5–4.10).

Dassier portrays his eminent scholars and statesmen with an informality that is unusual in the art of the medal. Parallels with the style of Roubiliac and other artists from the St Martin's Lane Academy (see cats 3.44–3.46) are clear.

The Foundling Hospital
3.37–3.43

In 1739 Thomas Coram obtained a royal charter for a Hospital for the Maintenance and Education of Exposed and Deserted Young Children. Orphanages had a long history on the Continent, but puritan England feared that young women would be encouraged into immorality if facilities were provided for unwanted children. Coram and his supporters represented a new concern for those in need, but pity was mixed with mercantile pragmatism and – after four years of wet-nursing and foster care in the country – foundlings were to be taught useful skills that would benefit society: girls were brought up to be

domestic servants; boys as seafarers. Survival rates were remarkably high in comparison with those of children left to the care of the parish under the old poor law system (see pp. 144–5).

Coram's first premises were in Hatton Garden, but building soon began on a 56-acre site in Bloomsbury, and in 1745 the Foundling Hospital opened. Costs had to be met by charitable donations, and fundraising was crucial to the enterprise. Patrons were encouraged to visit the hospital, and a group of artists, led by William Hogarth, recognized the advantage of exhibiting their work in a grand public building where potential clients would gather. They presented a number of impressive paintings: full-length portraits of Coram (by Hogarth), Dr Richard Mead (by Allan Ramsay) and others involved in the project; large history paintings of suitable subjects – *The Finding of Moses* (Francis Hayman), *Moses Brought before Pharaoh's Daughter* (Hogarth), *Hagar and Ishmael* (Joseph Highmore), *The Little Children before Christ* (James Wills); decorative views of other London hospitals by Thomas Gainsborough, Edward Haytley, Samuel Wale, Richard Wilson. The Foundling Hospital became, in effect, the first public art gallery in the country. The chapel with its magnificent organ, a gift from Handel, provided a setting for benefit concerts.

Harris and Simon is a useful introduction to the early years of the Foundling Hospital. See McClure for a more detailed history and Nicolson for a catalogue of the collection. At the time of writing the institution is in the process of developing a new Foundling Museum which will open in 2004. The Coram Foundation continues to provide valuable help for children in difficult circumstances, while the grounds of the Hospital and its colonnades form Coram's Fields, a playground purchased for local children (adults not admitted unless accompanied by a child) by Lord Rothermere after the Hospital was demolished in 1926.

3·37

James McArdell (1729–65) after William Hogarth (1697–1764)

Captain Thomas Coram, 1749

This state published by Laurie and Whittle, 1794

Mezzotint with some scratched lines and engraved lettering, 354 × 256 mm

C.S. 45 (iii); Goodwin 8

1902-10-11-3233 Bequeathed by William Eaton, 2nd Baron Cheylesmore

Thomas Coram (1668–1751) was born in Lyme Regis but made his fortune as a shipbuilder in Massachusetts, where he lived for about ten years from 1693. On his return to England he settled in Rotherhithe, maintaining his interests in America as a trustee of the colony of Georgia and through his scheme to settle unemployed artisans in Nova Scotia. His philanthropic concerns were soon focused, however, on the plight of abandoned children in London and he began a campaign that was to last nearly twenty years to set up an institution where they could be cared for.

Coram had become a national figure, and this print is one of a number based on Hogarth's portrait of 1740. The great wood-engraver Thomas Bewick recalled that in his childhood, around 1760, a woodcut of Captain Coram was among the portraits displayed on cottage and schoolroom walls 'of eminent men who had distinguished themselves in the service of the country, or in their patriotic exertions to serve mankind' (see O'Connell, fig. 4.20).

3·38

Foundling Tokens

ILLUSTRATED IN COLOUR, PLATE 9

Although the artistic collections of the Foundling Hospital remain impressive, the most poignant memorials of its early days are the small tokens left by mothers with their babies in order that they could be identified at a later date if a mother were to return and claim her child. Ledgers recording names and describing tokens are preserved in the Foundling Hospital papers at the London Metropolitan Archive. After 1760 a more systematic procedure was devised whereby each mother left a piece of the fabric of her baby's clothing that could be attached to the ledger. The tokens shown here have been lent by the Foundling Museum. They range from the simplest found objects to specially made mementoes of a mother's affection.

– Child's necklace of coral with a Spanish coin (a half-real of Philip V from the Mexico mint) dated 1736 and a metal clasp engraved with a tulip.

There was considerable use of foreign coin in London in the early to mid eighteenth century, mostly bought by favourable trade balances between Britain and the Portuguese and Spanish empires, though aided by the occasional capture of a French or Spanish treasure ship.

– Key

– Finger ring with a heart-shaped red stone and a tiny gold padlock and key

Will.ᵐ Hogarth Pinx.ᵗ · Ja.ˢ M.ᶜ Ardell Fecit.

Captain Thomas Coram.

Upon whose Petition and Sollicitation The Royal Charter, for y° FOUNDLING HOSPITAL was Granted by his MAJESTY King GEORGE y° Second

Published 1ˢᵗ May 1794 by LAURIE. 17 of October 1739. & WHITTLE, 53 Fleet Street London.

3.37

hanging from it, enamelled with gold lettering reading 'Qui me neglige me perd' ('Take care of me or you will lose me')

– Metal thimble

– Hazel nutshell carved into lobes

– Brass uniform button of a Coldstream Guardsman

– Half a silver shilling of Edward VI, 1550–3. Obverse with the head of Edward VI with the numeral XII (for twelve pence); reverse with legend [POSUI] DEU[M] AD IUTO[REM MEUM] (I have made God my helper).

These shillings and similar ones of Mary I were the only coins to survive Elizabeth I's recoinage of 1560 and were still in use until the great recoinage of 1696 which removed all old hammered coins from circulation and replaced them with machine-struck pieces. There is no obvious reason for the survival of this example for a further half-century, but sharing coins was a popular sentimental gesture and many Foundling tokens were coins clipped into easily identifiable shapes.

– The arm of a small black wooden doll

– Bone fish (a gambling token)

– Child's bracelet with padlock

– Child's silk purse embroidered with the letters 'M D'

– Parish school badge lettered 'St Ethelburga and St Swithin No.38'
Badges of this sort can be seen attached to the sleeves of charity school-children in cats oo and oo. The school must have been run jointly by two City parishes: St Ethelburga-the-Virgin within Bishopsgate and St Swithin London Stone in Cannon Street.

– Enamelled bottle ticket lettered 'Ale'

– Enamelled ticket with a child's face, lettered 'Ann Higs'

– Silver heart engraved 'You have my heart / Tho we must part / IW / Nat. 6 Sept 1759'

– Mother of pearl heart lettered on both sides 'E L' with a cross

This heart may have been left with Elizabeth Lodge who was admitted to the Foundling Hospital on 21 July 1757, as child no. 5199, and died of fits on 3 February in the following year.

– Mother of pearl fragment scratched 'James son of James Concannon Late or Now of Jamaica 1757'

3.39

François Morellon de la Cave (fl. 1725–66) after William Hogarth (1697–1764)

Power of Attorney for the Foundling Hospital, 1739

Etching with engraved lettering, 362 × 218 mm

Paulson 225

1868-8-22-1552 Bequeathed by Felix Slade

3.39

Myriads of Proselites sustain thy Cause;
Throng to thy Altars and obey thy Laws;
From hence, fair Venus, spring those sweet Supplys
To fill the Mansions which to thee arise.

These Mansions rais'd by Patrons kind & great,
Where Babes deserted find a safe Retreat:
Tho Frenchmen sneer; Their boasted first Design,
Brittish Benevolence shall far outshine.

To his Grace John Duke of Bedford, This Plate is humbly Inscrib'd *by his Graces most Dutiful and Obedient Servant Margrett Granville.*

3.40

This document has been described as a subscription ticket, but it is actually a power of attorney authorizing collectors of subscriptions or donations. It would doubtless have been displayed in gathering places such as the coffee houses listed in cat. 3.42; collectors were to pay subscriptions to the Hospital's account at the Bank of England.

Hogarth's design illustrates the pathos of mothers giving up their babies, the kindliness of Coram and the useful futures of the young people leaving the Hospital: girls carrying a spinning wheel, a paper (for keeping accounts) and a broom; boys with a rake and a scythe, or in sailors' uniforms carrying navigation instruments.

3.40
Charles Grignion (1721–1810) and Pierre Charles Canot (1710–77) after Samuel Wale (1721?–86)

A Perspective View of the Foundling Hospital with Emblematic Figures, 14 April 1749

Published by Margrett Granville

Etching and engraving with engraved lettering, 350 × 450 mm

Crace XXXI.67

1880-11-13-4786

The contemporary fame of the Foundling Hospital led to the publication of a great number of engraved views during the 1750s. Although many were purely commercial enterprises, this print and its pair (cat. 3.41) were evidently published in order to

encourage donations. It is dedicated to the Duke of Bedford, an important patron of the Hospital and local landowner (see p. 131). Happy children dance around an emblematic statue of Venus, who was responsible for their birth, and play near a statue of Diana of Ephesus symbolizing the charity that will support them. The verse has a topical anti-French flavour; the over-dressed French gentlemen standing to the right of a channel in the foreground contrast with unpretentious English visitors.

3.41

3.41

Charles Grignion (1721–1810) and
Edward Rooker (*c*.1712–74) after
Samuel Wale (1721?–86)

*A Perspective View of the Foundling
Hospital with Emblematic Figures,*
14 April 1749

Published by Margrett Granville

Crace XXXI.68

1880-11-13-4787

In this pair to cat. 3.40 a statue of
Fortune stands outside the Foundling
Hospital, while Charity stands within.
Sorrowful single mothers make their way
to leave babies at the gate.

3.42

3.42

William Hogarth (1697–1764)

Ticket for a performance of Messiah at the Foundling Hospital, 1750

Etching and engraving with engraved lettering, 115 × 213 mm (plate), 195 × 213 mm (sheet)

Paulson 236

1858-4-17-578

An impression of this ticket at the Handel House, Halle, is completed in manuscript for a performance of *Messiah* at 12 noon on 1 May 1750. The oratorio was first performed in Dublin in 1742; its first London performance was at the Covent Garden Theatre on 23 March 1743. Handel's performances of *Messiah* at the Foundling Hospital every year from 1750 to 1754 not only raised over £7,000 for the Hospital but established the lasting fame of the oratorio.

The note on the ticket asking gentlemen to come without swords and ladies without hoops suggests that it was expected that the chapel would be very crowded. Tickets were sold at 10s 6d at Arthur's Coffee House in St James's Street, Batson's Coffee House in Cornhill, and Tom's Coffee House in Devereux Court. The latter was run by Thomas Twining, whose descendants developed the famous tea company whose headquarters remain at the site of the eighteenth-century coffee house. The emblem of the Foundling Hospital combines the many-breasted Diana of Ephesus, symbolizing charity, and Britannia holding the liberty cap.

3.43

John Faber (1684–1756) after Thomas Hudson (1701–79)

George Frederick Handel, 1749

Published by John Faber at the Golden Head in Bloomsbury Square

Mezzotint with some scratched lines and engraved lettering, 353 × 252 mm

C.S. 175

1902-10-11-1504 Bequeathed by William Eaton, 2nd Baron Cheylesmore

3.43

The mid eighteenth century saw the first performances of two of the best remembered works by George Frideric Handel (1685–1759): *Messiah* (1743, see cat. 3.42) and the *Fireworks Music* (1749, see cat. 5.26). He had been at the centre of the London musical world since settling in the capital in 1712 and - as well as much public adulation - had attracted patronage at the highest level: in 1713 Queen Anne awarded him a pension of £200 a year; in 1717 he wrote the *Water Music* for a riverborne entertainment for George I; in 1727 he composed four anthems for the coronation of George II, including *Zadok the Priest*, which has been performed at every coronation since. From 1720 to 1741 Handel staged opera at the King's Theatre, Haymarket, as well as at the Theatre Royal, Covent Garden, and the Lincoln's Inn Theatre. Thereafter – the fashion for Italian opera having faded – his major works were oratorios, especially *Judas Maccabeus* (dedicated to William Augustus, Duke of Cumberland after the defeat of the Jacobite Rebellion in 1746) and *Messiah*. These were the highlights of Handel's enormously popular annual Lenten seasons at Covent Garden, and he continued to perform even after completely losing his sight.

This two-shilling print is one of two made by Faber after a portrait of 1748 by Thomas Hudson (Miles 34) that the composer took with him on a visit to Germany in 1750; it is now in the Staats- und Universitätsbibliothek, Hamburg. The rage for his music and for portraiture meant that Handel's image was produced in a range of media, from Roubiliac's great statue at Vauxhall Gardens (cat. 5.63) to medals and ceramic busts; for a satirical print see cat. 5.85. For Handel's life and work see Deutsch and Simon.

The St Martin's Lane Academy

3.44–3.46

During the winter of 1735 an Academy was opened in Peter's Court, St Martin's Lane, which was to provide the impulse for the flowering of the visual arts in Britain over the next thirty years. William Hogarth was the prime mover, and until 1747 he and John Ellys took charge of the Academy, but its democratic organizational model was closer to that of the many convivial male social clubs of the period than to a drawing school. Members paid an annual subscription of two guineas in the first year and one and a half guineas subsequently. Life classes with both male and female models took place every weekday evening except during the summer months, and subscribers took turns to set the pose of the model for the evening; sculpture and painting were introduced during the 1740s.

Bignamini lists a total of eighty-three members, between thirty and forty of whom would have been active at any time. The coming together of such a large group of artists provided a critical mass which meant that new artistic developments had immediate impact on a circle of peers. It was through the Academy that the Rococo style came to

London, introduced largely by the French draughtsman Hubert Gravelot, manager 1744–5. The St Martin's Lane artists were highly visible in the two great mid-century opportunities for public exhibition: Vauxhall Gardens (cats 5.45–5.67) and the Foundling Hospital. Artists meeting at the Academy and at the nearby Slaughter's Coffee House also campaigned for professional status through the establishment of a public academy on Continental lines where young artists could receive formal training and regular exhibitions could be held; Hogarth's opposition to the project – which came to fruition with the foundation of the Royal Academy in 1768 – was to alienate him from much of the London artistic community.

See Bignamini for a comprehensive discussion of the St Martin's Lane Academy and earlier London art institutions. For the place of the Society of Arts in developments towards the Royal Academy, as well as in the encouragement of more practical arts, manufactures and commerce, see pp. 18–27.

3.44

William Hogarth (1697–1764)

William Hogarth Serjeant Painter to his Majesty, 1758

Published by William Hogarth

Etching and engraving with engraved lettering, 403 × 352 mm

Paulson 204 (iii)

1847-5-8-2

3.44

This composition shows Hogarth the painter and theorist: his art is portrayed in classical terms in the image of Thalia, the muse of comedy, and his book, *The Analysis of Beauty* (1753), leans against the easel. The only indication that his fortune and reputation had been made in the less elevated trade of engraver is a burin resting on a shelf behind the easel. The small painting, now in the National Portrait Gallery, on which the print is based, originally included one of the artist's favourite pug dogs urinating on a pile of old master prints, but – perhaps in a bid for respectability – he painted out the dog in the final version.

Hogarth produced this self-portrait to celebrate his appointment to the post of Serjeant Painter to the King. The post had been held by his teacher and father-in-law James Thornhill who had been knighted the year after he was appointed, and the ever-ambitious Hogarth must have hoped for the same recognition. Perhaps because of his notoriously uncompromising attitude and his opposition to the idea of a royal academy which George III was to support, no such honour came his way. Subsequent states of the print chart increasing disillusion: Hogarth's face takes on a grimmer expression and, by the time he made the final alterations in the last year of his life, the muse Thalia held the mask of a mocking satyr and his title had been scratched through as though to suggest that it – or he – was worthless.

Carpentier p[t].

Lewis Francis Roubilliac

a proof touched by Mr. Martin

D. Martin fec
1765

3.45

3·45

David Martin (1737–97)
after Adriaen Carpentiers
(c.1739–78)

Louis-François Roubiliac, 1765

Published by David Martin

Mezzotint touched with white heightening, 377 × 255 mm

C.S.6 (i)

1852-10-9-224

Louis-François Roubiliac (1702–62), the great French Huguenot sculptor, settled in London about 1730. He came to fame in 1738 with his first major commission in Britain, the statue of Handel for Vauxhall Gardens in 1738 (see pp. 237–41). His style is a perfect Rococo blend of informality and grace, combined with a theatrical flair that is particularly evident in his grand funerary monuments in Westminster

Abbey and in the tomb of John Montagu, 2nd Duke of Montagu, at Warkton, Northamptonshire. Roubiliac's compositions – though extraordinarily lively and imaginative – demonstrate his wide knowledge of European sculpture, much of which would have been gained by studying prints. Roubiliac was manager of the St Martin's Lane Academy 1746–7, and he appears to have introduced some teaching of sculpture.

He is shown here working on the model for the marble figure of Shakespeare that he made for David Garrick in 1758; the model is now in the Folger Shakespeare Library in Washington D.C. and the sculpture was bequeathed by Garrick to the British Museum.

The portrait of Roubiliac by Carpentiers (now in the National Portrait Gallery) on which the mezzotint was based hung in the London house of the Scottish Member of Parliament Robert Alexander. David Martin was primarily a portrait-painter, but he made a number of mezzotints in the mid-1760s (see C.S.) when he was working in London as principal assistant to his fellow Scot and former master Allan Ramsay. Both artists were members of the St Martin's Lane Academy; each year from 1759 to 1761 Martin won Society of Arts premiums of up to ten guineas for drawings made at St Martin's Lane by artists under the age of twenty-four. In 1765 he was lodging with a hosier in Oxford Road (Street) opposite Poland Street, Soho. In his late forties Martin returned to Scotland, where he established himself as Edinburgh's leading portrait-painter.

3.46

Richard Earlom (1743–1822)
after James McArdell (1729–65)

James McArdell, 1771

Published by Robert Sayer, no. 53 Fleet Street

Mezzotint , 450 x 326 mm

C.S. 28 (i); Wessely 41

1902-10-11-894 Bequeathed by William Eaton, 2nd Baron Cheylesmore

James McArdell was the most talented of a group of Irish mezzotinters who came to London in the 1740s and raised the standards of what had become a somewhat tired medium; see 5.31 for a particularly fine example of McArdell's work. The technique had been invented in the mid seventeenth century as a means of reproducing the bold contrasts of light and shade of contemporary

3.46

paintings and was much used for portrait prints. McArdell formed a particularly fruitful professional relationship with the young Joshua Reynolds and made thirty-eight mezzotints after his portraits. Reynolds – the consummate professional – was aware of the importance of prints in spreading his reputation, and famously acknowledged that he would be 'immortalized' by McArdell. As painted portraits took on some of the pretensions of history painting so mezzotints increased in size, designed to be framed and hung on the wall rather than kept in albums. This print,

after a self-portrait drawing, was made by Richard Earlom six years after McArdell's premature death and demonstrates the increasing boldness and scale of the medium. He portrays himself not with a portrait print of the type that made up most of his production but with a print after an old master: Van Dyck's *Time Clipping Cupid's Wings* (Goodwin 209).

STAND COACHMAN, OR THE HAUGHTY LADY WELL FITTED.

At a Toy Shop hard by Charing Crofs t'other Day, | But being that Favour moft rudely denied. | The Mobb seeing this, they all laugh'd at the Whim, | The Lady much ruffled, soon alter'd her Tone,
A Lady's Coach ftood quite acrofs the Foot Way: | By John on the Box, and his Lady beside; | And fwore 'twas as free for the reft, as for him; | And call'd to her Coachman in hafte to move on:
A Person did civily th' Coachman intreat | The Gentleman, finding that Words would not do, | So hoifting each other, juft like a Ship's Crew | 'Tis hop'd the fair Ladies from hence will beware,
To pull up, and let him pafs over the Street: | He op'nd the Coach Doors, and genteely went thro': | Befpatter'd and dirty, began to march thro': | How they ftop a Free Pafsage with such haughty Air.
Taken from Life, and Publish'd according to Act of Parliament, for J. Wakelin in Flower de Luce Court, Fleet Street. Price 6.d —1750.

3.47

Charing Cross

3.47–3.54

3.47

Anonymous

Stand Coachman, or the Haughty Lady Well Fitted, 1751

Published by J. Wakelin in Flower de Luce Court, Fleet Street

Etching with engraved lettering, 205 × 290 mm

BM Satire 3085

1870-5-14-2833

For Samuel Johnson 'the full tide of human existence' was at Charing Cross. This sixpenny print shows something of the range of people who might be

encountered there: from a grand lady who owns a gilded coach to a diminutive chimney boy, a ragged newsboy, toothless crossing-sweeper, foppish wig-maker's man and a hurdy-gurdy player. The scene depicts a reportedly true incident that took place in the winter of 1750 outside Mary Chenevix's famous toyshop at the sign of the Golden Door, Suffolk Street: a lady refused to move her coach although it was blocking the path and so a gentleman opened the door of the coach and climbed through, only to be followed by 'the mob … bespattered and dirty' – the lady quickly moved on. Behind the coach is a glimpse of the shop, its window full of vases and decorative figures including a *budai*, like those bought by Hogarth's Viscountess Squanderfield (cat. 5.72). Eighteenth-century 'toyshops' were designed for

adults not children, selling jewellery and other small luxuries.

The 'great toy-shop … at the end of Suffolk Street, Charing Cross' was well established by 1729, when on 17 September the foundations of the building gave way owing to the collapse of a sewer in heavy rain (*Weekly Journal: or, British Gazetteer*, 20 September 1729); the sewer dated back at least to the 1660s (see Barton, pp. 62–7). The shop was owned by the Huguenot goldsmith Paul Daniel Chenevix (d. 1742), but it is likely that – as was common practice – he concentrated on practical work while his wife ran the shop and kept accounts. Mrs Chenevix was particularly well suited to that role, being the daughter of another toyshopman, John Deard (see cat. 5.83); she outlived her husband by thirteen years and continued to run the shop with great success. According to Horace Walpole she was 'famous for her high prices and fine language' (Common Place Book, Waldegrave collection); on 15 September 1746 Walpole wrote to Horace Mann that he had taken their mutual friend the Marquis Rinuncini to see the sights of the town: 'palaces and Richmond gardens and park, and Chenevix's shop'. A year later he took over from Mrs Chenevix the lease of the house near Twickenham that was to become Strawberry Hill (see p. 208).

The print was advertised in the *General Advertiser* on 18 January 1751.

3.48
Anonymous

Bill head of Peter Russel at Chenevix's Toy Shop facing Suffolk Street, Charing Cross, 1759

Etching and engraving with engraved lettering, 65 × 204 mm (plate), 162 × 207 mm (sheet)

Heal 119.30 Bequeathed by Sir Ambrose Heal, 1959

Peter Russel was married firstly to Hannah Hoare, sister of the painter William Hoare of Bath It seems that he was married secondly to Mary Chenevix, widow of Paul Daniel Chenevix (see cat. 3.47), but records conflict. This bill shows that Russel was running the former Chenevix shop in 1759; he is again recorded there in *Mortimer's Director* in 1763.

The bill is made out to Mrs Turnour, wife of the future Earl Winterton (see cat. 3.82), who has bought a pair of gold shoe buckles. The gold cost £1 6s while the work of making the buckles is charged separately, as was usual, at 13s. In 1759 Caroline Fox, wife of Henry Fox (cat. 4.21), purchased a pair of buckles, this time of silver, from Mrs Chenevix for her sister Emily, Countess of Kildare, who sent frequent commissions from Ireland for luxury goods to be purchased in London shops (Tillyard, pp. 171–2).

3.49
Bill head of Rachel Laggatt, 1759

NOT ILLUSTRATED

Engraved lettering, 72 × 154 mm (plate), 182 × 155mm (sheet)

Heal 66.41 Bequeathed by Sir Ambrose Heal, 1959

Rachel Laggatt's simple undecorated bill head suggests a less extravagant shop than Mrs Chenevix's. Situated a few hundred yards to the north in Great Newport Street near Leicester Square, the shop stocks: 'all sorts of the finest diamond cut glass, flint glasses, china, finest stone ware, English and Dutch tiles, Liverpool ware, and glass bottles, etc.'. The goods sold on this occasion were: 'two fine enamelled Chelsea china figures [see cats. 5.38–5.50], £1 10s, four white enamel beakers, 6s; one large brown tea pot and cover, 2s'.

The bill, dated 27 March 1759 – and, unusually, paid 'at the same time' – is made out to the future Earl Winterton (see cat. 3.82) and is receipted by the shopkeeper's son, Philip Laggatt. It is probable that what was for this wealthy family a small purchase was made by a servant: Tillyard (p. 175) records that in Henry Fox's household the housekeeper Mrs Fannen 'took charge of all household goods, and Emily [Fox's sister-in-law the Countess of Kildare, normally resident in Ireland] wrote directly to her when she needed crockery and china from London'.

3.50
Robert Clee (?1711–73)

Trade card of Maydwell and Windle's Cut-glass Warehouse, c.1755–65

Etching and engraving with engraved lettering, 268 × 190 mm

Heal 66.44 Bequeathed by Sir Ambrose Heal, 1959

The Maydwell family were in the glass business from at least 1675 when James Maydwell was a member of the Worshipful Company of Glass Sellers.

3.48

Two men named Glisson Maydwell are recorded successively at the King's Arms, Strand, from 1708 to 1736. Like Mary Chenevix, the widow of the second Glisson Maydwell ran the shop until about 1750, when it was taken over by George Maydwell & Company. Richard Windle became a partner in 1751 and the firm traded as Maydwell and Windle until about 1770. It continued under other ownership until 1810. Windle almost certainly had a family connection with the glassmakers Weatherby, Crowther, Quintin & Windle of East Smithfield, who supplied glass for cutting to specialists such as Maydwell and Windle or Betts (cat. 3.51); by 1765 there are thought to have been twelve glass-cutting workshops in London.

This elaborate Rococo card not only lists the 'curious glass-work' sold but shows examples of cut-glass salvers, jelly glasses, candelabra and a ewer similar to cat. 3.52. At the bottom of the sheet are two vignettes with workers at the glass-cutting machine and the glass-grinding machine; the man on the left is cutting a glass sphere for a chandelier using a wheel powered by an assistant, while on the right a man is grinding a decanter on a circular horizontal disk driven by a crank which he turns with his left hand.

Hilary Young has argued that, although many trade cards are made up of plagiarized elements, there is good reason to think that the objects shown here are authentic Maydwell and Windle pieces.

3.51
Anonymous
Bill head of Thomas Betts, Glass-cutter, 1747

NOT ILLUSTRATED

Etching with engraved lettering, 60 × 192 mm (plate), 169 × 211 mm (sheet)
Heal 66.4 Bequeathed by Sir Ambrose Heal, 1959

This bill is for 9s 6d to pay for '2 glasses fitted to silver', probably epergne dishes made for a silver stand, and a 'pair neat quarts stopt and hollo'd' (a pair of quart decanters, with stoppers, shallow cut). It is made out to Mr Clayton of Brook Street, Mayfair, and signed by Thomas Smith, one of Thomas Betts's employees.

Alex Werner's research into the documentary records of Betts's career (Werner 1985) tells us a good deal about his life in particular and the glasscutting trade in general. In 1742 he had moved from Hart Street, Bloomsbury, to the King's Arms Glass Shop opposite Pall Mall on the north side of Cockspur Street, Charing Cross, from which he issued this bill and where he was to remain until his death in 1765. The premises was still a glass shop as late as 1793. It consisted of two houses joined together and was insured by Betts for £200. He did not own a furnace, purchasing glass from the Whitefriars factory, near Fleet Street, and probably also from the makers of fine coloured glass in Southwark. In 1756 he took a lease on a house in Lewisham where he had access to water-power, making redundant the hand-operated machinery that he would have used previously (see cat. 3.50), and much of the work of glass-cutting must have moved out of town. Betts owned a punt which

3.50

would have carried glass along the Ravensbourne running from Kent to join the Thames at Deptford Creek; from there glass would have been shipped upstream to Charing Cross.

Betts's annual turnover was about £5,000. At his death in 1765 his stock in trade and equipment were valued at £3,094 14s 5¼d and other assets brought his estate up to more than £10,000. The probate inventory of the two houses listed four paintings, a number of framed prints including a set of Hogarth's *Harlot's Progress*, a chariot and a pair of grey coach horses with harness, clothes – including three pairs of spectacles – valued at £11, a gold watch and seal with a steel chain modestly valued at £8 8s, and eighty-nine books including Samuel Richardson's *Pamela*. Betts's possessions – comfortable, but by no means extravagant – portray him as a typical successful tradesman of the sort that Hogarth and Richardson admired; his Lewisham house would have been a suburban retreat as well as a workshop – like Hogarth's house at Chiswick – with three good bedrooms, one decorated with India paper (see cats. 3.68, 3.69) and a summer house in the garden.

Life was not so attractive for workers in the glass-cutting trade. A skilled cutter earned between £2 and £3 a week, while journeymen earned 15s and labourers (like the man turning the wheel in cat. 3.50) earned 12s. Colebron Hancock, the son of a poor clergyman, was apprenticed to Betts in 1752 (his indenture fee of £20 paid by a charity) and ten years later he was running his own shop in nearby Suffolk Street. Others did not succeed so well: on 18 October 1744 Betts put a notice in the *Daily Advertiser* reporting that an apprentice had run away and threatening action against anyone harbouring him, 'Andrew Pawl ... is tall, has a thin meagre look, is very much pockfretten, with very small grey eyes, and a large scar on his forehead; he had on when he went away, a cinnamon colour coat, and a Dutch frieze [coarse woollen cloth] waistcoat. Note – he is a Bohemian, and speaks good English.' Bohemian

cut-glass was renowned, and Pawl presumably came to Betts through some trading contact. In 1751 another young man applied successfully to the courts to be discharged from his apprenticeship with Betts. Richard Lidgley was suffering from lead poisoning from exposure to dust breathed in while working at a machine cutting and polishing glass which had a high proportion of lead: 'the motion [of the glass-polishing machine] was so exceeding swift that it forces or throws out a great effluvia of the pernicious particles from the lead which has not only affected the said Richard Lidgley's nerves but, as the said Richard Lidgley

was advised (by persons skilled in physick), his intestines also and that if the said Richard Lidgley should continue much longer in the said trade he must immediately die, having at several times had very severe fits occasioned by the said effluvias'.

3.52

Helmet-shaped jug with massive loop handle and domed foot, the body cut with a pattern of shallow diamonds and the rim with deep bevelled curves

Blue glass, height 250 mm
MME 2001,7-6,1

3.52

3.53

3.54

Jean Guien (fl. *c.*1762)

Page 6 of Livre d'Ouvrages de Joüaillerie, October 1762

Published by François Vivares

Etching and engraving with engraved lettering, 165 × 242 mm

1930-6-17-31

The designs shown here are for earrings, finger rings, buckles, the lid of a circular box and other decorative metalwork.

Jewellery and Toys
3.55–3.65

The following pieces have been chosen to indicate the luxury items that would have been offered for sale in Chenevix's and other toyshops in mid-century London. Cats 3.57–3.64 are close to designs in the pages of Jean Guien's *Livre d'Ouvrages de Joüaillerie* shown above. Cats 3.65 and 3.66 would have been copied from prints engraved after paintings and intended primarily as reproductions of works of art rather than as designs for artisans.

This beautiful jug is one of a pair that were formerly the property of Lord Suffield of Gunton Park, Norfolk, and may have been acquired from Betts by his ancestor Sir William Harbord (d. 1770). The other jug of the pair is now in the Corning Museum of Glass, New York. They are attributed to Thomas Betts on stylistic grounds. Betts's probate inventory (see Werner 1985) lists two large blue ewers 'unfinished' in his ware room at Lewisham. A similar jug appears on Maydwell and Windle's trade card.

snuff box, to either side at the top are two designs for circular lids and below them elaborate seals; see cats 00 – 00 for similar pieces.

The book, consisting of six sheets sewn together, sold for 3s. Pattern books of this sort made to suggest ideas to artisans were a large but specialised field within print publishing from its earliest days and they played a major role in the rapid transmission of new designs throughout Europe.

3.53

Jean Guien (fl. *c.*1762)

Title page of Livre d'Ouvrages de Joüaillerie, October 1762

Published by François Vivares

Etching and engraving with engraved lettering, 165 × 242 mm

1930-6-17-26

The London jeweller Jean Guien is known only from this ornament book. He was very likely a member of the Huguenot community that was centred on Soho, and the patterns shown here are typical of the period. At the centre of the title page is a design for the lid of an oval

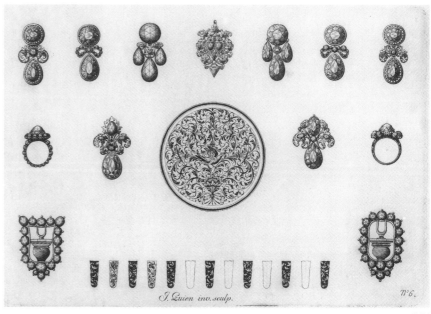

3.54

3.55

3.55
Buckle, c.1762

Silver set with paste, width 41 mm

Hull Grundy 86

MME 1978,10-2,1212 Presented by
Professor and Mrs John Hull Grundy

3.56
Finger ring,
first half of 18th
century

3.56

Gold, enamelled, set with diamonds,
diameter 22 mm

Dalton 2089

MME Af.2061 Bequeathed by Sir
Augustus Wollaston Franks, 1897

3.57
Finger ring,
first half of the
18th century

3.57

Gold with a ruby set in
silver with sparks of diamond,
diameter 25 mm

Dalton 2090

MME 1872,6-4,444 Castellani collection

3.58
*Finger ring
commemorating the
wedding of George III
and Queen Charlotte*, 1761

3.58

Gold and white enamel, set with garnets,
diameter 18 mm

Dalton 1420

MME Af.1492 Bequeathed by Sir
Augustus Wollaston Franks, 1897

The bezel is in the form of two hearts
joined together and surmounted by a
crown, all in garnets. The hoop is
inscribed 'George & Charlotte United
1761', reserved in gold on a ground of
white enamel.

3.59
*Seal die, the handle in the form of
the head of an African*, mid 18th
century

Sard with gold mount, the handle of agate
and gold set with rubies and amethysts,
length 210 mm

Tonnochy 397

MME 1927-2-16-183 Presented by Mill
Stephenson; ex-collection G.B. Croft
Lyons

The seal has an unidentified coat of arms
impaling that of Choke of Avington.

3.60
Seal die, mid 18th century

Sard with gold mount, length 175 mm

Tonnochy 400

MME 1927-2-16-185 Presented by Mill
Stephenson; ex-collection G.B. Croft
Lyons

The seal has the coat of arms of
Codrington.

3.61
Seal die, mid 18th century

Sard with gold mount, length 140 mm

Tonnochy 396

MME 1927-2-16-188 Presented by Mill
Stephenson; ex-collection G.B. Croft
Lyons

The seal has the coat of arms of
Chetwynde impaling Grober.

3.62
Seal die, mid 18th century

Sard with gold mount, length 200 mm

Tonnochy 423

MME 1927-2-16-184 Presented by Mill
Stephenson; ex-collection G.B. Croft
Lyons

The seal has the coat of arms of Fellow
impaling Germin or Holgrave.

3.59   3.60   3.61   3.62

3.63

3.64

3.63

Ishmael Parbury (*c.*1697–1746)

Plaque with a scene of Alexander and Roxanna after Antoine Coypel, 1745

Gold, 62 × 83 mm (now set as the lid of a 19th-century tortoiseshell box)

MME 1997,7-7,1 Purchased with the help of the Heritage Lottery Fund and the British Museum Friends; ex-collection George III

Parbury was one of the most accomplished gold-chasers of his generation. George Vertue (III, pp. 62 and 134) made the following obituary note mentioning this box: 'Mr Ishmael Parbury. Gold chaser of watches, etc. of Salisbury Court [near Fleet Street] deceased in September 1746 ... He was a man in his art of great excellency in the neatness and finishing correctness of his works, which gained him great esteem above any other Englishman and by that means he obtained the highest prices for his works. One piece, or rather master piece, being top of a gold snuff box he kept till his death (dated 1745) with his name to it, was sold at the sale of his collections. His collections sold for 258 pounds ... [he] was a man near fifty years of age.' Parbury was evidently a close friend of the other leading chaser of the time, the

Swiss George Michael Moser who acted as his executor.

Chasing is the technique of modelling metal with hammer and steel tools. By the mid eighteenth century it was well-established as a fashionable means of decorating gold, especially small objects such as boxes and watch-cases.

The scene shown is the marriage of Alexander the Great and Roxanna, the daughter of a king whom he had defeated. It is based on a tapestry cartoon of 1684–6 by Antoine Coypel (now in the Mobilier National, Paris), probably through the intermediary of a print by François Morellon de la Cave; a print of the subject was included in the posthumous sale of Parbury's collection.

The plaque was in the collection of George III, who had it mounted as a presentation snuff box before giving it to his private secretary Sir Herbert Taylor in the early nineteenth century.

For gold-chasing of the period see Edgcumbe.

3.64

Henry Manly (fl. 1730s–*c.*1772)

*Watch-case with a scene of the Sacrifice of Iphigenia, c.*1760

Gold, diameter 54 mm

MME 1888,12-1,249 Bequeathed by Octavius Morgan

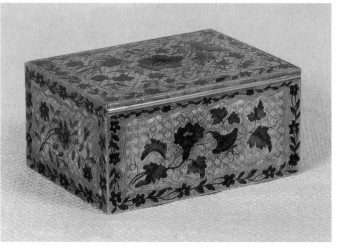

3.65

Manly was another leading London chaser of the mid-century. His work is known today from about twenty-five pieces, chiefly watch-cases. He was evidently based in the City in the early years of his career when he married Sarah Brawne on 13 August 1733 at St Benet's, Paul's Wharf, but by 1737 he was living in the western suburb of Knightsbridge.

For Iphigenia see cat. 5.34.

3.65
Box, 1760s

Gold and enamel, 630 × 450 × 300 mm
MME 1873,3-22,3 Bequeathed by Lady Frances Vernon Harcourt

This box is based on a French design, but was probably made in Germany. It is said to have belonged to Queen Charlotte and to have been given by her to a member of the Harcourt family.

Print-sellers
3.66–3.69

3.66
Anonymous

Trade card of Dorothy Mercier, Printseller and Stationer, c.1760

Etching with engraved lettering, 254 × 150 mm
Banks 100.69
D.2-3391 Sarah Banks collection, presented 1818

Dorothy Clapham married the painter and printmaker Philip Mercier (c.1689–1760) in 1735. They were based in York from 1739 to 1751, and he – presumably with his wife – visited Ireland, Scotland and Portugal between 1747 and 1752 before returning to London where he died eight years later.

The card shows the elegant interior of Mrs Mercier's shop in Windmill Street, Soho, with prints on the wall and stacked on shelves. The proprietress is dressed

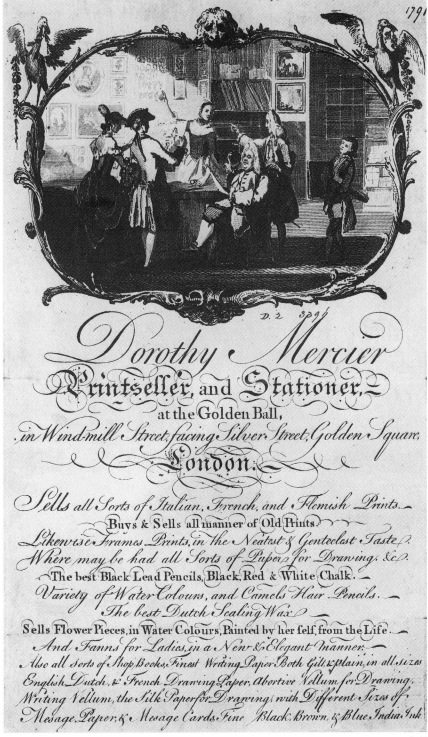

Dorothy Mercier Printseller, and Stationer, at the Golden Ball, in Wind-mill Street, facing Silver Street, Golden Square, London.

Sells all Sorts of Italian, French, and Flemish Prints. Buys & Sells all manner of Old Prints. Likewise Frames Prints, in the Neatest & Genteelest Taste. Where may be had all Sorts of Paper for Drawing, &c. The best Black Lead Pencils, Black, Red & White Chalk. Variety of Water Colours, and Camels Hair Pencils. The best Dutch Sealing Wax. Sells Flower Pieces, in Water Colours, Painted by her self from the Life. And Fanns for Ladies, in a New & Elegant manner. Also all sorts of Shop Books, Finest Writing Paper Both Gilt & plain, in all sizes English, Dutch, & French Drawing Paper, Abortive Vellum for Drawing, Writing Vellum, the Silk Paper for Drawing, with Different Sizes of Mesage Paper, & Mesage Cards, Fine Black, Brown, & Blue India Ink.

3.66

modestly in cap and plain dress in contrast to her female customer with her fashionable hat and lace-trimmed sleeves and the men with their extravagant wigs. A foot-boy stands to one side holding a large portfolio and roll of prints.

Unlike most printsellers, Dorothy Mercier did not publish prints, although she did sell her own watercolours of flowers, and ladies' fans perhaps also painted by herself. The prints she sold were imported from Italy, France and Flanders and she bought and sold 'all manner of old prints'. She also framed prints and sold the full range of drawing materials, different types of paper and vellum, pencils and brushes, chalks, watercolours and inks, as well as stationery for genteel uses – message cards, writing paper and vellum and shop books.

3.67

Anthony Walker (1726–65)

*Trade card of Thomas Jefferys, Engraver, Map and Printseller, c.*1750

Etching with engraved lettering, 261 × 189 mm (cropped)

Banks 100.64 Sarah Banks collection, presented 1818

This elegant trade card advertises stock of a high quality: portfolios of fine prints, including engravings by William Hogarth, Thomas Major, Andrew Lawrence, and Jacques-Philippe le Bas; mezzotints by John Faber, James McArdell, John Simon; maps by Herman Moll and John Senex. Thomas Jefferys (*c.*1719–71) was an ambitious, and largely successful, publisher – he was Geographer to Frederick Prince of Wales at the age of twenty and to George III from 1761 to the end of his life – but in 1766 he over-extended himself with an expensive project to publish a series of county maps. Robert Sayer saved him from bankruptcy by helping to pay his debts and, evidently in return, acquired control of much of Jefferys' stock. Two years later the two men were involved in

3.67

an incident that illuminates a corner of the international print trade of the period: they travelled to Paris with a stock of maps and prints for sale, but their trip ended after two months with an early-morning visit from the Commissioner of Police and the Inspector of the Book Trade, who seized three bundles of what were described as indecent prints. Although Jefferys and Sayer may have been selling pornography, it is much more likely that the prints showed no more than the sort

of mildly titillating images that were commonplace in London and Paris, and that the real objection of the Parisian authorities was that they were competing with French publishers. See Pedley for an account of the incident and references to manuscript sources in Paris.

In the Royal collection is a drawing by Paul Sandby of Jefferys asleep on a chair; another informal drawing of him by Sandby (whose prints Jefferys stocked) is in the British Museum.

3.68

Matthew Darly (*c*.1720– *c*.1779)

Trade card of Matthew Darly's Manufactory for Paper Hangings at the Acorn facing Hungerford, Strand, 1750s

Etching and engraving with engraved lettering, 253 × 183 mm

Banks 91.7

D.2-3238 Sarah Banks collection, presented 1818; ex-collection Joseph Gulston

Matthew Darly is best remembered for satirical prints published with his wife Mary in the 1760s and 1770s, but this card indicates that for a while at least he concentrated on the new fashion for wallpaper, as well as jobbing engraving of 'visiting tickets, coats of arms, seals, book plates, frontispieces and shop-keepers bills', the latter term referring to the type of trade card shown here. Darly's stock was not always so innocuous: in 1749 he had been prosecuted for selling obscene and seditious prints. In 1754 he engraved the plates for Thomas Chippendale's *Director* (fig. 3) and his own *New Book of Chinese Designs*, which was used at the Bow and Worcester porcelain factories by enamellers and textile printers. By 1762 the Darlys had taken the sign of the Acorn (shown on this card) to Ryder's Court, Fleet Street (Clayton, p. 215), but by 1772 they had returned to a shop in the Strand – no. 39 on the corner of Buckingham Street, almost opposite the old Manufactory for Paper Hangings. No. 39 Strand appears as the Macaroni Print Shop in Darly's print after Edward Topham of 1772 (BM Satire 4701).

Wallpaper developed in the late seventeenth century and improved over the following decades, especially when manufacturers started to paste sheets together before printing so that paper could be bought in rolls as shown on this card. By the middle of the eighteenth century it had replaced gilded leather, and to a large extent textiles, for lining the walls of fashionable houses. John

3.68

Baptist Jackson set up a company in 1752 to market 'paper hangings, printed in oils' and in 1753 George Bickham advertised 'China pictures' that would 'join top, bottom, and sides … to make one running grand subject' (Clayton, p. 98). Wallpaper was used in decoration of Buckingham House in 1763. The Lord Chamberlain's accounts (quoted in Smith, p. 76) show that the Prince of Wales's nursery was hung with 'fine verditure [vert de terre or terre-verte, a bluish green] blue' at a cost of £1 10s. Other rooms were decorated with chintz paper, gothic paper, green varnished

paper and crimson mock-embossed paper, all with borders, for equally modest sums, but £84 3s was paid for 611 yards of 'fine linen covered with Cumberland and Imperial paper printed four times over a fine verdeterre blue', to decorate three roooms on the ground floor, and this was accompanied by a further outlay of £76 1s 6d for 830 feet of 'broad papier machee border, very rich in burnished gold'.

The verso of this card is annotated with a number 'N.13245' and price, 3*d*, identifying it as coming from the enormous collection of Joseph Gulston

3.69

Anonymous

Trade card of Masefield's Original Mock India Paper Hanging and Papier Machée Manufactory in the Strand, 1758

Etching with engraved lettering, 327 × 244 mm (cropped)

Banks 91.20

D.2-3231 Sarah Banks collection, presented 1818

Richard Masefield's card is designed to emphasize wallpaper as appropriate for genteel interior decor. The shop is elegantly appointed, and expensively dressed women choose papers from a large selection.

The Strand to Fleet Street
3.70–3.84

3.70

Thomas Sandby (1723–1798)

*View of Beaufort Buildings looking towards the Strand, c.*1765

ILLUSTRATED IN COLOUR, PLATE 10

Watercolour with pen and ink, 451 × 616 mm

Crace XVII.65; Stainton 15

1880-11-13-2854

(1745–86; Lugt 2986). The price was evidently Gulston's estimate of value rather than an indication of how much he paid. A further note in the same hand reading 'Westminster' suggests that the card was classified in some sort of topographical arrangement. Gulston's omnivorous appetite for prints explains the unusual inclusion of ephemeral printed material in his collection. Trade cards, broadsides and the like usually survive in collections put together specifically to illustrate topography or contemporary history (like those of Samuel Pepys, see Aspital; for other collections of ephemera see

O'Connell, pp. 192–202). Sarah Banks (1744–1818) collected large quantities of printed ephemera, as well as metal tickets and tokens (see cat. 5.24); according to her annotation on the verso of this card, she acquired it in 1791, presumably at the sale of prints from Gulston's collection held on 18 August 1791. Most of his collection had been sold shortly before his death five years earlier.

In the early 1680s the newly created Duke of Beaufort demolished his sixteenth-century riverside mansion, Worcester House (the family had been Earls and then Marquises of Worcester), and developed the site with new residential terraces. It was still a respectable street in the mid eighteenth century when the novelist Tobias Smollett and the composer Thomas Arne lived there. The houses shown here – carefully delineated by Thomas Sandby, who was primarily an architect – are substantial buildings conforming to the various regulations introduced since the Great Fire of 1666: lamps to light the street fixed to brackets outside houses, railings and grilles over basement openings and exterior shutters on ground-floor windows. The striking red colour of the bricks was fashionable in the early eighteenth century, but by the 1750s most new houses were faced with bricks of a yellowish-grey. As is the case with other ambitious watercolours shown in this exhibition, this is a joint production, and the pavements in front of Beaufort Buildings (themselves an up-to-the-minute feature of the best streets of London) are peopled by figures who have been transferred from other scenes and from the sketchbooks of Paul Sandby.

A View of Somerset House, with St Marys Church in the Strand London. Vüe de la Maison royale de Somerset avec l'Eglise de St Marie dans le Strand a Londres.

3.71

The BEAUX DISASTER.

Ye Smarts, whose Merit lies in Dress,
Take warning by a Beaux Distress,
Whose Pigmy Size, & ill-tun'd Rage
Ventur'd with Butchers to engage.

But they unus'd Affronts to brook,
Have hung poor Fribble on a Hook,
While, foul Disgrace! expos'd in Air,
The Butchers Shout, & Ladies stare,

Satyr so strong, ye Fops, must strike you
How can you think ye Fair will like you,
Women of Sense, in Men despise
The Anticks, they in Monkeys prize.

3.72

175

3.71

Thomas Bowles (1712?–67)

A view of Somerset House with St Mary's Church in the Strand, 1753 (this edition after 1768)

Published by Carington Bowles, 69 St Paul's Churchyard, Robert Wilkinson, 58 Cornhill, and Robert Sayer in Fleet Street

Etching with engraved lettering, 262 × 402 mm

Crace XVII.102

1880-11-13-2891

The view is dominated by St Mary-le-Strand, built to James Gibbs's design in 1714–17 as a result of the Tory campaign to create fifty new churches in London; St Mary's was one of only twelve churches that were actually built (see also cat. 5.70). The print was made as a *vue d'optique* and designed to be seen through a viewing machine; the deliberately distorted perspective exaggerates the size of the church so that it appears to dominate the façade of old Somerset House to the right. To the left of the print is the row of shops that was swept away in 1900 for the creation of the Aldwych; Somerset House was rebuilt by William Chambers after 1776.

Like cat. 3.2 this view is a late impression of a print that would originally have been a joint publication of John and Thomas Bowles and Robert Sayer.

3.72

Anthony Walker (1726–65)

The Beaux Disaster, 1747

Etching and engraving with engraved lettering, 184 × 286 mm

BM Sat 2880

1868-8-8-3852 Edward Hawkins collection

Garrick's Fribble (see cat. 3.6) appears again in this sixpenny print. The effeminate character has got into an altercation with a group of butchers who have hung him from a hook above a stall. The scene takes place in Butchers' Row just north of the east end of the Strand,

leading towards Temple Bar. The bustling shambles with its drain in the middle of the cobbled street contrasts with the quiet residential Beaufort Buildings just a few hundred yards to the west; shop signs hang over the street and pot plants stand on ledges above the racks displaying joints of meat.

The print evidently appeared shortly after the publication in the *British Magazine,* 1747, of 'Beau's Sunday Morning Walk' (quoted by Hallett, p. 94), a narrative that follows the satirical tradition of describing life in London through the eyes of an observant passer-by (see also 5.96): the beau is trapped in a 'narrow passage, where, to

crown my vexation, what should present itself to my view, staring me as it were full in the face, but a smoking buttock of beef ... all was smoke, stink, and the steam of reeking victuals, on the one side; all beggars, vermin, nastiness, and stinks of another kind, on the other ... figure to yourself the extreme delicacy of my taste, the ticklish tenderness of my paltry stomach ... added to the plague of unmannerly gaping fools about me'. Hallett – in the context of a pioneering art-historical analysis of mid-century satirical prints – draws attention to Walker's subversion of the topographical view (such as 3.71): the fact that the setting for this print is identifiable serves

3.73

not as a focus for civic pride but to add immediacy to the class conflict that is being played out in the street between the fashionable strollers, the butchers and a group of women in ragged dresses.

3·73
Anonymous

The Heads of Townley and Fletcher on Temple Bar, c.1746

Hand-coloured etching, 192 × 146 mm (cropped)

BM Satire 2799

1868-8-8-3799 Edward Hawkins collection

This print focuses on an object that can be seen in the background of the previous print: Temple Bar, the City gate rebuilt by Christopher Wren at the junction of the Strand and Fleet Street. The heads of two Jacobites were exposed there – at a prominent entrance to the

City – as a warning against rebellion. Francis Townley, George Fletcher and other officers of the Manchester Regiment who supported the Jacobite Rebellion (see cats 2.15–2.17 and 3.27) were hanged, drawn and quartered on Kennington Common on 2 August 1746. The heads of Townley and Fletcher were the last to be exposed on a city gate; twenty years later on 9 December 1766, *The Annual Register* recorded that 'This morning between two and three o'clock, a person was observed to watch his opportunity of discharging musket-balls from a steel cross-bow, at the two remaining heads upon Temple Bar'.

This print would have been made shortly after the execution, when anti-Jacobite feeling was still strong. The design mixes the emblematic tradition with naturalism: the topographical view of the gate is presented as a vignette supported on either side by the all too realistically portrayed heads on their

posts, while decorative banners give the names of the rebels and above them a lively devil holds a flag with the Jacobite motto 'A Crown or a Grave'.

3·74
Anonymous

The Gates of London c.1760

Etching with engraved lettering, 210 × 325 mm

Crace XXXVII.22

1880-11-13-5626

Most of the elaborate gates in the City walls were removed in the year 1760–61 to allow freer access to traffic; Newgate remained until 1776–7 and Temple Bar until 1878. Much of the remaining medieval walls was also pulled down in the 1760s. This was part of the modernizing of London that also saw the removal of street signs, the numbering of

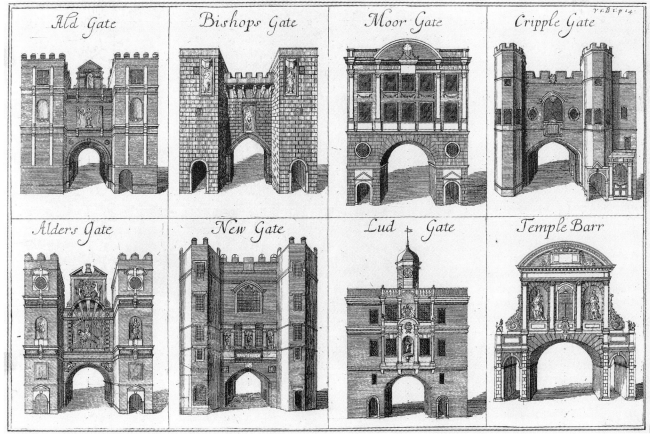

3.74

houses, planned street lighting and paving of roads (see p. 52).

(see p. 52)

The gates are shown topographically from Aldgate in the east to Temple Bar at the western boundary of the City.

3·75
Samuel Johnson (1709–84)
A Dictionary of the English Language, 1755

Printed by William Strahan for J. and P. Knapton, T. Longman, C. Hitch and L. Hawes, A. Millar and R. and J. Dodsley

Two folio volumes, 422 × 260 mm

Lent by Dr Johnson's House

Johnson's *Dictionary* appeared on 15 April 1755 and immediately became the standard work on the English language. The first edition of two thousand copies sold out immediately, and five further editions were published in Johnson's lifetime. Its intellectual context was the urge to amass and to classify knowledge that the British Museum represents in concrete form. The impetus was also manifest in encyclopaedias (Chambers' published in 1728, Diderot's, 1751–72, and the *Britannica*, 1768), and in more popular form, in magazines, newspapers and directories with their potted facts. The social context of the *Dictionary* was the expanding world of publishing where a clever writer could earn a relatively independent living. Johnson supported himself largely as a journalist writing hundreds of essays for magazines.

The *Dictionary* project demonstrates how intellectual activity had ceased to be dominated by the aristocratic elite. In his pamphlet announcing 'The Plan of a Dictionary of the English Language addressed to the Right Honourable Philip Dormer, Earl of Chesterfield' (1747) Johnson recalled 'times in which princes and statesmen thought it part of their honour to promote the improvement of their native tongues, and in which dictionaries were written under the protection of greatness', but Chesterfield famously delayed his

support until it was too late to be of value and the *Dictionary* was funded by a consortium of publishers. Their fee of £1,575 allowed Johnson to employ six assistants at 23s a week to transcribe quotations from 'the best writers' illustrating the meanings of words. It was not until 1762 that Johnson finally received patronage in the form of a pension of £300 a year from the King.

Johnson lived at a number of London addresses after his arrival from Lichfield in 1737 (with his friend and former pupil David Garrick). Most were in the vicinity of Temple Bar and the *Dictionary* was produced in Gough Square just inside the City boundary. Boswell met Johnson in 1763 and his biography is the source for many of the lexicographer's famous comments on life and on London.

Watchmaking

In the eighteenth century a variety of clocks and watches were available for purchase depending on the depth of one's pocket, ranging from a simple timepiece in a brass and leather case to the finest gold pair-cased watch with added complications, such as an alarm, a striking mechanism or a repeating mechanism which would sound the hours and quarters when the pendant was depressed. In terms of timekeeping technology, the major step forward was the horizontal or cylinder escapement introduced by George Graham in about 1725. This innovation improved accuracy and was used in higher-class watches. For cheaper watches, however, the more robust verge escapement continued to be commonly used.

In the middle of the century the London watch and clock trades were centred in the streets immediately to the north of the Strand and Fleet Street. The trade was already divided among a mass of specialists: the man whose name appeared on the watch and sold it in his shop would have assembled it from parts made by a number of highly skilled artisans, including movement frame-makers, fusee chain-makers, repeating motion-makers, bell-makers, dial-

The Art of Making Clocks & Watches.

Design'd & Engrav'd for y̆ Universal Magazine according to Act of Parliament 1748. for J. Hinton at the Kings Arms, in S.t Pauls Church Yard, London

3.76

3.77

makers, case-makers, engravers, gilders and enamellers; the crucial task of putting all these parts together was the responsibility of a finisher, and this work too might be contracted out. There were close ties with Liverpool watch-movement and component manu-facturers who supplied many of the leading London watchmakers and clock-makers. During the second half of the century the concentration of workshops moved eastwards to the area around the Old Bailey, gradually moving north to Clerkenwell, where many remained until the mid twentieth century.

For the development of clocks and watches through the ages see Bruton; for English watches Clutton and Daniels (with a glossary of technical terms), Jagger and Britten.

3.76

Anonymous

The Art of Making Clocks and Watches from the Universal Magazine, February 1748

Published by J. Hinton in *The Universal Magazine* at the King's Arms in St Paul's Churchyard

Etching with engraved lettering, 204 × 236 mm

Y.4-431 Sarah Banks collection, presented 1818

The main purpose of this illustration seems to be to emphasize the genteel nature of the clockmaking art, performed in a panelled room by a bewigged crafts-man sitting on a graceful chair. It is full of inaccuracies and technical errors, most prominently in the schematic display above the workbench showing the wheel-work of a spring-driven clock. The display is based on the frontispiece engraved by J. Mynde for the 1734 edition of William Derham's *The Artificial Clockmaker*, one of the classic books in the field. The present illustra-tion is one of many which copied Mynde; the errors continued to be repeated in illustrations until at least 1825, when the display appeared in the second edition of *The Operative Mechanic and British Machinist* by John Nicholson.

The letter (from Philo Chronos, 4 February 1748) that the print accompanies is similarly unhelpful in its description of clock mechanisms. For *The Universal Magazine* see cat. 1.79.

3.77

George Graham (1673–1751)

Pair-cased cylinder watch, 1750

Tortoiseshell-covered brass outer case with gold decoration, plain gold inner case (with the maker's mark of John Ward), gilt brass dust cap, white enamel dial, blued-steel beetle and poker-style hands, overall diameter 50 mm

Graham's number 6460; hallmark London 1750 (both on inner case)

MME CAI 1807 ex-collection Courtenay Adrian Ilbert

The famous clockmaker and watchmaker George Graham was born at Kirklington, Cumberland. In 1688 he was apprenticed in London to Henry Aske. In 1695 he was admitted to the Clockmakers' Company and entered the employment of the great Thomas Tompion at the Dial and Three Crowns at the corner of Water Lane and Fleet Street, eventually becoming Tompion's partner. In 1713 Graham and his wife Elizabeth, who was Tompion's niece, inherited the business, moving it in 1720 to new premises across the road. Graham's reputation as a scientific instrument-maker and clockmaker led to his election as a fellow of the Royal

3.79

Society, and he was honoured by being buried with Tompion in Westminster Abbey.

This is a typical high-quality cylinder watch from the Graham workshops. The outer case is lined with red silk and contains a small silk roundel with a verse in praise of friendship signed by J.T. Wood:

Oh! yes, there is a heaven below
'Tis when we do real friendship know
A Heaven on earth is this!
To act toward each a friendly part
And feel their kindred touch our heart,
Doth constitute our bliss.

3.78

George Graham (1673–1751)

Manuscript bill addressed to Samuel Bennett, 13 June 1748

NOT ILLUSTRATED

Pen and ink, 81 × 207 mm

Heal 39.39 Bequeathed by Sir Ambrose Heal, 1959

Samuel Bennett, a partner in Gosling's Bank, Fleet Street (see cat. 1.35), has been charged 12s by Graham for mending and cleaning a gold watch made by Windmills and Bennett (their number 7991). The bill is receipted by Samuel Barkley on Graham's behalf; Barkley and Thomas Colley were to succeed to Graham's business when he died three years later.

3.79

Thomas Mudge (1715–94)

Triple-cased minute repeating cylinder clock-watch, c.1755

Brass outer case with leather covering and pierced and gold decoration, two gold inner cases both pierced and engraved, white enamel dial, blued-steel hands, gilded-brass movement and dust-cover, diameter 75 mm

Mudge's number 407

MME 1984,0301.1

This magnificent watch was made by Thomas Mudge, the most extraordinary watchmaker of his time. He learnt his trade as an apprentice to George Graham and in 1750 was running his own business at the sign of the Dial and One Crown nearby at the eastern corner of Fleet Street and Bolt Court; he remained at the same address until he left London for Plymouth in 1771.

In 1752 Mudge received what must have been tremendous encouragement with an open-ended commission from Ferdinand VI of Spain to produce elaborate timepieces with complex mechanisms – the king had first come across Mudge's work in the form of a watch that he had made for John Ellicott and which Ellicott (as was normal practice for a contractor) had signed. Mudge was a great horological innovator: his new lever escapement, invented about 1754, is still used by

leading Swiss manufacturers. From 1755 Mudge worked in partnership with William Dutton who dealt with run-of-the-mill business, while Mudge concentrated on producing fine and complicated items. The present example has repeating mechanisms that sound the time to the nearest minute.

Doubtless inspired by John Harrison's famous marine timekeeper displayed in Graham's shop in the 1730s, Mudge also applied himself to solving the problem of maintaining accuracy during long sea voyages. Improved navigation was vital for a nation that relied on naval power and international trade, and in 1714 the Board of Longitude offered a prize of £20,000 for a 'practicable and useful' means of determining longitude. Astronomers had tried for centuries to develop a system using the position of the moon or the stars, but the prize was eventually won by a clock that allowed mariners to gauge their longitude by comparing local time according to the sun with time at their home port. John Harrison's development of his clock between 1730 and 1759 is described by Andrewes.

For documents relating to Mudge's career see Turner and Crisford with further references.

3.80

of the King's Arms and Dial in Russell Street, Covent Garden. Daniel Grignion was a member of the Society of Arts (see pp. 18–27) and in 1759 presented a precision timekeeper. His son Thomas (1713–84) became a partner in the 1730s. Thomas Grignion's most famous clock was a turret clock made for St Paul's, Covent Garden; it was destroyed in the fire which severely damaged the church in 1795, but was replaced by another clock by his son Thomas Grignion junior who carried on the business until 1825.

The card shown here was probably amended to add the name of Thomas Grignion when he became a partner; its style suggests that it dates from the 1720s, as does the use of French which gradually became less common among Huguenots, and by the 1750s was rarely used; the fanciful dials probably imitate the shop sign.

3.81
Daniel and Thomas Grignion (1684–1763 and 1713–84)

Movement, dial, dust-cap and bell of a cylinder watch with quarter-repeat, 1752

White enamel dial, blued-steel beetle and poker hands, silver dust-cap, gilded brass and steel movement, diameter 36 mm

Grignion's number 1205

MME CAI 1634 ex-collections Malcolm Gardener, Robert Atkinson and Courtenay Adrian Ilbert

3.80
Anonymous

Trade card of Daniel and Thomas Grignion, Watchmaker

Etching and engraving with engraved lettering, 154 × 127 mm

Heal 39.46 Bequeathed by Sir Ambrose Heal, 1959

Daniel Grignion (1684–1763) arrived in London as a Huguenot refugee from Poitou at the age of four. According to this trade card and inscriptions on several table clocks, he worked for the leading Quaker clockmaker and watch-maker Daniel Quare (d. 1724) before setting up on his own account at the sign

3.81

This watch movement, with fusee and cylinder escapement, is a fine example of the Grignions' work. It has the added refinement of a quarter-repeat mechanism designed to sound the hours and the quarters. The bell is signed by Drury of Islington, a specialist in bells for watches. The silver dust-cap is a relatively unusual feature; in the eighteenth century these were commonly made from gilded brass.

In 1953 this watch was recorded as having gold pair-cases hallmarked London 1752, the outer case was chased with a depiction of Britannia and signed by George Michael Moser, the leading gold-chaser; it is likely that these cases were removed and placed on another watch with the name of a more collectable maker such as George Graham.

3.82

Daniel and Thomas Grignion (1684–1763 and 1713–84)

Manuscript bill addressed to Edward Turnour Esq. (later Lord Winterton), February 1756

NOT ILLUSTRATED

Pen and ink, 144 × 146 mm

Heal 39.43 Bequeathed by Sir Ambrose Heal, 1959

The Grignions have charged Edward Turnour £63 for a gold-chased repeater bearing their names, and £2 2s 6d for work on two watches made by Harvey and Freeman. A reduction of 13s 6d was made to allow for the value of the gold in a watch by Harvey given in exchange by Turnour; the remainder of the bill was paid on 6 April 1756 and receipted by Thomas Grignion. Turnour's watch was a relatively expensive one, but as much as a hundred guineas could be paid for elaborate gold watches.

A number of bills paid by Edward Turnour (created Earl of Winterton in 1766) survive in the Heal collection and they give an indication of the sort of sums spent on luxury goods by a member of the upper classes. In 1756 Turnour married Anne, daughter of Thomas,

Lord Archer, and they set up home in Brook Street, Mayfair (their house was on the present site of Claridge's Hotel). Between March and June Turnour spent £1,656 17s on silver cutlery and other tableware purchased from Thomas Gilpin, Goldsmith, at the Acorn in the Strand (Heal 67.163). Jewellery purchased from Peter Dutens at the Golden Cup, Chandois Street, Covent Garden, in March 1756 (Heal 67.126) amounted to £1,903, including a pair of earrings costing the staggering sum of £650. The following year Dutens was to supply Ferdinand VI of Spain with a cane handle with a striking watch by Thomas Mudge (Turner and Crisford, p. 581).

3.83

Daniel and Thomas Grignion (1684–1763 and 1713–84)

Manuscript receipt addressed to Edward Turnour Esq. (later Lord Winterton), 23 April 1757

NOT ILLUSTRATED

Pen and ink, 80 × 180 mm

Heal 39.45 Bequeathed by Sir Ambrose Heal, 1959

This note, signed by Thomas Grignion, records the sale of a horizontal gold watch made by Grignion; he was paid eighteen guineas plus a gold watch given in exchange. Unfortunately Grignion's number for the new watch is not recorded. This is an early mention of the term 'horizontal watch', in this case the watch was undoubtedly a cylinder watch. The cylinder escapement was first used by George Graham in about 1726 following an earlier design by his former partner and mentor, Thomas Tompion, in 1695. This new escapement was employed by the leading London watchmakers in their best-quality watches. Not only did it afford greater accuracy than the verge escapement, commonly used at the time, but also it allowed watches to be made smaller and thinner.

3.84

Thomas Grignion (1713–84)

Manuscript bill addressed to Edward Turnour Esq. (later Lord Winterton) covering the period 29 June 1758 to 15 June 1759

NOT ILLUSTRATED

Pen and ink, 162 × 160 mm

Heal 39.42 Bequeathed by Sir Ambrose Heal, 1959

Grignion appears to have delayed charging Turnour 15s for cleaning and mending an old clock in June 1758 until the account had built up. In the following June he cleaned and mended another old clock for 7s 6d and sold Turnour a man's gold chain for £5 15s 6d, a lady's gold chain with five swivels (a chatelain) for £6 16s 6d, and a 'best gilt' watch key for 2s 6d. The total of £13 17s was paid on 3 August and the bill receipted by Grignion.

Visitors to London
3.85–3.87

The great metropolos of London, attracted people from far and near. Ten per cent of all Britons lived there at some point in their lives. Many were seasonal workers helping with the harvest in suburban fields and market gardens, others were ambitious young people keen to make their way in the capital like James Boswell from Scotland, George Graham from Cumberland or the Irish James Maclaine. There were children of expatriates such as William Beckford, born in Jamaica, and William Chambers, born in Sweden, or Britons – from Thomas Coram to Robert Clive – who returned to London after making fortunes overseas. Wealthy foreigners, such as Pierre-Jean Grosley and Giacomo Casanova, came as tourists; others, such as Canaletto or Handel, were established in their professions at home and came to London to find a wider audience; economic migrants sought a better living – sailors from ports

William Ansah Sessarakoo Son of John Bannishee Corrantee Ohinnee of Anamaboe and of Eukobah Daughter of Ansah Sessarakoo King of Aquamboo & Niece to Quishadoo King of Akroan. He was Sold at Barbadoes as a Slave in y̆ Year 1744 Redeem'd at the Earnest Request of his Father in the Year 1748, and brought to England.

This Plate is most Humbly Inscrib'd to the Right Hon.ble the Earl of Hallifax, First Lord Commissioner for Trade & Plantations, and one of his Majesty's most Hon.ble Privy Council. by his most obedient & most hum. Serv.t

Price 1:6.d   Gabriel Mathias.

3.85

around the world, Savoyard hurdy-gurdy players, Bohemian glass-cutters; young black slaves were purchased as exotic accessories for fashionable households.

The three visitors shown here are an Austrian musical prodigy who stayed for over a year, an eminent American who spent several years in London, and an African who enjoyed brief fame.

3.85

John Faber (1684–1756) after Gabriel Mathias (d. 1803)

William Ansa Sasraku, 1749

Published by Gabriel Mathias

Mezzotint with some scratched lines and engraved lettering, 328 × 225 mm

C.S. 323 (ii)

1902-10-11-1867 Bequeathed by William Eaton, 2nd Baron Cheylesmore

The Akwamu, Denkyira, Akim and Fanti people of what is now Ghana were involved throughout the eighteenth century in wars to control trading links with Europeans on the coast. In the mid-century Nana Ansa Sasraku, King of the Akwamu, defeated his neighbours and came to dominate a vast stretch of land from Denkyira to the Accra plains, at one stage even driving European traders out of their coastal fortress. Conquest of the peoples around him was not sufficient in itself to guarantee power in the region: it was essential to achieve effective communication with the main trading partners – the Europeans. Sasraku realized that he needed a trusted English-speaking mediator and so arranged for his son to be educated in England. Prince William Ansa Sasraku was put on board a British ship, but instead of delivering him safely to England the captain took the young man to Barbados and sold him into slavery. Luckily for the prince, his father's control of West African trade was important enough for William to be retrieved and taken to London as promised. He was the toast of the town and his story was told in prints, poems,

newspaper reports and a book entitled *The Royal African*. Garrick exploited the story by reviving Thomas Southerne's *Oroonoko* (1695), based on Aphra Benn's novel in which an African prince is sold into slavery, and the *Gentleman's Magazine* reported a visit by William Ansa Sesraku on 9 May 1749 to the Drury Lane Theatre, where members of the audience were moved as much by the prince's tearful reaction to the tragedy on stage as they were by the play itself.

The European trade in African slaves began in the sixteenth century in order to service sugar plantations in Brazil and later the Caribbean. Successful marketing had changed the perception of sugar – a native plant of Indonesia – from a luxury item to a staple food that was grown, processed and exported on a huge scale. The plantations required large numbers of strong manual workers who could withstand a hot, humid climate. Although European indentured workers and transported criminals were employed, Africans proved far more satisfactory. Slaves had long been high-status possessions in Africa and Europe – and the presence of exotically dressed black attendants in many portraits (see, for instance, cat. 00) demonstrates the continuation of this attitude – but on the plantations they were treated as beasts of burden and with systematic cruelty.

By the mid eighteenth century sugar was the most valuable import into England; William Beckford (1709–70), Member of Parliament and twice Lord Mayor of London, inherited a huge fortune earned from Caribbean sugar and left an estate worth a million pounds. Hans Sloane had begun his career as a physician in Jamaica (1687–8) and married the widow of a planter; his *Voyage to the Islands of Madera, Barbados, Nieves, St Christopher and Jamaica* (1707–25) discusses the medical and musical skills of the forty thousand Africans already living in Jamaica and describes the harsh conditions under which they lived and worked. The London-based Royal African Company held the monopoly of the British slave trade from the 1660s until 1730, but by

the middle of the century Bristol had become the main slaving port, and for most Londoners it was all too easy to ignore the inhumanity on which sugar wealth was based. Thoughtful individuals, such as Samuel Johnson (1709–84) – who left his manuscripts and much of his property to his (free) black servant Francis Barber – opposed slavery, but the first moves towards emancipation did not occur until the 1770s, and the Society for Effecting the Abolition of the Slave Trade was not founded until 1787.

Faber's mezzotint was based on a painting by Gabriel Mathias, an artist of German origin who held an appointment in the office of the Privy Purse and after 1769 administered George III's subsidies to the Royal Academy.

For black people in eighteenth-century England see Gerzina; for a history of slavery based on contemporary accounts see Hogg.

3.86

James McArdell (1729–65) after Benjamin Wilson (1721–88)

Benjamin Franklin, 1761

Mezzotint with some scratched lines and engraved lettering, 350 × 250 mm

C.S. 73; Goodwin 86

1902-10-11-3268 Bequeathed by William Eaton, 2nd Baron Cheylesmore

Benjamin Franklin (1706–90) is remembered by history for his central role in the establishment of the United States of America, but long before the War of Independence he was a well-known figure. He had established a successful business as a printer and publisher, in particular of the popular *Poor Richard's* almanacs with their homilies advocating the bourgeois values of thrift and industry that were coming to dominate society. He was also an active experimental scientist and Fellow of the Royal Society. This portrait, after a painting of 1759, makes reference to Franklin's theories on electricity and the experiment of 1752 when he flew a kite into a

The diminutive Wolfgang Amadeus Mozart, aged eight, is shown here at the harpsichord – poised for performance; his twelve-year-old sister, Maria Anna ('Nannerl'), sings and their father Leopold plays the violin. This is one of a number of early autograph copies of a watercolour (now in the main archive of Carmontelle's work in Chantilly) that was made in Paris shortly before the Mozart family arrived in London in April 1764 (see Davies, pp. 22–3).

London was at that time an active and lucrative musical market, and Leopold was assured of great artistic and financial rewards following the family's highly successful tour of the Continent. Performances included concerts at Ranelagh Gardens, and the Great Room in Spring Gardens, Charing Cross, and the family played at least twice before George III: on 27 April – within a month of their arrival – and again on 17 May 1764. The Mozarts also visited the new British Museum to which Wolfgang dedicated a motet, 'God is our refuge', his first sacred composition, written in July 1765.

The family spent its first night in London at the well-known White Bear Inn, Piccadilly, and the next day moved to the house of a barber, John Cousins, in Cecil Court, St Martin's Lane. In the summer, they moved for the sake of Leopold's health to the suburban calm of Five Fields Row (now Ebury Street), Chelsea, where they remained until late September 1764. Mozart is said to have written his first symphony there. They then moved to Frith Street, Soho, where they remained until the end of their visit in July 1765.

On 4 April 1764 Leopold Mozart recorded that Christian von Mechel was working on a print after the watercolour (Bauer and Deutsch, p. 142), but only a print by Jean-Baptiste Delafosse is known.

B. Wilson pinx.ᵗ   _J. Mc Ardell fecit._

B. Franklin of Philadelphia
L.L.D. F.R.S.

3.86

thundercloud to attract the lightning. Franklin was not alone in his experiments with electricity: in May 1746 the Duchess of Bedford wrote to the Duke, 'I supped at the Duchess of Montagu's on Tuesday night, where was Mr [Henry] Baker of the Royal Society, who electrified; it really is the most extraordinary thing one can imagine.' (Thomson, p. 290); in 1780 Anne Keppel, Countess of Albemarle, aged seventy-seven, was helped to recover from a stroke by being administered electric shocks.

3.87
Louis Carmontelle (1717–1806)

Wolfgang Amadeus Mozart with his father Leopold and sister Maria Anna, 1777 (version of a drawing of 1764)

ILLUSTRATED IN COLOUR, PLATE 11

Watercolour and bodycolour,
325 × 200 mm

1994-9-14-48 Transferred from the National Gallery, ex-collection Caroline Fitzroy, Lady Lindsay

IV

WESTMINSTER

Westminster has been the seat of national government since the eleventh century, when King Edward the Confessor rebuilt the abbey church that gave the area its name and moved his London residence to a new palace beside it. In 1066 William the Conqueror was crowned at Westminster Abbey and every subsequent coronation has taken place there. In 1220 another rebuilding of the Abbey was begun; it was to proceed in fits and starts until 1745 when the western towers were erected to Nicholas Hawksmoor's design. Today, the last remaining parts of the old palace of Westminster are Westminster Hall (1097) and the Jewel Tower (1366), but in the eighteenth century other buildings survived, most notably the fourteenth-century St Stephen's Chapel serving as the House of Commons and the White Chamber, where the House of Lords met.

In 1530 the royal Court had moved a few hundred yards north to the complex of buildings known as Whitehall Palace, previously the London residence of the Archbishops of York and splendidly rebuilt by Cardinal Wolsey. After a fire in 1698 destroyed most of the palace (Inigo Jones's Banqueting House of 1622 was the only substantial survivor), the Court moved to St James's Palace and Kensington, and the huge and very desirable site beside the river was parcelled out by the Crown to favoured courtiers who built grand town houses.

By the mid eighteenth century the river front from Charing Cross to Westminster Hall consisted almost entirely of fine new buildings, and a great new bridge spanned the Thames. The wide thoroughfare of Whitehall was

modernized by the removal of the two gates that narrowed the passage: King Street Gate, which stood where the road divided into two near Downing Street, was demolished in 1723, and the Holbein Gate in front of the Banqueting House (see cat. 4.15) in 1759. Government offices were beginning to be conspicuous: the two most important new buildings were Horse Guards, headquarters of the army general staff, and the Screen shielding the Admiralty from Whitehall.

The move of the royal Court to St James's in 1698 proved to be of symbolic significance. Power was shifting from the monarch to Parliament. Robert Walpole's long tenure as First Lord of the Treasury from 1721 to 1742 had established the importance of a post that was effectively that of prime minister. Powerful politicians of the mid-century challenged the King's supremacy and in particular George II's use of British resources to defend Hanover: Henry Pelham got his way by engineering a mass resignation of ministers, and William Pitt the Elder succeeded in overthrowing George III's favoured minister the Earl of Bute. Foreign trade was bringing huge wealth to merchant families and, although government was in the hands of the landowning aristocracy, many had links to trade: Pitt's family fortune derived from a grandfather who grew rich as governor of the East India Company's settlement in Madras, and he maintained close links to the City.

George II led troops to battle at Dettingen in 1743, and his son William, Duke of Cumberland, was commander in chief of the army until 1757 – notably successful in 1746 at Culloden against

the rebellion led by his cousin Prince Charles Edward Stuart – but military and particularly naval leaders were beginning to include men who, however well connected socially, had earned promotion from the junior ranks. The most dramatic rise in status was that of Robert Clive, who was brought up in genteel poverty and began his career as a clerk in the service of the East India Company (see cat. 4.14). The reasons for war expanded from disputes over ancestral European domains to the control of colonies and trade around the world: the War of Austrian Succession (1739–48) was triggered by Maria Theresa's claim to succeed to the Habsburg lands of her father, Emperor Charles VI, whereas the Seven Years War (1756–63) was fought for the possession of India, Canada and islands in the Caribbean, for silk, spices, tea, fish, fur, slaves and sugar.

Whitehall: the Army and the Navy

4.1–4.14

4.1

Francis Patton (fl. 1760s) after Robert Adam (1728–92)

The Admiralty Screen, 20 February 1761

Published by Robert Adam and sold by A. Millar in the Strand

Etching and engraving with engraved lettering, 405 × 646 mm (cropped)

Crace XVI.94

1880-11-13-2774

The first major building at the north end of Whitehall is the Admiralty, which lies on the west side backing on to St James's Park. Naval administration has been conducted on the site since the early seventeenth century, but the present building, to the designs of Thomas Ripley, dates from the 1720s. In 1759–61 an elegant neoclassical screen was erected to protect the building from Whitehall. It was the first public commission of the young Scottish architect Robert Adam, who had recently settled in London after spending three years in Rome. The publication of the engraved plan and elevation of the Admiralty Screen was part of Adam's assiduous self-promotion (see cat. oo for a letter making it clear that he saw the value of prints in publicizing his work); the print sold for 2s 6d, a price suggesting that it was aimed at a market with a serious interest in architecture. The introduction of antique ships as decorative motifs in the pediments on either side of the screen trumpets Adam's classical learning.

Adam's career developed rapidly. In 1761 he was appointed joint architect of the King's Works with William Chambers and was already working on the remodelling of Syon House to the

west of London for the Duke of Northumberland, and other commissions throughout the country.

Adam became one of the leading European architects of his generation. He was to transform London. The Adelphi development (built with his brother James in the 1770s) on the riverside near Charing Cross was a particularly innovative model for urban planning in its combination of human-scale residential and commercial accommodation within an architectural composition of a grandeur that looked back to ancient Rome.

4.2

Giovanni Antonio Canaletto (1697–1768)

Old Horse Guards from St James's Park, 1749

ILLUSTRATED IN COLOUR, PLATE 12

Pen and ink and wash over black chalk, 346 × 688 mm

Constable 734

1868-3-28-305

Next to the Admiralty stands Horse Guards, in the eighteenth century the headquarters of the army's general staff.

This drawing shows the late seventeenth-century Horse Guards building, demolished in 1749. The view is taken from St James's Park with the Admiralty to the left, buildings at the end of Downing Street (official home of the First Lord of the Treasury since 1732) in the foreground to the right, and a glimpse of the Treasury behind them. As in his Thames subjects, Canaletto has created a grandeur and spaciousness that had not previously been associated with London views; his images of Westminster must have gladdened the hearts of propagandists seeking to enhance the reputation of government. Close examination reveals that this composition was carefully constructed on the basis of a series of vertical lines ruled in black chalk; for Canaletto's use of compasses or dividers in drawings of Westminster Bridge see cats 4.25, 4.26.

At least three paintings relate closely to this composition: they show, respectively, old Horse Guards, the new building under construction and the new building complete. The first painting (now belonging to the Andrew Lloyd Webber Art Foundation), which is an impressive canvas two and a half metres wide, is probably the 'View of St James's Park' that Canaletto advertised (*Daily*

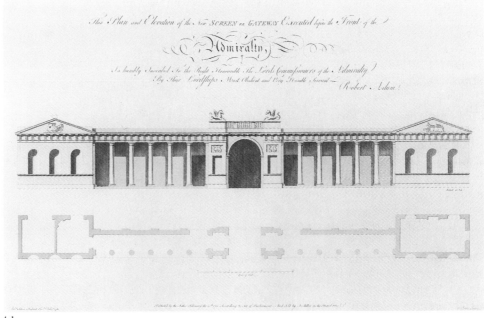

4.1

Advertiser, 25 July 1749) as being available for viewing at his lodgings at the house of Mr Wiggan, a cabinet-maker, in Silver Street, Golden Square (now Beak Street), Soho. The later versions (both in private collections) are much smaller. Robert Sayer published a print of the view in two states, during rebuilding and after completion.

A drawing of this subject, perhaps the present one, was sold in 1766 for £4.

4.3

4·3
Attributed to John Woolfe (fl. 1750–93)
The west front of Horse Guards, 1760s

Pen and ink and wash, 274 × 652 mm
Crace XII.50
1880-11-13-2302

This is a preliminary drawing for plates 7 and 8 of *Vitruvius Britannicus*, volume 5, published in 1771 by James Gandon and John Woolfe (Adams 45). It is likely to have been made by Woolfe, like the other plates of Horse Guards.

Colen Campbell's three-volume *Vitruvius Britannicus* of 1715–25 (Adams 24) contained three hundred engravings of plans and elevations of British architecture from Inigo Jones onwards; it was effectively a manifesto for the Palladian style. In 1767 and 1771 Gandon and Woolfe issued their two volumes illustrating recent buildings as a continuation of Campbell's series. See 5.12 for other books of architectural engravings.

4·4
John Vardy (1718–65) after William Kent (1684–1748)
The west front of Horse Guards, 1752

Published by John Vardy
Etching with engraved lettering, 361 × 578 mm (cropped)
Crace XII.49
1880-11-13-2301

4.4

Kent's Horse Guards and George Dance's Mansion House were London's two major public buildings of the 1750s. The Mansion House stands on a busy City street, but Horse Guards has sufficient open space on both its east and west sides for it to be appreciated and, more particularly, to give scope for Kent's talent for creating a grand setting. Kent and his patron, Richard Boyle, Earl of Burlington, developed a rational Palladian architecture in which classical proportions mattered more than function: Summerson (pp. 116–18), although granting that Horse Guards is the outstanding building of the period, points out that it is designed from outside in, a piece of stage scenery whose exterior bears little relation to the rooms within. Hogarth made pointed fun of the impracticalities of his old enemy's building in *Canvasssing for Votes* (1754/7), where a coachman is decapitated, his head flying through the air as he drives through the low central arch. Horse Guards may have proved inconvenient, but Kent unarguably succeeded in creating a setting for military display and, as this print shows, that was always an important function – the west front of Horse Guards still provides the backdrop for the annual Trooping of the Colour, one of London's prime royal occasions.

Kent had died two years before building began in 1750. Supervision was in the hands of John Vardy who had worked with Kent since 1736 and succeeded him as architect to the Board of Works. During Kent's lifetime in 1744 Vardy published an ambitious volume of engravings, *Some Designs of Mr Inigo Jones and Mr William Kent* that linked Kent with his great precursor. Vardy came from a poor family in Durham and his career was an example of how trade – architecture was not yet seen as a profession – could provide a route to financial and social success for a talented and energetic man. The law, the Church, Parliament, and the upper levels of the army and navy, on the other hand, were open only to members of the landed classes.

The Seven Years War and Victory Medals

The Seven Years War of 1756–63 was the first to be fought on a global scale. Britain was a major player, but there were no battles on home soil. Although the protagonists were European – Britain and Prussia against France, Austria, Russia, Sweden and Saxony – the theatre of operations stretched from India to the Caribbean, from West Africa to North America. Parliament in Westminster raised an army of ninety thousand men and a navy of seventy thousand and the funds to pay for them; the 'year of victories' of 1759 was purchased with a military budget of £12,500,000. By 1763 Britain had acquired what came to be called the first British Empire.

The medals shown here were made to commemorate some of the victories of the final stages of the war. Cats 4.6 and 4.9 are two of the nine medals designed for the Society of Arts (see pp. 18–27) between 1758 and 1765. The Society's encouragement of medal-making was led by Thomas Hollis, who also commissioned medals privately as part of a personal campaign to promote Whig ideals of civil and religious liberty by distributing medals, books and prints to individuals and institutions throughout the world. Hollis worked closely with James 'Athenian' Stuart and Giovanni Battista Cipriani as designers, and with the two leading medal-making families, the Pingos and the Kirks. Hollis's collections of coins and prints provided sources for images, and inscriptions were taken from classical texts. See Eyres for Hollis's medallic programme.

Until the 1730s most medals made in England had been struck in the Mint by coin engravers. In the 1740s Thomas Pingo established himself as an independent medallist, making presentation medals for institutions as well as commemorative medals for collectors, although much of the family income came from run-of-the-mill work cutting seals, punches and stamps. Eimer attributes seventy medals to Pingo and his sons, John and Lewis, amounting to

thirty per cent of the eighteenth-century London output of medals; he attributes sixty-eight medals to the Kirks (see cats 1.43–1.46). Many issues numbered no more than two hundred medals.

4.5
Thomas Pingo (1714–76)
Louisbourg Taken, 1760

Bronze, diameter 44 mm
MI, ii, p. 685, 404; Eimer 10

The fall of the French colony of Louisbourg on 26 July 1758 was the first step in the expulsion of the French from Canada. On the obverse of this medal a soldier and a sailor point to the position of Louisbourg on the globe, at their feet lies a naked female figure representing France. The reverse illustrates the final stages of the siege when, after six weeks' bombardment by British troops under General Wolfe, sailors from Admiral Boscawen's fleet boarded two French ships. The medal was exhibited at the Society of Arts in 1760, but the source of the commission is unclear.

4.5

4.6

Lewis Pingo (1743–1830) after James 'Athenian' Stuart (1713–88)

Guadeloupe Surrenders, 1762

Bronze, diameter 40 mm
MI, ii, p. 697, 427; Eimer 22

This medal won Pingo the Society of Arts premium of twenty guineas for a medal commemorating the taking of the French West Indian island of Guadeloupe on 1 May 1759. The subject was suggested by Hollis and the Committee for Polite Arts two years after the event when it seemed likely that the Treaty of Paris might return Guadeloupe to France.

Stuart's innovative neoclassical design shows Pallas Athene on the obverse holding a military standard and a trident representing the navy; it is inscribed with the names of Commodore John Moore and Major-General John Barrington, and that of the Society. On the reverse a female figure holding sugar canes kneels before Britannia.

4.7

John Kirk (1701?–61)

The French beaten at Minden: Protestants Rejoicing

Bronze, diameter 30 mm
MI, ii, p. 702, no. 433

Prince Ferdinand of Brunswick, shown on the obverse of this medal, led the combined British, Hanoverian and Hessian forces in Europe. During 1758 and the first months of 1759 they drove the French army out of Hanover in a series battles culminating on 1 August 1759 in the decisive victory at Minden, Westphalia. More than a hundred thousand soldiers took part in the battle.

The inscription, 'Protestants Rejoicing', above the battle scene on the reverse is a reminder that religious differences still played an important part in popular propaganda.

4.8

John Kirk (1701?–61) after Isaac Gossett (1713–99)

James Wolfe, 1760

Bronze, diameter 37 mm
MI, ii, p. 706, 440

News of the death of General Wolfe at the siege of Quebec on 13 September 1759 reached London more than a month later. Wolfe's victory was a turning point for the North American campaign, but it was his death that made him a popular hero. There was a demand for portraits in every medium. Gossett's wax model was sold as an independent work of art, as well as serving as the basis for the obverse of this medal. The reverse shows an urn and military trophies surrounded by the words *In Victoria Caesus* ('Struck down at the moment of victory') and *Pro Patria* ('For his Country').

4.9

John Pingo (1738–1827)

Canada subdued, 1761

Bronze, diameter 39 mm
MI, ii, p. 711, no. 448; Eimer 15

This medal commemorates the capture of Montreal – and with it all Canada – on 8 September 1760 just a few weeks before the death of George II whose head is shown on the obverse. The subject was offered by the Society of Arts in 1761 (hence the inscription 'S P A C', Society for the Promotion of Arts and Commerce) with the requirement that

4.6

4.8

4.7

4.9

the reverse should be based on the 'Judea Capta' coinage of imperial Rome that had been made to mark the fall of Jerusalem in AD 70; John Pingo replaced the palm of Judea with a pine tree with a beaver at its foot. Pingo was awarded a premium of thirteen guineas.

4.10

Thomas Pingo (1714–76) after James 'Athenian' Stuart (1713–88)

Pondicherry Taken, 1761

Bronze, diameter 39 mm

BHM, i, no. 72; Eimer 20

While British forces had driven the French out of Bengal in the 1750s (see cat. 4.14), the Compagnie des Indes remained powerful in south-east India until the fall of Pondicherry on 15 January 1761. Inscriptions on the reverse refer to the 'total expulsion of the French from India', and to Colonel Eyre Coote and the naval commander Rear-Admiral Charles Steevens. Stuart's design shows a figure of Victory standing between two palms with water flowing from urns representing the Indus and Ganges Rivers. The new king, George III, appears on the obverse.

Pondicherry was returned to France in 1763, but Britain remained the dominant power in India.

4.11

4.10

4.11

John Faber (1684–1756) after John Wootton (1682–1764) and Thomas Hudson (1701–79)

William Augustus, Duke of Cumberland

Published by John Faber

Mezzotint with scratched lines and engraved lettering, 503 × 534 mm

C.S. 102

1902-10-11-1332 Bequeathed by William Eaton, 2nd Baron Cheylesmore

William Augustus, Duke of Cumberland (1721–65), was the fourth son of George II. Like his father (see cat. 5.1) he led the cavalry into battle, not only with success at Dettingen in 1743, as shown here, and at Culloden in 1746, but also to defeat at Fontenoy in 1745, at Laffeldt in 1747 and at Hastenbeck in 1757. This last battle allowed the French to take over Hanover, and Cumberland was relieved of his role as commander of the so-called Army of Observation (made up of British, Hanoverian, Hessian and other contingents) to be replaced by Prince Ferdinand of Brunswick; Hanover was regained in 1758. Cumberland is remembered as 'Butcher Cumberland' for the summary executions and destruction of homes in the Scottish Highlands after the defeat of the Jacobite rebellion, but to contemporary England he was a hero. His reforms of the army were of lasting importance.

This print is based on a painting (Miles 20, still in the Royal collection, see Millar 554) commissioned by Cumberland's older brother, Frederick, Prince of Wales, in 1744. It was a joint production by John Wootton, who specialized in equestrian subjects, and the portraitist Thomas Hudson who painted the head and shoulders of the Duke. This print became the prime image of Cumberland as a victorious general; it was the source for a vast number of less expensive versions – from Faber's own version of the head of the Duke alone, to numerous cheap prints and inn signs (see cat. 1.9).

4.12

James McArdell (1729–65) after
Sir Joshua Reynolds (1723–92)

George Lord Anson, 1755

Published by James McArdell at the Golden Head in Covent Garden

Mezzotint with scratched lines and engraved lettering, 354 × 250 mm

C.S. 2 (ia); Goodwin 43 (ii)

1902-10-11-3175 Bequeathed by William Eaton, 2nd Baron Cheylesmore

The career of George Anson (1697–1762) combined spectacular exploits at sea with an administrative talent that enabled him to effect essential reforms to the organization of the navy. His name was always associated with the circumnavigation of the world between 1740 and 1744. The expedition was a harrowing one involving the loss of nearly eight hundred of the 961 men who

The Rt. Honble George Lord Anson . Baron of Soberton
Firft Lord Commiffioner of the Admiralty . Vice Admiral of Great Britain
Admiral of the Blue Squadron & one of . his Majefty's moft Hon.ble Privy Council.

4.12

left England, but it was celebrated as a triumph with a procession through London carrying £500,000-worth of Spanish treasure captured in the Pacific. Three years later Anson led the Channel fleet to victory over the French off Cape Finisterre and carried home another £300,000-worth of booty that had been destined for America and the East Indies. He had joined the Admiralty in 1744 and, although he did not become First Lord until 1751, immediately set about instituting reforms. The command

structure of the fleet was completely overhauled; a corps of marines under the jurisdiction of the Admiralty replaced the old marine regiments; the administration of the dockyards was improved; and new articles of war were drawn up which remained naval law until 1865. His role as an administrator was essential to the victories of 1759 which turned the Seven Years War in Britain's favour.

The print is based on a painting in the National Portrait Gallery (Mannings 67a).

4.13

James McArdell (1729–65) after Sir Joshua Reynolds (1723–92)

Admiral Boscawen, 1758

Mezzotint with scratched lines and engraved lettering, 506 × 349 mm

C.S. 24 (i); Goodwin 59

1902-10-11-3213 Bequeathed by William Eaton, 2nd Baron Cheylesmore

Edward Boscawen (1711–61) joined the navy at the age of fifteen. He served at the famous battles of Portobello (1739) and Cartagena (1741). His role as senior captain at the battle of Cape Finisterre in 1747 earned him the command of a fleet off India; in 1748 both the young Robert Clive and Hannah Snell, the 'female soldier' (cat. 2.13), served under him at the unsuccessful siege of Pondicherry – though it is very unlikely that he was aware of either. In April 1755 Boscawen was involved in precipitating what was to become the Seven Years' War when he took two French ships off Newfoundland in an attempt to blockade the St Lawrence river and prevent supplies reaching French colonies inland. In 1758 he was promoted to the rank of admiral and contributed to the capture of Louisburg. In 1759, in one of the triumphs of the 'year of victories', he commanded the fleet that engaged the French off Lagos, Portugal, and in 1760 was promoted to general of marines. He died the following January.

4.14

James McArdell (1729–65) after Thomas Gainsborough (1727–88)

Robert, Lord Clive, ?1763

Published by John Ryall at Hogarth's Head, Fleet Street (inscription on published state)

Mezzotint, 465 × 313 mm

C.S. 42 (i); Goodwin 100 (i)

1950-5-20-230 Presented by F. W. B. Maufe and Mrs G. B. Lane

In 1753 Robert Clive (1725–74) arrived in London in glory having led British and Indian troops of the East India Company to victory over the French and their allies in the south of India, most spectacularly at the defence of Arcot in 1751 where his force, only a few hundred strong, had stood against an army of thousands. Although Britain and France were not officially at war after 1748, the trading companies conducted what amounted to a proxy war. Clive was a courageous soldier and a cunning strategist, with a talent for exploiting local rivalries in fragmented India to the advantage of British interest. The victory at Arcot turned events decisively in Britain's favour.

After Clive's return to India in 1756, attention shifted northwards to the immensely wealthy province of Bengal. On 20 June 1756, a number British men and women died imprisoned by allies of the French in the notorious Black Hole of Calcutta after the capture of the East India Company's settlement. In January 1757, Clive, leading nine hundred British troops and fifteen hundred

The Honorable Edward Boscawen Admiral of the Blue Squadron of His Majesty's Fleet, And One of the Lords Commissioners of the Admiralty

4.13

4.14

in the East India Company, dominating affairs at the Company headquarters in Leadenhall Street. This print is based on a lost portrait by Thomas Gainsborough painted during this period; this is a proof before letter, but the published state is dedicated to 'the Honourable the Court of Directors of the United Company of Merchants of England Trading to the East Indies'.

News of corruption and instability in the Company's affairs in India sent Clive back in 1765 to restore order. It was during this last stay – of less than two years – that the British took formal control of Bengal when the Mughal emperor in Delhi granted the diwani (the right to collect revenues) to Clive on behalf of the Company, thus reducing the Nawab to a subsidiary position. The East India Company was amassing profits of some two million pounds a year enabling so-called 'nabobs', extremely wealthy Company men – often, like Clive, from relatively humble origins – to build grand houses in London, favouring the still-undeveloped land north of Oxford Street around Portman Square. Clive's own London home was in Berkeley Square.

Clive's final return to England in 1767 was a contrast to his earlier glorious welcomes. The climate of opinion was changing from one where every British gain was greeted as an unequivocal good, and he was met with severe criticism of the means by which he had enriched himself. His health failed and he succumbed to opium addiction and depression, finally committing suicide at the age of forty-nine. From 1766 the Treasury had contrived that some of the wealth of India came directly to the Exchequer; Acts of Parliament of 1773 and 1784 began a process of transfer of East India Company activities to the British government, finally to be completed after the so-called Indian Mutiny of 1857.

sepoys (Indian soldiers), recovered Calcutta. The following June, his victory at Plassey over Siraj-ud-Daulah, Nawab of Bengal, effected a crucial change in the role of the British in India: formerly simply powerful traders, they now became political overlords. A new Nawab, Mir Jaffir, was installed, and Clive became the Company's local governor. Mir Jaffir, although nominally ruler of the state, was dependent on the Company and he made large presents, including a personal gift to Clive of more than £200,000; he also transferred back to Clive the sum of £30,000 a year that the Company paid in rent for its territories south of Calcutta (the jagheer). Criticism over his acceptance of these payments was to dog the last years of Clive's life, but his return to London in 1760 was triumphal. He was created Baron Clive of Plassey and wielded political power both as a Member of Parliament and as a major stock-holder

Whitehall and the Privy Garden

4.15–4.17

4.15

Thomas Sandby (1723–98)

*Whitehall, c.*1750

ILLUSTRATED IN COLOUR, PLATE 12

Watercolour with pen and ink over graphite, 326 × 606 mm

1941-6-18-1 Presented by the National Art Collections Fund

Sandby presents a calm, expansive view of Whitehall with the Banqueting House on the right; the so-called Holbein Gate (built in 1532 and demolished 1759) spans the roadway. Like many of the Sandby brothers' watercolours, this example includes a number of figures by Paul Sandby that appear in other sketches. Again, not unusually in the Sandbys' oeuvre, there are several other watercolour versions of the composition: one in the Guildhall Library (see http://collage.nhil.com) and two in the Royal Library (Oppe Sandby, 165 and 166).

4.16

John Boydell (1719–1804)

A View of the Privy Garden, 1751

Published and sold by John Boydell, Engraver, at the Unicorn, the corner of Queen Street, Cheapside, London

Etching with engraved lettering, 260 × 427 mm (cropped)

Crace XVI.47

1880-11-13-2727

This and the following print come from the series of one-shilling views of London engraved by John Boydell after his own designs at the beginning of his career as an independent publisher. Although the prints give an informative description of mid-century London – in this case showing the former private garden of old Whitehall Palace – their

A View of Privy-Garden Westminster. Veuë du Privy-Garden à Westminster.

4.16

composition is naive and formulaic. Boydell has attempted to go beyond simple topography by putting dramatic shadows in the foreground and to one side to create a repoussoir effect taking the eye into the distance, but he fails to exploit buildings of architectural interest (here, for instance, the imposing bulk of the Banqueting House is rendered as a two-dimensional façade) or to find compositional potential in the shapes and textures of an everyday urban scene. Canaletto's magnificent paintings of this view from the opposite direction are at Goodwood and Bowhill (Constable 438 and 439).

For a note on Boydell's career see cat. 2.4.

4.17

John June (fl. *c.*1747–70) after J. L'Agneau (fl. 1750s)

Lusus Naturae [the light of nature] or Caricaturas of the Present Age, 5 March 1752

Published by Bispham Dickinson on Ludgate Hill

Etching with engraved lettering, 316 × 466 mm

BM Satire 3187

1868-8-8-3925 Edward Hawkins collection

This print, which also shows the Whitehall Privy Garden, derives from a type of group portrait popular among Grand Tourists in Italy around 1750 where the image is subverted by exaggerating facial features, and enlarging heads. The best-known examples are paintings by Joshua Reynolds (Mannings 1962–1969) and Thomas Patch. The taste for caricature had developed in Italy in the late sixteenth century, and became a commercial proposition in the hands of Pier Leone Ghezzi (1674–1755), whose drawings, and prints after them, sold well to English milordi. Amateur artists, most notably George, Marquess Townshend (1724–1807), adapted the style to political satire when they returned home and involved themselves in affairs of state.

This print is an early example of caricature designed in London by a professional artist (see also cat. 5.20). The figures outside 'Whitehall Chapel' (the Banqueting House was used as the Chapel Royal throughout the eighteenth century, and as the Horse Guards Chapel for most of the nineteenth) include Dr John Hill, the gossip columnist (see cat. 5.20), who appears to be leaving the scene, to left, with a young prostitute (her short skirts indicate that she is not a respectable woman). The other figure identified by a contemporary inscription is Sir Samuel Prime, serjeant-at-law, who, according to the inscription, married his cook – this is further suggested by the newsvendor's sheet with the title 'A Genuine Account of Sir Simon Pride and his Cook Maid Mary'. Others taking the air in Whitehall include a bearded Jewish man (in eighteenth-century London only Jews wore beards) holding three pairs of spectacles and talking to a portly clergyman. Features, though exaaggerated, clearly belong to individuals and remain to be identified. Topographical accuracy was clearly not of particular importance in

this print and John June has allowed it to be reversed in the printing process.

The designer J. L'Agneau's interest in prurient subject matter (cat. 5.20 also includes prostitutes) is confirmed by the fact that on 27 March 1752 he announced in the *General Advertiser* that he had published a print with the title *Flagellation. Lusus Naturae* and *A View of the Mall* were both published by Bispham Dickinson. In the newspaper advertisement L'Agneau gave his address as 'at the Golden Sugar Loaves, the Corner of Shoemaker Row [now

Carter Lane], Blackfriars'; the prints were also to be found at the Green Canister in Hanover Street (now Endell Street), Long Acre, Covent Garden. These three prints, all published in March 1752, are all that is known of L'Agneau, and it is possible that the name was a pseudonym, although in the 1780s a print-seller styling himself L'Agneau le Jeune advertised English and French prints for sale in the rue de l'Orangerie, Paris.

The Palace of Westminster: Government 4.18–4.24

4.18

John Boydell (1719–1804)

New Palace Yard, Westminster, 1751

Published by John Boydell, Engraver, at the Unicorn, the corner of Queen Street, Cheapside, London

Etching with engraved lettering, 262 × 432 mm

Crace XV.74

1880-11-13-2662

The ancient Westminster Hall is shown here as part of the streetscape with a clutter of small shops in front and beyond. The Hall housed the law courts from the fourteenth century until 1882, when they moved to the Strand, but there were also stalls selling prints and other luxuries.

Government

In the mid eighteenth century the party system of government and opposition was not yet fully evolved. Members of the loosely organized Whig party were in power for most of the century, but factions within the party provided opposition to successive ministries. The notoriously bad relations within the royal family formed rallying positions

4.17

4.18

for groups of disaffected politicians: Leicester House – the London home, and rival court, of successive Hanoverian Princes of Wales – was a focus for opposition, first to George I and Walpole, later to George II and by the end of the century to George III. The wealthier classes dominated the electorate: land tax was unpopular with the great landowners while excise tax could have drastic effects on trade (Robert Walpole had almost lost power when he introduced new excise charges in 1733). War was the heaviest drain on the Exchequer, and so the landed classes tended to support peace, while merchants broadly saw money spent on war as a worthwhile investment towards gaining new opportunities for trade. For the disenfranchised poor the only political weapon was riot; government was always wary of public opinion, see cat. 1.90, pp. 95 and 200.

4.19

Richard Houston (1722–75) after John Shackleton (d. 1767)

Henry Pelham and John Roberts, 1752

Published by Joseph Edmondson, at his house in Warwick Street, Golden Square, St James

Mezzotint with scratched lines, 388 × 385 mm

C.S. 87 (i)

1902-10-11-2680 Bequeathed by William Eaton, 2nd Baron Cheylesmore

Henry Pelham (1696–1754) served as First Lord of the Treasury from 1743 to 1754; his secretary, John Roberts, M.P. for Harwich (d. 1772), was a skilled party manager who proved invaluable to Pelham's brother, the Duke of Newcastle, when he took over government in 1754. The aftermath of Robert Walpole's long years of skilfully managed government (1730–42) involved a certain amount of jockeying for power, but Pelham's Whig ministry was relatively stable. The chief conflict was with George II over British involve-

4.19

ment in the War of Austrian Succession, which was seen as diverting British taxes and increasing the national debt in order to protect the King's possessions in Hanover. Pelham demonstrated his opposition to the King's demands by calling for a mass resignation of ministers on 11 February 1746 – at a point when the defeat of the Jacobite Rebellion was by no means clear; he was recalled after three days when the King's ally, John Carteret, Earl Granville, was unable to form a government. A general election called in 1747 confirmed Pelham's position. When the War of Austrian Succession was brought to an end in 1748, Pelham reduced the military establishment, lowered land tax and consolidated the national debt.

Shackleton's painting, which does not seem to have survived, was based on Van Dyck's double portrait of the Earl of Strafford with his secretary, Sir Philip

Mainwaring (itself derived from compositions by Titian and Sebastiano del Piombo).

4.20

James McArdell (1729–65) after William Hoare (1706–92)

Thomas Pelham-Holles, Duke of Newcastle

Published by James McArdell

Mezzotint with a few scratched lines, 387 × 274 mm

C.S. 136 (i); Goodwin 176

1863-1-10-178 Bequeathed by William Eaton, 2nd Baron Cheylesmore

Thomas Pelham-Holles (1693–1768) was created Duke of Newcastle-upon-Tyne in 1715 as a reward for his support of the Hanoverian cause at the time of the first Jacobite Rebellion, and in 1718 was made a Knight of the Garter; he is shown here in splendid traditional Garter robes. In 1711 he had inherited, as adopted heir, the enormous wealth of his uncle John Holles, 1st Duke of Newcastle. His annual income included £25,000 from rents alone. He held office under Robert Walpole from the age of thirty-one and was one of the lords regent who ran affairs of state during the frequent absences in Hanover of both George I and George II.

After the sudden death of his brother Henry Pelham in 1754, Newcastle succeeded him as First Lord of the Treasury. War was brewing with the French who took advantage of the fact that most of the British fleet was in either the Channel or the Bay of Biscay to take the British Mediterranean island of Minorca in 1756. Admiral Byng, who failed to save the island, was shot 'pour encourager les autres' (as Voltaire acidly commented in *Candide*); Newcastle, who had failed to predict the French attack,

resigned, but was compensated with the additional title of Duke of Newcastle-under-Lyme. He was out of office for only seven months, but, despite his return to power, William Pitt, who had led the government in the interim, continued to dominate the House of Commons until the accession of George III in 1761. In 1762 Newcastle was driven to resignation and was replaced by John Stuart, Earl of Bute, whose influence over the young King was deeply unpopular (see cats 00–00). Newcastle returned to office for only one further year, 1765/6, when he was Lord Privy Seal under Lord Rockingham. In 1768 he died after a stroke at his house in Lincoln's Inn Fields.

Power resided in the power of patronage that came with high office and by modern standards eighteenth-century politicians were shockingly corrupt. Although Newcstle had many critics, according to James McMullen Rigg

(*DNB*) he 'undoubtedly was, according to the standard of his age, an honest politician … and died £300,000 the poorer for nearly half a century of official life'.

This relatively expensive five-shilling print was based on a painting still in the family collection; Hoare's preliminary drawing is in the British Museum.

4.21

James McArdell (1729–65) after Allan Ramsay (1713–84)

Henry Fox, 1762

Mezzotint with some scratched lines, 374 × 277 mm (cropped)

C.S. 72; Goodwin 93

1902-10-11-3267 Bequeathed by William Eaton, 2nd Baron Cheylesmore

Henry Fox (1705–74) was one of the most powerful politicians of the mid-century, holding high office successively under Walpole, Pelham, Newcastle and Bute. As paymaster-general of the forces from 1757 to 1765, Fox – unlike his predecessor Pitt, but like most of his contemporaries in office – amassed a huge fortune; those reponsible for large public funds had personal control of the balances and of the interest on them. At the end of 1762 Fox's skill at political manipulation pushed through the controversial vote in Parliament in favour of ending the Seven Years War. He was rewarded by George III with the title Baron Holland of Foxley, but gained the lasting enmity of the City which was furious that trading opportunities won through battle were ceded in the Treaty of Paris. In 1769 Lord Mayor William Beckford described him in a petition to the King as 'the public defaulter of unaccounted millions'.

Tillyard shows a more appealing side of the cunning politician as a loving husband and father. His wife was Caroline, daughter of Charles Lennox, 2nd Duke of Richmond, who had refused permission for the wedding of his daughter to a commoner; the couple eloped and in 1753 Fox opposed

4.20

4.21

4.22

Hardwicke's Marriage Act (cats 1.67–1.70), which would have prevented his marriage. His son was the radical politician Charles James Fox (cat. 5.17).

4.22
Richard Houston (1722–75) after William Hoare (1706–92)

*William Pitt, c.*1754–6

Published by Richard Houston at the Golden Head in Broad Court, Covent Garden

Mezzotint with scratched lines, 387 × 278 mm

C.S. 92 (a i)

1902-10-11-2685 Bequeathed by William Eaton, 2nd Baron Cheylesmore

William Pitt (1708–78) was known by the epithet 'The Great Commoner' from his impressive performance in, and influence on, the House of Commons. His family's

fortune was based on the success of his grandfather, 'Diamond' Pitt, so called because he had acquired the world's largest diamond when governor of the East India Company's settlement in Madras. William Pitt entered Parliament in 1735 as one of the 'boy patriots' gathered around Richard Temple, Viscount Cobham, and Frederick, Prince of Wales, in opposition to Robert Walpole. He identified with the City and demanded a more active (that is bellicose) pursuit of trading interests in the East and West Indies, but – to the fury of George II – opposed support of Hanover against the French in the War of Austrian Succession (1740–8). He achieved office in 1746 as vice-treasurer of Ireland (at a salary of £3,000 a year) and as paymaster general of the forces (at £4,000 a year) and impressed public opinion by administering funds with transparent honesty. He was dismissed in 1755 after attacking Newcastle's

ministry, but in 1756 the outbreak of the Seven Years War brought him back, as Secretary of State.

Pitt proved an enormously effective leader of a war that was fought on opposite sides of the earth. He supported Robert Clive's campaigns against the French in India, sent troops to North America, and fleets to the West Indies, Africa and the coasts of France, and subsidized the armies of Frederick the Great of Prussia to defend British interests in Continental Europe. But the new king, George III, and his adviser Lord Bute who became Secretary of State in 1761 and First Lord of the Treasury in 1762, were determined to end the war, and behind them were the great landowners – paying huge taxes for a war whose purpose was to enhance trade, a matter they saw as having no direct relevance to their way of life. Pitt resigned in 1761. His later years were dogged by ill-health, but he remained active in Parliament.

He pleaded in defence of constitutional liberty in 1763 on behalf of John Wilkes and in 1766 in support of the American colonists who resisted the imposition of the Stamp Act. In 1766 he was created Earl of Chatham and served as First Lord of the Treasury for two years. His son William Pitt the Younger was to become Prime Minister in 1783.

There are several versions of Hoare's painting, see Kerslake 1050.

John Wilkes

On 18 June 1762 John Wilkes (1727–97), Member of Parliament for Aylesbury, and Charles Churchill (1731–64), satirical poet and former clergyman, launched a weekly journal entitled *The North Briton* (i.e., the Scot). Its main target was the Scottish Earl of Bute, the young King's mentor, who had been appointed a month earlier as First Lord of the Treasury and was determined to bring the Seven Years War to a speedy end. *The North Briton* no. 17 (25 September 1762) criticized Hogarth for his print *The Times*, Plate 1 (cat. 1.37) in favour of ending the war. On 10 February 1763 the Peace of Paris was signed. Opposition mounted and Bute resigned. Issue no. 45 of *The North Briton* appeared on 23 April with what was virtually a direct attack on George III. Three days later a general warrant was issued for 'apprehending and seizing the authors, printers, and publishers of a seditious libel, together with their papers'. Wilkes was imprisoned in the Tower, but released on the grounds of his privilege as a Member of Parliament. On 6 May he was escorted from the court at Wesminster Hall to his home nearby in Great George Street by a crowd of thousands shouting the new slogan of radicalism: 'Wilkes and Liberty!'. Wilkes set up a printing press in his house to publish a collected edition of *The North Briton*, and also to print his *Essay on Woman*, a parody of Pope's *Essay on Man*, addressed to Fanny Murray (cats 3.12, 3.16, 3.17). It was this porno-

graphic and blasphemous verse that was to turn the balance of influential opinion against him. Meanwhile, on 3 December, *The North Briton*, no. 45, was burnt by the common hangman at the Royal Exchange in the City and a riot ensued; further charges were brought, but postponed until the new year while Wilkes

recovered from a bullet wound received in a duel with fellow M.P. Samuel Martin who felt that he had been libelled in *The North Briton*. Wilkes fled to France on Christmas Day and on 20 January 1764 was expelled from Parliament; in February an arrest warrant was issued for printing the

4.23

Essay on Woman and for re-publishing *The North Briton*, no. 45. Wilkes remained abroad until 1768, when his election as M.P. for Middlesex heralded the radicalism of the last decades of the century.

Much has been written about Wilkes, but for a full account of the events of 1762–3, see Rudé 1962, pp. 17–37.

4.23

William Hogarth (1697–1764)

John Wilkes, 1763

Pen and ink over graphite, 355 × 216 mm

1936-10-15-1 ex-collection Samuel Ireland

Hogarth included Wilkes and Churchill as minor elements in his pro-Bute satire *The Times*, Plate 1, and he was deeply hurt by their retaliation in *The North Briton*, no. 17. He took the opportunity to express his feelings by making this hostile sketch of Wilkes in Westminster Hall on 6 May 1762 and a week later publishing a print of it at 1s.

4.24

William Hogarth (1697–1764)

John Wilkes, 16 May 1763

Published by William Hogarth

Etching and engraving with engraved lettering, 341 × 220 mm (cropped)

Paulson 214

1868-8-8-4315 Edward Hawkins collection; ex-collection Joseph Gulston (verso inscribed 'No 1619', Lugt 2986)

In the *London Chronicle* for 14–17 May 1763 and the *Public Advertiser* for 16 May the following notice appeared: 'This day was published, price 1s., a whole-length print of John Wilkes, Esq., drawn from the life, and etched by William Hogarth. To be had at the Golden Head in Leicester Fields. This print is in direct contrast to a print of Simon, Lord Lovat, first published in the year 1746, and is of the same size and etched in the same manner …' Hogarth was drawing on the popular genre of the convict print

(see O'Connell, pp. 93–6), and the advertisement makes it clear that he was likening Wilkes to a traitor who had lost his head on the block at Tower Hill (see cat. 2.17).

The print sold in huge numbers, but it was not a success in Hogarth's terms. Wilkes's many supporters did not read the print as Hogarth had intended; the audience took the grinning figure with the cap of liberty at face value, failing to read the irony in what was for Hogarth a rare caricature. The image became an icon of the radical cause copied in cheap prints and other media for decades – forever associated with the cry 'Wilkes and Liberty!'. See Rauser for a discussion of the print's reception.

4.24

Westminster Bridge and the River at Westminster

4.25–4.27

4.25

Giovanni Antonio Canaletto (1697–1768)

The Thames and Westminster Bridge from the north

ILLUSTRATED IN COLOUR, PLATE 13

Pen and ink with wash over black chalk, 345 × 738 mm

Constable 749a

1868-3-28-306

This splendid drawing is a reminder that the grandest approach to Westminster was by river – whether following tradition in a richly decorated shallop or passenger barge, or by taking advantage of the most striking addition to mid-eighteenth-century London and crossing the new bridge. It was this elegant marvel of engineering that would have impressed the contemporary viewer. The palaces of Lambeth and Westminster, centres of ecclesiastical and political power, dominate the skyline, but their medieval architecture was of only anti-quarian interest. The new Westminster Bridge not only opened up the western part of town but also stood as a symbol for the shift of the capital away from the commercially focused City with its ancient crowded bridge inhabited by shopkeepers to the home of political power on a worldwide scale.

Close examination reveals something of Canaletto's technique. The architec-ture is carefully constructed with ruled black chalk lines, and pinpricks indicate that the arches of the bridge have been measured with dividers. These mechanical preliminaries are overlaid with lively detail freely drawn in pen and brown ink, and varied tones of grey wash create an illusion of three-dimension-ality. The wooded hills on either side are compositional inventions.

The drawing is one of three versions of the same view; the others are in the Royal collection and at Stourhead. The view is shown also in a painting in the collection of Lady Vestey, and in another which was painted for William Barnard, Bishop of Derry. See pp. 127–9 for a discussion of the new bridge and Canaletto's depictions of it.

4.26

Giovanni Antonio Canaletto (1697–1768)

The western arches of Westminster Bridge

ILLUSTRATED IN COLOUR, PLATE 13

Pen and ink with wash over black chalk, 414 × 731 mm

Constable 752

1905-5-20-1 Presented by Henry Joseph Pfungst through the National Art Collections Fund

This drawing shows the western end of Westminster Bridge. Work is still taking place on the parapet, and a barricade prevents access to the roadway. It is probably based on studies made shortly after Canaletto's arrival in England in the summer of 1746, but may have been executed later. As is the case with cat. 4.25, the main structure of the drawing is provided with black chalk underdrawing, and incised arcs outlining the arches are visible in a raking light. The appearance of the drawing is distorted by the fact that the brown ink used for outlines has eaten into the paper and shows as light lines in the darker shadows.

The close focus on a relatively small part of a major public structure would have surprised a contemporary audience. As prints and drawings in this exhibition demonstrate, urban views were expected to be descriptions of important architec-tural features or of noteworthy events, or they were amusing depictions of street life. Canaletto's acute observations of previously unconsidered detail must have puzzled the average picture buyer, but they fascinated fellow artists and brought a new sort of subject matter to prominence.

4.27

Samuel Scott (1702–72)

Westminster Bridge, 1744

ILLUSTRATED IN COLOUR, PLATE 14

Brush drawing in grey wash with watercolour over graphite, 351 × 1110 mm

ECM 6; Kingzett D97; Stainton 7

1865-6-10-1324

This drawing must date from before the beginning of 1745 when the abutments of the arches of Westminster Bridge where finished. It was used, however, as the basis for five paintings showing the bridge as it appeared after completion at the end of 1750 (Kingzett, pp. 60–2).

The buildings on the north bank are houses fronting on to a series of small but elegant streets between the river and Parliament Street: Manchester Court, Dorset Court and Derby Court. What appears to be a large stone-built house with a pediment was in fact a terrace of three substantial houses in Dorset Court with gardens running down to the river and stairs where boats could tie up. The scene is only some three hundred yards upstream from Scott's view of Montagu House; the stretch of river bank can be seen in the illustration of the first part of cats 2.31 and 2.32.

See Section II: The River for other views of Westminster Bridge.

V

ST JAMES'S AND MAYFAIR

In Westminster the upper classes dealt with the serious business of state; in the area to the west – St James's, Mayfair and beyond in the pleasure gardens of Ranelagh and Vauxhall – they relaxed. The magnet that had originally drawn them westward was the transfer of the Court to the Tudor St James's Palace after fires at Whitehall Palace in the 1690s, but the area also had the advantage of clean air (prevailing westerly winds took the smoke of the City eastwards) and, for the very richest, offered opportunities to create gardens and to enjoy open outlooks over parkland.

By the middle of the eighteenth century almost all the grandest families had moved their London residences from the City or the Strand. The fields to the north-east of St James's Palace had been developed at the time of the Restoration to create St James's Square and the surrounding streets; mansions were built along the ancient highway of Piccadilly – Burlington House (1660s onwards), Devonshire House (1730s, replacing Berkeley House of 1664), Egremont House (1756–63) – but Mayfair was an entirely eighteenth-century creation, built by aristocratic landowners in what had been open fields. There were mansions – notably Chesterfield House (1747–52) – but more typical were speculative developments of elegant terraces in streets and squares. Noble and wealthy residents would often take leases for relatively short periods – spending the winter season in town and summers at their country estates. Further west in Chelsea, the grounds of a mansion built by Lord Ranelagh in the 1690s were developed in the 1740s, not as residential property but

as a pleasure garden which rapidly overtook the less exclusive Vauxhall Gardens as the most fashionable venue for promenading, masquerading and intrigue.

Thorold gives a useful account of the financial and social underpinning of successive building booms and depressions in post-Fire London, especially of the expansion to the west. Summerson remains the most helpful architectural overview, but the forthcoming volume 6 of Pevsner will undoubtedly bring much information to light.

St James's

5.1–5.9

5.1

Simon François Ravenet (1706/21–74) after Pierre David Morier (c.1705–70)

*George II, c.*1745

Published by I. Wesson

Etching and engraving with engraved lettering, 620 × 454 mm

1870-10-8-2574

The King is shown as a military hero. A contemporary viewer, familiar with horses and classical riding, would have been impressed by his impeccable yet subtle control. The horse is engaged in the *passage*, trotting with balance and sustained precision, as illustrated in contemporary riding manuals such as François Robichon de la Guérinière's *Ecole de Cavalerie*, 1733. In cat. 4.11 the Duke of Cumberland, in a similar display of equestrian skill, rides a Spanish

charger, the most highly prized war horse of the early eighteenth century. The King's horse is a larger animal with an oriental head. It might even have been bred at the state stud at Celle in Hanover and descended from horses seized from the Ottoman army as it retreated from Vienna in 1683. State studs were set up throughout Europe in the early eighteenth century in order to provide a good supply of military horses, but in Britain – more concerned with its navy than with its cavalry – horse-breeding was largely a private amusement indulged in by those with a passion for racing and hunting.

George II was the last English king to lead his army in battle, at Dettingen in 1743. His campaigns in the War of Austrian Succession and support for what was to become the Seven Years War were driven by concern for Hanover rather than for the sake of British interests. His frequent absences in Germany, together with the expense of these wars for the British taxpayer, made him unpopular.

Both Morier and Ravenet arrived in London from France in the early 1740s.

5.2

Thomas Bowles (1712?–67)

View of St James's Palace and Pall Mall, 1750s

Etching with engraved lettering, 246 × 389 mm (cropped)

Crace XI.28

1880-11-13-2135

St James's Palace was built in the 1530s. It was the official royal residence from

George the Second, King of Great Britaine, &c. &c. &c.

5.1

A View of St James's Palace Pall-Mall, &c. | Vue du Palais royal de St Jacques Pall-Mall, &c.

5.2

A View of St James's Square London | Vue de la Place de Ste Jaques a Londres.

5.3

the Whitehall Palace fire of 1698 until the 1820s when George IV rebuilt Buckingham House. This print, a *vue d'optique* to be viewed with a special apparatus (see cat. 1.21), shows the main entrance to the palace from the foot of St James's Street, with Pall Mall stretching towards the church of St Martin-in-the-Fields. St James's Street was noted for coffee and chocolate houses and gambling clubs, including the surviving White's.

5.3

Thomas Bowles (1712?–67)

View of St James's Square, 1750s (this edition from after 1768)

Published by Robert Wilkinson in Cornhill, Carington Bowles in St Paul's Churchyard and Robert Sayer in Fleet Street

Etching with engraved lettering, 261 × 398 mm

Crace XI.95

1880-11-13-2202

St James's Square was laid out by Henry Jermyn, Earl of St Albans, in the 1660s. Many of its grand residences changed hands and were rebuilt during the following century by owners wanting town houses in the most up-to-date and lavish style. The Music Room from Norfolk House in the south-east corner of the Square (shown on the right of this print) can be seen at the Victoria and Albert Museum and gives some sense of the splendour behind the restrained exteriors.

The first house on the site was Jermyn's own mansion. It was purchased by the 8th Duke of Norfolk in 1722 for £10,000. Frederick, Prince of Wales, rented it for a while after being expelled from St James's Palace in 1737, and his son, the future George III, was born there in the following year. In 1748 the 9th Duke of Norfolk bought neighbouring Belasyse House for £1,830, demolished both buildings and employed Matthew Brettingham to build a new house at a cost of £18,575. Norfolk

House was complete by the beginning of 1756. Horace Walpole attended the celebratory party: 'All the earth was there last Tuesday … In short, you never saw such a scene of magnificence and taste. The tapestry, the embroidered bed, the illumination, the glasses, the lightness and novelty of the ornaments, and the ceiling are delightful.'

But residents needed practical amenities as well as magnificence and taste. A local Act of Parliament in 1726 allowed them to levy rates for paving and maintaining the Square and to create the ornamental reservoir, supplied with water pumped from the Thames by the York Buildings Waterworks.

5.4

5.4

Edward Fisher (1722–82) after Joshua Reynolds (1723–92)

The Ladies Amabel and Mary Jemima Yorke, 1762

Published by Edward Fisher in Great Newport Street, Leicester Square

Mezzotint with some scratched lines and engraved lettering, 451 × 359 mm (cropped)

C.S. 61 (i)

1838-7-14-40 ex-collections Thomas Lawrence, John Rushout, Baron Northwick

This fine mezzotint is based on a portrait of the daughters, aged four and nine, of Philip, Viscount Royston and his wife

Lady Jemima Campbell, painted by Joshua Reynolds in 1760 for a fee of eighty guineas (Mannings 1956). In 1761 Horace Walpole saw the painting hanging in the family house in St James's Square; it is now in the Cleveland Museum of Art, Ohio.

The family were typically aristocratic residents of the Square. Viscount Royston was the son of Lord Chancellor Hardwicke (cat. 1.67) and succeeded him as 2nd Earl of Hardwicke in 1764. His wife had a longer and more elevated pedigree, her father being 3rd Earl of Breadalbane and her mother, Amabel, the daughter of Henry de Grey, Duke of Kent, who had inherited from her maternal grandfather the titles Baroness Lucas and Marchioness de Grey which unusually passed through the female line. In 1772, twelve years after Reynolds's portrait was painted, Lady Amabel married Alexander, Viscount Polwarth, son of the Earl of Marchmont; she inherited her mother's titles and in 1816 was created Countess de Grey. In 1780 Lady Mary Jemima married Thomas Robinson, 2nd Lord Grantham.

5.5

T. Miller (fl. 1760s) after John Vardy (1718–65)

North West view of Spencer House, 1763

Published by John Vardy (inscription on finished state)

Etching with engraved lettering, 302 × 343 mm

Crace XI.16

1880-11-13-2123

The richest Londoners built their own mansions in town. By the mid eighteenth century these would be on the Thames at Westminster (see cat. 2.36), in newly developing Mayfair, or near to the palace and the park in St James's. Among the wealthiest young couples in the country were John Spencer and Margaret Poyntz, who married in 1755 when he had just come of age at twenty-one and she was eighteen. Nine years earlier John

5.5

Spencer had inherited a fortune which included 100,000 acres that brought him an income of £35,000 a year, as well as the family's ancestral home at Althorp, a hunting lodge at Pytchley in Northamptonshire and a villa at Wimbledon Park. The Spencers' first London home was in Grosvenor Street, but in the year of their marriage the architect John Vardy sold Spencer a building lease on a site fronting what is now Green Park (its previous owner, Henry Bromley, 1st Baron Montfort, had shot himself after getting into financial difficulties). Spencer House, built at a cost of £50,000, between 1756 and 1763, is the grandest London house of the period to survive.

The west front of Spencer House, shown here, overlooks what is now Green Park; the apparent scale of the building is reduced by the giant pediment stretching over five bays and gives the town mansion the air of a suburban villa appropriate to its quasi-rural setting. The interiors illustrate the mid-century transition from Palladian to neoclassical taste. Vardy's rooms on the ground floor are characterized by robustly carved and moulded detail,

culminating in the spectacular southern-most room on the Park front where a screen of columns is transformed into a group of naturalistic palm trees. The room immediately above is the most lavish of those decorated by James 'Athenian' Stuart, who took over the interior decoration in 1758. The contrast could scarcely be more marked. Stuart's decoration is almost entirely two-dimensional, or in very low relief, with delicate – though richly gilded – neoclassical motifs inspired by Raphael's Vatican Loggie as well as by recent discoveries at Herculaneum; the chimney piece is a copy of the *Aldobrandini Wedding*, a Roman painting excavated in 1605.

For an account of the house see Friedman.

5.6

James Watson (1740–90) after Joshua Reynolds (1723–92)

Viscountess Spencer and her daughter, Georgiana, c.1765

Published by Robert Sayer at the Golden Buck, near Serjeants Inn, Fleet Street

The RIGHT HONOURABLE

Georgiana Lady Viscountess Spencer, and Her Daughter the Hon. Miss Georgiana Spencer.

London, Printed for Robt Sayer, Map & Printseller, at the Golden Buck near Serjeants Inn, Fleet Street.

5.6

Mezzotint with some scratched lines and engraved lettering, 505 × 354 mm

C.S. 132 (ii)

1902-10-11-6503 Bequeathed by William Eaton, 2nd Baron Cheylesmore

In 1757 the Spencers' first child, Georgiana, was born. This mezzotint is based on a portrait (Mannings 1677) painted by Joshua Reynolds for Margaret Spencer's brother William Poyntz. Reynolds's notebooks for September 1761 record four appointments for the mother, but only one – separate – appointment for the child. Reynolds was paid his fee of seventy guineas in June 1763. The pose, which seems so natural, was obviously contrived by Reynolds but he conveys what was evidently a particularly affectionate mother and child relationship. He has combined his study in Italy of images of the Virgin presenting the Christ Child with a French Rococo asymmetry and the sort of tender informality that Ramsay brought to female portraits.

Georgiana was to grow up to be – as Duchess of Devonshire – one of the celebrities of her age; see Foreman for an account of her extraordinary life.

The print, sold for 7s 6d, would have been made in 1765 when Spencer was created Earl; the publisher's address, still without a street number (see p. 52), indicates that it cannot date from later than 1768.

Horace Walpole and his Circle

Horace Walpole (1717–97) was the youngest son of Robert Walpole, First Lord of the Treasury from 1721 to 1742, and he enjoyed a position at the centre of society. He was born in Arlington Street, St James's; from 1779 he made his London home in Berkeley Square.

Walpole's *Memoirs of the Reign of George II*, *Memoirs of the Reign of George III* and more especially his extensive correspondence provide a precise and witty commentary on life in eighteenth-century England; his publication of George Vertue's notebooks, as *Anecdotes of Painting*, was the first history of British art, and his *Castle of Otranto* the first gothic novel. His fanciful villa, Strawberry Hill, near Twickenham – acquired from Mrs Chenevix, the toyshop keeper (cat. 3.47) in 1747 – became the focus for the eighteenth-century revival of the gothic style in architecture.

The standard biography is Ketton-Cremer; Mowl discusses Walpole's homosexual orientation and its effect on his life and work. Much of Walpole's collection was gathered together by Wilmarth Sheldon Lewis at Farmington, Connecticut (now the Lewis-Walpole Library, Yale University); more than two hundred items were brought together for an exhibition in 1980; see Calloway *et al*.

5.7

McArdell's studio together with the plate and all impressions. In 1787 he heard that the print had been copied for a magazine, but age had made him more sanguine: 'It was originally my own fault … if one will make an exposition of one's self, one must not complain if one's head serves for a signpost'.

5.8
Richard Bentley (1708–82)

A letter with sketches of Chinese buildings

Pen and ink and wash, 310 × 193 mm
1962-7-14-8 Bequeathed by Iolo Williams

Bentley was the son of the renowned classical scholar of the same name. In 1748 he met Walpole, and with John Chute the three men formed the 'Committee of Taste' that was responsible for the early, and perhaps the most imaginative, development of Strawberry Hill. Bentley's continual financial problems and optimistic money-making schemes – as well as his forceful wife and his six children – irritated Walpole and they saw little of each other after 1760.

5.7
James McArdell (1729–65) after Joshua Reynolds (1723–92)

Horace Walpole, 1757

Mezzotint with engraved lettering,
352 × 250 mm
Private plate
C.S. 186 (ii); Goodwin 63 (ii)
Q.2-57 ex-collection Joseph Gulston (Lugt 2986)

This mezzotint is based on one of three versions of a portrait painted by Reynolds in 1756 and 1757 (Mannings 1819–21), probably the one painted for Grosvenor Bedford (now in the National Portrait Gallery). Walpole commissioned the print as a private plate (not for publication) so that he could distribute impressions among friends. On 9 November 1757 it came to his attention that McArdell had told people about the print and he wrote to Bedford that he was 'extremely angry', demanding that the painting be removed from

5.8

209

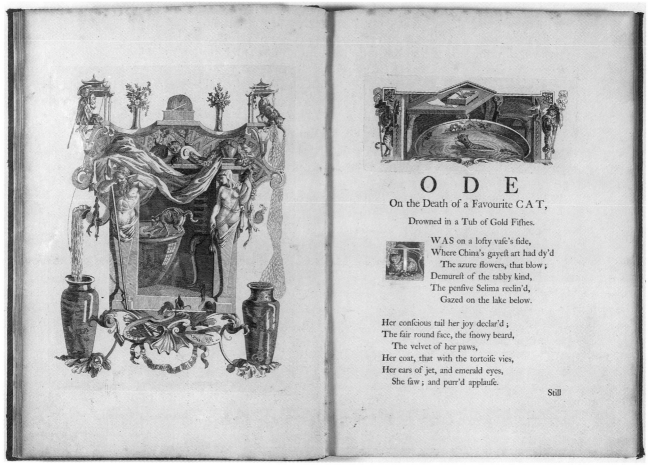

ODE

On the Death of a Favourite CAT,

Drowned in a Tub of Gold Fishes.

WAS on a lofty vase's side,
Where China's gayest art had dy'd
The azure flowers, that blow;
Demureft of the tabby kind,
The penfive Selima reclin'd,
Gazed on the lake below.

Her confcious tail her joy declar'd;
The fair round face, the fnowy beard,
The velvet of her paws,
Her coat, that with the tortoife vies,
Her ears of jet, and emerald eyes,
She faw; and purr'd applaufe.

Still

5.9

Bentley's letter reads: 'Dear Sir / and am vastly sorry I cannot / have the pleasure of attending you tomorrow. I am / your most obedient servant / R. Bentley / it was impossible for me / to give you earlier notice.' The two rapid sketches of pagodas may have some relation to those in cat. 5.9.

5.9
Johann Sebastian Müller
(c.1715–92) after Richard Bentley
(1708–82)

Designs by Mr. R. Bentley, for six poems by Mr. T. Gray open at Ode on the Death of a Favourite Cat by Thomas Gray, 1753

Etching, 268 × 210 mm (full page illustration), 79 × 180 mm (headpiece)
Published by Robert Dodsley in Pall Mall
1868-7-11-6 to 30 (165 b 6)

This exceptionally fine publication contains six poems by Thomas Gray (1716–71): *Ode on the Spring*; *Ode on the Death of a Favourite Cat*; *Ode on a Distant Prospect of Eton College*; *A Long Story*; *Hymn to Adversity*; *Elegy Written in a Country Churchyard*. Each is illustrated with a full-page engraving and head- and tailpieces by Müller or Charles Grignion after Richard Bentley's extraordinarily inventive designs in the gothic-Rococo taste. An 'Explanation of the prints' by Horace Walpole follows.

Gray was a friend of Walpole's from their schooldays at Eton. In 1739–41 they travelled together in France and Italy, but they quarrelled and were not reconciled until 1745. Gray spent the rest of his life as a Cambridge don; although he became well known – largely through the popularity of the *Elegy* – he avoided the limelight and in 1757 declined the post of Poet Laureate.

The volume shown here appeared only after a great deal of persuasion on Walpole's part. Gray was reluctant to be seen to be promoting his own work and insisted that the title should stress Bentley's designs. Walpole was already considering setting up his own press and Dodsley's splendid publication must have encouraged him; in 1757 Gray's *Progress of Poesy* and *The Bard* were the first works printed at Strawberry Hill.

Robert Dodsley (1703–64) was the leading bookseller and publisher of the day. His shop at Tully's Head in Pall Mall was a centre for the publication of the poetry from Alexander Pope to translations of Virgil. He was also a co-publisher of Johnson's *Dictionary* (cat. 3.75), and published the first translations of Voltaire and Rousseau; he ran four periodicals, *The Public Register*, *The Museum*, *The World* and

The Annual Register, as well as partly owning *The London Evening Post*, *The London Magazine* and *The London Chronicle*; his *Oeconomy of Human Life*, a collection of moral precepts, was the best-selling book of the eighteenth century. Dodsley's promotion of poetry did much to create a British canon, in which Gray's *Elegy* holds an important place. The *Ode on the Death of a Favourite Cat*, written for Walpole in 1747, is less well known, but its final phrase has passed into the language: 'From hence, ye Beauties undeceiv'd. / Know, one false step is ne'er retriev'd, / And be with caution bold. / Not all that tempts your wand'ring eyes / And heedless hearts, is lawful prize; / Nor all that glisters gold.' For Dodsley's career see Solomon.

Bentley's designs have a remarkable inventiveness. The death of the favourite cat is illustrated with emblematical whimsy perfectly embodying the Rococo taste for chinoiserie. Two cats fish from pagodas on either side of a large mousetrap; the moment before Selina meets her end is framed by a river god and a female figure of Fate cutting the thread of life. Below mice rejoice, one climbing on a spent candle; Gray, the poet, is represented by a lyre and Bentley, the artist, by a palette. On the headpiece to the poem two cat pall-bearers with black crepe ribbons round their hats frame the last moments of the cat as she flounders in the Chinese fishbowl. At the end of the poem a tailpiece shows Charon rowing the cat across the Styx to where a slavering Cerberus awaits her.

Princess Augusta and Gardens

5.10–5.13

In 1736 Princess Augusta (1719–72), daughter of the Duke of Saxe-Gotha, married Frederick, Prince of Wales (1707–51). Irreconcilable differences between the Prince and his parents led in the following year to the young couple's expulsion from St James's Palace. The Prince already owned Carlton House in Pall Mall and a suburban villa at Kew, but he also acquired three country residences – Cliveden in Berkshire, Park Place near Henley-on-Thames and Durdans near Epsom. After making a London home for five or six years at Norfolk House, St James's Square (see cat. 5.3), the family moved in 1743 to Leicester House in Leicester Fields

A View of the Garden &c at Carlton House in Pall Mall, a Palace of Her Royal Highness the Princess Dowager of Wales. To whom it is most humbly Inscribed by Her Royal Highness's Allegd and most obedient Servant John Tinney.

Vûe du Jardin de Carlton House, Palais de S.A.R. La Princesse Douairiere de Galles.

5.10

(now Leicester Square). George II had set up a rival court there when he was Prince of Wales, and Frederick followed the pattern. Leicester House remained a focus of political intrigue after Frederick's sudden death in 1751, until in 1764 Princess Augusta moved to Carlton House.

5.10

William Woollett (1735–85)

A View of the Garden at Carlton House in Pall Mall, July 1760

Published by John Tinney at the Golden Lion, Fleet Street, and sold by Thomas Bowles, St Paul's Churchyard, John Bowles and Son, Cornhill, and Robert Sayer, Fleet Street

Etched with engraved lettering,
377 × 553 mm
Fagan 33 (ii)
1866-12-8-102

In the 1730s the 12-acre garden of Carlton House, on the northern edge of St James's Park, had been laid out for Frederick, Prince of Wales, by William Kent in the new informal style. The busy street of Pall Mall is just a hundred yards away, but the spire of St Martin-in-the-Fields rising above the trees is the only indication that this garden is in town. The plan, as can be seen clearly on Rocque's map (pp. 44–5), consisted of a strong central axis leading to a Palladian temple, while on either side dense plantations of trees are threaded through with irregular paths.

This is one of a number of prints of aristocratic gardens published by John Tinney and others from the late 1740s onwards. They would have been designed not only to appeal to owners and their immediate circle but also to those of the respectable middling class who were allowed to visit such gardens and the public rooms of grand houses while their owners were away. The fact that Tinney joined Robert Sayer and the Bowles family to publish this print indicates a large market.

This is one of Woollett's earliest prints. He was to go on to become one of the greatest British printmakers. Many of Woollett's prints were reproductions of paintings – then the most prestigious area of the trade – but in this case he worked after his own design. The print is dedicated to Princess Augusta, but she is not shown in her garden; the focus is on gardeners sweeping the lawn and sieving grass cuttings, their quiet concentration on the task in hand enhancing the air of bucolic calm. The image is entirely etched. Woollett – in a technical tour-de-force – has created a range of textures to suggest the hard surfaces of the garden sculpture and the distant temple as well as a wide range of foliage.

Carlton House and the garden were remodelled by the future George IV, before being demolished in 1827 and replaced by Nash's Carlton House Terrace.

5.11

T. Miller (fl. 1760s,) after William Chambers (1723–96)

The Great Pagoda from the Gardens and Buildings at Kew, 1763

Published by William Chambers
Etching with engraved lettering,
580 × 428 mm
1863-5-9-263 (242.c.14)

In 1731, shortly after his arrival in England, Frederick, Prince of Wales had leased a seventeenth-century house at Kew. He employed William Kent to enlarge and embellish it, but did not begin any extensive work on the grounds until 1750. By the time of his death on 20 March 1751 he had planted, according to George Vertue, 'many curious and foreign trees'; he had erected the 'House of Confucius' to the design of Joseph Goupy and was planning other garden buildings and sculpture. Princess Augusta continued the work under the guidance of Lord Bute (see cat. 1.37), an ardent gardener and botanist. In

1758 she commissioned the 'Alhambra' from William Chambers and by 1763 he had designed – as well as a number of hothouses or 'stoves' – a mosque, a ruined arch, several Roman temples and the spectacular 163 foot Great Pagoda shown here and still in situ.

Horace Walpole claimed that Augusta spent between £30,000 and £40,000 on Kew. After her death the gardens were joined to the adjacent royal gardens of Richmond Lodge, already redesigned by Capability Brown. In succeeding decades, under the supervision of Sir Joseph Banks, they were to become the Royal Botanic Garden.

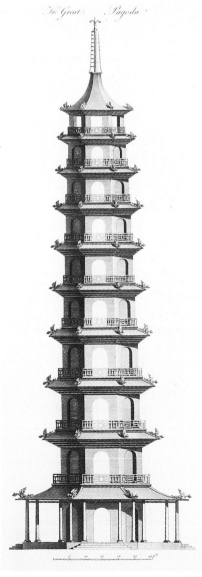

5.11

With this fine volume Chambers was advertising his talents as an architect and making the buildings at Kew available to be copied. Publication was expensive, and the young George III supported Chambers with a contribution of £800, no doubt persuaded of the value of promoting advanced British design and expertise. The volume follows a number of influential books of architectural engravings published earlier in the century: Colen Campbell's *Vitruvius Britannicus*, 1715–25, William Kent's *Designs of Inigo Jones*, 1727, James Gibbs's *Book of Architecture*, 1728, John Vardy's *Some Designs of Mr Inigo Jones and Mr William Kent*, 1744. Chambers's own *Designs of Chinese Buildings, Furniture, Dresses*, 1757, recorded buildings he had seen in China in the 1740s.

For the history of Kew gardens see Desmond; for Chambers see Harris.

5.12

Lancelot ('Capability') Brown (1716–83)

Manuscript bill addressed to Lord Winterton, 11 February 1762

NOT ILLUSTRATED

Pen and ink, 228 × 187 mm

Heal 74.2 Bequeathed by Sir Ambrose Heal, 1959

Brown was born in Northumberland and established his career in the 1740s working as head gardener for Richard Temple, Viscount Cobham, at Stowe. From 1751 he lived in Hammersmith, then a village to the west of London, in reach of the town houses of patrons whose country estates he was already transforming. By 1762 when he sent this bill to Lord Winterton (cat. 3.82), Brown had become extremely fashionable. His hallmark was to integrate the country house into a landscape of undulating lawns, carefully placed clumps of trees and broad stretches of water. In 1764 he was appointed Master Gardener for the royal estates at Richmond and Hampton Court. His

name is associated with about two hundred English estates.

Brown has charged Winterton £84 3s for a survey of his estate, Shillinglee Park, near Kirdford, Sussex. The estate had come into the Turnour family by marriage in the mid seventeenth century and was no doubt ripe for modernization after a hundred years. The bill totals £84 3s: £12 13s for the survey itself at 4d per acre; £40 for the plan; £31 10s for several journeys and for Brown's men's time. François de la Rochefoucauld writing a year after for Brown's death, recorded that 'on riding around a park for an hour he could conceive a design for the whole place, and that afterwards half a day sufficed for him to mark it out on the ground'.

See Stroud for a biography of Brown.

5.13

François Vivares (1709–80) after Pierre Bourguignon (fl. 1750s–80s)

*Trade card of James Scott at Turnham Green. c.*1754

Etching with engraved lettering, 240 × 180 mm

Heal 74.41

5.13

While wealthy garden owners were fascinated by botanical experiments and fashionable landscape, gardens were also essential for the provision of food. Aristocratic gardens contained kitchen gardens where fruit and vegetables were grown, and from the seventeenth century market gardening on a commercial scale developed around the edges of the built-up area of London, fertilized by the loads of the night-soil men (cat. 1.89) and by horse manure carried by boat from Dung Wharf, near Blackfriars. Nurserymen provided seeds and developed new varieties. The range of vegetables and fruits was mouth-watering: a seed catalogue issued by Jacob Wrench of Lower Thames Street (Banks 74.39) includes seventeen varieties of peas, ten varieties of cabbage, thirteen lettuces, twenty-eight peaches, thirty plums, forty-two pears, thirty-eight apples 'and divers others'. James Scott lists such exotics as pineapples as well as melons, grapes and apricots and advertises that he will build stoves (hothouses) for forcing such fruit.

For a brief history of growing, marketing and eating vegetables in London see R. Weinstein, 'London's Market Gardens in the Early Modern Period', in Galinou, pp. 80–99; for the seasonal workers employed in market gardens see George, pp. 145–6; for an aristocratic kitchen garden see Thomson, pp. 352–3.

The New King and Queen and Young Aristocrats

5.14–5.17

George II died on 25 October 1760. His son, Frederick, Prince of Wales, had died nine years earlier and so the throne passed to his grandson, the twenty-two-year-old George III. A suitable queen had to be found for the young king, and on 8 September 1761 the seventeen-year-old Princess Charlotte of Mecklenburg-Strelitz arrived from Germany. The wedding

took place that evening in the chapel of St James's Palace and the coronation in Westminster Abbey two weeks later on 22 September.

Although the wedding was a private affair, the coronation was an occasion for public spectacle: the aristocracy appeared at its most extravagant in splendid formal robes, glittering with gold, silver and precious stones. It was an opportunity exploited by mercers, lacemen, jewellers, robe and mantua makers who were eager for commissions. A letter in the Duchy of Bedford archives blends the obsequiousness

that was expected in any approach to a member of the aristocracy with the assertiveness of a confident tradesmen: Benjamin Day of Long's Warehouse, at the corner of Tavistock Street, Covent Garden, wrote on 16 July 1761 to the Duke of Bedford's agent, Robert Butcher, pointing out that 'His Grace has now an opportunity which may possibly never happen again, which is to employ him in making the coronation robes for my Lord Duke's family, as we have all the patterns of the last coronation, at which time they was in general made at Long's Warehouse.

5.14

He hopes my Lord Duke will not take it amiss that he takes this method to apply, as Mr Day is at this time afflicted with the gout and not able to wait on him in person.' New ermine-lined robes – using refurbished ermine from his old robes and sixty new skins – were ordered for the Duke from Day at a cost of £26 19s 6d; Andrew Hunter provided new coronets for the Duke and Duchess; James Spilsbury of Pritchard's Warehouse made the Duchess's robes, a skirt of 'silver stuff' and a silver coat trimmed with *point d'espagne* lace; Kempe Brydges, laceman, at the Three Crowns at the corner of Bedford Street, Covent Garden, provided silver net and gold and silver tassels (Thomson, pp. 294–7).

5.14

Thomas Frye (1710–62)

Queen Charlotte, 24 May 1762

Published by Thomas Frye at the Golden Head, Hatton Garden

Mezzotint with a few scratched lines and engraved lettering, 594 × 430 mm (cropped)

C.S. 1 a I (proof before letter)

1872-1-13-844

This print is one of the finest examples of the art of mezzotint. Frye has created a variety of textures, from the young Queen's skin and hair to her ermine gown and rich lace, to the pearls and diamonds which she wears in abundance. Horace Walpole described her appearance at Court on the evening of her arrival in London on 8 September 1761: she was dressed in white and silver with 'an endless mantle of violet-coloured velvet, lined with ermine, and attempted to be fastened on her shoulder by a bunch of large pearls … On her head was a beautiful little tiara of diamonds; a diamond necklace, and a stomacher of diamonds, worth threescore thousand pounds, which she is to wear at the coronation too.' Charlotte's love of jewellery became legendary and was to provide

fuel for critics of the monarchy in the radical 1790s.

This is the largest of three versions of the portrait that Frye produced at the same time. The plates, together with those of George III after Frye's drawing (see cat. 5.15), and those for Frye's series of mezzotint heads were acquired by John Boydell after Frye's death. For Frye's career as a printmaker and porcelain manufacturer see cat. 2.5.

5.15

William Pether (1738–1821) after Thomas Frye (1710–62)

George III, 1 November 1762

Mezzotint with etching and engraved lettering, 615 × 428 mm

Published by John Boydell, Engraver, in Cheapside, and Henry Parker and Elizabeth Bakewell in Cornhill

C.S. 17 (ii)

1845-7-24-117

HIS Most Excellent Majesty George III King of GREAT-BRITAINE

5.15

George III was the first Hanoverian king to be born in Britain, but he was unpopular at the start of his reign. His determination (and that of his mentor, John Stuart, 3rd Earl of Bute, who became First Lord of the Treasury, see cat. 1.37 and p. 200) to bring a speedy end to the Seven Years War was seen as overturning the victories of 1759, and as excessive interference by the monarch in government. But by the mid-1760s Bute's influence had waned and George matured into a king who was largely respected for his personal integrity.

George III took a serious interest in scholarship and built up an immense library (passed to the British Museum by George IV and now in the British Library) which was open to readers on application; Samuel Johnson was a regular reader. In 1762 he purchased for £20,000 the magnificent art collection of the Venetian consul Joseph Smith which included the great works by Canaletto that remain among of the treasures of the royal collection. Frye died before making mezzotints of the young King as pairs to those of the Queen, and his drawings were engraved by his pupil William Pether.

5.16

Edward Fisher (1722–82) after Joshua Reynolds (1723–92)

Lady Elizabeth Keppel, 1761

Published by Edward Fisher at the Golden Head, the South Side of Leicester Square

Mezzotint with scratched lines and engraved lettering, 582 × 362 mm

C.S. 36 (v)

1902-10-11-2173 Bequeathed by William Eaton, 2nd Baron Cheylesmore

Lady Elizabeth Keppel, (1739–68) was the daughter of William Anne van Keppel, 2nd Earl of Albemarle. She is shown here in the dress she wore as one of ten bridesmaids at the wedding of George III and Queen Charlotte. Her dress is an example of the *corps de robe*

5.16

worn for formal Court occasions.
Although the pose created by Reynolds
suggests lively movement, in reality
such dress must have been heavy and
uncomfortable: the fabric was weighted
down with embroidery in silver thread,
the upper part (the 'body') was stiffened
so that the wearer would have to stand
rigidly upright, and the train descending
up to three yards from the waist required
assistance from a page.

Less than three years later, on 8 June
1764, Elizabeth married Francis Russell,
Marquis of Tavistock, and settled into a
country residence, Houghton House,
near Ampthill, Bedfordshire, and a town
mansion, Thanet House, Great Russell
Street (the Russells – Dukes of Bedford
– remained in Bloomsbury until 1800).
But her happiness was short-lived: in
March 1767, while she was pregnant
with her third child, her husband was
killed in a riding accident and she died
less than two years later.

For life in the Russell household see
Thomson.

The print sold for the high price of
15s. Fisher's lengthy address points to
the confusion possible before numbering
was introduced: Hogarth also used the
sign of the Golden Head at his house in
Leicester Square, at the southern end of
the east side. Joshua Reynolds also lived
in Leicester Square. His notebooks
record sittings for the painting on which
this print is based: eight for Lady
Elizabeth and two for her black servant.
The painting remains at Woburn Abbey,
the Russell country house (Mannings
1052).

5.17

5·17

James Watson (1740–90) after
Joshua Reynolds (1723–92)

*Charles James Fox with Ladies
Sarah Lennox and Susan
Strangways*, 1762

Published by James Watson, no. 16 Craven
Buildings, Drury Lane, and John Bowles,
Cornhill, and Carington Bowles, St Paul's
Churchyard, and Robert Sayer, Fleet
Street (lettering on finished state)

Mezzotint with a few scratched lines and
engraved lettering, 630 × 428 mm

C.S. 91 (i)

1832-12-11-77

Sarah Lennox was renowned as a great
beauty, and the future George III had
been infatuated with her before being
diverted into a more suitable marriage
with a German princess. She is shown
here a few months after the royal
wedding – aged seventeen and herself

about to marry Sir Charles Bunbury –
leaning out of a window at Holland
House, the Jacobean mansion beyond the
western edge of London where Henry
Fox (cat. 4.21) had set up home in 1746.
Fox was married to Sarah's much older
sister Caroline. Their son Charles James
Fox, who was to grow up to become a
leading radical politician, is shown here
as a thirteen-year-old looking admiringly
at his older cousin Susan Fox-
Strangways. The group portrait alludes

to a much-praised Latin poem that Charles James wrote as an Eton schoolboy; in it he wished that a pigeon would carry a letter of love to Susan.

The elaborate gowns of the young women are examples of fashionable day dress, without the heavy embroidery that made formal wear so uncomfortable, but involving a complicated arrangements of several garments. Upper-class women could not dress or arrange their hair without assistance. Underwear consisted of a fine linen shift, stays (or 'bodies') made of leather, a hooped petticoat and stockings supported by garters; on top was a silk outer petticoat, an open-fronted gown (Susan Fox-Strangways's gown is trimmed on either side of the front with a long strip of raw-edged gathered silk arranged in a serpentine scroll) pinned to the stiff triangular stomacher that covered the front of the stays; further trimmings included lace ruffles that were tacked to the sleeves of the shift so that they could be removed for washing, 'handkerchiefs' worn across the shoulders, and caps of lace or gauze– Sarah wears a fashionable style called the 'Ranelagh mob' while Susan's cap is wired to stand out from her head. See Hart and North for a detailed account of fashionable dress of the period.

Both these young women were to transgress social proprieties and to spend years ostracized from polite circles. In 1764 Susan eloped at the age of twenty-one with William O'Brien, a popular actor; her parents disowned her and the couple were obliged to spend six miserable years exiled in New York on an allowance from Henry Fox. In 1769 Sarah hit the headlines when she left her husband for Lord William Gordon, the father of her child; the affair was short-lived, but it was many years before she was accepted in society. At the end of her life, widowed after a happy second marriage, she received a pension of £800 a year from the aged King.

The print, sold for 10s 6d, reproduces a painting made for Henry Fox by Joshua Reynolds at a cost of £120; it remains in the family collection. Reynolds painted Sarah again in 1764 in a pseudo-classical composition, *Lady Sarah Bunbury sacrificing to the Graces*; her first husband Sir Charles Bunbury paid Reynolds £250 for the painting.

For the lives of the Lennox sisters based on their letters and family papers see Tillyard.

St James's Park
5.18–5.30

St James's Park, a wedge-shaped piece of land to the south of the Palace and west of Whitehall, was opened to the public by Charles II, who had it redesigned and created a canal from several small ponds. By the middle of the eighteenth century it was known as a night-time haunt of prostitutes (see cat. 5.20), but by day it could still be seen as an almost rural retreat: 'In this park are stags and fallow deer that are so tame as to take gently out of your hand and each end of the Mall there are stands of cows, from whence the company at small expense, may be supplied with warm milk' (*London in Miniature*, 1755).

Buckingham House (later Palace) lies on the western side of St James's Park facing the avenue of the Mall, more than half a mile long and a fashionable place for promenading. The House had been built at the beginning of the century for John Sheffield, Duke of Buckingham and Normanby, and in 1762, it was bought for £28,000 by George III. It served as the principal London residence of the royal family, removed from the state

A View of the Canal in S.t James's Park, Buckingham House &c. | Vue du Canal et de la Maison de Buckingham dans le Parc de taken from the Parade. | S.t James.

5.18

functions of St James's Palace, and was often described as the Queen's House. Ownership was transferred to Queen Charlotte in exchange for her interest in Somerset House (which had been the official home of the Queen since the seventeenth century) when it was rebuilt in 1775.

5.19

5.18

John Stevens (fl. *c.*1750) after Antonio Canaletto (1697–68)

A view of the canal in St James's Park

Etching with engraved lettering, 252 × 398 mm

Crace XII.85

1880-11-13-2337

This is one of a group of prints after drawings by Canaletto published by Sayer in 1751 (see cat. 1.3). A lost drawing of St James's Park by Canaletto which was perhaps the source for this print appeared in the sale of the collection of Charles Rogers on 24 April 1799 (Lot 62).

5.19

Anthony Walker (1726–65)

A Park Shower, or the Beau Mond in Distress, 22 September 1755

Etching with engraved lettering, 254 × 384 mm

Published by John Smith at Hogarth's Head, Cheapside

Crace XII.89

1880-11-13-2341

It is unusual for prints to show London in the rain. Here the fashionable world gathered in the Mall is thrown into panic by a sudden shower. A woman on the right is being revived with smelling salts (see cat. 1.78).

5.20

5.20

John June (fl. *c.*1747–70) after J. L'Agneau (fl. 1750s)

A view of the Mall, 23 March 1752

Published by Bispham Dickinson on Ludgate Hill

Etching with engraved lettering, 323 × 474 mm

BM Satire 3188

1865-6-10-1096

This decidedly inelegant view of the Mall was published in the City after a design by a City designer and print-seller (for L'Agneau see cat. 4.17) and is suggestive of how leisured promenading in St James's Park might have been seen by those at the workaday end of town. Pompous gentlemen – evidently caricatures of identifiable people – are propositioned by provocatively dressed women; one woman is thrusting forward a young girl. The Park had a reputation

5.21

The Cock Pit

5.21

William Hogarth (1697–1764)
Cock Pit, 5 November 1759

Published by William Hogarth

Etching with engraved lettering,
314 × 382 mm

Paulson 206

1868-8-22-1618 Bequeathed by Felix
Slade, 1868

Cockfighting was enjoyed by all levels
of society. Hogarth shows the blind
Lord Albemarle Bertie (*c.*1720–65),

brother of the Duke of Ancaster (see
cats 2.16 and 5.31), in a crowd that
includes a butcher, a chimney-sweep,
a sow gelder, a black footman, a
coachman and a jockey; women were
not admitted. James Boswell, a young
Scot in London, saw the sport as a
peculiarly English pastime. On
15 December 1762 he went to the Royal
Cockpit: 'I was sorry for the poor cocks.
I looked round to see if any of the
spectators pitied them when mangled
and torn in a most cruel manner, but I
could not observe the smallest relenting
sign in any countenance … Thus did I
complete my true English day, and came
home pretty much fatigued and pretty

as a resort of prostitutes. James Boswell,
who lodged nearby in Downing Street,
recorded in his diary for Friday
25 March 1763: 'As I was coming home
this night, I felt carnal inclinations
raging through my frame. I determined
to gratify them. I went to St. James's
Park, and … picked up a whore. For the
first time did I engage in armour [used a
condom, see cat. 3.20], which I found but
a dull satisfaction. She who submitted to
my lusty embraces was a young
Shropshire girl, only seventeen, very
well-looked, her name Elizabeth Parker.
Poor thing, she has a sad time of it!'

much confounded at the strange turn of this people.'

The Royal Cockpit was built in the late seventeenth century on the south side of St James's Park, off Birdcage Walk. It was demolished in 1816.

5.22
Rules and Order of Cocking, 1756

Body colour on vellum, 278 × 306 mm
Private collection

Hugh Phillips records what may be this sheet – or a facsimile – in a public house in Dartmouth Street, near the site of the Royal Cockpit, in the 1960s (Phillips 1964, pp. 266–7). Rule number 12 explains the shadow over the pit in Hogarth's print: 'Should any man make a wager and lose, but not pay his dues and make another wager, he shall be put in a basket and hung up to the eaves of the main [fighting area], where all men shall see him, and there shall remain till the end of the session, when he shall be cut down and banished from the main.'

5.23
Admission ticket for a cock pit, c.1765

Silver, height 37 mm
Private collection

Season tickets to places of entertainment were commonly made of some durable material, often copper alloy, silver or even gold (see cats. 5.60–5.67 for season tickets to Vauxhall Gardens). The obverse of this silver ticket shows a figure of a cock standing; the reverse is engraved with the name 'Lord Milton'.

The cockfighting owner of the ticket was probably Joseph Damer, 1st Lord Milton, later Earl of Dorchester (1715/19–1798). Milton employed the architect William Chambers at his house in Tyburn Lane (now Park Lane) in 1769–71 and at his country seat at Milton Abbey in Dorset, 1771–6; the architect described his patron as 'this unmannerly imperious Lord, who treats me as he does every body, ill' (Colvin, p. 237). Milton's son, John Damer, married the sculptor Anne Seymour Damer, and in

1776 he shot himself after he and his two brothers had contracted a debt of £70,000.

5.24
Two admission tickets for a cock pit, 18th century

Copper alloy, 38 × 50 mm
CM J.2955 Sarah Banks collection, presented 1818
MME MG 1162 Presented by Montague Guest, 1907

The obverse of these cheaper cock pit tickets shows a figure of a cock standing; the reverse shows two cocks fighting and is engraved 'Ye Royal Sport'.

5.23

5.22

5.24

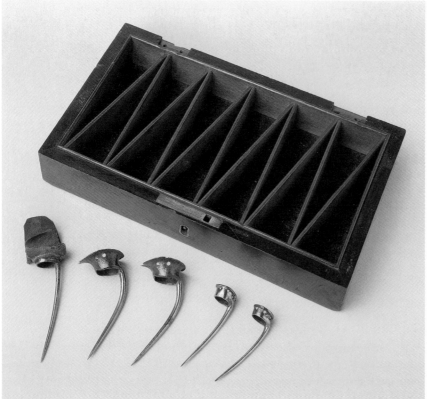

5.25

5.25
A set of cockspurs, 18th century

Steel, in a wooden box
Museum of London, A 5850 a–e

Cocks have on their legs a natural projection or spur which is used when fighting, but artificial spurs of steel, brass or even silver were fastened to the legs to enhance their prowess in the cockpit. Birds were carefully prepared for fights – 'cut out for battle' – by being clipped, having comb and wattles cut off, tail feathers cut, and wing feathers sheared 'slope-wise' to sharp points.

Cockfighting was banned in 1822, but bull- and bear-baiting continued until 1835. The best-known animal-baiting pits were at Tothill Fields, Westminster, and Hockley-in-the-Hole, Clerkenwell, while duck-hunting – where spaniels were set on a duck tethered in a pond – was enjoyed by Londoners in Green Park, at the Field of Forty Footsteps on the present site of Russell Square and at

the Dog and Duck tavern in Lambeth on the present site of the Imperial War Museum.

Fireworks

In October 1748 a treaty was signed at Aix-la-Chapelle ending the War of Austrian Succession. The war – sparked off in 1740 by Maria Theresa's claim to inherit the Habsburg territories from her father Emperor Charles VI – was an episode in the manoeuvring for position by European powers that continued throughout the century. Britain's main interest was to gain access to and maintain the lucrative trade routes to the Americas that were controlled by France and Spain. The treaty failed to settle matters, and skirmishing continued through the early 1750s, erupting again into all-out war in 1756 (see pp. 189–91).

The official celebration of the Peace of Aix-la-Chapelle took place on 17 April 1749 in the northern part of St James's Park, now called Green Park. A huge

temporary structure was erected for a firework display organised by the famous Italian pyrotechnist Giovanni Niccolo Servandoni, in collaboration with the Royal Laboratory at Woolwich. £8,000 was spent and ten thousand rockets were let off, but the evening ended in chaos when one wing of the structure caught fire. However, the large number of souvenir prints published – few of which record the accidental fire – ensured that the display would not be forgotten, and its design became an emblem for 'fireworkers' for some time afterwards. But the most enduring success of the day was the overture specially composed by Handel for the celebrations – the *Music for the Royal Fireworks*.

Ogborn (pp. 236–8) discusses the ambiguity of the Royal Fireworks, at once a symbol of monarchical power and a commercial enterprise.

5.26
Anonymous
A View of the Public Fire Works, 1749

Etching, 454 × 1162 mm
Published by Henry Overton at the White Horse without Newgate, London
1877-6-9-2060

This print depicts the climax of the firework display when, according to the official programme of events (Simon 200), the words 'Vivat Rex' appeared in 'bright fire' in the central sunburst. The structure, built of wood and canvas with allegorical statues in plaster, was 410 feet wide and 176 feet high. Beyond are the 101 cannon which fired the royal salute; to the left, the viewing stand (admission 10s 6d) and Buckingham House; to the right, St George's Hospital, Hyde Park Corner and houses in Piccadilly. The crowd is kept back by a line of soldiers.

The site for the display was marked out five months in advance and news-paper reports and prints recorded the progression of building work (Crace XII. 104–16). The Board of Ordnance commissioned George Vertue to engrave

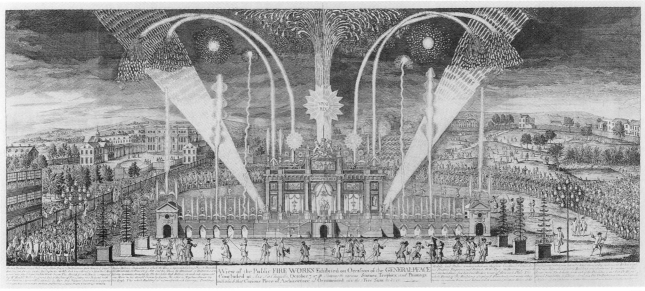

5.26

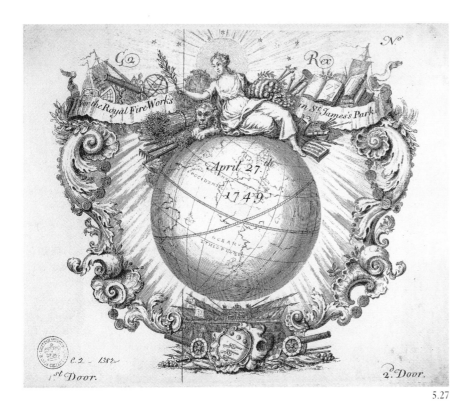

5.27

a volume of twenty high-quality architectural plates as an official record, but in the event only one was published (Simon 199). This is a much less fine print, but it is of interest as a rare survival of a two-sheet print of the sort that appear in large numbers in the catalogues of the cheap and middle-range print publishers. Large prints were intended for display and few were preserved.

5.27

Anonymous

Ticket for the Royal Fireworks, 1749

Etching and engraving with engraved lettering, 179 × 218 mm

C.2-1382 Sarah Banks collection, presented 1818

This elaborate ticket allowed admission to the viewing stand shown at the left of cat. 5.26. The image of the globe, and of the Atlantic Ocean in particular, is a reminder that for Britain the war that had just ended, though triggered by disputes in Europe, was fought over trade routes to the Americas. The personification of Plenty, leaning against the British Lion and the Union Flag, is surrounded by emblems of war and navigation, as well as agriculture and the arts, drenched in the light of a glorious sun.

Sarah Banks was five years old in 1749, and it is possible that she attended the Royal Fireworks herself; as a child in London (the family home was in Argyle Street, off Oxford Street) she would almost certainly have known of such an exciting event. There are two impressions of the ticket in her collection of ephemera. One was given to her in 1791 by John Charles Brooke, Somerset Herald. In a letter kept with the ticket, Brooke offers to procure for Miss Banks, in addition to the Fireworks ticket, 'a dinner ticket for Painters Hall in 1689, with different devices engrav'd from that he formerly gave her, if she has not already got one.' This letter makes it clear not only that Banks kept the printed ephemera that she came across in the course of everyday life but that she actively collected earlier material.

5.28

Anonymous

Souvenir fan of the Royal Fireworks, 1749

ILLUSTRATED IN COLOUR. PLATE 15

Hand-coloured etching on paper, with ivory sticks, 160 × approx. 420 mm

Schreiber 4

1891-7-13-76 Presented by Lady Charlotte Schreiber, 1891

Folding fans became an important fashion accessory at the beginning of the eighteenth century, and by the 1720s huge numbers were being printed for sale at 1*s* 6*d* plain or 2*s* 6*d* coloured. Although many were purely decorative, publishers would use well-known prints – Hogarth's *Harlot's Progress, Midnight Modern Conversation,* for instance – or satires on political events which would be marketed at particular audiences. They were cheap fashion accessories which could be replaced at will by ladies wanting to demonstrate that they were up to date with the latest fashionable concern – whether a political controversy, or a popular event.

5.29

5.29

Anonymous

*Trade card of Samuel Clanfield, firework engineer, at the Royal Fireworks in Hosier Lane, West Smithfield, c.*1750

Etching with engraved lettering, 167 × 237 mm

Heal 62.4 Bequeathed by Sir Ambrose Heal, 1959

5.30

Anonymous

*Trade card of Benjamin Clitherow, Fireworker, c.*1750

Etching with engraved lettering, 331 × 203 mm

Banks 62.6

D.2-2276 Sarah Banks collection, presented 1818

Although neither of the firework manufacturers whose trade cards are shown here was involved in the famous Royal Fireworks of 1749, both attempt to associate themselves with it: Clanfield uses the structure built in St James's Park as his shop-sign, while Clitherow uses the King's Arms as his sign but

shows the central arch of the 1749 structure surmounted by the words 'Vivat Rex' ('Long live the King'). They present themselves as rivals, both claiming to have organized firework displays at Ranelagh (cats 5.31–5.37) and Marylebone Gardens (flourishing in the grounds of the old manor house of Marylebone from 1650 to 1778) – Clanfield calls himself the 'original engineer', Clitherow the 'real engineer'. Clanfield showed his fireworks at the notorious Cuper's Gardens, near the present site of the Festival Hall (see Phillips 1951, pp. 208–9); Clitherow had a more elevated audience in Frederick, Prince of Wales and his family at Kew (see pp. 211–12). Their lists of fireworks, indoor and outdoor, are very similar, both including the 'China fire that represents a beautiful fruit tree in full bloom and will extend its flowers from 10 to 40 feet high'. Each uses the typical tradesman's claim to exclusivity: Clanfield, 'it's only sold by me'; Clitherow, 'They are all counterfeit that has not this mark'.

5.30

Chelsea

5.31–5.53

Ranelagh Gardens

In 1740 James Lacy, Garrick's partner at the Drury Lane Theatre, acquired the mansion built by Lord Ranelagh in the 1690s immediately to the east of the Royal Hospital, Chelsea. Lacy, with Sir Thomas Robinson (known as 'long Sir Thomas' to distinguish him from Thomas Robinson, 1st Baron Grantham, his neighbour on the riverfront at Whitehall) developed the grounds as the most fashionable of the London pleasure gardens. Ranelagh's most conspicuous feature was the rotonda or amphitheatre designed by William Jones, 150 feet in diameter, with a central stage for an orchestra and two tiers of fifty-two boxes around the walls. Horace Walpole described his first impression in a letter to Horace Mann of 26 May 1742: 'Two nights ago Ranelagh Gardens were opened at Chelsea; the prince, princess, duke [Frederick, Prince of Wales, Princess Augusta, William, Duke of Cumberland], much nobility, and much mob besides were there. There is a vast amphitheatre, finely gilt, painted, and illuminated; into which everybody that loves eating, drinking, staring, or crowding is admitted for twelve pence.

The building and disposition of the gardens cost sixteen thousand pounds. Twice a week there are to be ridottos [assemblies with music and dancing] at guinea tickets, for which you are to have a supper and music.' Two years later Walpole was still impresed: 'Every night constantly I go to Ranelagh; which has totally beat Vauxhall. Nobody goes anywhere else – everybody goes there. My Lord Chesterfield is so fond of it that he says he has ordered all his letters to be directed thither … You can't set your foot without treading on a Prince, or Duke of Cumberland' (letter to Henry Seymour Conway, 29 June 1744). Ranelagh remained open until 1804.

5.31

James McArdell (1729–65) after Thomas Hudson (1701–79)

Mary, Duchess of Ancaster, 1757

Mezzotint with some scratched lines, 507 × 353 mm
Published by James McArdell at the Golden Head, Covent Garden
Goodwin 62 (i); C.S. 1 (i)
1902-10-11-3172 Bequeathed by William Eaton, 2nd Baron Cheylesmore

Mary Panton, illegitimate daughter of Thomas Panton, Master of the King's running horses at Newmarket, married Peregrine Bertie, 3rd Duke of Ancaster, in 1750. Their London home was in Berkeley Square. She was a leader of fashion and in 1761 was appointed Mistress of the Robes to the young Queen Charlotte.

The Duchess of Ancaster is shown here in a fine proof of one of McArdell's best mezzotints after one of Hudson's best portraits (Miles 58). She is dressed as if for a masquerade at Ranelagh – the amphitheatre is in the background – wearing a variation of the fashionable 'Van Dyck dress' in which artists had portrayed sitters since the 1730s. The feathered hat and fan, the puffed sleeves and the arrangement of the skirt pinned up at the sides are all taken from the costume worn in a portrait then thought

5.31

5.32

Anonymous

Ranelagh Gardens and the Grand Amphitheatre, 1764

Published by John Ryall at Hogarth's Head in Fleet Street

Etching with engraved lettering, 334 × 479 mm

Crace XIII.81

1880-11-13-2462

In this shilling print the Ranelagh amphitheatre is shown as a monumental building worthy of the comparison to the glories of Rome made in the verse below, though much of its appeal to visitors to Ranelagh would have been as a place to be entertained indoors on rainy days. The architect, William Jones (fl. 1736–d. 1757), made deliberate echoes of the Colosseum in the arcaded exterior of the amphitheatre and of the Pantheon in its huge dome. It is his best-known building, but he was responsible for other notable London buildings of the mid-century: Surgeons' Hall, Old Bailey; Berkeley Chapel, Berkeley Square; and warehouses and offices for the East India Company in Leadenhall Street. See Colvin for a brief account of his career and further references.

5.33

Anthony Walker (1726–65) after William Newton (1735–90)

The Amphitheatre, Ranelagh Gardens, 29 August 1761

Published by William Newton

Etching with some engraved lines and engraved lettering, 350 × 576 mm

Crace XIII.80

1880-11-13-2461

Walker, whose figures always have a French elegance, has given Ranelagh a far more stylish air than suggested in cat. 5.33: his visitors are people of fashion and the grand architecture is framed by a fanciful theatrical curtain. Walker trained with John Tinney, who sold prints imported from France as well

to show Helena Fourment and to be by Van Dyck (it is now identified as Susanna Fourment and attributed to Rubens), but the seventeenth-century ruff has been reinterpreted so that it is merely hinted at in the lace around the Duchess's neck. The Fourment costume was often repeated as a formula by drapery specialists who would never see the sitter, but here the treatment is unusually convincing. It is possible that the Duchess actually had such a costume made for a masquerade at Ranelagh. In

1742 Horace Walpole described seeing at a masquerade given by the Duchess of Norfolk: 'quantities of pretty Vandykes, and all kinds of old pictures walked out of their frames' (letter to Horace Mann); see also a portrait of Fanny Murray in Van Dyck dress (cat. 3.16). Hudson's portrait of the Duchess remains in the family collection at Grimsthorpe Castle, Lincolnshire. The print was sold for 5*s.*

as others made by himself and a talented group of pupils, including William Woollett, the greatest engraver of his generation (see cat. 5.10).

William Newton was apprenticed to William Jones, the architect of Ranelagh. After completing his training, he worked in the London office of Matthew Brettingham where he would have been involved in the building of a number of grand houses in St James's and Piccadilly. He was practising on his own by 1764. He did not attract the same kind of aristocratic clientele as Brettingham,

but he designed a number of buildings in London and the Home Counties including, in 1768, an eating room and ballroom for the London Tavern (see cat. 1.87). He had scholarly inclinations, visiting Rome in 1766, and in 1771 publishing the earliest English translation of the first five books of Vitruvius; he also helped to edit and complete the second volume of James Stuart's *Antiquities of Athens*, 1788. Newton worked with Stuart at Greenwich Hospital from 1782, but ended his days aggrieved that he did not receive the

recognition he felt he deserved for his architectural role there. See Colvin for further information.

5.34

Anonymous

Iphigenia, 1749

Etching with stipple and engraved lettering, 334 × 249 mm

BM Satire 3032

1868-8-8-3894 Edward Hawkins collection

This print focuses on the interior of the amphitheatre at Ranelagh and a particularly notorious masquerade costume. The contemporary manuscript note enlarges on the engraved title: 'Miss Chudley Maid of Honour to the Princess of Wales in the character of Iphigenia, at the Italian Masquerade in the daytime at Ranelagh Gardens in June 1749'. Elizabeth Chudleigh (1720–68), a member of the Royal Household, chose a classical subject for her extraordinarily revealing costume: she appears as Iphigenia, the daughter of Agammenon sacrificed by her father in order to placate Artemis as the Greek fleet sailed for Troy.

This sixpenny print is of unusually high quality for its price. Delicate stippling has been used to emphasize the soft texture of Chudleigh's flesh and the elaborate architectural detail is carefully described. She wears a convincingly classical robe, while the men beside her are wearing conventional masquerade masks and dominoes (cloaks) in the Venetian manner. Rather more staid masqueraders behind them are dressed as Punch and Mother Shipton (see cat. 1.65).

Chudleigh was a great beauty, and the protection of a series of aristocratic lovers allowed her to rise from genteel poverty to great wealth. Her semi-naked appearance at Ranelagh was one of the most notorious episodes in a life that was a succession of scandals, culminating in 1776 in a conviction for bigamy. A print by John Hamilton Mortimer (BM Satire 5362) satirizing Chudleigh at the time of

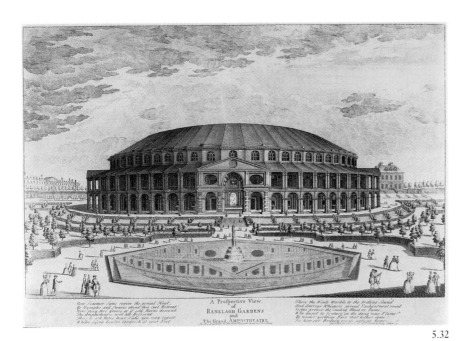

A Prospective View of RANELAGH GARDENS and The Grand AMPHITHEATRE

5.32

A Prospective View of the Inside of the AMPHITHEATRE In Ranelagh Gardens, at Chelsea.

5.33

her trial shows her as short and stout, but recalls the Ranelagh masquerade by referring to her as Iphigenia. She fled the country and spent the remaining years of her life travelling throughout Europe; she bought an estate in St Petersburg, where she was well received by Catherine the Great, and acquired a grand house in France from Louis XVI's brother. She died in Paris less than a year before the Revolution.

During her years as maid of honour to Augusta, Princess of Wales, Elizabeth Chudleigh lived with her mother in Conduit Street, Mayfair; after becoming the mistress (and later putative wife) of the extremely wealthy Duke of Kingston she built a mansion just to the south of Hyde Park.

5·35
Anonymous
Miss Chudly, 1749

Etching with engraved lettering,
318 × 192 mm (cropped)
BM Satire 3033
1868-8-8-3879 Edward Hawkins
collection

In this print Elizabeth Chudleigh is shown wearing what appears to be a revealing version of contemporary theatrical costume, quite different from the classical chiton she wears in the more carefully produced cat. 5.34. According to the note below, she had been assisted in designing her costume by Susannah Maria Cibber (1714–66), famous as a singer in oratorio and as a tragic actress. Cibber had herself been the subject of a

scandal ten years earlier when her husband, the actor Theophilus Cibber, brought a legal action against her lover; he claimed £5,000 in damages but was awarded only 10s.

5·36
Charles Grignion (1721–1810) after Giovanni Antonio Canaletto (1697–1768)
Ranelagh Gardens with the Masquerade, 2 December 1751

Published by Robert Sayer at the Golden Buck opposite Fetter Lane, Fleet Street
Etching with engraved lettering,
260 × 401 mm
Crace XIII.69
1880-11-13-2450

5.34

5.35

A View of the Canal, Chinese Building, Rotundo, &c. in RANELAGH GARDENS, with the MASQUERADE. | Vüe du Canal, du Bâtiment, Chinois, de la Rotunda, &c. des JARDINS de RANELAGH un jour de MASQUARADE.

5.36

5·37
Anonymous

A Night Scene at Ranelagh, 1752

Etching and engraving with engraved lettering, 324 × 207 mm

Published by H. Carpenter

BM Satire 3183

1868-8-8-3926 Edward Hawkins collection

This elaborate print was published on 29 May 1752, three weeks after the event shown. It was part of a 'paper war' precipitated by John Hill (1716?–75), the 'Inspector', whose gossip column in the *London Advertiser and Literary Gazette* had libelled a Mr Mountfort Brown. Brown is shown here having pulled off

This print is one of a number based on drawings by Canaletto that were published by Sayer in December 1751 (see cat. 1.3). Ranelagh is shown with visitors in fanciful masquerade dress, the grand amphitheatre obscured by trees and the foreground taken up by a whimsical Chinese building that had been built on the canal in 1750.

Canaletto's drawing, which does not survive, may have been made when he was working on a painting of 'the Representation of Chelsea-College [i.e., the Royal Hospital], Ranelagh House and the River Thames' that he advertised as being available for viewing on 31 July 1751 (since divided into two parts, one now in a private collection, the other at Blickling Hall, National Trust). Canaletto's drawings of the exterior and interior of the amphitheatre were also engraved for Sayer in 1751. Two paintings of the interior followed: one in the collection of Lord Trevor, the other made for Thomas Hollis in 1754 and now in the National Gallery.

5.37

Hill's wig and challenging him to a duel; on the left is the master of ceremonies of Ranelagh, attempting to make peace. In 1753 Hill became involved in the Elizabeth Canning case (cats 1.59–1.66), taking the side of the 'Old Gypsy' against Canning, or, more specifically, against Henry Fielding. Hill went on to develop a career as a botanist, publishing a number of ambitious botanical works culminating in the 26-volume *Vegetable System* (1759–75), a complete classification of the plant kingdom. In 1761, through the influence of Lord Bute, he was appointed gardener at Kensington Palace at a salary of – according to Walpole – £2,000 a year.

Although sold for only 6*d*, the print is carefully engraved and, incidentally, provides a detailed view of the interior of the amphitheatre at Ranelagh.

Chelsea Porcelain

On 5 March 1745 the *Daily Advertiser* announced: 'We hear that the china made at Chelsea is arrived to such perfection, as to equal if not surpass the finest old Japan, allowed so by the most approved judges here; and that the same is in so high esteem of the nobility, and the demand so great, that a sufficient quantity can hardly be made to answer the call for it.' From 1744 to 1784 the Chelsea porcelain factory occupied premises (just off the lower left-hand corner of Rocque's map) between Church Lane East (now Old Church Street) and Lawrence Street. Details of the factory's history are still emerging, but Adams incorporates much new material.

The factory was run by Nicholas Sprimont (1716–71), a Flemish Huguenot, originally a silversmith, who is first recorded in London in 1742. He seems to have begun the factory in collaboration with Charles Gouyn, another Huguenot, but the two men separated in 1750; see Adams, pp. 42–63, for their acrimonious battle in the press and for Gouyn's recently identified St James's porcelain factory. Consider-

able support for the Chelsea factory came from Sir Everard Fawkener, secretary to the Duke of Cumberland, who seems to have been the main financial backer. His withdrawal from the business a year before his death in 1758 precipitated the first of a series of cash-flow crises. Fawkener's social contacts doubtless assisted sales, and he also arranged the loan – in order to be copied – of a large number of pieces of Meissen porcelain (see p. 107) belonging to Sir Charles Hanbury-Williams, the British envoy to the Court of Saxony in Dresden.

Chelsea is sometimes thought of as the English equivalent of the court porcelain factories of Saxony or France, but it was an entirely commercial enterprise. Although more prestigious than Bow (cats 2.5–2.11), the Chelsea factory was a smaller set-up: Chelsea's total assets were never insured for more than £5,000 (in 1754), while the Bow factory and its stock were valued at £8,650 in 1755. While Bow had an outlet in the City, Sprimont sold his work at a West End showroom: from 1751 to 1755 in Pall Mall, and for the next three years in Piccadilly. He also developed a novel way of selling by auction (see cat. 5.78), at first at Chelsea, in the mid-1750s at Richard Ford's auction rooms in the Haymarket and later at David Burnsall's in Charles Street, Berkeley Square.

Some of the earliest Chelsea pieces were designed by Sprimont himself and imitate his work in silver (see Snodin 1984, p. 114, G.17, and Adams, fig. 3.2), but he employed a number of talented modellers and decorators to produce work of a superb standard. Joseph Willems, a fellow Fleming, was at Chelsea from 1748 to 1766 and was probably responsible for all the figures modelled during that period. Leading painters were John Donaldson, William Duvivier, Jean Le Febre and Jeffryes Hamett O'Neale (see Adams, p. 196 for a list of all those known to have worked at the factory). The quality of the gilding on Chelsea porcelain was much admired, and in 1765 Josiah Wedgwood wrote to his brother John, hoping that they could discover the method used: 'I believe it is

neither a secret, or very curious art, for women only are employed in it at Chelsea' (quoted by Adams, p. 160).

Porcelain figures were essential items for the elegant interior: in January 1750 Mrs Elizabeth Montagu wrote to her sister that 'ornaments of Chelsea china or the manufacture of Bow … make a room look neat and furnished'. On 7 February 1752 Horace Walpole wrote an essay in *The World* explaining how grand dining tables were decorated: 'Jellies, biscuits, sugar plums and creams have long given way to harlequins, gondoliers, Turks, Chinese and shepherdesses of Saxon China … toymen and china shops were the only fashionable purveyors of the last stage of fashionable entertainments; women of the first quality came home from Chenevix's [cats 3.47–3.48] laden with dolls and babies.' Chelsea's output was largely of figures and in 1752 Sprimont wrote a pamphlet putting the case for the prohibition of competitive imports from Meissen. No Act was passed in his favour, but by the late 1750s taste moved away from Meissen (the factory was, in any case, badly affected by the Seven Years War) towards the French style of Vincennes (founded 1738) and Sèvres (1756). These factories developed rich coloured glazes and elaborate gilding that were quickly imitated at Chelsea (see cats 5.46–5.50). Most of the pieces shown here are from this later period when Chelsea porcelain was at its most lavish.

The earliest Chelsea pieces, from *c*.1745–9, were marked with an incised triangle (there is also a rare crown and trident mark); from *c*.1750 to 1752 a raised anchor was used; from 1753 to 1758 an anchor painted in red, and from 1759 to 1772 a gold anchor. Pieces can also be dated not only on style but also by the changing compositions of the porcelain body and glazes.

Throughout the 1760s the factory was in difficulties and Sprimont was suffering from ill health. It was finally taken over in 1770 by William Duesbury (who bought the Bow factory in 1776) and was run in tandem with his porcelain factory at Derby until 1784.

5.38

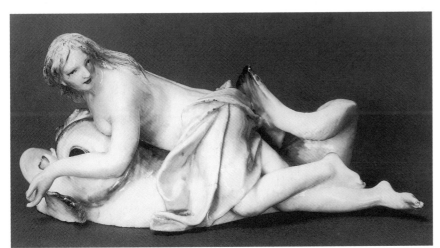

5.39

5.40

5.38

Octagonal cup and saucer with scenes from Aesop's Fables, c.1752–3

Soft-paste porcelain, painted in overglaze colours, height 55 mm (cup), diameter 136 mm (saucer)

Porc. Cat. II, 76

MME 1887,3-7,II.76 Presented by Sir Augustus Wollaston Franks

Subjects from Aesop's *Fables* appeared on Chelsea porcelains from around 1750 onwards. This cup and saucer are painted with scenes from the Fables of the Wolf, Goat and Sheep and the Lion and the Frog. The octagonal form was based on Japanese porcelain and has been identified as the 'new shape' advertised by Sprimont in 1750 (Adams, pp. 64–6).

5.39

Leda on a dolphin, c.1755

Soft-paste porcelain, painted in overglaze colours, length 220 mm

MME 1938,3-14,69 Bequeathed by Wallace Elliot

This is typical of the simply modelled mythological figures of the red-anchor period. Leda would have ridden her dolphin on the dining table, as Horace Walpole explained, 'on oceans of looking-glass, or seas of silver tissue'. Another version in the Victoria and Albert Museum has Leda looking back over her shoulder.

5.40

Large plate with moulded border, 1753–8

Soft-paste porcelain, painted in overglaze colours, diameter 323 mm

MME 1981,1-1,230 Bequeathed by Miss Constance Woodward

This red-anchor plate has a moulded border pattern forming three cartouches in which are painted landscape scenes. The pattern continued in use into the gold-anchor period with a variety of painted decoration.

5.41

Helmet-shaped jug and basin,
c.1759–60

Soft-paste porcelain, painted in overglaze colours and gilt, height 209 mm (jug), width 348 mm (basin)

MME 1923,12-8,4 Bequeathed by Charles Borradaile

The gold-anchor period saw gilding on almost every piece made at Chelsea. It was applied in the form of finely ground gold mixed with honey; the piece would then be fired to a temperature that would amalgamate the mixture with the glaze.

5.42

Scent bottle with commedia dell'arte
figures, 1752–8

Soft-paste porcelain, painted in overglaze colours and gilt, gold mount, height 91 mm

Porc. Cat.II,128; Dawson 24

MME 1887,3-7,II.128 Presented by Sir Augustus Wollaston Franks, before 1888

Miniature items called 'toys' were produced from the 1750s onwards: expensive trifles that would have served as gifts and often bear amorous or flirtatious inscriptions. This scent bottle takes the form of a dovecote with playful *commedia dell'arte* figures, the Doctor, Clown and Harlequin hiding in a kennel. The base is inscribed 'stratageme d'amour' ('subterfuge of love').

5.43

Scent bottle with two doves billing,
1750s

Soft-paste porcelain, painted in overglaze colours and gilt, gold mount, height 67 mm

Porc. Cat.II, 141

MME 1887,3-7,II.141 Presented by Sir Augustus Wollaston Franks

The base of this bottle is inscribed 'imite nous' ('imitate us').

5.41

5.42   5.43   5.44

5.45

5.46

5.46

Virgin and Child group on a stand,
c.1758–61

Soft-paste porcelain, painted in overglaze colours and gilt, the stand in underglaze blue, gilt, height 312 mm

Dawson 8

MME 1948,12-3,57 Bequeathed by Sir Bernard Eckstein

This piece bears the gold-anchor mark but examples of the group are known with the red anchor, indicating that the model was made in the late 1750s. Joseph Willems created the model, probably in clay, from which the mould was made. This group and a Chelsea *Pietà* of about the same date are unusual examples of apparently Roman Catholic imagery.

5.47

Heart-shaped box and cover,
1759–69

Soft-paste porcelain, painted in underglaze blue and overglaze colours, gilt, length 120 mm

Porc. Cat. II, 175

MME 1887,3-7,II.175 Presented by Sir Augustus Wollaston Franks

The deep mazarine blue used as a ground on this box and on cat. 5.46 was copied as early as 1756 from porcelain produced at

5.44

Scent bottle in the form of a stove
with two putti, 1750s

Soft-paste porcelain, painted in overglaze colours and gilt, gold mount, height 84 mm

Porc. Cat.II, 108

MME 1887,3-7,II.108 Presented by Sir Augustus Wollaston Franks

This bottle is inscribed 'mon feu durera toujours' ('my fire will last for ever').

5.45

Figure of a shepherd with two
dogs, 1759–69

Soft-paste porcelain, painted in overglaze colours and gilt, height 285 mm

Porc. Cat. II, 43

MME 1900,11-15,2 Bequeathed by Sophia Lutener

Shepherds and shepherdesses were favourite Rococo subjects. On the back of this figure is what seem to be the remains of a candleholder, and it may have been intended for use as a candlestick.

5.47

Vincennes and Sèvres. The handle
continues the playful theme of the
miniature scent bottles.

5.48

*Broth bowl and cover with stand,
1759–69*

Soft-paste porcelain, painted in overglaze
colours on a gold ground, height 140 mm
(bowl), diameter 182 mm (stand)

Porc. Cat. II, 95

MME 1887,3-7,95 Presented by Sir
Augustus Wollaston Franks

Gold-ground pieces are some of the most
spectacular products of Chelsea,
decorated with flowers taken from life
and painted in natural colours. There are
gilt flowers inside this bowl.

5.48

5.49

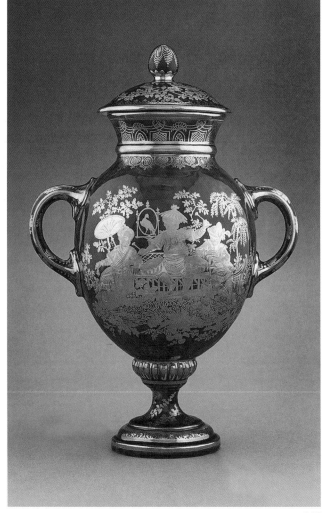

5.50

5.49

Fortune teller group, after Watteau,
c. 1760

Soft-paste porcelain, painted in overglaze
colours, gilt, height 290 mm

MME 1945,12-1,1 Presented by Mrs F.
Lowenadler

Groups became more complex in the
gold-anchor period, and stylized foliage
(*bocage*) was introduced to suggest a
rustic setting. These figures were not
table decorations of the type Walpole
described, but intended for display in
cabinets.

5.50

*Vase and cover, c.*1759–60

Soft-paste porcelain, painted in overglaze
colours, gilt, height 292 mm

MME 1948,12-3,60 Bequeathed by Sir
Bernard Eckstein

This vase is an extremely rare example
of a Chelsea turquoise ground. In 1760
Sprimont advertised 'a few pieces of
some new colours which have been found
this year … at very great expense,
incredible labour, and close application,
all highly finished, and heightened
with the gold peculiar to that fine and
distinguished manufactory'. One side,
shown here, has Chinese children at
play; the other (Adams, fig. 11.12) shows
a group of exotic birds.

5.51

John Haynes (fl. 1753–67)

The Botanic Gardens at Chelsea,
30 March 1751

Published by John Haynes at Michael
Angelo's Head in Buckingham Court near
Charing Cross

Etching and engraving with engraved
lettering, 611 × 480 mm

Crace IV.4

1880-11-13-1224

In 1673 the Company of Apothecaries
leased ground in Chelsea in order to
create a physic garden for the cultivation
of medicinal plants. In 1712 the manor
of Chelsea was purchased by Hans
Sloane, and the following year he gave
the freehold of the Physic Garden to the
Company; they still maintain the
Garden.

The statue of Sloane shown here in the
centre of the Gardens has been replaced
with a replica, and the original is now in
the British Museum.

John Haynes was a land surveyor
(see his trade card, Banks 76*. 9) and he
has presented the 'Botanic Gardens at
Chelsea' in the combination of plan, view
and decorative border that he would have

used for surveys of country estates. The
two aloes framing the view are examples
of the rare plants grown in the Garden.
They are based on drawings by Jacobus
van Huysum (*c.*1685/9–1746) showing
plants at the Physic Garden (examples
are in the library of the Royal Society,
and in an album from Hans Sloane's
collection in the British Museum
(Sl. 5283)).

For much of the eighteenth century
Chelsea Physic Garden was the
country's principal botanic garden,
receiving exotic specimens from abroad
and despatching them to other British
gardens.

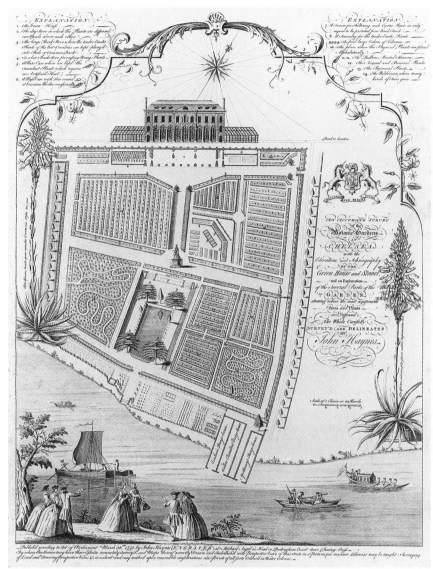

5.51

5.52

Anonymous

David Loudon's Chelsea Bun House,
1750s

Etching with engraved lettering,
207 × 370 mm

Crace XIII.39

1880-11-13-2420

The famous Bun House was just to the
north of Ranelagh Gardens in Jews Row,
now Pimlico Road. Chelsea buns were a
popular eighteenth-century treat made
with eggs, sugar, lemon peel and spice.
The House shown here was demolished
in 1839 to be replaced by the 'New Bun
House', which survived until the early
twentieth century.

The print is an attractive mixture of
measured drawing, naturalistic representation and emblem. The Bun House is
shown in an architectural elevation,
made on a scale of 1:80, with genteel
customers walking along the colonnade
outside the building. The upper part of
the print is taken up by the royal coat of
arms flanked by soldiers on guard, and
on either side freemasons hold masonic
devices. By the mid eighteenth century
there were over a hundred freemasons'
lodges meeting in taverns all over
London, but there is no record of
meetings in the Bun House; it is likely
that Loudon's allusions to freemasonry
were intended to proclaim his own
membership of the society.

5.53

John Boydell (1719–1804)

A View of Chelsea Water Works,
1752

Published by John Boydell, Engraver, at
the Unicorn, the corner of Queen Street,
Cheapside

Etching with engraved lettering,
264 × 424 mm

Crace XIII.63

1880-11-13-2444

In 1723 the Chelsea Waterworks was set
up to supply Westminster and adjacent

5.52

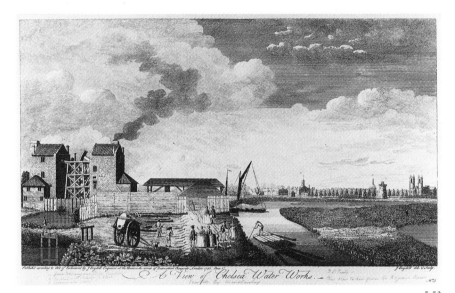

5.53

areas. Water flowed from the Thames at
high tide into a system of small canals
which allowed sediment to settle –
there was no filtration. At the present
site of Victoria railway station was an
impressive steam-driven engine that
pumped the water into channels running
to the north and east. Over the next few
years further reservoirs were built in
Green Park and Hyde Park. Water was
conveyed beneath the streets through
hollowed tree trunks joined by iron
ferrules or unions, which frequently
leaked or burst underground. A man is
shown here poling a number of timber
pipes upstream like a raft.

By using dramatic contrasts of light
and shade Boydell has attempted to

create a more sophisticated composition
than the simple descriptions of the
London views published, for instance,
by the Bowles family, but this remains
primarily a topographical view of interest
for its depiction of the Waterworks with
its curious steam-engine. Londoners
strolled out of town to see this new
phenomenon, but the marshy area
between Westminster and Chelsea – part
of the Grosvenor Estate (see cat. 5.71) –
remained largely untouched until the
1830s.

Vauxhall Gardens
5.54–5.67

Spring Gardens at Vauxhall was opened to the public by 1661. Visitors crossed the Thames by boat to find 'a pretty contrived plantation' (John Evelyn, *Diary*, 2 July 1661) where 'a man may go to spend what he will, or nothing, all is one – but to hear the nightingales and other birds, and here fiddles and there a harp, and here a jews trump, and here laughing, and there fine people walking, is mighty divertising' (Samuel Pepys, *Diary*, 28 May 1667). In 1728 the twenty-one-year-old Jonathan Tyers took a lease on the gardens at an annual rent of £250; he bought the freehold in 1758, and the gardens remained in his family until 1821, closing in 1859.

Tyers was responsible for the series of whimsical buildings and special effects for which Vauxhall was well known. Designed to be seen at night by the light of over a thousand oil lamps and to the music of a fine orchestra, as well as an organ and caged song-birds that augmented the song of the nightingales that Pepys had enjoyed, the effect must have been exhilarating. There were arcaded gothic or Chinese 'temples' where visitors could dine in supper boxes; the orchestra stand raised on delicate columns (replaced in 1758 by a larger gothic structure); a 'Turkish Tent' supported on twenty Ionic and Doric columns and lit by five large glass chandeliers; a series of triumphal arches; an artificial waterfall.

London artists – eager to show their work at a time when there were no public exhibitions – were delighted at the opportunities that Tyers offered. The graceful informality of the Rococo style emanating from St Martin's Lane Academy (cats 3.44–3.46) was perfectly in keeping with Tyers's aims. Louis-François Roubiliac made his name with the statue of Handel commissioned by Tyers for £300 and set up at Vauxhall in 1738 (now in the Victoria and Albert Museum). In the early 1740s Francis Hayman (1708–76), a successful

theatrical scene-painter, relaunched his career with a series of large supper-box paintings of children's pastimes and other light-hearted subjects (Allen, pp. 180–2, provides a check-list of forty-seven recorded paintings). Tyers no doubt commissioned the paintings as a response to the opening of the rival Ranelagh Gardens, and he continued to create new attractions to lure visitors across the river. A letter of 1759 from the architect Robert Adam to his brother James demonstrates the significance of a Vauxhall commission for an up-and-coming young man – and indicates the importance of prints in spreading a reputation: 'I am now scheming another thing, which is a temple of Venus for Vauxhall which Mr Tyers … proposes to lay out £5,000 upon and is happy in my doing it. You shall hear more of this when I know of it myself; but you may easily judge that it is one of the most critical undertakings for a young beginner and requires more to be perfect than anything I know. For here the universe are judges, whereas in a private garden it is only the narrow public and clamour. However if I can satisfy myself and Paul Sandby and the proprietor, who has genius and fancy, I doubt not but it will please all and Sandby will make it public over all by Rooker and him engraving it.' The project does not appear to have come to fruition, and Vauxhall is not included among the large views of London made by Edward Rooker after Sandby in the early 1760s (see cat. 3. 4).

Vauxhall was, however, an extremely popular subject with print publishers and – with Tyers's encouragement – prints and illustrated song sheets had appeared since the 1730s. They could be bought at Vauxhall as well as in printshops in town: a print of the Gardens published by George Bickham in 1741 (BM Satire 2465) gives the print-seller's address as 'at Vauxhall Gardens', as well as at his house in May's Buildings, Covent Garden; on 7 May 1752 Rober Sayer advertised in the *General Advertiser* that Canaletto's views (cats 5.56–5.59) would be sold

'in the avenues at Vauxhall'. The most substantial publications were the series of prints of eighteen of the supper-box paintings engraved by Antoine Benoist, Charles Grignion, Richard Parr, Louis Truchy and François Vivares, and published in 1743 by Thomas and John Bowles (see fig. 2).

The prints described below come from two series that appeared late in 1751. Their publishers may well have been encouraged by the increase in attendance at Vauxhall after the opening of Westminster Bridge a year earlier. Cats 5.54 and 5.55 were part of a series published on 21 November 1751 by John Bowles after drawings by Samuel Wale; cats 5.56–5.59 were published less than two weeks later by Robert Sayer after drawings by Canaletto, who provided Sayer with a number of drawings of London views shortly after his return from Venice the preceding summer. Mid-century prints of Vauxhall, together with cheaper copies, continued to be listed in publishers' catalogues until at least the 1790s.

For accounts of Vauxhall Gardens and further references see D. Coke, 'Vauxhall Gardens', in Snodin, pp. 75–81, with related catalogue entries, pp. 71–2 and 82–98, and Edelstein.

5.54

Johann Sebastian Müller
(*c*.1715–92) after Samuel Wale
(1721?–86)

A General Prospect of Vauxhall Gardens, 21 November 1751

Published by John Bowles at the Black Horse, Cornhill

Etching with engraved lettering, 287 × 406 mm

Crace XXXV.131

1880-11-13-5465

The print is a clear, if rather pedestrian, view of the layout of Vauxhall looking eastwards. A double doorway in a typical Georgian terrace leads into the Gardens, the well-kept walks, flourishing trees and exotic buildings contrasting with

A General Prospect of Vaux Hall Gardens. Shewing at one View the disposition of the whole Gardens.

Vüe Detaillée des Jardins de Vaux Hall. Printed for John Bowles at the Black Horse in Cornhill.

5.54

the bleak surrounding landscape. A comparison with the plan of the Gardens shown on Rocque's map completed in 1746 (pp. 44–5) shows that Tyers had recently expanded into the area to the north-west of the plantations of trees, shown on the left of the print. The former appearance of the area was described by John Lockman as 'the rural downs … in the form of a long square; with little eminences … In these downs were three openings, (last season) covered with shrubs; whence some styled them the musical bushes, while others called the subterraneous sounds heard there, the fairy music.' By the winter of 1751/2 the underground orchestra had been abandoned in favour of a series of fanciful buildings: the circular Music Room with its pointed roof, the adjoining Pillared Saloon and the gothic colonnade with its pavilions, or 'temples'. The rectilinear plan of the Gardens is otherwise largely the original seventeenth-century one, with the exception of another semicircular colonnade of supper-boxes encroaching on the plantation of trees on the south side (cat. 5.59).

5.55

Henry Roberts (fl. 1737–68) after Samuel Wale (1721?–86)

The Elegant Music Room in Vauxhall Gardens, 1751

ILLUSTRATED IN COLOUR, PLATE 14

Published by John Bowles at the Black Horse in Cornhill, and Carington Bowles in St Paul's Churchyard, London

Hand-coloured etching with engraved lettering, 292 × 437 mm

Crace XXXV.146

1880-11-13-5480

The Music Room, or Rotonda, 70 feet in diameter, was built in 1749. Although only half the size of the amphitheatre at Ranelagh, its sumptuous interior was impressive. According to George Vertue, the elaborate plasterwork was designed by the gold-chaser George Michael Moser and executed by 'French and Italians'. The print shows the festoons of flowers painted on the ceiling, some of the sixteen sash windows with busts and vases on carved brackets beneath, and some of the sixteen looking-glasses each with two sconces for candles. Not shown is the chandelier 11 feet in diameter with a further seventy-two candles.

The Pillared Saloon beyond,

measuring 70 by 34 feet, was added in 1750. In 1752 John Lockman described the screen of columns dividing the two structures: 'embellished with foliage, from the base a considerable way upwards; and the remaining part of the Shaft, to the capital (of the Composite Order) is finely wreathed with gothic balustrade, where boys are represented ascending it'. There were two cupolas in the roof, each of which let in light through ten glazed skylights framed in the gothic style and painted with classical gods.

The giant plasterwork frames on the walls of the Saloon (measuring 12 by 15 feet) were probably intended for paintings of the life of Frederick, Prince of Wales, ground landlord of Vauxhall and an important patron whose visits did much to enhance the status of the Gardens. Frederick's untimely death in 1751 meant that the subject was no longer appropriate, and the frames were filled between 1761 and 1764 by four paintings by Francis Hayman celebrating recent British victories in Canada and India. Commissions for history paintings were rare in England, and on such a scale were almost unheard of; in providing an opportunity for Hayman, Tyers played another significant part in the development of British art. All four paintings are lost, but the compositions of three of them are known from preliminary studies and from a print by Simon François Ravenet. For a full account of the paintings in the Pillared Saloon see Allen, pp. 62–70.

5.56

Johann Sebastian Müller (c.1715–92) after Giovanni Antonio Canaletto (1697–1768)

A View of the Temple of Comus in Vauxhall Gardens, 2 December 1751

Published by Robert Sayer (publication line erased from this late impression)

Etching with engraved lettering, 252 × 398 mm

Crace XXXV.138

A View of the Temple of Comus &c. in Vauxhall Gardens. Vue du Temple de Comus dans le Jardins de Vauxhall

5.56

A View of the Grand Walk &c. in Vauxhall Gardens, taken from the Entrance. Vue de la Grande Allée du Jardin de Vauxhall prise de l'Entrée.
London: Printed for & Sold by Rob.t Sayer, at the Golden Buck, opposite Fetter Lane, Fleet street.

5.57

o'clock – was a spectacular moving picture with sound effects: 'a most beautiful landscape in perspective in hilly country with a miller's house and a water mill, all illuminated by concealed lights; but the principal object that strikes the eye is a cascade or water fall. The exact appearance of water [created by releasing strips of tin] is seen flowing down a declivity, and turning the wheel of the mill, it rises up in a foam at the bottom, and then glides away' (*A Description of Vauxhall Gardens*, 1762, quoted in Edelstein, p. 20)

The Temple of Comus and the colonnade on either side differ in many architectural details from the building shown in cat. 5.54. The prints were published within a few days of each other and one, at least, must have been based on an earlier drawing.

5.57

Edward Rooker (*c.*1712–74) after Giovanni Antonio Canaletto (1697–1768)

A View of the Grand Walk in Vauxhall Gardens, 2 December 1751

Published by Robert Sayer at the Golden Buck opposite Fetter Lane, Fleet Street

Etching with engraved lettering, 257 × 399 mm

Crace XXXV.137

Canaletto's painting of this view (Constable 431, collection of Lord Trevor) appears to have been painted later than this print; it differs in detail but is substantially the same view.

At the east end of the Grand Walk was a gilded statue of Aurora, goddess of the dawn. By 1762 this had been removed and replaced with the gothic obelisk that stands at the end of the southernmost walk, the 'Dark Walk' shown on the right of cat. 5.54.

Canaletto's views of Vauxhall have a much lower viewpoint than Samuel Wale's. We are inside the Gardens and, like its visitors, are protected from the reality of the world outside. This is a daytime scene and the Gardens' visitors are respectable families, but a visit to a Temple dedicated to Comus – a pagan god invented by Milton – was more appropriate for an evening of dalliance. Milton has Comus introduce a night of revelry: 'What hath night to do with sleep? / Night hath better sweets to prove, / Venus now wakes, and wakens

Love / Come, knit hands, and beat the ground / In a light fantastic round' (*Comus: A Maske Presented at Ludlow Castle*, 1637).

The Temple was decorated inside 'with a whimsical piece of painting; the subject being Vulcan, catching Mars and Venus in his net, the whole drawn in the Chinese taste' (Lockman). It was the centrepiece of Tyers's new extension to the Gardens, the colonnade on either side leading from the Pillared Saloon to the Cascade in the Cross Walk. The Cascade – revealed each evening at nine

239

A View of the Center Cross Walk &c in Vauxhall Gardens. *Vüe du Centre de la Grande Allee du Jardin de Vauxhall.*

5.58

A View of the Grand South Walk in VAUX HALL GARDENS, with the Triumphal Arches, Mr Handels Statue, &c. *Vüe de la Grande promenade du Coté du Sud, des JARDINS DE VAUXHALLE, avec l'Arch. de Triomphe, la Statue de Mr Handels, &c.*

5.59

5.59

Johann Sebastian Müller
(*c*.1715–92) after Giovanni Antonio
Canaletto (1697–1768)

A View of the Grand South Walk in Vauxhall Gardens, 2 December 1751

Published by Robert Sayer, Map and Printseller at the Golden Buck opposite Fetter Lane, Fleet Street

Etching with engraved lettering, 258 × 398 mm

Crace XXXV.140

Canaletto's viewpoint is near to the west end of the South Walk with its succession of triumphal arches designed by 'an ingenious Italian' (Lockman) and made from wood covered with painted canvas. At the far end of the Walk in 1751 was another trompe l'oeil painting showing a temple of Neptune, his statue surrounded by gods, tritons and boy genii; by 1754 this had been replaced by a painting of the recently discovered ruins of Palmyra. Roubiliac's statue of Handel can be seen just to the right of centre, standing alone in front of the newly erected semicircular colonnade shown on the right of cat. 5.54. A print of 1744 by J. Maurer (see Snodin, p.87, no. F13) shows the statue as it was originally installed some six years earlier, in more or less the same position but placed in an elaborate niche that served as a screen to the trees beyond.

Admission Tickets to Vauxhall Gardens

When Jonathan Tyers took over Vauxhall Gardens he introduced an admission charge of 1s in order to deter undesirables. In March 1737 he advertised the issue of one thousand annual season tickets at one guinea each; each ticket admitted two. By 1740 the price had risen to £1 5s, by 1748 to two guineas. Ticket designs evidently changed each year, and those issued in 1749, 1750 and 1751 were dated. A number of tickets survive with the

5.58

Edward Rooker (*c*.1712–74) after Giovanni Antonio Canaletto (1697–1768)

A View of the Center Cross Walk in Vauxhall Gardens, 2 December 1751

Published by Robert Sayer (publication line erased from this late impression)

Etching with engraved lettering, 259 × 394 mm

Crace XXXV.139

This is a view of the northern end of the Cross Walk where the dull suburban fields were screened by a theatrical backcloth with a view of a ruined viaduct and a lake and waterfall beyond. The backcloth can be seen on the extreme left of cat. 5.54.

names of holders engraved on the reverse. Most are made of silver or copper alloy, but the life ticket given by Tyers to his friend William Hogarth (cat. 5.67) is made of gold.

Fourteen different designs were catalogued by Wroth in 1898, including three designs identified by Sarah Banks whose connection with Vauxhall Wroth doubted. A further group of similar tickets in the Department of Coins and Medals may also include examples from Vauxhall. Only one Vauxhall ticket is signed by the designer, a ticket showing the muse Thalia by Richard Yeo (d. 1779), who went on to become chief engraver to the Royal Mint in 1775. Other designs are traditionally given to Hogarth, but there is no contemporary evidence for such an attribution.

5.60

Ticket with a design of the muse Calliope, 1749

Silver, height 48 mm

Wroth 8

CM J.3032 Edward Hawkins collection, purchased 1860

The reverse of the ticket is engraved with the name 'Mr John Hinton', the number '212' and the date '1749'. The owner may have been the publisher of the *Universal Magazine* (cats 1.79 and 3.76).

5.60

5.61

5.62

5.61

Ticket with a design of three cupids, 1750

Silver, height 43 mm

Wroth 5

CM J.3029 Edward Hawkins collection, purchased 1860

The obverse of the ticket is engraved with the motto from Horace (*Odes*, III, iii, 23), 'Iocosae conveniunt lyrae' ('The cheerful lyres play their part'). On the reverse is the name 'Mrs Wood', the date '1750' and the number '64'. The ticket may have belonged to Tyers's daughter, Elizabeth, who married John Wood at around this time. An example of the same ticket was recorded by Wroth with the name 'Mr Wood' and the number '63'.

Francis Hayman's painting of Jonathan Tyers with John and Elizabeth Wood is at the Yale Center for British Art.

5.62

Ticket with a design of Orpheus, 1751

Silver, height 42 mm

Wroth 6

MME MG 684 Presented by Montague Guest, 1907

The reverse of the ticket is engraved with the name 'Mr John Robinson', 'No. 68' and, in relief, the date '1751'.

5.63

Ticket with a design of the statue of Handel at Vauxhall

Silver, height 44 mm

Wroth 1

MME MG 680 Presented by Montague Guest, 1907

Roubiliac's statue of Handel is the most important survival of Vauxhall Gardens, but for Tyers its appearance on an admission ticket would have been intended as much as a reminder of the fine music played in the Gardens, as to demonstrate the works of art to be seen there. In 1740 Handel wrote a hornpipe for Vauxhall, and on 21 April 1749 he held a rehearsal there for his *Music for the Royal Fireworks* (cat. 5.26) with a hundred musicians in front of an audience of twelve thousand.

The obverse of the ticket is engraved with the motto from Horace (*Odes*, I,

5.63

xxiv, 13), 'Blandius Orpheo' ('Sweeter than Orpheus'). The reverse is engraved with the name 'Sr. Jon. English Barnt.' and the number '592'.

5.64

Ticket with a design of Arion on a dolphin

Silver, height 40 mm

Wroth 2

MME MG 675 Presented by Montague Guest, 1907

Among the tokens left at the Foundling Hospital (see cat. 3.38) is an example of this ticket engraved with 'Richard Arnold esq.' and '184'.

5.65

Ticket with a design of a female figure representing Spring

Silver, height 48 mm

Wroth 3

CM J.3027 Edward Hawkins collection, purchased 1860

The obverse of the ticket is engraved with a motto from Horace (*Odes*, I, iv, 1) on Spring, 'Grata vice veris' ('The happy turning point of Spring'). On the reverse is the name 'Mr R Wright' and the number '305'.

5.66

Ticket with a design of a female figure representing Summer

Silver, height 40 mm

Wroth 4

CM J.3028 Edward Hawkins collection, purchased 1860

The obverse of the ticket is engraved with a motto from Virgil's *Georgics*, 'Frondosa reducitur aestas' ('Leafy summer returns'). In the background is a lamplit arch like those at Vauxhall; over a thousand oil lamps were used in the Gardens in the middle of the eighteenth century. On the reverse is the name 'Mr Parris' and the number '256'.

5.67

Attributed to Richard Yeo (d. 1779)

Ticket with a design of female figures representing Virtue and Pleasure

Gold, height 44 mm

Wroth 7

MME 1913,5-15,1 Presented by Charles Fairfax Murray

The obverse of the ticket is engraved with the words 'Virtus' (Virtue), 'Voluptas' (Pleasure) and 'Felices una' ('Happy together'), and the reverse 'Hogarth' and 'In perpetuam beneficii memoriam' ('In everlasting memory of his support'). This ticket was given by Jonathan Tyers to William Hogarth.

Hogarth married Jane Thornhill around 1730 and the couple lived for a while in Lambeth not far from Vauxhall Gardens at the time when the young Tyers was working on his initial improvements. Hogarth's precise involvement is unclear though he certainly advised and encouraged Tyers.

Mayfair
5.68–5.79

In the 1680s an annual fair held in the first half of May was transferred from Haymarket to an open field north of Piccadilly and the area became known as Mayfair. In 1764 the fair was supressed as a result of the development of a new and fashionable area of London that had sprung up in a matter of a few decades. The vast majority of houses were built as speculative developments by builders and landowners whose names remain familiar from the streets and squares they created: Lady Berkeley of Stratton, Sir Thomas Bond, Lord Burlington, Sir Nathaniel Curzon, Lord Dover, Sir Richard Grosvenor, Edward Shepherd and Margaret Stafford. In the 1750s few houses were more than thirty-five years old.

5.64

5.66

5.65

5.67

The MILITARY PROPHET: or A FLIGHT from PROVIDENCE.

Address'd to the FOOLISH and GUILTY, who *timidly* WITHDREW themselves on the *Alarm* of another EARTHQUAKE, *April* 1750.

SAD stupid Age! alike in Church and State;
Too *credulous* the *Low*, meer *Apes* the Great;
Conscious of Ill, each other they can't truft,
So fly the GRAND SUPREME, All-Good and Juft.
Thro' their own *jaundic'd* Eyes the Scene they view,
And VICE tints all Things with its own *pale* Hue;
Offending HEAVEN whilft on Earth they ftay,
They bear their *Future* Pains and fhun the Day;
In Night's dark Gloom fair VIRTUE *fhines* moft clear,

In Mid-day Sun GUILT *clouded* will appear.
When dread Convulfions fhook this Earthly Ball,
The *juft* alone on *Nature's Lord* did call;
With deep Contrition thought on Failings paft,
And fhrunk not, tho' that Sun had fhone the *laft*.
Dauntlefs they ftay'd, nor fear'd the coming Day,
None but the WEAK or WICKED fneak'd away.
Difmay'd, aghaft, they fly their own Abodes,
And throng in difmal Groupes thro' different Roads.

Vain Wretches! blufh, Kneel down, confefs your Shame;
Know PROVIDENCE *is ev'ry where the fame.*
BRITONS no more your Diffidence betray,
Eclipfes, Shadows, dancing Lights difmay;
To try your Faith, firft *Bottle Conj'rers* rife
And laft a *craz'd Enthufiaft* blinds your Eyes.
Rife from your lurking Holes, each daftard Fool,
Creep back to Town, and go to Wifdom's School;
There learn, that HEAV'N's Decrees are hid in Night,

Not fram'd for *Knaves* or *Dupes* to bring to Light;
Learn ONE juft FEAR, the Fear of *doing ill,*
Or acting t'offend th'*Almighty Will*;
His Will which inftantly bid Nature rife
And governs her each Work all-good, all-wife.
Or, if ftill Wizard Tales your Judgment blind,
And future *Earthquakes* fright the *tender Mind,*
As *Panicks* drew ye forth, ye *Pigmy Race!*
Fly *quite away,* nor more our ISLE DISGRACE.

5.68

5.68

Attributed to Louis Philippe Boitard (fl. 1733–67)

The Military Prophet: or a flight from Providence, 12 April 1750

Etching with letterpress, 189 × 334 mm (image, cropped), 246 × 334 mm (sheet, cropped)

Published by Bispham Dickinson, at the corner of the Belle Savage Inn, Ludgate Hill

BM Satire 3076

1868-8-8-3903 Edward Hawkins collection

There was a slight earthquake in London on 8 February 1751; on 8 March, a somewhat stronger one. During the following month panic rose in anticipation of a third earthquake, and on the night of 7/8 April thousands left London to sleep in open country. This satire shows Piccadilly crammed with coaches which – presumably by an oversight on the printmaker's part – are heading eastwards into town, rather than west towards Hyde Park. The precise location is at the top of St James's Street with the Palace in the distance and the sign of the White Horse Inn standing above the heads of the crowd.

The verse below mocks a credulous populace that sees the hand of providence in natural occurences, falls for the notorious Bottle Conjuror (a hoax that had drawn huge crowds in January 1749) and follows 'a craz'd Enthusiast' (presumably a reference to George Whitefield, see cat. 3.29). The print's title refers to a trooper who predicted the third earthquake.

5.69

Attributed to Anthony Walker (1726–65)

Hanover Square from the north

Published by Robert Sayer, Print and Mapseller, at the Golden Buck in Fleet Street

Etching and engraving with engraved lettering, 270 × 411 mm

Crace XXIX.72

1880-11-13-4533

Hanover Square was the first of the Mayfair squares, laid out between 1717 and 1719 by the elderly Whig general Richard Lumley, 1st Earl of Scarborough. In 1688 Lumley had signed the invitation to William III to take over the throne, and he was subseqently – as demonstrated in the name of

A North View of Hanover Square, London. Veüe du Nord de la Place d'Hanover, a Londre.
London Printed for Rob.t Sayer Print & Map seller at the Golden Buck in Fleet street.

5.69

A View of St Georges Church Hanover Square, Vue de l'Eglise de Saint George dans le Carré de Hanover, from Conduit Street London. près de l'dit Rüe Conduit à Londres.
London Printed for Ia.s Boydell Engraver Cheapside.

5.70

planning of most of eighteenth-century London.

The square as shown in this print is peopled by fashionable young men, and even the tired chair-men are drawn with a refined Rococo line. The contrast with Bowles's prosaic view of Grosvenor Square (cat. 5.71) is marked. As with Canaletto's views of Vauxhall (cats 5.56–5.59), the viewpoint is low and we are brought into the scene with the help of bold shadows in the foreground. The concern is less with providing a clear description of the new development than with giving a sense of urban elegance.

5.70

Anonymous

View of St George's Church, Hanover Square, from Conduit Street, c.1751

Originally published by Thomas Jefferys, this impression published by John Boydell, Engraver, Cheapside

Etching with engraved lettering, 281 × 420 mm

Crace XXIX.73

1880-11-13-4534

Although the development of Hanover Square was a Whig project, the church of St George (1720–4) was a product of the Tory Act of 1711 providing for the building of fifty new churches. The High Church ascendancy was short-lived but the twelve fine churches that were built as a result of the act remain conspicuous London landmarks.

The livestock being driven past the church and the open view in the distance are reminders that London's West End was being developed piecemeal in open fields. Ambitious plans for Cavendish Square, immediately to the north of Hanover Square on the other side of Oxford Street, had been thwarted by the bursting of the South Sea Bubble in 1720 and it was not completed until 1770. The owner of the land was Robert Harley, 1st Earl of Oxford, whose library of manuscripts was one of the foundation collections of the British Museum.

his building development – a supporter of the Hanoverian succession. The Square and adjacent streets immediately became a desirable residential area; by 1725 the parish contained nine dukes, two marquesses, twenty-one earls, six viscounts, thirteen barons and two bishops.

This print showing the square in the 1750s might be intended to illustrate the description of a commentator of some fifteen years earlier: 'the view down George-Street, from the upper side of the square, is one of the most

entertaining in the whole city: the sides of the square, the area in the middle, the breaks of building that form the entrance of the vista, the vista itself, but, above all, the beautiful projection of the portico of St George's Church, are all circumstances that unite in beauty, and make the scene perfect' (J. Ralph, 1734, quoted in Summerson, p. 100). What Ralph calls the 'vista' – the broadening of the street between the church and the Square – remains impressive today, a theatrically Baroque motif that contrasts with the rectilinear

A View of Grosvenor Square London. | Vüe de la Place de Grosvenor a Londres.

5.71

5.71

Thomas Bowles (1712?–67)

A View of Grosvenor Square, 1751

Etching with engraved lettering,
256 × 400 mm (cropped)

Crace XXIX.105

1880-11-13-4566

Grosvenor Square was created by Sir Richard Grosvenor between 1725 and 1731 as the centrepiece of a development which took in the whole north-west section of Mayfair. The 100-acre estate, as well as a further 400 acres in Pimlico and what is now Belgravia, had come into the Grosvenor family in 1677 with the marriage of Sir Thomas Grosvenor to Mary Davies, twelve-year-old heiress to a City fortune.

The Grosvenor development in Mayfair followed the usual system of letting plots of land on building leases at rents which were reduced for the first year or two while building was in progress. Grosvenor Square was divided into fifty-one sites and thirty builders were involved; houses were large and expensive, costing up to £7,500. Although standards were set very high (and have been maintained by Sir Richard's descendants, later Dukes of Westminster, who still own what remain the most exclusive areas of London), it was not possible to prescribe detailed designs in such circumstances. There was some attempt to create an architectural whole – the east side of the Square (on the right of the print) was planned as a symmetrical unit – but mid-eighteenth-century London developments have none of the uniformity of, for instance, Nash's early nineteenth-century Regent's Park. The Grosvenor family themselves retained their London residence on Millbank until 1806 when they built a house in Park Lane.

Bowles gives no sense of the huge scale of Grosvenor Square, which is far larger than St James's or Hanover Squares, enclosing a space of 8 acres. It was the first square in London to be designed with a central garden. Grosvenor and his lessees spent nearly £3,000 on the wall and fence, gravel paths, turf, thousands of flowering shrubs, neat elm hedging and trees clipped to a maximum height of 8 feet to allow unencumbered views. For London garden squares and the eighteenth-century arguments for and against this aspect of *rus in urbe* see Longstaffe-Gowan, pp. 183–233.

Invented Painted & Published by W.ᵐ Hogarth *Marriage A-la--Mode.* (Plate II) *Engraved by B. Baron* *According to Act of Parliament April 1ˢᵗ 1745*

5.72

Luxury

5.72

Bernard Baron (1696–1762) after
William Hogarth (1697–1764)

Marriage A-la-Mode, Plate II,
1 April 1745

Published by William Hogarth

Etching and engraving with engraved
lettering, 388 × 462 mm

Paulson 159 (ii)

1868-8-22-1561 Bequeathed by Felix
Slade, 1868

Hogarth does not give an address for the
fictional Viscount Squanderfield and his
wealthy bride, but there is no question
that such a couple would have lived
anywhere but in St James's or Mayfair.
The luxury of their home contrasts
dramatically with the old-fashioned
drabness of the City house where the
bride had been brought up (cat. 1.15).

Hogarth set out in *Marriage A-la-
Mode* to satirize the lifestyle of the
wealthy. In earlier conversation pieces,
such as *The Cholmondeley Family*, 1732,
or *A Performance of 'The Indian
Emperor'*, 1732–5, he had portrayed
grand interiors as fitting settings for his

patrons, but here he shows splendid
decor as a contrast to the trivial pursuits
of the young aristocrats: paintings of
martyred saints overlook card-tables; the
dignified bust of a Roman matron is
surrounded by amusing oriental figures
bought by a flighty young bride with her
stays undone and hair falling over her
brow (a loose curl was added in pen to
early states of the print). In his *Analysis
of Beauty* (1753, p. 35) Hogarth noted
that 'A lock of hair falling thus cross the
temples ... has an effect too alluring to be
strictly decent, as is very well known to
the loose and lowest class of women'.
A Letter of Genteel and Moral Advice to a

246

Marriage A-la-Mode (Plate IV)

Invented Painted & Published by Wm. Hogarth
Engraved by S. Ravenet
According to Act of Parliament April 1st 1745

5.73

Young Lady by the Reverend Wettenhall Wilkes (1740) indicates how the young woman's negligent attitude would have been read by a contemporary audience: 'Never appear in company without your stays. Make it your general rule to lace in the morning, before you leave your chamber. The neglect of this is liable to the censure of indolence, supiness of thought, sluttishness – and very often worse. Leaning and lolling are often interpreted to various disadvantages ... The negligence of loose attire, may oft' invite to loose desire.'

Although Hogarth's warnings of the risks to women of contravening behavioural norms were conventional, his criticism of conspicuous consumption was at odds with a society which revelled in increasing wealth. The series was not received as well as his more traditional moral tales, *A Harlot's Progress* (1732) and *A Rake's Progress* (1735). The series of *Marriage A-la-Mode* paintings was not sold until 1751 and then for only a hundred and twenty guineas rather than the £500 or £600 that Hogarth had hoped for.

5·73
Simon François Ravenet (1706/21–74) after William Hogarth (1697–1764)

Marriage A-la-Mode, Plate IV, 1745

Published by William Hogarth

Etching and engraving with engraved lettering, 390 × 464 mm

Paulson 161 (ii)

1868-8-22-1563 Bequeathed by Felix Slade, 1868

The Countess (now elevated by the death of her father-in-law) holds a morning levée in the manner of the French court, receiving guests as she conducts her toilette. Copies of old master paintings of erotic subjects (Cavallino's *Lot and his Daughters*, Correggio's *Jupiter and Io* and Michelangelo's *Jupiter and Ganymede* – all of which would have been known to Hogarth from reproductive prints) make an ironic background to the performance of a castrato singer and to the lawyer's invitation to the Countess to meet him at a masquerade. As in cat. 5.72, attention is drawn to the rich young woman's casual acquisitiveness: spread on the floor is an incoherent group of purchases from an auction sale including a 'merman' (see cat. 5.79), a small bronze of Actaeon and a dish decorated with a scene of Leda and the swan by Giulio Romano, whose name was associated with explicit prints of the loves of the gods. Among the Countess's other fashionable accessories are two black servants.

The Squanderfields' Purchases

5.74

Bust of a Roman matron, perhaps Julia, daughter of Emperor Titus, 1st century AD

Parian marble, height 425 mm

Smith Sculpture 1892

GR 1865-1-3-51 ex-collection Count James Alexandre de Pourtalès-Gorgier

Roman antiquities found their way to London with returning Grand Tourists, and dealers exploited their taste. Sculpture was often damaged (sometimes deliberately so in order to facilitate the acquisition of export licences), and this bust, like the one in Hogarth's print, has a broken nose. See Kenworthy-Browne for a case study of the activities of Matthew Brettingham (1725–1803), son of the architect of the same name referred to in cat. 5.3, who was in Rome from 1747 to 1754. Brettingham acted as agent for his father, for Thomas Coke, Earl of Leicester, and on his own account in the purchase of antique sculpture and

plaster casts as well as pictures; according to Robert Adam, Brettingham 'had commissions, when at Rome, for near £10,000 for statues, etc.'. Other well-known British expatriates who sent antiquities back home for sale were the painters Gavin Hamilton (1723–98) and Thomas Jenkins (1722–98).

5.75

A group of twenty-six pieces of Qing dynasty porcelain and other eighteenth-century Chinese export ware

Chinese porcelain found a market in Europe from the fourteenth century onwards. During the eighteenth century the British East India Company came to dominate the trade, based in a small area of Canton and dealing with Chinese merchants licensed by the Emperor to deal with Europeans. Sea voyages lasted six months or more, and the goods carried were luxuries: porcelain, silk, and most of all from the mid seventeenth century, tea. Blue and white Chinese porcelain was used as everyday table ware in wealthy London households: for instance, in cat. 5.72 the Countess has been using a Chinese tea set, and in cat. 5.73 her friends drink chocolate from Chinese cups.

In cat. 5.72 Hogarth portrays a collection of vases and figures as a hotch-potch of odd shapes crowded on to a mantelpiece. The taste for Chinese design – whether genuine pieces or European chinoiserie – was well established: ornamental Chinese porcelain appeared in inventories of Burghley House in 1688 and 1690, in Mary II's collection at Kensington Palace and Hampton Court, and in the collection of Hans Sloane as well as in less elevated contexts – the brothel-keeper Elizabeth Haddock (d. 1752) had an enormous collection of porcelain including blanc-de-Chine groups of boys, men on horseback, figures on camels, dragons, tigers and lions.

The pieces are listed here as they appear in the illustration, left to right.

Snuff bottle

Red and yellow glass, and stone (realgar imitation), stopper made of gilded metal, height 57 mm plus stopper

OA 1948,1019.6

Snuff bottle

Porcelain with underglaze blue, stopper made of coral, height 70 mm

OA 1945,1017.365

One of a pair of joss-stick holders in the form of Buddhist lions

Blanc-de-Chine porcelain, height 120 mm

OA 1980,0728.118

Budai

Bronze, height 69 mm

OA 1952,1219.13

Budai was a figure from popular Chinese religion, commonly, but misleadingly, known as 'the laughing buddha'.

Water vessel in the form of a European with a crane

Blanc-de-Chine porcelain, height 76 mm

OA Franks.1397

Figure of St Anthony of Padua with the Christ child

Blanc-de-Chine porcelain, height 229 mm

OA 1928,0718.7

Iohan figure, with rosary incised on knee

Blanc-de-Chine porcelain, height 150 mm

OA 1980,0728.53

One of a pair of beakers of gu form, decorated with pheasants, magnolia and other flowers

Porcelain painted in underglaze blue, height 248 mm

OA Franks.125

5.74, 5.75

Guanyin figure

Ivory, height 279 mm

OA 1937,0416.205

Guanyin or Guanshym, the mother goddess or the 'Bodhisattva who hears the cries of the world', appears here in one of her Chinese manifestations as the *songzi* or child-giving Guanyin. The image was influenced by Spanish figures of the Virgin and Child, and it appears on shipping lists as the 'Sancta Maria'.

Snuff bottle

Brown and gold glazed porcelain with metal stopper, height 85 mm

OA Franks.115.+

One of a pair of vases with lids, decorated with birds and flowers

Porcelain painted in underglaze blue, height 280 mm

OA Franks.124

Snuff bottle

Blue and white porcelain, with red stopper

OA 1963,0731.16

Snuff bottle with stand

Glass

OA 1943,0213.26

Snuff bottle

Red and yellow glass, height 580 mm

OA +.6510

Snuff bottle

Glass

OA 1945,1017.331

One of a pair of vases with lids, decorated with birds and flowers

Porcelain painted in underglaze blue, height 280 mm

OA Franks.124

Figure group of two Europeans

Blanc-de-Chine porcelain

OA Franks.579

Guanyin figure with child

Blanc-de-Chine porcelain, height 300 mm

OA 1980,0728.24

Snuff bottle

Brown and yellow glass

OA 1886,1013.13

Budai

Blanc-de-Chine porcelain

OA 1980,0728.49

One of a pair of beakers of gu form, decorated with pheasants, magnolia and other flowers

Porcelain painted in underglaze blue, height 248 mm

OA Franks.125

Figure of St Anthony of Padua with the Christ child, on a hexagonal flower-decorated pedestal

Blanc-de-Chine porcelain, height 270 mm

OA 1980,0728.74

Joss-stick holder with two Europeans wearing tricorne hats

Blanc-de-Chine porcelain, height 850 mm

OA 1980,0728.102

Snuff bottle and stopper decorated with a scene of Immortals crossing water

Porcelain painted in underglaze blue, with stopper made of wood, height 51 mm

OA Franks.421.+

One of a pair of joss-stick holders in the form of Buddhist lions

Blanc-de-Chine porcelain, height 120 mm

OA 1980,0728.119

Snuff bottle

Glass

OA 1886,1013.12

5.76

5.76

Pack of fortune telling cards, 1745–56

Etching and engraving with engraved lettering, 94 × 57 mm

Schreiber Playing Cards, E.82

1896-5-1-942* Bequeathed by Lady Charlotte Schreiber

This pack of cards was designed to tell fortunes by supplying answers to each of twenty questions listed on the Kings of each suit. One of the questions on the card of the King of Clubs (Pharaoh) is 'Whether they shall succeed in love'; by following a tortuous set of rules the player arrives at the answer 'This match decline, they'll ne'er be thine'. The Kings and Queens are illustrated by ancient monarchs but the Knaves include comparatively recent anti-royalists Wat Tyler (see cat. 1.16) and John Hewson, one of the regicides who signed the death warrant for Charles I.

Pip cards have astrological spheres and the names of astrologers or sibyls and the answers to the players' questions.

The pack is associated with the name of the well-known vendor of playing cards John Lenthall (1683 – after 1762), but there is no evidence that he actually made these or any other cards. He was a member of the Stationers' Company and it is more likely that he was a publisher. The pack is first recorded in an advertisement of November 1690; Lenthall advertised it from 1711 to 1720, but it was advertised by other dealers from 1736 to 1754. The garter tax stamp still visible on the Ace of Spades indicates that this particular pack was issued between 1745 and 1756 (see cat. 5.77). It is well thumbed and has clearly been used a good deal.

5·77
Patent copper-plate cards, 1765–76

ILLUSTRATED IN COLOUR, PLATE 15

Etching and engraving with engraved lettering, 89 × 64 mm

Published by Rowley & Co.

Willshire E.169

1982.u.4627

The pack was obviously made for the top of the market and would have cost at least 5s before tax. It is unusual in that – like cat. 5.76 – it was printed from intaglio plates. In standard packs, court cards were printed from woodblocks, and the pips stencilled; in this pack even the pips are printed – on the court cards from separate plates. Court cards are differentiated: the King of Hearts is George III, with Queen Charlotte and a Yeoman of the Guard as the Knave; Spades represent the French monarchy; Clubs are Austria with the double-headed eagle on the Knave's hat. The pips combine the French suits (used in Britain) with the Latin, so that Hearts are superimposed on chalices or cups, and Spades take the form of a spear-head. There is subtle differentiation in the colour of the ink used for the pips of each suit; only the Ace of Spades, printed at the Stamp Office, is in black ink.

The Ace of Spades allows this pack to be dated. It is of the type introduced in 1765 to show that stamp duty had been paid, and it was superseded in 1776. Duty on playing cards was introduced in 1711, initially at 6d per pack, but increasing in 1756 to 1s, and in 1776 to 1s 6d. Various labels and seals were used to provide proof of payment, together with four different hand-stamps on the Ace of Spades used successively between c. 1712 and 1765 (see cat. 5.76). In 1765 hand-stamps were replaced by engraved Aces of Spades printed from plates at the Stamp Office on the maker's own paper. For an account of tax marks on English playing cards see Berry, IV, 1–5.

5·78
Catalogue of the collection of shells, ores, fossils, minerals, and natural curiosities, of Mr Daniel Furzer for sale by auction by Abraham Langford, the Great Piazza, Covent Garden, 16–17 June 1756

NOT ILLUSTRATED

Letterpress, 10 pages, 195 × 125 mm

Sc.A.1.3/23

Hogarth's Countess (cat. 5.73) has bought a basketful of bric-a-brac from the collection of 'the late Sir Timothy Babyhouse'. She may have met her lawyer, Silvertongue, at the auction. Auction houses were one of the new developments of the mid eighteenth century that allowed the mixing of different classes – in this case the middling and upper classes. Auctioneers, as well as their customers, provided rich material for satirists: the popular image was that of the plausible Peter Puff who happily exploited the gullible wealthy in Samuel Foote's play Taste of 1748.

Daniel Furzer was probably a lawyer; he is described on the title page of the catalogue as 'of New Inn', one of the Inns of Chancery beyond the western boundary of the City (New Inn was close to Somerset House) that served as social clubs for solicitors and attorneys. His collection consisted chiefly of scientific specimens, but there were also curiosities: Lot 23, 'a Persian hubble bubble, 2 pipes, a pair of Turkish boots, an Indian fan, and a canister'; Lot 26, 'a pair of Chinese cows, a pair of mandarins, a shaking figure, and a mandarin in brass'.

Abraham Langford (1711–74), the leading auctioneer of the day, took over the Covent Garden premises of Christopher Cock in 1748. James Christie (1730–1803) held his first sale in Pall Mall in 1766. John Sotheby (1740–1807) became associated in 1780 with the firm founded in Covent Garden by his uncle Samuel Baker, a specialist book and print auctioneer. See Pears for the development of the English art trade.

5.79

5·79
'Merman'

Dried monkey with fish tail, length 380 mm

Department of Ethnography, 1942 AS 1.1

Presented by HRH Princess Arthur of Connaught, ex-collection Seijiro Arisuye

Mermaids and mermen have appeared in popular mythology from the earliest times, and they were among the many phenomena – artificial and otherwise – exhibited in eighteenth-century shows (see O'Connell, pp. 98–108). A number of 'mermen' survive from the period, evidently constructed in east Asia, and Hogarth's inclusion of an example suggests they were well known in London.

This example was said to have been caught in the sea off Japan. Radiographic examination has revealed that the 'merman' was modelled from clay or plaster around two metal armatures. The skin of a small monkey – still with some hair – covers the upper part, but the jaw of a fish with several rows of teeth has been inserted The tail is that of a large fish with large scales; the lower backbone remains.

Richard Siddall Chymist.
at the Golden Head in Panton Street,
near the HAY-MARKET,
Makes and Sells all manner of
Chymical and *Galenical Medicines,*
With all Sorts of Druggs:
Wholesale & Retail, at very Reasonable Rates.
N.B. The Elixir for the Asthma, as also
for the Gout and Rheumatism

R.ᵈ Clee Fecit

5.80

Shopkeepers

5.80–5.90

The new residential developments of St James's and Mayfair were catered to by shops selling a wide range of luxury goods, and shopkeepers advertised their businesses with attractive trade cards. Bills demonstrate not only the high prices paid but also the length of time between purchase and payment. Hogarth satirizes the aristocrat's casual attitude in *Marriage A-la-Mode*, Plate II (cat. 5.72), where the steward holding a clutch of bills despairs of gaining his employers' attention.

5.80

Robert Clee (1711?–73)

Trade card of Richard Siddall, Chemist, at the Golden Head in Panton Street, near the Haymarket

Etching with engraved lettering, 245 × 182 mm

Heal 35.64 Bequeathed by Sir Ambrose Heal, 1959

According to Tillyard (pp. 40–2), 'by the mid-eighteenth century fashionable society was drowning in a tidal wave of potions and syrups', although the expensive prescriptions provided by doctors 'were scarcely distinguishable from the cheaper remedies offered by quacks who toured the streets' (see cats 1.30 and 1.75). Siddall's shop-sign is the head of Galen, the second-century Greek physician.

This elaborate trade card is based on a painting entitled *La Pharmacie*, one of a series by Jacques de Lajoue made for the Duc de Picquigny in 1735 and known in London from a print of 1738 by Charles Nicolas Cochin. The engraver Robert Clee was a neighbour of Siddall in Panton Street; as well as making prints, he engraved silver and between 1769 and 1773 he was paid up to £345 a year by the silversmiths John Parker and Edward Wakelin, also of Panton Street (see cat. 5.84).

5.81

5.81

Anonymous

Trade card of Elizabeth Godfrey, Goldsmith, Silversmith and Jeweller, at the Hand, Ring and Crown, in Norris Street, St James's Haymarket

Etching with engraved lettering, 245 × 203 mm

Heal 67.168 Bequeathed by Sir Ambrose Heal, 1959

Elizabeth Godfrey traded at the sign of the Hand, Ring and Crown from 1741 to 1758. The accounts of Benjamin Mildmay, Earl Fitzwalter (Essex Record Office, transcribed in *Antiquarian*

Horology, V, March 1967, pp. 198–9), record a payment on 4 May 1745 to Mrs Godfrey of £2 for a large silver milk jug.

5.82

George Bride (1739–c.1812)

Trade card of Morris, Jeweller, Goldsmith and Toyman, at the King's Arms, the corner of Norris Street, in St James's Haymarket

Etching with engraved lettering, 244 × 182 mm

Heal 67.284 Bequeathed by Sir Ambrose Heal, 1959

5.82

Anonymous

*Trade card of William and Mary
Deards, at the Star, the end of Pall
Mall near St James's Haymarket*

Etching with engraved lettering,
192 × 154 mm

Heal 119.11 Bequeathed by Sir Ambrose
Heal, 1959

The Deards or Deard family business
flourished throughout the eighteenth
century dealing in jewellery, gold, silver
and porcelain. John Deard (d. 1731) had
a toyshop in Fleet Street – 'toys' at that
time referred to all manner of small
luxury objects – and another in the
fashionable spa town of Tunbridge Wells
that was run by his daughter, the future
Mrs Chenevix (see cat. 3.47). It was
probably Deard's widow whose shop in
Bath caught the eye of Lady Mary
Wortley Montagu in 1736: 'Farewell to
Deard's and all her toys which glitter in
her shop / Deluding traps to girls and
boys, the warehouse of the fop'. Another
daughter became Mrs Bertram, whose
toyshop in Bath was referred to in
Alexander Pope's lines to Lady Fanny
Shirley. William Deard (d. 1761) ran the
London business by 1740: following the
westward move of wealthy clients, he set
up shop firstly in the Strand and then, in
the late 1750s, in Pall Mall as advertised
in this card. The accounts of Benjamin
Mildmay, Earl Fitzwalter (see 5.81),
record a payment of £5 15s 6d on 9
February 1741 to 'Mr Deards for a cane
with a little gold head with my crest upon
it'; Fielding mentions in *Joseph Andrews*
(1742) that 'one of Mr Deard's best
workmen, whom no other artificer can
equal … hath made all those sticks which
the beaus have lately walked with about
the Park in a morning'. Another William
Deard is recorded in 1760 and 1777
running a china shop at the corner of
Dover Street, Piccadilly; John Deard,
jeweller of Davis Street, Piccadilly, died
in 1794.

The card shows examples of the sort of
pieces that would have been sold in a
luxury toyshop and a vignette of a
workshop with a workbench beneath a
long window and a machine for drawing
gold wire.

 The card was engraved by George
Bride, who is otherwise recorded as a
decorative engraver on gold and silver.
The apprentice books held at
Goldsmiths' Hall record that George
·Bride, son of Richard Bride, a dyer of the
parish of St Luke, Middlesex, was
apprenticed to Francis Garden (see
cat. 1.86) in 1754 and was made free on

4 July 1770 (information from Laurence
Worms). His apprenticeship would have
lasted seven years, but he evidently spent
the 1760s working as a journeyman until
he was ready to set up his own business.
In 1770 his address was given as
Blackmore Street, Clare Market; in 1775
he was recorded at Norris Street,
running west from the Haymarket (in the
same street as Morris's shop advertised
here), and from 1781 to 1805 at 23
Oxenden Street, just to the east.

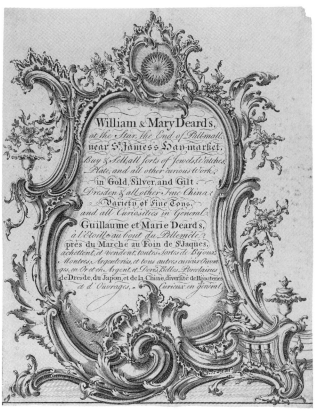

5.83

5.84

5.84

Anonymous

Trade card of George Wickes and Samuel Netherton, Goldsmiths, Jewellers and Silversmiths, in Panton Street, near St James's Haymarket, 1750

Etching with engraved lettering, 205 × 147 mm

Heal 67.428 Bequeathed by Sir Ambrose Heal, 1959

George Wickes was one of the great gold-smiths of the age, and several of his pieces survive. Most notable are a two-hundred-piece silver dinner service made for James Fitzgerald, 20th Earl of Kildare (later 1st Duke of Leinster), between 1745 and 1747 (private collection, see Barr, pp. 197–205), and a silver-gilt table centrepiece made in 1745 for Frederick, Prince of Wales, after a design by William Kent, at a cost of £695 14s 4d (Royal Collection).

Wickes was in partnership with Samuel Netherton by 1751. In 1760 they were succeeded by Edward Wakelin and John Parker, and in 1792 Robert Garrard took over. The firm still bears his name. Ledgers going back to Wickes's time (Victoria and Albert Museum) formed the basis for an illuminating study of his career by Elaine Barr.

5.85

Joseph Goupy (1678/89–before 1770)

*The Harmonious Boar, c.*1754

Etching with engraved lettering, 469 × 315 mm

BM Satire 3272; Simon 8

1868-8-8-3974 ex-collection Edward Hawkins

This print satirizes Handel's famous greed for food. It shows the musician as a gigantic pig playing an organ inscribed 'O che Tocca' ('What a touch') on which hang a leg of ham and a goose; a barrel of oysters is on the floor behind him and he sits on a cask of brandy. A monkey holds a mirror indicating Handel's vanity, and cannon and a braying jackass satirize the loudness and discordance of his music. The print is based on a pastel in the Fitzwilliam Museum, Cambridge. There were at least two related prints of the subject, one of which is dated 1754.

Handel and Joseph Goupy would have known each other since at least 1727, when Goupy worked at the King's Theatre, Haymarket, on the scenery for Handel's *Riccardo I*. A portrait by Goupy of Handel (present whereabouts unknown) was in the collection of his patron Frederick, Prince of Wales, by 1742 (Rorschach. p. 73, no. 152). Horace

Walpole noted a quarrel between the two men; according to a later writer Handel provided Goupy with a simple meal at his house only to be found secretly tucking in to an array of delicacies. The verse in Italian at the bottom of the sheet translates as 'Anger is justified when the cause is just'.

Handel lived for thirty-six years at 25 Brook Street, Mayfair. Goupy was at least in 1750 a close neighbour when he advertised prints for sale from King's Row on the western edge of Mayfair opposite Grosvenor Gate; by 1765 he was living in Kensington.

5.86

John Fougeron (fl. 1761–70)

Trade card of Domenico Negri, Confectioner, at the Pineappple in Berkeley Square, c.1760–5

Etching with engraved lettering, 162 × 190 mm

Heal 48.43 Bequeathed by Sir Ambrose Heal, 1959

This lively example of Rococo chinoiserie advertises one of the Italian tradesmen who provided good food for eighteenth-century Lonodners. Italian retailers worked at all levels of the market (see cat. 1.53), but Negri was catering to the most discriminating palates. He was the leading London confectioner of the second half of the eighteenth century, when there were a number of such businesses catering to wealthy West End customers. He provided a range of dried and crystallized fruits, biscuits, ice creams and water ices. Ice would have been collected from lakes and ponds in the winter and stored in underground ice houses. Negri's one-time partner, James Gunter, took over the business about 1800 and it flourished for another 150 years; Gunter's ices were renowned as the best in London until Second World War rationing destroyed such luxury foods.

See David, pp. 310–72, for a history of London confectioners.

5.85

5.86

5.88

5.87

Anonymous

Bill head of Domenico Negri, Confectioner, at the Pot and Pineapple in Berkeley Square, 1760

NOT ILLUSTRATED

Etching with engraved lettering, 65 × 182 mm (engraved plate), 335 × 212 mm (sheet)

Heal 48.42

Bequeathed by Sir Ambrose Heal, 1959

This bill head carries an account for Mr Clayton, a resident of Brook Street, Mayfair, from 18 March to 13 May 1760. Among his extravagant purchases were dried apricots at 8*s* a pound, dried sweetmeats at 5*s* a pound, savoy biscuits at 3*s* a pound, and four peaches in brandy for 6*s*. It is estimated that prices in general are about a hundred times higher today than in the mid eighteenth century, but luxury foods such as those listed here were comparatively far more expensive than they are today: a jar of peaches in brandy at Fortnum and Mason's costs £8, a pound (500 grams) of dried apricots costs £3. It might also be noted that in the 1750s a skilled tradesman would not expect to earn more than 18*s* a week, and 5*s* was thought to be sufficient to support a poor family for a week.

5.88

Anonymous

Bill head of Bartolommeo Valle and Brother at the Old Italian Warehouse, St James's Hay Market, 1753

Etching with engraved lettering, 255 × 2133 mm (sheet)

Banks 89.46

D.2-1196 Sarah Banks collection, presented 1818

This is a bill made out to the 'Revd. Mr. Cook' for 5 pints of 'fine [olive] oil' at 6*s* 10½*d*, two pounds of anchovies at 2*s* 6*d*, and half a pound of mustard with a bottle at 1*s* 1*d*. It is dated 5 June 1753 and was paid on 23 July. The elaborate billhead shows Bartolommeo Valle's shop-sign, the Orange Tree and Two Oil Jars, with salami, Parma ham and wine bottles encased in raffia baskets. A similar bill in the Bedford archives records purchases of Florence oil, Provence oil, cheese, capers, anchovies, macaroni, plums, bottled mangoes, isinglass and soap purchased for a total of £5 12s 9½d in 1769 (Thomson, p. 251). The shop – already described as the 'old Italian warehouse' – was well known into the nineteenth century, and Thomas Rowlandson made a lively watercolour of the interior. The firm was taken over by Robert Jackson & Co. of Piccadilly in 1911; in the 1920s that company still sold 'Barto Valle's Cream Virgin Olive Oil'.

5.89

Trade card of Bartolommeo Valle and Brother at the Old Italian Warehouse, at the Orange Tree and Two Oil Jars in St James's Hay Market, near Panton Street, 1763

NOT ILLUSTRATED

Letterpress, 264 × 219 mm

Heal 89.159 Bequeathed by Sir Ambrose Heal, 1959

This stock list contains not only Italian goods but delicacies from further afield: Cyprus wine, maraschino cherries from Corfu, mangoes from the East Indies, Japanese soy, Russian caviar and botargo from North Africa, as well as olives and oil from Provence, hams from Westphalia and Bayonne, Spanish olives, Durham mustard, French apricots, prunes and Hungary Water, toilet waters from Paris and Dutch snuff. On the back of the list is a bill of 1763 made out to Lord Winterton (see cat. 3.82) for 6 pounds of anchovies at 10s, ¼ pound of morels at 3s 6d and ¼ pound of truffles at 2s 6d.

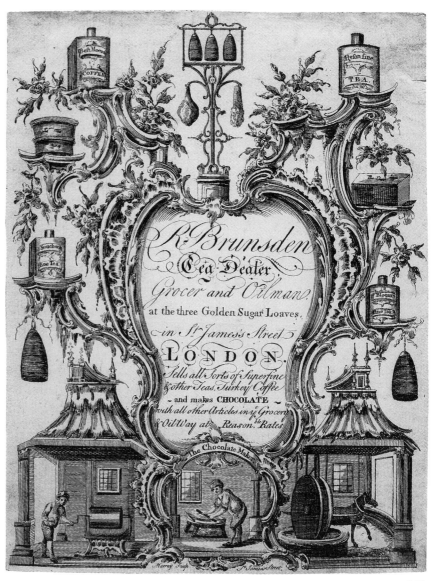

5.90

5.90

Murray (fl. 1750s)

Trade card of R. Brunsden, Tea Dealer, Grocer and Oilman at the Three Golden Sugar Loaves in St James's Street

Etching with engraved lettering, 193 × 154 mm

Heal 68.45 Bequeathed by Sir Ambrose Heal, 1959

The Rococo cartouche supports goods sold by Brunsden: coffee from Mokha in the Yemen; tea from China; chocolate and sugar – his sign is three hanging

sugar loaves – from the West Indies. Grocers were not simply retailers but wholesale traders who sometimes owned West Indian plantations – though tea would have had to be bought from Chinese merchants (see cat. 5.75). Brunsden announces that he makes chocolate, and three vignettes show men roasting chocolate beans and cracking their shells to extract the cocoa nibs which are then ground by a horse-powered mill. Chocolate was introduced to England in the 1650s as a drink. Hans Sloane, who had developed an interest in the medicinal properties of chocolate while in Jamaica in the 1680s, was the first to combine milk with chocolate; solid eating chocolate was not made until 1847. The engraver Murray of St James's Street is not otherwise recorded.

Tyburn and James Maclaine, the Gentleman Highwayman

5.91–5.98

Beyond Mayfair at the north-east corner of Hyde Park was Tyburn, a place of execution since the twelfth century. The 'triple-tree', the triangular gallows shown in cat. 5.96, stood there from 1571 to 1759; from 1760 to 1783 a movable gallows was put up and taken down for each execution. Residents in fashionable Mayfair objected to the proximity of public executions and the rowdiness that

accompanied them, and in 1783 the principal place of execution for London was moved to the wide space of the Old Bailey outside Newgate Prison. Executions ceased to be public in 1868.

The death penalty applied to about two hundred offences, but its main function was to act as a deterrent. During the 1750s a total of 281 people were executed; one-third of those sentenced were reprieved.

James Maclaine (1724–50) came from a respectable Irish clergy family, but in his early twenties he took to highway robbery. In 1748 he set himself up in lodgings in St James's Street – with his accomplice Plunket taking the part of his servant – and for two years he passed in society as a wealthy gentleman. One of Maclaine's victims was Horace Walpole, whom he robbed of a gold watch in Hyde Park in November 1749. He was finally

caught on 27 July 1750 when attempting to dispose of fine clothing taken from a passenger on the Salisbury coach at Turnham Green a month earlier. Quantities of stolen goods were found at his lodgings and he was found guilty at the Old Bailey on 13 September. The trial caused a tremendous stir among those who had been taken in by his gentlemanly appearance; according to Horace Walpole three thousand people visited him in Newgate on the Sunday after his trial. He was hanged at Tyburn on 3 October. The story gave rise to a large number of prints, broadsides, pamphlets and newspaper accounts. Plunket was never apprehended.

5.91

Anonymous

The Ladies Hero or the Unfortunate James McLeane Esq., 1750

Published by T. Harrison

Etching and engraving with engraved lettering, 350 × 249 mm

1851-3-8-408

The print claims to have been made from a drawing belonging to Mr Salt, keeper of the Westminster Gatehouse where Maclaine was imprisoned after his arrest. The prison, opposite the west end of Westminster Abbey, was built in 1370. In 1761 Dr Johnson described it as a disgrace to the magnificence of the city; it was eventually demolished in 1776.

5.92

Charles Mosley (fl. 1737–56)

Maclaine, the highwayman, robbing Lord Eglinton, 13 August 1750

Published by P. Angier, Engraver and Print-seller, at the Plume of Feathers in Windmill Street, St James's, London

Etching and engraving with engraved lettering, 248 × 350 mm

1894-6-11-79

The print – priced at 6d plain, 1s coloured – shows Maclaine and Plunket

The Ladies Hero or the Unfortunate James McLeane Esq.
Done from the Original late in the possession of Mr Salt Keeper of the Gate House — Publish'd according to Act of Par:

5.91

holding up the coach of Alexander Seton, 10th Earl of Eglinton, on Hounslow Heath on 26 June 1750. They are wearing elegant Venetian masks of the sort worn at masquerades; a similar mask lies at Maclaine's feet in cat. 5.91.

5.93

Anonymous

James Macleane, the Gentleman Highwayman at the Bar, 29 September 1750

Published by T. Fox in the Old Bailey

Etching with engraved lettering and letterpress, 248 × 250 mm (image), 407 × 255 mm (sheet)

1851-3-8-407

The text recounts the story of Maclaine's life, his crimes and his apprehension. It describes how when asked 'what he had to urge why sentence should not be passed upon him', Maclaine was too terrified to give his prepared speech. Thomas Gray alluded to this in his *Long Story* (cat. 5.9): 'A sudden fit of ague shook him / He stood as mute as poor McLean.' This print was sold for 6*d* plain, 1*s* coloured. The copper-plate was adapted four years later for a view of the trial of Elizabeth Canning (cat. 1.64).

5.94

Anonymous

Newgate's Lamenation or the Ladies' Last Farewell of Maclean, 1750

Etching with engraved lettering, 200 × 248 mm

1851-3-8-411

This cheap etching illustrates Horace Walpole's complaint, 'You cannot conceive the ridiculous rage there is of going to Newgate, the prints that are published of the malefactors, and the memoirs of their lives set forth' (letter to Horace Mann, 18 October 1750). James Boswell was uncharacteristically subdued by his experience of Newgate on 3 May 1763, when he saw Paul Lewis,

another highwayman who began life in genteel circumstances as the son of a clergyman: 'He was dressed in a white coat and blue silk vest and silver, with his hair neatly queued [tied back] and a silver-laced hat, smartly cocked. An acquaintance asked him how he was. He said, "Very well"; quite resigned. Poor fellow! I really took a great concern for him and wished to relieve him. He walked firmly and with a good air, with his chains rattling upon him …' The following day Boswell went to see Lewis hanged at Tyburn.

Unlike Hogarth's prints of Lord Lovat or John Wilkes (cat. 4.24), this is clearly

An Exact Reprefentation of MACLAINE the Highwayman Robbing LORD EGLINGTON on Hounflow Heath on the 26ᵗʰof June 1750.

5.92

Newgates Lamentation or the Ladys Last farewell of Maclean.

5.94

5.93

not based on a portrait of the prisoner. The composition is derived from Hogarth's painting of *The Beggar's Opera* (1728), Maclaine taking the place of Macheath standing in shackles surrounded by admiring women.

5.95

William Hogarth (1697–1764)

Preliminary drawing for Plate 11 of Industry and Idleness, 1747

ILLUSTRATED IN COLOUR, PLATE 16

Pen and ink with grey wash over graphite, with a splash of bodycolour, indented for transfer, 227 × 388 mm

Oppé 63, ECM 41

1896-7-10-25 ex-collection Horace Walpole

Hogarth's complex composition is fully worked out in this drawing and the indented lines suggest that it was transferred directly to the copper-plate. A few details remain to be finished, most notably the figure of the enthusiasic Methodist preacher (see cats 3.29–3.31) who is accompanying the prisoner in the cart, while the Newgate chaplain (the 'Ordinary') travels more comfortably by carriage. In the published series the Idle 'Prentice is called Tom Idle, but Hogarth must have decided on that name at a very late stage; in this drawing the execution broadside seller in the foreground cries 'The Last Dying Speech and Confession of Thomas Fowler'. For a discussion of execution broadsides see O'Connell, pp. 89–98; see also the execution broadsides in cats 1.15 and 3.17.

5.96

William Hogarth (1696–1764)

Industry and Idleness, Plate 11: *The Idle 'Prentice executed at Tyburn*, 30 September 1747

Published by William Hogarth

Etching and engraving with engraved lettering, 272 × 403 mm

Paulson 178 (ii)

The IDLE 'PRENTICE Executed at Tyburn.

5.96

1868-8-22-1582 Bequeathed by Felix Slade, 1868

Hogarth's view of a Tyburn execution parallels that of the anonymous writer of *A Trip through London*, published in 1745. The description begins at Newgate:

'At last out set the criminals, and with them a torrent of mob bursting through the gate, like a west-country barge with a flash of Thames water. Thousands were pressing to mind the looks of them. Their quondam companions more eager than others, break through all obstacles to take leave: and here you see young villains, that are proud of being so, (if they know any of them) tear the clothes off their backs by squeezing and creeping through the legs of men and horses to shake hands with them; and not to lose before so much company the reputation there is, in having had so valuable an acquaintance. All the way from Newgate to Tyburn, is one continued fair,

for whores and rogues of the meaner sort. Here the most abandoned rascals may light on women as shameless: here trollops all in rags may pick up sweethearts of the same politeness. Where the crowd is the least, which among the itinerants is nowhere very thin, the rabble is the rudest; and here jostling one another and kicking dirt about are the most innocent pastimes. Now you see a fellow, without provocation, push his companion in the kennel; and two minutes after the sufferer trip up the other's heels, and the first aggressor lies rolling in the more solid mire.

No modern mob can long subsist, without their darling cordial, the grand preservative of sloth, geneva [gin]. The traders who vend it among them, on these occasions, are commonly the very rubbish of the creation, the worst of both sexes, but most of them weather-beaten fellows, that have mispent their youth. Here stands an old sloven in a wig actually putrified, squeezed up in a corner, recommending a dram of it to the goers by: there another in

rags as rusty as a non-juring clergyman's cassock, with several bottles in a basket, stirs about with it where the throng is the thinnest, and tears his throat like a flounder fellow with crying his commodity: and further off you may see the head of a third, who has ventured in the middle of the current and minds his business as he is fluctuating in the irregular stream: whilst higher up, an old decrepit woman sits dreaming with it on a bulk, and over-against her, in a soldier's coat, her termagant daughter sells the sot's comfort with great dispatch.

It is incredible what a scene of confusion this often makes, which yet grows worse near the gallows, and the violent efforts of the most sturdy and resolute of the mob on one side, and the potent endeavours of rugged sheriff's officers, constables and headboroughs to beat them off on the other; the terrible blows that are struck, the pieces of swingeing sticks and blood that fly about the men that are knocked down and trampled upon, are beyond imagination.

After all, the Ordinary and Executioner having performed their different duties, with small ceremony and equal concern, seem to be tired, and glad it is over.'

5·97

John Hamilton (d. 1777)

View of an execution at Tyburn,
14 October 1767

ILLUSTRATED IN COLOUR, PLATE 16

Pen and ink and watercolour, 126 × 359 mm

1883-7-14-103

According to the note at the top of the drawing, Tyburn is shown here on 'October 14th 1767 – the day that Guest the banker's clerk was hanged'. The artist's main interest seems to be in the structures erected for spectators, especially in the curious arrangements described in a later inscription at the foot of the sheet: 'it was the custom of lamplighters in those days to erect their ladders together – for persons to mount them at 2d. and 3d. each to see the executions. Some of their parties frequently pulled down the ladders to get fresh customers to mount.'

This drawing – inscribed 'J. Hamilton' – has been tentatively attributed to Captain John Hamilton who served in Canada during the Seven Years War (see Sloan, pp. 120–1).

5·98

Williiam Hogarth (1697–1764)

Reward of Cruelty, 1 February 1751

Published by William Hogarth

Etching and engraving with engraved lettering, 378 × 318 mm

Paulson 190

S.2-126

James Maclaine hangs in the form of a skeleton in the background of Hogarth's print of the dissection of a criminal after execution. Such dissections were public events, given for the purpose of the study of human anatomy, but also providing much prurient interest. Dissection was

THE REWARD OF CRUELTY.

5.98

also intended to serve as an additional deterrent to crime – resurrection on Judgement Day was believed to require the body to be intact.

Opposite Maclaine in this early state of the print hangs the skeleton of Gentleman Harry (Henry Simms) who was executed on 17 June 1747. In the published state, Hogarth changed the name above the skeleton to the more topical James Field. The boxer Field was hanged within days of the publication of the print; he appeared in Plate 2 of the series in an advertisement for a fight with George Taylor (cat. 3.31).

Tom Nero, who had begun his career with cruelty to animals (cat. 3.25), is shown here as reduced to something less than human in the hands of the anatomists – and a dog takes final revenge by chewing at Nero's heart. The hall has been identified as the Cutlerian theatre of the Royal College of Physicians in Warwick Lane, near Newgate, which the Surgeons' Company used from 1745 to 1751 after separating from the old Barber-Surgeons' Company. At the end of the century the Surgeons' Company, shortly to become the Royal College, was given custody of the great anatomical collection of John Hunter which is still on show in Lincoln's Inn Fields.

CHRONOLOGY 1745–1765

1745   Prince Charles Edward Stuart leads a Jacobite army as far south as Derby

Hawksmoor completes the west towers of Westminster Abbey

Hogarth paints *Marriage A-la-Mode*

1746   The Battle of Culloden ends the Jacobite Rebellion

Canaletto arrives in London (stays until 1755)

1747   Garrick takes over the Drury Lane Theatre (remains until 1776)

1748   The Treaty of Aix-la-Chapelle ends the War of Austrian Succession

Pompeii is discovered

1749   Handel writes *Music for the Royal Fireworks* for the peace celebrations in St James's Park

Henry Fielding becomes Bow Street magistrate; his novel *Tom Jones* is published

John Cleland's novel *Fanny Hill, or the Memoirs of a Woman of Pleasure* is published

1750   The Jockey Club is founded at the Star and Garter Coffee House, Pall Mall

1751   Frederick, Prince of Wales, dies

The Gin Act restricts the retail of spirits

Thomas Gray's poem *Elegy Written in a Country Churchyard* is published

1752   The 'New Style' Gregorian calendar replaces the 'Old Style' Julian calendar; the year begins on 1 January rather than 25 March and, in order to equalize dates with those of Europe, eleven days, 3–13 September, are omitted in 1752

1753   The British Museum is founded

The Marriage Act is passed, requiring the licensing of ministers and calling of banns

The Jewish Naturalization Act allowing civil rights to Jews is passed in June and repealed in December

1754   Samuel Johnson's *Dictionary of the English Language* is published

Thomas Chippendale's *Gentleman and Cabinet Maker's Director* is published

John Fielding succeeds his brother as magistrate at Bow Street

1756   The Seven Years War begins: Britain loses Minorca to the French (Admiral Byng is shot for cowardice the following year); dozens of British captives die in the Black Hole of Calcutta where they have been confined overnight by Indian allies of the French; Britain is driven from the Canadian Great Lakes

The New Road is built from Marylebone to Islington to bypass London

1757   The Battle of Plassey, Bengal, is the turning point for the British in India: Robert Clive leads British and Indian troops to defeat the French allies under Siraj-ud-Daula

1758   Britain pays £670,000 to Frederick the Great of Prussia to maintain troops in Germany; Fort Duquesne is captured by British troops from the French and renamed Pittsburgh

1759   This is the 'annus mirabilis' or 'year of victories' in which the course of the Seven Years War turns in Britain's favour

The public is first admitted to the British Museum

Laurence Sterne's novel *Tristram Shandy* is published

1760   Montreal is captured from the French, and Canada comes under British control

George II dies

1761   George III marries Charlotte of Mecklenberg-Strelitz

Pondicherry falls to British troops, and French dominance in Madras is ended

1762   Britain takes Grenada from the French

George III buys Buckingham House

1763   The Treaty of Paris ends the Seven Years War: Britain retains Canada, Nova Scotia, Florida, Dominica, Grenada and Tobago

1764   Hogarth dies

Mozart, aged eight, arrives in London for a stay of over a year

1765   The Stamp Act imposes taxation on American colonists

BIBLIOGRAPHY AND ABBREVIATIONS

Place of publication is London unless otherwise noted.

Ackroyd P. Ackroyd, *London: The Biography*, 2000

Adams 1983 B. Adams, *London Illustrated 1604–1850: A Survey and Index of Topographical Books and Their Plates*, 1983

Adams 2001 E. Adams, *Chelsea Porcelain*, 2nd edn, 2001

Adams and Redstone E. Adams and D. Redstone, *Bow Porcelain*, 1981

Alford V. Alford, 'Rough music or charivari', *Folklore*, CXX, 1959, pp. 505–18

Allan, thesis D. G. C. Allan, *The Society for the Encouragement of Arts, Manufactures and Commerce: Organization, Membership and Objectives in the First Three Decades (1755–84)*, Ph.D. thesis, University of London, 1979

Allan 1979 D. G. C. Allan, *William Shipley, Founder of the Royal Society of Arts*, 2nd edn, 1979

Allan 1992 D. G. C. Allan, 'Artists and the Society', in J. L. Abbott and D. G. C. Allan, *The Virtuoso Tribe of Arts and Sciences: Studies in the Eighteenth-century Work and Membership of the London Society of Arts*, Athens, Georgia, 1992

Allen 1987 B. Allen, *Francis Hayman*, exhibition catalogue, Yale Center for British Art, New Haven and Kenwood, 1987

Allen 1991 B. Allen, 'The Society of Arts and the first exhibition of contemporary art in 1760', *RSA Journal*, CXXXIX, 1991, pp. 265–9

Altick R. D. Altick, *The Shows of London: A Panoramic History of Exhibitions, 1699–1862*, Cambridge, Massachusetts, and London, 1978

Anderson F. Anderson, *Crucible of War: The Seven Years' War and the Fate of the Empire in British North America, 1754–1766*, 2000

Andrew D. T. Andrew, *Philanthropy and Police: London Charity in the Eighteenth Century*, Princeton, New Jersey, 1990

Andrewes J. H. Andrewes (ed.), *The Quest for Longitude*, 1993

Andrews 1967 J. H. Andrews, 'The French school of Dublin land surveyors', *Irish Geography*, V, 1967, pp. 275–92

Andrews 1977 J. H. Andrews, 'Two maps of 18th-century Dublin and its surroundings by John Rocque', introductory notes to accompany facsimiles by Harry Margary, 1977

Apling H. Apling, 'The "Lima" coinage of George II', *Seaby's Coin and Medal Bulletin*, March 1970, pp. 82–7.

Apology M. Kitson, 'Hogarth's "Apology for Painters"', *Walpole Society*, XLI, 1968, pp. 46–111

Appleby 1992 J. H. Appleby, 'Mills, models and magdalens – the Dingley brothers and the Society of Arts', *RSA Journal*, CXL, 1992, pp. 267–9

Appleby 1995 J. H. Appleby, 'Charles Dingley's sawmill, or public spirit at a premium', *RSA Journal*, CXLIII, 1995, pp. 54–6

Aspital A. W. Aspital, *Catalogue of the Pepys Library at Magdalene College, Cambridge, III.i, Prints and Drawings, General*, Cambridge, 1980

Ball J. Ball, *Paul and Thomas Sandby: Royal Academicians*, Cheddar, 1985

Banks Index of trade cards in the British Museum chiefly from the collection of Sarah Banks (unpublished manuscript in the Department of Prints and Drawings)

Barr E. Barr, *George Wickes, 1698–1761: Royal Goldsmith*, 1980

Barrell J. Barrell, *The Political Theory of Painting from Reynolds to Hazlitt*, 1986

Barton N. Barton, *The Lost Rivers of London*, revised edn, 1992

Bauer and Deutsch W. A. Bauer and O. E. Deutsch (eds), *Mozart: Briefe and Aufzeichnungen, Gesamtausgabe*, Basel, 1962

Beall K. Beall, *Cries and Itinerant Trades*, Hamburg, 1975

Beattie J. Beattie, *Policing and Punishment in London, 1660–1750*, Oxford, 2001

Belsey H. Belsey, *Gainsborough's Family*, Sudbury, 1988

Benhamou R. Benhamou, 'Public and private art education in France, 1648–1793', *Studies on Voltaire and the Eighteenth Century*, CCCVIII, Oxford, 1993, pp. 90–112

Berry J. Berry, *Playing Cards of the World: A Catalogue of the Worshipful Company of Makers of Playing-cards on Deposit at Guildhall Library*, 1995

Bewick I. Bain (ed.), *A Memoir of Thomas Bewick Written by Himself*, Oxford, 1975

BHM L. Brown, *British Historicial Medals, 1760–1960*, 1980–7

Bignamini I. Bignamini, 'Art institutions in London, 1689–1768', *Walpole Society*, LIV, 1988, pp. 1–148

Bindman D. Bindman, *Hogarth and His Times*, exhibition catalogue, British Museum, 1997

Bisschop W. R. Bisschop, *The Rise of the London Money Market, 1640–1826*, New York, 1968

Black J. Black, *Pitt the Elder: The Great Commoner*, 1992

Bleackley H. Bleackley, *Ladies Fair and Frail: Sketches of the Demi-monde during the Eighteenth Century*, 1909

BM Satire *Catalogue of Personal and Political Satires in the British Museum, 1870–1954* (vols I–V by F. G. Stephens; VI–XI by M. D. George)

Borer 1975 M. C. Borer, *Mayfair: The Years of Grandeur*, 1975

Borer 1976 M. C. Borer, *Hampstead and Highgate: The Story of Two Hilltop Villages*, 1976

Boswell F. A. Pottle (ed.), *Boswell's London Journal, 1762–1763*, 1950

Boulton W. Biggs Boulton, *The Amusements of Old London: being a survey of the sports and pastimes, tea gardens and parks, playhouses and other diversions of the people of London from the Seventeenth to the beginning of the Nineteenth century*, 1901

Brewer 1870 E. C. Brewer, *A Dictionary of Phrase and Fable*, 1870 (revised by I. H. Evans, 1970)

Brewer 1973 J. Brewer, 'The misfortunes of Lord Bute: a case-study in 18th-century political argument and public opinion', *The Historical Journal*, XVI, 1973, pp. 3–43

Brewer 1997 J. Brewer, *The Pleasures of the Imagination: English Culture in the Eighteenth Century*, 1997

Bromberg R. Bromberg, *Canaletto's Etchings: Catalogue Raisonné*, 2nd edn, San Francisco, 1993

Bronze Cat. H. B. Walters, *Catalogue of Bronzes, Greek, Roman and Etruscan in the British Museum*, 1899

Burford 1992 E. J. Burford, *Wits, Wenchers and Wantons, London's Low Life: Covent Garden in the Eighteenth Century*, 1992

Burton E. Burton, *The Georgians at Home*, 1967

Byrd M. Byrd, *London Transformed: Images of the City in the Eighteenth Century*, 1978

Cain and Hopkins P. J. Cain and A. G. Hopkins, *British Imperialism: Innovation and Expansion, 1688 and 1914*, 1993

Calloway et al. S. Calloway, M. Snodin and C. Wainwright, *Horace Walpole and Strawberry Hill*, exhibition catalogue, Orleans House Gallery, Twickenham, 1980

Campbell R. Campbell, *The London Tradesman*, 1747

Carter S. Carter, *Purchasing Power: Representing Prostitution in Eighteenth-century English Popular Print Culture*, forthcoming

Casanova G. Casanova (trans. W. R. Trask), *History of My Life*, 6 volumes, 1967–72

Castro J. P. de Castro, *The Gordon Riots*, 1926

Challis C. E. Challis (ed.), *A New History of the Royal Mint*, Cambridge, 1992

Clark 1983 P. Clark, *The English Alehouse: A Social History, 1200–1830*, 1983

Clark 1988 P. Clark, 'The "Mother Gin" controversy in early 18th-century England', *Royal Historical Society Transactions*, XXXVIII, 1988, pp. 63–84

Clark 2000 P. Clark, *British Clubs and Societies 1580–1800: The Origins of an Associational World*, Oxford, 2000

Clayton T. Clayton, *The English Print, 1688–1802*, 1997

Coke D. Coke, 'Vauxhall Gardens', in M. Snodin (ed.), *Rococo: Art and Design in Hogarth's England*, exhibition catalogue, Victoria and Albert Museum, 1984, pp. 74–98

Colley L. Colley, *Britons: Forging the Nation, 1707–1837*, 1992

Colvin H. Colvin, *A Biographical Dictionary of British Architects, 1600–1840*, 3rd edn, 1995

Constable W. G. Constable, *Canaletto: Giovanni Antonio Canal, 1697–1768*, 2nd edn revised by J. G. Links, Oxford, 1976 (with Supplement, 1997)

Coutu J. Coutu, 'William Chambers and Joseph Wilton', in J. Harris and M. Snodin (eds), *Sir William Chambers, Architect to George III*, 1997

Crace J. G. Crace, *A Catalogue of Maps, Plans and Views of London, Westminster and Southwark, collected and arranged by Frederick Crace*, 1878

Crellin J. Crellin, 'Dr James's Fever Powder', *Transactions of the British Society for the History of Pharmacy*, 1974, pp. 136–43

Cruikshank and Burton D. Cruikshank and N. Burton, *Life in the Georgian City*, 1990

C.S. J. Chaloner Smith, *British Metzotinto Portraits*, 1883

Dalton O. M. Dalton, *Catalogue of the Finger Rings in the British Museum*, 1912

Davies M. Davies, *National Gallery: The French School*, 2nd edn, 1956

David E. David, *Harvest of the Cold Months: The Social History of Ice and Ices*, 1994 (references to 1996 Penguin edition)

Davis D. Davis, *A History of Shopping*, 1966

Davison et al. L. Davison, T. Hitchcock, T. Keirn and R. B. Shoemaker (eds), *Stilling the Grumbling Hive: The Response to Social and Economic Problems in England, 168–1750*, Stroud, 1992

Dawson A. Dawson, *Eighteenth-century English Porcelain in the British Museum*, 1987

Defoe D. Defoe (ed. P. Rogers), *A Tour through the Whole Island of Great Britain*, 1971

Desmond R. Desmond, *Kew: The History of the Royal Botanic Gardens*, 1995

Dickson P. G. M. Dickson, *The Financial Revolution in England: A study in the Development of Public Credit, 1688–1756*, 1967

Dillon P. Dillon, *The Much-lamented Death of Madam Geneva: The Eighteenth-century Gin Craze*, 2002

Dossie R. Dossie, *Memoirs of Agriculture and other Oeconomical Arts*, 1768

Dyos H. J. Dyos, *Victorian Suburb: A Study of the Growth of Camberwell*, Leicester, 1966

Earle 1976 P. Earle, *The World of Defoe*, 1976

Earle 1994 P. Earle, *A City Full of People*, 1994

ECM E. Croft-Murray, *Catalogue of British Drawings in the British Museum: Artists Born 1665–1715* (unpublished manuscript in the Department of Prints and Drawings)

Edelstein T. J. Edelstein, *Vauxhall Gardens*, exhibition catalogue, Yale Center for British Art, New Haven, 1983

Edgcumbe R. Edgcumbe, *The Art of the Gold Chaser in Eighteenth-century London*, Oxford, 2000

Egan P. Egan, *Boxiana; or Sketches of ancient and modern pugilism*, 1812

Eimer 1991 C. Eimer, 'The Society's concern with "The Medallic Art" in the 18th century', *RSA Journal*, CXXXIX, 1991, pp. 753–62

Eimer 1994 C. Eimer, 'The first RSA medal', *RSA Journal*, CXLII, 1994, pp. 18–19

Eimer 1998 C. Eimer, *The Pingo Family and Medal Making in Eighteenth-century Britain*, 1998

Einberg and Egerton E. Einberg and J. Egerton, *Tate Gallery Collections, Volume II: The Age of Hogarth – British Painters Born 1675–1709*, 1988

Emerson R. L. Emerson, 'The scientific interests of Archibald Campbell, 1st Earl of Ilay and 3rd Earl of Argyll (1682–1761)', *Annals of Science*, LIX, 2002, pp. 21–56

Eyres P. Eyres, '"Patriotizing, strenuously, the whole flower of his life"': the political agenda of Thomas Hollis's medallic programme', and 'Celebration and Dissent: Thomas Hollis, the Society of Arts and Stowe Gardens', *The Medal*, XXXVI, Spring 2000, pp. 8–23, and XXXVIII, Spring 2001, pp. 31–50

Fagan L. Fagan, *A Catalogue Raisonné of the Engraved Works of William Woollett*, 1885

Foreman A. Foreman, *Georgiana, Duchess of Devonshire*, 1998

Forrer L. Forrer, *Biographical Dictionary of Medallists*, 1907

Fox 1984 C. Fox, *Specimens of Genius Truly English*, exhibition catalogue, Galdy Galleries, New York, 1984

Fox 1987 C. Fox, *Londoners*, 1987

Friedman J. Friedman, *Spencer House: Chronicle of a Great London Mansion*, 1993

Gabszewicz A. Gabszewicz, *Made at New Canton: Bow Porcelain from the Collection of the London Borough of Newham*, exhibition catalogue, Christie's, Newham Museum and elsewhere, 2000

Galinou M. Galinou (ed.), *London's Pride: The Glorious History of the Capital's Gardens*, 1990

Gee 1998 T. Gee, *Up to Scratch: Bareknuckle Fighting and Heroes of the Prize-ring*, Harpenden, 1998

Gee 1999 T. Gee, 'Fresh light on Jack Slack', in B. J. Hugman (ed.), *The British Boxing Board of Control Yearbook*, 1999

George M. D. George, *London Life in the Eighteenthth Century*, 1925, revised 1965 (references to the Penguin edition, 1992)

Gerzina G. Gerzina, *Black England: Life before Emancipation*, 1995

Gibbon E. Gibbon (ed. G. A. Bonnard), *Memoirs of my Life*, 1966

Godfrey J. Godfrey, *A Treatise upon the Useful Science of Defence*, 1747

Goodwin G. Goodwin, *James McArdell*, 1903

Gregory and Stevenson J. Gregory and J. Stevenson, *The Longman Companion to Britain in the Eighteenth Century, 1688–1820*, Harlow, 2000

Griffiths 1984 A. Griffiths, 'A checklist of catalogues of British print publishers', *Print Quarterly*, I, 1984, pp. 4–22

Griffiths 1989 A. Griffiths, 'Early mezzotint publishing in England, I: John Smith', *Print Quarterly*, VI, 1989, pp. 243–57.

Griffiths 1996 A. Griffiths (ed.), *Landmarks in Print Collecting: Connoisseurs and Donors at the British Museum since 1753*, exhibition catalogue, Museum of Fine Arts, Houston, and elsewhere, 1996

Griffiths 1998 A. Griffiths, The *Print in Stuart Britain*, exhibition catalogue, British Museum, 1998

Guillery and Herman P. Guillery and B. Herman, *Deptford Houses, 1650 to 1800: Report for the Royal Commission on the Historical Monuments of England*, 1998

Gwynn J. Gwynn, *An Essay on Design*, 1749

Hallett M. Hallett, *The Spectacle of Difference: Graphic Satire in the Age of Hogarth*, 1999

Halsband R. Halsband, *Lord Hervey: Eighteenth-century Courtier*, Oxford, 1973

Harley and Walters J. B. Harley and G. Walters, 'English map collecting, 1790–1840', *Imago Mundi*, XXX, p. 37, 1978

Harris 1970 J. Harris, *Sir William Chambers*, 1970

Harris 1974 C. Harris, *Islington*, 1974

Harris and Simon R. Harris and R. Simon (eds), *Enlightened Self-interest: The Foundling Hospital and Hogarth*, exhibition catalogue, Thomas Coram Foundation for Children, 1997

Hart and North A. Hart and S. North, *Historical Fashion in Detail: The Seventeenth and Eighteenth Centuries*, 1998

Hayward and Kirkham J. Hayward and P. Kirkham, *William and John Linnell: Eighteenth-century London Furniture Makers*, 1980

Heal Index of trade cards in the British Museum from the collection of Ambrose Heal (unpublished manuscript in the Department of Prints and Drawings)

Heal 1957 A. Heal, *Sign Boards of Old London Shops*, 1957 (reissued 1988)

Henderson T. Henderson, *Disorderly Women in Eighteenth-century London*, 1999

Herrmann L. Herrmann, *Paul and Thomas Sandby*, 1986

Hibbert C. Hibbert, *George III: A Personal History*, 1998

Hicks C. Hicks, *Improper Pursuits: The Scandalous Life of Lady Di Beauclerk*, 2001

Highfill et al. P. H. Highfill, K. Burnim and E. Langhaus, *A Biographical Dictionary of Actors, Actresses, Musicians, Dancers, Managers and Other Stage Personnel in London, 1660–1800*, 16 vols, Carbondale, Illinois, 1973–93

Hobson R. L. Hobson, *Catalogue of the Collection of English Porcelain in the British Museum*, 1905

Hodson D. Hodson, *County Atlases of the British Isles Published After 1703*, 3 volumes, 1984–97

Hogarth W. Hogarth, *The Analysis of Beauty*, 1753

Hogg P. Hogg, *Slavery: The Afro-American Experience*, 1979

Howgego J. Howgego, *Printed Maps of London, circa 1553–1850*, Folkestone, 1978

Hudson and Luckhurst D. Hudson and K. W. Luckhurst, *The Royal Society of Arts, 1754–1954*, 1954

Hull Grundy C. Gere et al., *The Art of the Jeweller: A Catalogue of the Hull Grundy Gift to the British Museum*, 1984

Hyde 1982 R. Hyde, *The A–Z of Georgian London*, 1982

Hyde 1985 R. Hyde, *Gilded Scenes and Shining Prospects*, exhibition catalogue, Yale Center for British Art, New Haven, 1985

Hyde 1994 R. Hyde, *The Prospect of Britain: The Town Panoramas of Samuel and Nathaniel Buck*, 1994

Hyde Prospects R. Hyde, *Prospects and Panoramas of British and Irish Towns*, in preparation

Inwood S. Inwood, *A History of London*, Basingstoke, 1998

Isaacs P. Isaacs, 'Pills and print', in R. Myers and M. Harris (eds), *Medicine, Mortality and the Book Trade*, New Castle, Delaware, and Folkestone, 1998, pp. 25–47.

Jenkins 1975 S. Jenkins, *Landlords to London: The Story of a Capital and Its Growth*, 1975

Jenkins I. Jenkins, 'Dr Richard Mead', in R. Anderson, M. Caygill and L. Syson (eds), *Enlightening the British: Knowledge, Discovery and the Museum in the Eighteenth Century*, forthcoming

Johnson S. Johnson (ed. N. Rudd), *Juvenal, London and The Vanity of Human Wishes*, Bristol, 1981

Kalm P. Kalm (ed. J. Lucas), *Account of His Visit to England on His Way to America in 1748*, 1892

Kent J. P. C. Kent, 'The circulation of Portuguese coins in Great Britain', *Actas do III Congresso National de Numismatica*, Lisbon, 1985, pp. 389–405.

Kenworthy-Browne J. Kenworthy-Browne, 'Matthew Brettingham's Rome Account Book 1747–1754', *Walpole Society*, XLIX, 1983, pp. 37–132

Kerslake J. Kerslake, *National Portrait Gallery: Early Georgian Portraits*, 1977

Ketton-Cremer R. W. Ketton-Cremer, *Horace Walpole*, 1940

Kingzett R. Kingzett, 'A catalogue of the works of Samuel Scott', *Walpole Society*, XLVIII, 1982, pp. 1–134

Krahl and Harrison-Hall R. Krahl and J. Harrison-Hall, *Ancient Chinese Trade Ceramics*, exhibition catalogue, Taiwan, National Museum of History, 1994

Lambert S. Lambert (ed.), *Pattern and Design: Designs for the Decorative Arts, 1480–1980*, 1983

Lane J. Lane, *The Masonic Records, 1717–1894*, 1895

Langford 1986 P. Langford, *Walpole and the Robinocracy*, Cambridge, 1986

Langford 1989 P. Langford, *A Polite and Commercial People: England 1727–1783*, Oxford, 1989 (references are to the paperback edition, 1992)

Larwood and Hotten J. Larwood and J. C. Hotten, *History of Signboards*, 1867

Lennox-Boyd C. Lennox-Boyd, G. Shaw and S. Halliwell, *Theatre: The Age of Garrick*, exhibition catalogue, Courtauld Institute Galleries, 1994

Lillywhite 1963 B. Lillywhite, *London Coffee Houses: A Reference Book of Coffee Houses of the Seventeenth, Eighteenth and Nineteenth Centuries*, 1963

Lillywhite 1972 B.Lillywhite, *London Signs*, 1972

Lindsay J. Lindsay, *The Monster City: Defoe's London, 1688–1730*, 1978

Linebaugh P. Linebaugh, *The London Hanged: Crime and Civil Society in the Eighteenth Century*, 1991 (references to the Penguin edition, 1993)

Links J. G. Links, *Canaletto*, 2nd edn, 1994

Linnaeus J. E. Smith, *A Selection of Correspondence of Linnaeus and other Naturalists*, 1821

Lippincott 1983 L. Lippincott, *Selling Art in Georgian London: The Rise of Arthur Pond*, 1983

Lippincott 1988 L. Lippincott, 'Arthur Pond's Journal of Receipts and Expenses, 1734–1750', *Walpole Society*, LIV, 1988, pp. 220–333

Little and Kahrl D. M. Little and G. M. Kahrl (eds), *The Letters of David Garrick*, 1963

Liversidge and Farrington M. Liversidge and J. Farrington, *Canaletto and England*, exhibition catalogue, Birmingham Museums and Art Gallery, 1993

Lloyd S. Lloyd, *Richard and Maria Cosway: Regency Artists of Taste and Fashion*, Edinburgh, 1995

Lockman J. Lockman (published anonymously), *A Sketch of Spring-Gardens, Vaux-Hall, in a Letter to a Noble Lord*, 1752

Longstaffe-Gowan T. Longstaffe-Gowan, *The London Town Garden, 1700–1840*, 2001

Lugt F. Lugt, *Les Marques des collections*, Amsterdam, 1921, and Supplement, The Hague, 1956

McClellan J. E. McClellan III, *Science Reorganized: Scientific Societies in the Eighteenth Century*, New York, 1985

McClure R. K. McClure, *Coram's Children: The London Foundling Hospital in the Eighteenth Century*, 1981

MacGregor A. MacGregor (ed.), *Sir Hans Sloane: Collector, Scientist, Antiquary, Founding Father of the British Museum*, 1994

Mackenzie G. Mackenzie, *Marylebone: A Great City North of Oxford Street*, 1972

Mackintosh I. Mackintosh with G. Ashton, *The Georgian Playhouse: Actors, Artists, Audiences and Architecture, 1730–1830*, exhibition catalogue, Hayward Gallery, 1975

MacIntyre I. MacIntyre, *Garrick*, 1999

Malcolm J. Malcolm, *London Redivivum*, 1802–7

Mannings D. Mannings and M. Postle, *Sir Joshua Reynolds: A Complete Catalogue of His Paintings*, 2000

Mason and Jackson-Stops P. Mason and G. Jackson-Stops, *Designs for English Picture Frames*, 1987

MG *Catalogue of the Montague Guest Collection of Badges, Tokens and Passes*, 1930

MI E. Hawkins, *Medallic Illustrations of the History of Great Britain and Ireland to the Death of King George II*, 1885

Miles E. Miles, *Thomas Hudson, 1701–1779, Portrait Painter and Collector*, exhibition catalogue, Iveagh Bequest, Kenwood, 1979

Millar 1963 O. Millar, *The Tudor, Stuart and Early Georgian Pictures in the Collection of Her Majesty the Queen*, 1963

Millar 1980 O. Millar and C. E. Miller, *Canaletto*, exhibition catalogue, Queen's Gallery, Buckingham Palace, 1980–1

Mortimer T. Mortimer, *The Universal Director*, 1763

Morton and Wess A. Q. Morton and J. A. Wess, *Public and Private Science: The King George III Collection*, Oxford, 1993

Mowl T. Mowl, *Horace Walpole: The Great Outsider*, 1996

Murdoch T. Murdoch, *The Quiet Conquest: The Huguenots 1685 to 1985*, exhibition catalogue, Museum of London, 1985

Nicolson B. Nicolson, *The Treasures of the Foundling Hospital*, 1972

Norton R. Norton, *Mother Clap's Molly House: The Gay Subculture in England 1700–1830*, 1992

O'Connell S. O'Connell, *The Popular Print in England*, 1999

O'Donoghue F. O'Donoghue and H. M. Hake, *Catalogue of Engraved British Portraits in the British Museum*, 6 volumes, 1908–25

Oldys J. Yeowell (ed.), *A Literary Antiquary: Memoir of William Oldys, Esqr., Norroy King-at-Arms*, 1862

Oppe 1947 A. P. Oppe, *The Drawings of Paul and Thomas Sandby ... at Windsor*, 1947

Oppe 1948 A. P. Oppe, *The Drawings of William Hogarth*, 1948

Palmer A. Palmer, *The East End: Four Centuries of London Life*, revised edn., 2000

Parreaux A. Parreaux, *Smollett's London*, 1968

Paulson 1974 R. Paulson, *Hogarth: His Life, Art and Times*, 1974

Paulson 1989 R. Paulson, *Hogarth's Graphic Works*, 3rd edn, 1989

Paulson 1991 R. Paulson, *Hogarth*, 3 volumes, 1991–3

Pearce D. Pearce, *London's Mansions: The Palatial Houses of the Nobility*, 1986

Pears I. Pears, *The Discovery of Painting: The Growth of Interest in the Arts in England 1680–1768*, 1988

Pedley M. Pedley, 'Gentlemen abroad: Jefferys and Sayer in Paris', *The Map Collector*, XXXVII, 1986, pp. 20–2

Pennant T. Pennant, *Some Account of London*, 1790

Pennington R. Pennington, *A Descriptive Catalogue of the Etched Work of Wenceslaus Hollar*, Cambridge, 1982

Penny N. Penny (ed.), *Reynolds*, exhibition catalogue, Royal Academy of Arts, 1986

Peters G. J. Peters, *The Life and Work of Humphrey Gainsborough*, Henley-upon-Thames, 1948

Pevsner N. Pevsner (founding ed.), *The Buildings of England: London*, 1991 continuing

Phillips 1951 H. Phillips, *The Thames About 1750*, 1951

Phillips 1952 H. Phillips, 'John Rocque's career', *London Topographical Record*, XX, 1952

Phillips 1964 H. Phillips, *Mid-Georgian London*, 1964

Pickard L. Pickard, *Dr Johnson's London: Life in London, 1740–1770*, 2000

Plumb J. H. Plumb, *The Commercialization of Leisure*, Reading, 1973

Pointon M. Pointon, *Hanging the Head: Portraiture and Social Formation in Eighteenth-century England*, 1993

Porter 1982 R. Porter, *English Society in the Eighteenth Century*, 1982

Porter 2001 R. Porter, *London: A Social History*, 2001

Priestley M. Priestley, *West African Trade and Coast Society: A Family Study*, 1969

Raines 1980 R. Raines, 'Peter Tillemans: life and work, with a list of representative paintings', *Walpole Society*, XLVII, 1980, pp. 21–59

Raines 1987 R. Raines, 'Notes on Egbert van Heemskerk and the English taste for genre', *Walpole Society*, LIII 1987, pp. 119–42

Rauser A. Rauser, 'Embodied Liberty: why Hogarth's caricature of John Wilkes backfired', in B. Fort and A. Rosenthal (eds), *The Other Hogarth: Aesthetics of Difference*, Princeton, 2001

Reddaway T. F. Reddaway, *The Rebuilding of London After the Great Fire*, 1940

Reynolds J. Reynolds (ed. R. Wark), *Discourses on Art*, 1975

RIBA J. Lever et al., *Catalogue of the Drawings Collection of the Royal Institute of British Architects*, 19 vols, 1964–84

Rickards M. Rickards (ed. M. Twyman), *The Encyclopedia of Ephemera: A Guide to the Fragmentry Documents of Everyday Life for the Collector, Curator and Historian*, 2000

Robertson B. Robertson, *The Art of Paul Sandby*, exhibition catalogue, Yale Center for British Art, New Haven, 1985

Rogers 1972 P. Rogers, *Grub Street: Studies in a Subculture*, 1972

Rogers 1989 N. Rogers, *Whigs and Cities: Popular Politics in the Age of Walple and Pitt*, Oxford, 1989

Rorschach K. Rorschach, 'Frederick, Prince of Wales (1707–51) as collector and patron', *Walpole Society*, LV, 1993, pp. 1–76

Roscoe S. Roscoe, *John Newbery and his Successors 1740–1814: A Bibliography*, Wormley, 1973

Rothstein N. Rothstein, *Silk Designs of the Eighteenth Century in the Collection of the Victoria and Albert Museum*, 1990

Rudé 1952 G. Rudé, *Paris and London in the Eighteenth Century*, 1952

Rudé 1962 G. Rudé, *Wilkes and Liberty*, Oxford 1962

Rudé 1971 G. Rudé, *Hanoverian London, 1714–1808*, 1971

Rule J. Rule, *The Vital Century: England's Developing Economy, 1714–1815*, 1992

Rumbelow 1971 D. Rumbelow, *I Spy Blue: The Police and Crime in the City of London from Elizabeth I to Victoria*, 1971

Rumbelow 1982 D. Rumbelow, *The Triple Tree: Newgate, Tyburn, and Old Bailey*, 1982

Sands M. Sands, *Invitation to Ranelagh, 1742–1802*, 1946

Saur *Allgemeines Künstler-Lexikon*, Leipzig, 1992 continuing

Schwartz 1983 R. B. Schwartz, *Daily Life in Johnson's London*, Madison, Wisconsin, 1983

Schwartz 1992 D. Schwartz, *London in the Age of Industrialisation: Entrepreneurs, Labour Force and Living Conditions, 1700–1850*, Cambridge 1992

Scouten A. H. Scouten (ed.), *The London Stage 1729–47*, Part 3 of *The London Stage 1660–1800*, Carbondale, Illinois, 1960 etc.

Sheppard 1958 F. Sheppard, *Local Government in St Marylebone, 1688–1835: A Study of the Vestry and the Turnpike Trust*, 1958

Sheppard F. H. W. Sheppard (gen. ed.), *The Survey of London*, 1900 continuing

Shesgreen S. Shesgreen, *Images of the Outcast: The Urban Poor in the 'Cries of London'*, Manchester, 2002

Short M. Short, *Windmills in Lambeth: An Historical Survey*, 1971

Shute 1977 N. Shute, *London Villages*, 1977

Shute 1981 N. Shute, *More London Villages*, 1981

Simon J. Simon (ed.), *Handel: A Celebration of his Life and Times 1685–1759*, exhibition catalogue, National Portrait Gallery, 1985

Sloan K. Sloan, *A Noble Art: Amateur Artists and Drawing Masters, c.1600–1800*, exhibition catalogue, British Museum, 2000

Smart 1992 A. Smart, *Allan Ramsay: Painter, Essayist and Man of the Enlightenment*, 1992

Smart 1999 A. Smart (ed. J. Ingamells), *Allan Ramsay: A Complete Catalogue of His Paintings*, 1999

Smith 1759 A. Smith, *The Theory of Moral Sentiments*, 1759 (ed. D. D. Raphael and A. L. Macfie, Oxford, 1976)

Smith 1776 A. Smith, *The Wealth of Nations*, 1776

Smith 1791 J. T. Smith, *Antiquities of London and Its Environs*, 1791–1800

Smith 1828 J. T. Smith, *Nollekens and His Times*, 1828

Snodin 1984 M. Snodin (ed.), *Rococo: Art and Design in Hogarth's England*, exhibition catalogue, Victoria and Albert Museum, 1984

Snodin 1986 M. Snodin, 'Trade cards and the English Rococo', in C. Hind (ed.), *The Rococo in England: A Symposium*, 1986, pp. 82–103

Snodin and Howard M. Snodin and M. Howard, *Ornament: A Social History Since 1450*, 1996

Sobel D. Sobel, *Longitude*, 1996

Solkin 1993 D. Solkin, *Painting for Money: The Visual Arts in the Public Sphere in Eighteenth-century England*, 1993

Solkin 2001 D. Solkin, 'The Fetish over the Fireplace: disease as a genius loci in Marriage A-la-Mode', in B. Fort and A. Rosenthal (eds), *The Other Hogarth: The Aesthetics of Difference*, Princeton and Oxford, 2001

Solomon H. M. Solomon, *The Rise of Robert Dodsley: Creating the New Age of Print*, Carbondale, Illinois, 1996

Southworth J. G. Southworth, *Vauxhall Gardens*, New York, 1941

Stainton L. Stainton, *British Landscape Watercolours*, 1985

Stewart L. Stewart, *The Rise of Public Science: Rhetoric, Technology and Natural Philosophy in Newtonian Britain, 1660–1750*, Cambridge, 1992

Stone 1980 L. Stone, 'The residential development of the West End of London in the 17th century', in B. C. Malament (ed.), *After the Reformation*, Manchester, 1980, pp. 167–212

Stone 1960 G. W. Stone, *The London Stage, 1747–76*, Part 4 of *The London Stage, 1660–1800*, Carbondale, Illinois, 1960 etc.

Stone and Kahrl G. W. Stone and G. M. Kahrl, *David Garrick: A Critical Biography*, Carbondale, Illinois, 1979

Stow 1753 J. Stow, *Survey of the Cities of London and Westminster*, 5th edn, 1753

Stow 1754 J. Stow, *Survey of the Cities of London and Westminster*, 6th edn, 1754

Stroud D. Stroud, *Capability Brown*, revised edn, 1975

Summerson J. Summerson, *Georgian London*, 3rd edn, 1978

Summerson Wren J. Summerson, *Sir Christopher Wren*, 1953

Tait H. Tait, *Bow Porcelain 1744–1776*, 1959

Thompson F. M. L. Thompson, *Hampstead: Building a Borough, 1650–1964*, 1974

Thomson G. S. Thomson, *The Russells in Bloomsbury, 1669–1771*, 1940

Tillyard S. Tillyard, *Aristocrats: Caroline, Emily, Louisa and Sarah Lennox, 1740–1832*, 1994 (references to the 1995 paperback edition)

Tonnochy A. B. Tonnochy, *Catalogue of British Seal-dies in the British Museum*, 1952

Treherne J. Treherne, *The Canning Enigma*, 1989

Turner and Crisford A. J. Turner and A. C. H. Crisford, 'Documents illustrative of the history of English horology: two letters addressed to Thomas Mudge', *The Antiquarian Horological Society*, X, 1977, pp. 580–2

Varley J. Varley, 'John Rocque, engraver, surveyor, cartographer, and mapmaker', *Imago Mundi*, V, 1948, pp. 83–91

Vertue G. Vertue, *Notebooks*, I–VI (Walpole Society), Oxford, 1930–52

Wagner P. Wagner, *Eros Revived: Erotica in the Age of Enlightenment*, 1986

Walker R. J. B. Walker, *Old Westminster Bridge*, 1979

Walpole W. S. Lewis et al. (eds), *The Yale Edition of Horace Walpole's Correspondence*, 48 volumes, New Haven, 1937–83

Walpole, Memoirs H. Walpole (ed. J. Brooke), *Memoirs of King George II*, 3 volumes, New Haven, 1985

Weber W. Weber, *Music and the Middle Class: The Social Structure of Concert Life in London*, Paris and Vienna, 1975

Weinreb B. Weinreb and C. Hibbert (eds), *The London Encyclopaedia*, 1983 and further editions (referencesto the 1988 printing)

Weinstein R. Weinstein, 'Feeding the City: London's market gardens in the early modern period', in M. Galinou (ed.), *London's Pride: The Glorious History of the Capital's Gardens*, 1990, pp. 79–99

Werner 1985 A. Werner, 'Thomas Betts: an 18th-century glasscutter', *Journal of the Glass Association*, I, 1985, pp. 1–16

Werner 1999 A. Werner, *Immoral Earnings Eighteenth-century Style: Elizabeth Haddock, Her Bagnios and Country House*, paper given at a conference for the Luxury Project, Warwick University, May 1999 (unpublished manuscript, courtesy the author, Museum of London)

Wessely I. E. Wessely, *Richard Earlom: Verzeichniss seiner Radirungen und Schabkunstblätter*, Hamburg, 1886

White et al. C. White, D. Alexander and E. D'Oench, *Rembrandt in Eighteenth-century England*, exhibition catalogue, Yale Center for British Art, New Haven, 1983

Williams 1980 E. N. Willliams, *The Penguin Dictionary of English and European History 1485–1789*, 1980

Williams 1973 R. Williams, *The Country and the City*, 1973

Wilson D. Wilson, *The British Museum: A History*, 2003

Wilton-Ely J. Wilton-Ely, *Giovanni Battista Piranesi: The Complete Etchings*, San Francisco, 1994

Wind B. Wind, 'Hogarth's Industry and Idleness reconsidered', *Print Quarterly*, XIV, 1997, pp. 235–51

Withers P. and B. Withers, *British Coin-weights*, Llanfyllin, 1993

Worms L. Worms, 'Thomas Kitchin's "Journey of Life": hydrographer to George III, mapmaker and engraver', *The Map Collector*, LXII, 1993, pp. 2–8, and LXIII, Summer 1993, pp. 14–20

Wrigley E. A. Wrigley, 'A simple model of London's importance in changing English society and economy, 1650–1750', *Past and Present*, XXXVII, 1967, pp. 44–70

Wroth W. Wroth, 'Tickets of Vauxhall Gardens', *Numismatic Chronicle*, XVIII, 1898, pp. 73–92

Young H. Young, 'An 18th-century London glass-cutter's trade card: its parallels and derivatives', *Apollo*, February 1998, pp. 41–6

INDEX